Absolute Stationery Design

and Integrated Identity Graphics

GINGKO PRESS

Absolute Stationery Design
and Integrated Identity Graphics

ISBN 978-1-58423-505-7

First Published in the United States of America
by Gingko Press by arrangement with
Sandu Publishing Co., Ltd.
Text edited by Gingko Press.

Gingko Press, Inc.
1321 Fifth Street
Berkeley, CA 94710 USA
Tel: (510) 898 1195
Fax: (510) 898 1196
Email: books@gingkopress.com
www.gingkopress.com

First published in 2013 by Sandu Publishing

Sponsored by Design 360°
- Concept and Design Magazine

Edited and produced by
Sandu Publishing Co., Ltd.

Book design, concepts & art direction by
Sandu Publishing Co., Ltd.

sandu.publishing@gmail.com
www.sandupublishing.com

Cover project by Berger & Föhr

Printed and bound in China

TIANA VASILJEV

www.tianavasiljev.com

I was first contacted by Sandu Publishing a few years ago to submit some of my design work for one of their publications. At the time, I was not very familiar with Sandu Publishing, but have since grown very fond of many of their titles. Having recently taken on a full-time role in developing Beautiful Pages — an online design store I founded in 2011 — has exposed me to an extensive range of quality design publications. It has been a very rewarding journey. During this time, I've watched Sandu Publishing build up an international reputation for featuring and promoting an enormous collection of high-level design work from around the world.

I am delighted to be writing this foreword to a book about stationery design. I am delighted for a number of reasons. Stationery design plays such a crucial role in the corporate identity of a company. Not only does it make a business look organized and professional, it also displays a company's sense of identity, which is used by clients as a form of brand recognition. Stationery performs the important task of attracting a viewer's attention, engaging their interest and at its absolute best, can sell the intended company's service or product. When designed and created correctly it can enhance a company's identity, strengthen their credibility and launch their marketing achievements.

When you receive a letter from a company in the mail or when you pick up their business card, it is the item's visual appeal, rather than its content, that first strikes you. A business card, a letterhead, even an envelope has the power to convey a company's beliefs, how they think, speak and communicate. A well-designed stationery system entices you as soon as you look at it. It invites you to pick it up, to observe it, to wonder and to learn about everything it has to say. This is the true power of design.

What is interesting about design is that it is too often taken for granted. I believe that design is hugely undervalued in our society. It can work so well that we often tend to forget all the effort that was involved to bring it into existence. Sometimes, like with the invention of the wheel, it is so simple and so basic that it seems obvious to us all and we tend to forget that at some point in history it never existed. We forget that billions of human hours have been invested into getting it to the stage that it is at today. Every great design has a powerful history. It also has behind it a designer (or more often a team of designers) who used their time and skills to make the world a better place to experience, by solving one problem or another.

To take on the challenge of creating genuinely great stationery takes remarkable focus, dedication and discipline. Designers aren't artists. We focus on other people's problems, rarely on those of our own invention. However, in order to create a successful solution for other people's problems, we must first strive to understand them.

Looking through the selection of stationery designs that Sandu Publishing has collected within this unique volume has sparked in me some serious design envy. The designers showcased in this book are featured because they have all done things differently. They've proved that it is well-worth investing time and effort into researching, designing and developing a company's corporate identity and accompanying stationery. These creatives all possess the artistic ability and the creative mind to create eye-catching and most importantly intelligent design solutions. Their work leaves memories, it impresses and most importantly stands out in a society where everyone and everything is increasingly screaming for our time and attention.

Sandu Publishing's *Absolute Stationery Design* shows us how some of today's best designers are reshaping the way we see businesses, corporations, products and services. These featured creatives are constantly raising the bar by composing powerful messages and delivering these through striking stationery designs.

Absolute Stationery Design is another soulful Sandu Publishing volume that provides us with endless inspiration. It is a book to be enjoyed, absorbed and appreciated. I hope this volume sparks inspiration in you, motivates you and strengthens your belief in the power of great design.

This publication and the work it so beautifully contains truly is absolute.

DAVE SEDGWICK

www.designbydave.co.uk

Being asked to write the foreword to *Absolute Stationery Design* is a real privilege and something I am proud of and honoured to be able to do. I'm also thrilled to be a part of this book. A read through each of the pages and it's very obvious that I am in very good company.

As an independent graphic designer I would go as far as to say that I still get the biggest and most satisfying feeling from working on and completing identity projects. Please don't get me wrong; we all enjoy finalizing any work. The feeling of completing a brief, answering all the questions, presenting and showcasing the fruits of our labour is always one of fulfillment and satisfaction.

However, there is just something truly unique about identity work.

Perhaps it's because it gives us the chance to influence and shape a business, initiative or enterprise through our own design work. The opportunity, as creatives, to contribute to something new, original and full of life. The initial meetings with the client when you begin to gain an insight into their world. Scribbling notes frantically. Listening to every sentence. Anticipation and excitement rolled into one. You can almost see it now – the signage, the uniforms, the vehicle livery, the website, the business cards, everything and anything. Right down to the pencils, notebooks or even the email signature.

I often can find myself attempting to explain to a new client why it is that they don't simply need a logo, that they need an identity. "But surely that is a logo" they often say, "I just want a logo, a little icon or symbol or something".

We, as designers, are hopefully very much aware how wrong this idea is, the idea that a logo is just a tiny (although still important) part of the overall identity. It is, how I often explain, as simple as a person's signature. It can be unique of course, but it also says very little about that person. It could just as easily be an X.

This is where the overall identity comes into play and how good and often great design can really come to life. It is how the "signature" can be used, or how it often can't be used (brand guidelines can be the bane of our lives sometimes). How it sits comfortably on the page, what colours it can be reproduced in. What other elements can be used to complement it, work together with it.

It's about the paper stock, the pantone colours, the imagery and photography and even down to the overall tone of voice. It is every single detail which enables an identity to prosper and develop and how by doing so, a client's core values, philosophy and brand statement is projected openly to their target market.

The book you are currently holding showcases some of the best identity work and brand design from all over the world. It aims to highlight and promote how various designers and studios select all the different elements required in order to produce the best conceptual and considered solutions for their clients' needs.

You will of course see styles and themes across the book. But no single piece is alike. This is the beauty of the design industry. The best designers and agencies are always looking to produce individual and bespoke work for their own clients.

We don't like to imitate and we try hard to find the answers to each of the individual questions when beginning the design process. We don't always succeed, not every time. But when we do, we are proud of our work and proud to show it off just like a newborn baby. Complete of course with gold foil blocking and double hit Pantone colours...

The work featured within also has a very global feel to it brought about through the selection of designs from countries such as the UK, Finland, Russia, Canada, Germany and Norway as well as many more places around the world.

Through books such as *Absolute Stationery Design* we are now able to gain a real insight into design trends and movements across the world. The obvious rise and rise of the Internet has helped to facilitate this, as we are now much more connected than ever before. One click of a mouse and I can see the work of design studios from Manchester to Mozambique ...

However, the chance to still own something we can touch and feel - something we can quickly flick through for inspiration and enjoyment is, and always will be, the beauty of printed books and the reason why most of us have extra large bookcases in almost every room in the house.

It forms a great inspirational and informative reference for us as designers, as well as those clients who are still prepared to stand out in a competitive and crowded marketplace. And for those same clients to whom design is a valuable and worthwhile commodity.

Enjoy this book, and as designers we really do owe it to ourselves and each other to continue to push the boundaries of identity design, to continue to gently persuade all clients to try something different and most importantly to be unique. After all, isn't that what having your own identity is all about...

Thank you.

Contents

Identity Frame Publishers

Frame Publishers is an internationally-acclaimed publishing house based in Amsterdam, the Netherlands. In advance of a major re-launch of its website, we were commissioned to create a new visual identity for the publisher which would be used in all corporate literature, business cards and – importantly – to also form the basis for the new visual identity for its three major magazine titles on the new company website. The three magazines are: *Frame*, from which the company takes its name and which is all about interior design; *Mark*, all about architecture; and *Elephant*, the newest title, which is all about art and culture.
We decided to focus on each of the three aspects as a unique entity and we assigned each a distinctive, bright and vibrant colour and this was then used as the core aspect of the design. The existing logo of Frame Publishers was not redesigned but it was incorporated into the new identity by always having it as white text against one of each of the three colours: *Frame*, pink; *Mark*, blue; and *Elephant*, green.

FRAME
Frame Publishers
Laan der Hesperiden 68
1076 DX Amsterdam
The Netherlands
T +31 20 4233 717
F +31 20 4280 653
frameweb.com
Frame Publishers
Laan der Hesperiden 68
1076 DX Amsterdam
The Netherlands
Frame Publishers
FRAME
Benjamin Verheijden
Circulation Manager
T +31 20 4233 717
benjamin@frameweb.com
FRAME

DESK IDEA
Travesera de Gracia 111
08008 Barcelona
T. 93 184 72 14
F. 93 550 44 10
deskidea@deskidea.com
deskidea.com

DESK IDEA
deskidea.com
ID
deskidea.com

IDEA
DESK
DESK

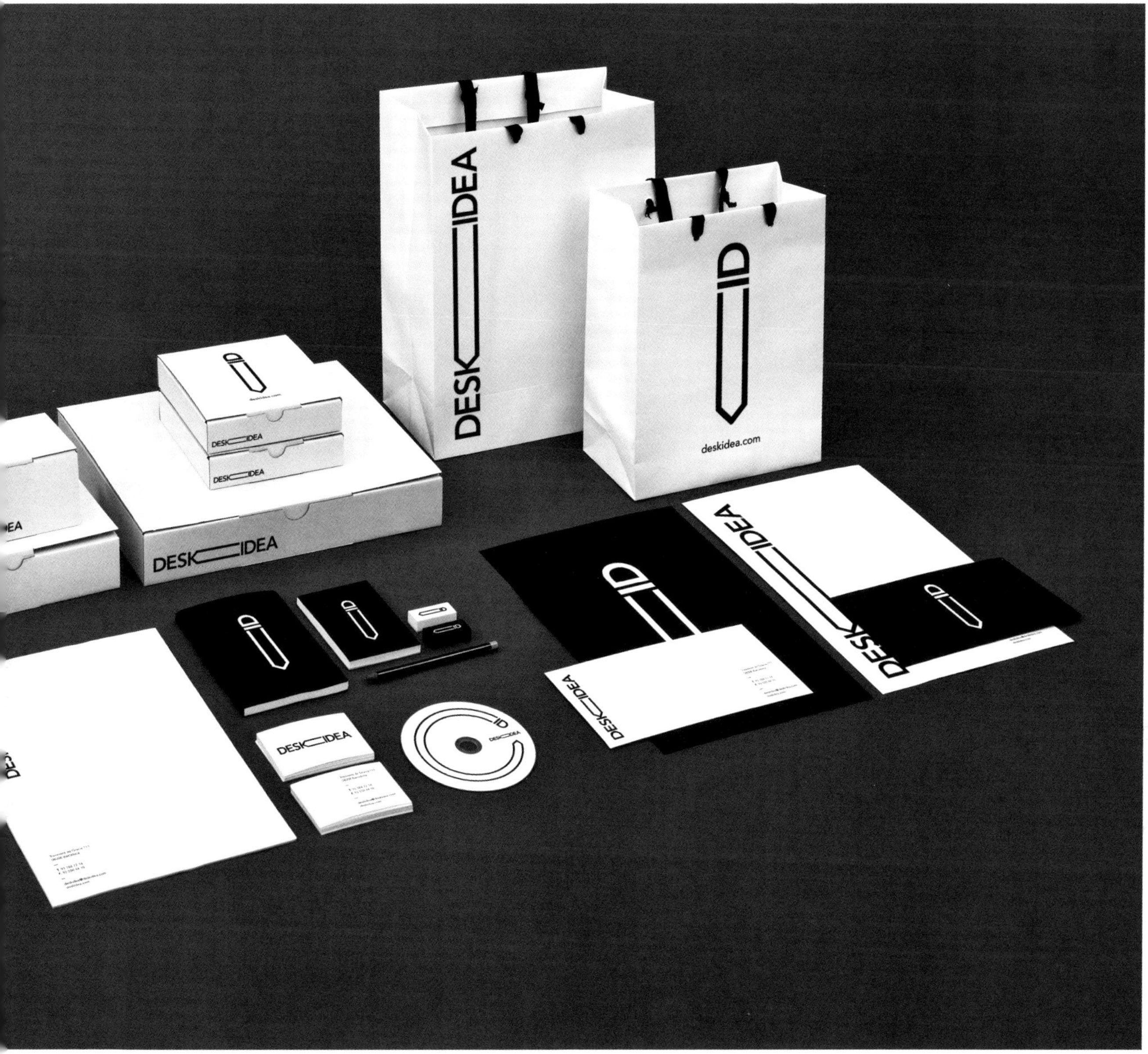

Deskidea

Deskidea is a Barcelona-based office that supplies e-commerce where the primary aim is to get a sense of simplicity from the very first purchase until the arrival of the product. The brand was designed to boost this simplicity value and the graphic solution came from the name itself, Deskidea. The idea was to convey its value using basic office objects, like the pencil. The different corporate applications are based on the pencil as a symbol, operating by itself or embedded within the brand. Photography by Susana Gellida.

Harri Koskinen Works

The branding created for the Finnish designer Harri Koskinen and his own furniture collection, Works, is practical and innovative like the designer himself.

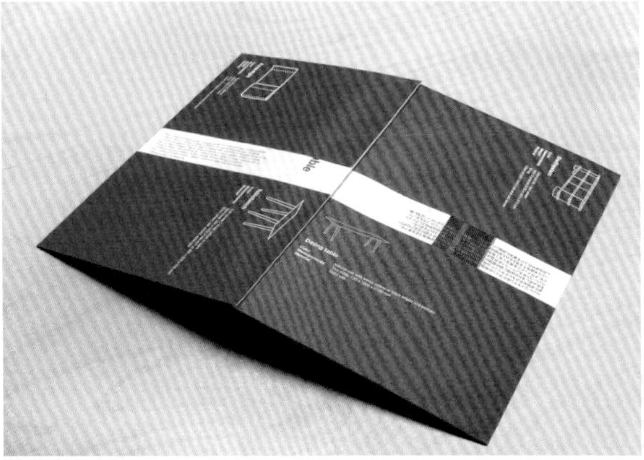

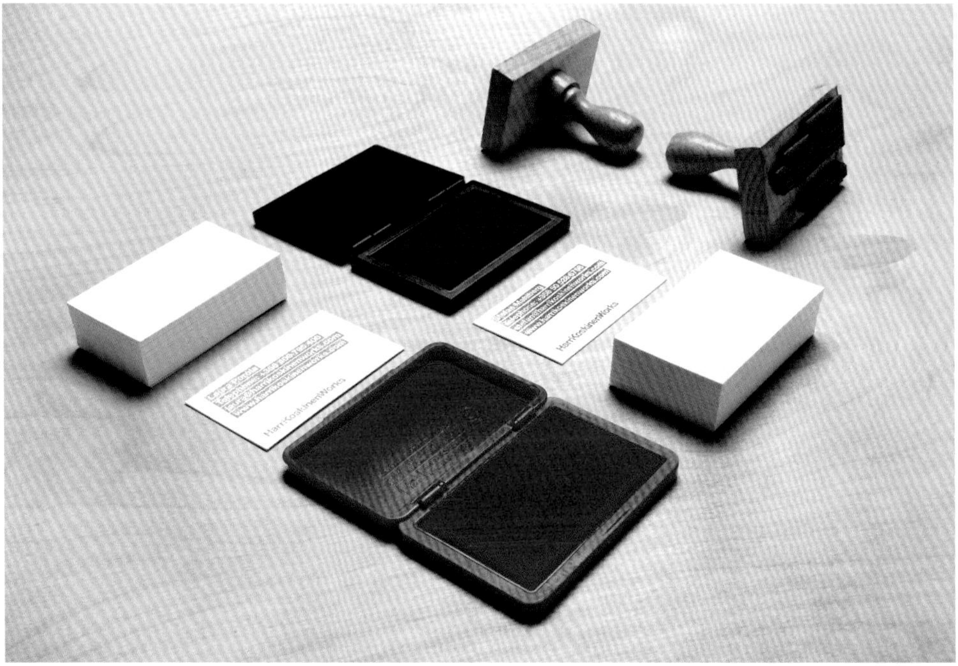

Stefan Mahlberg
Telephone: +358 50 528 6758
stefan@harrikoskinenworks.com
www.harrikoskinenworks.com
HarriKoskinenWorks

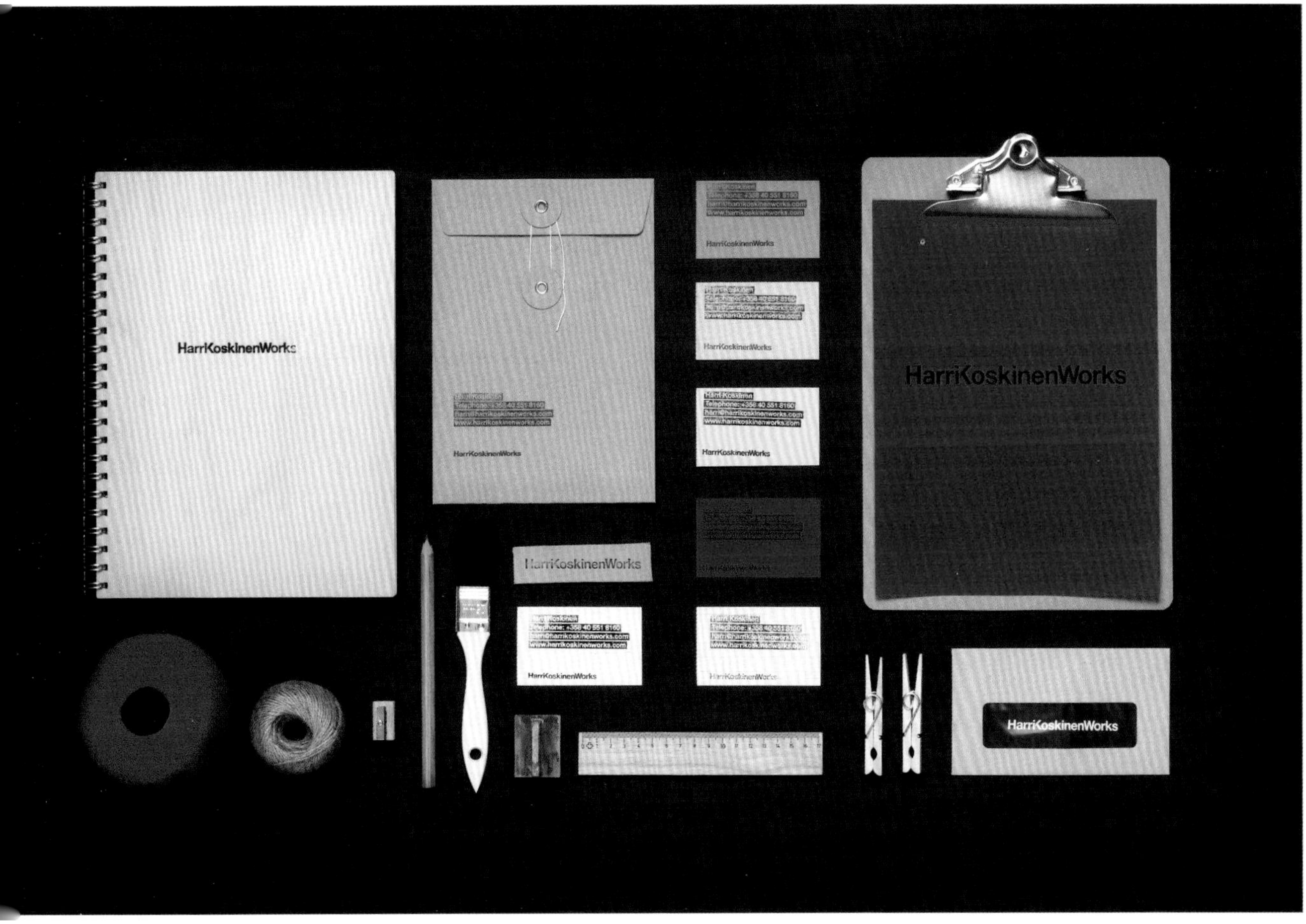
HarriKoskinenWorks
HarriKoskinenWorks
HarriKoskinenWorks
HarriKoskinenWorks

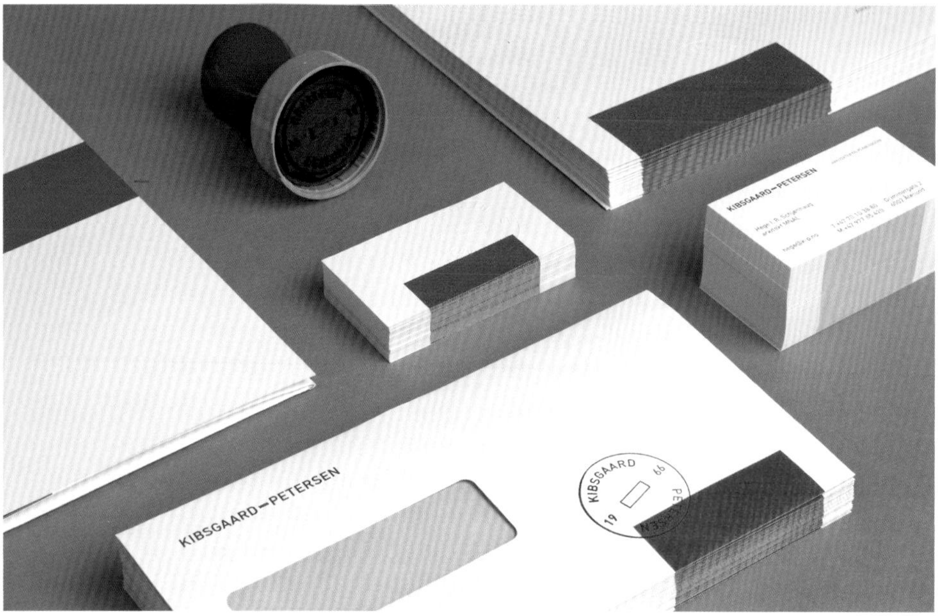

Kibsgaard–Petersen

A full range architecture company that works on both public as well as private housing, founded in Aalesund in 1966. The identity, based on the hyphen, communicates a bold and strong architectural language and visualizes the energy that represents Kibsgaard-Petersen, through young innovation combined with years of experience. Their solid red color combined with stamping and embossing tools tells a story of a modern company with solid traditions.

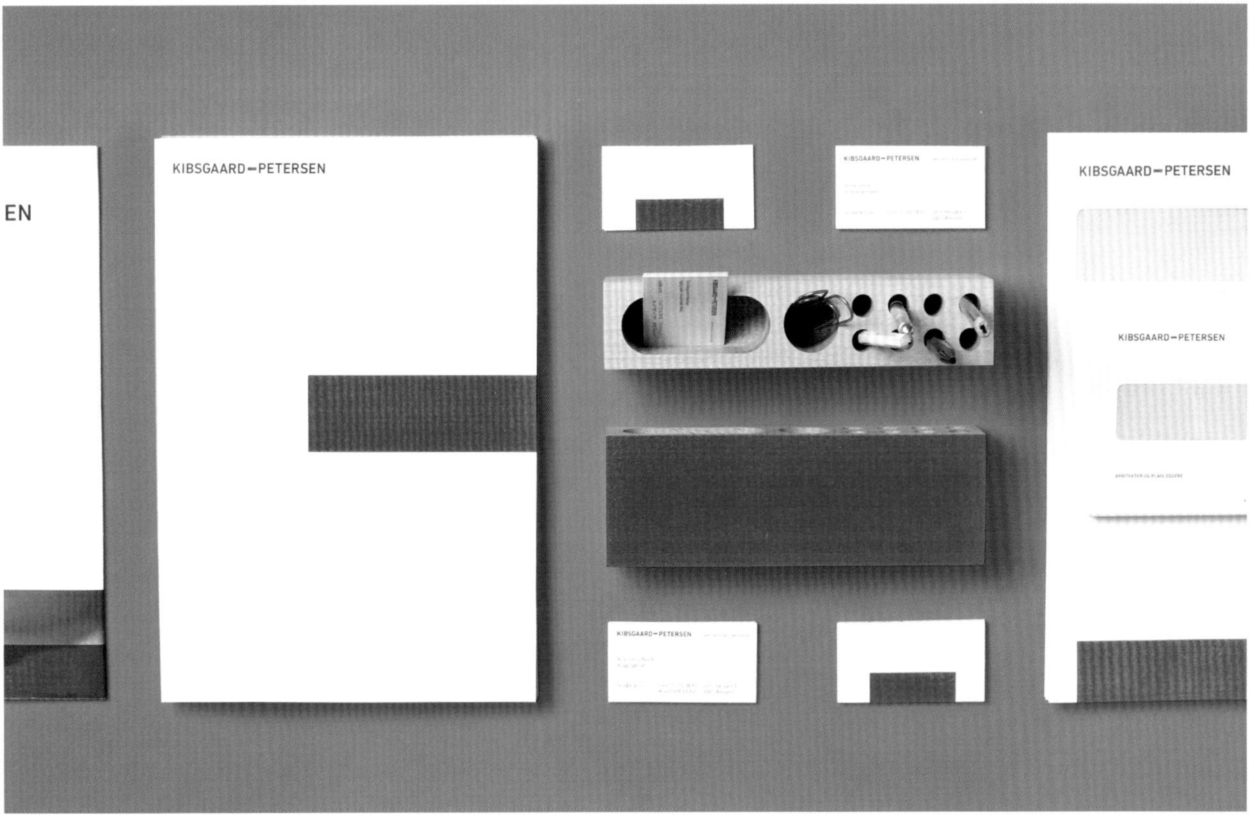
EN
KIBSGAARD—PETERSEN
KIBSGAARD—PETERSEN
KIBSGAARD—PETERSEN
KIBSGAARD—PETERSEN
KIBSGAARD—PETERSEN
KIBSGAARD—PETERSEN

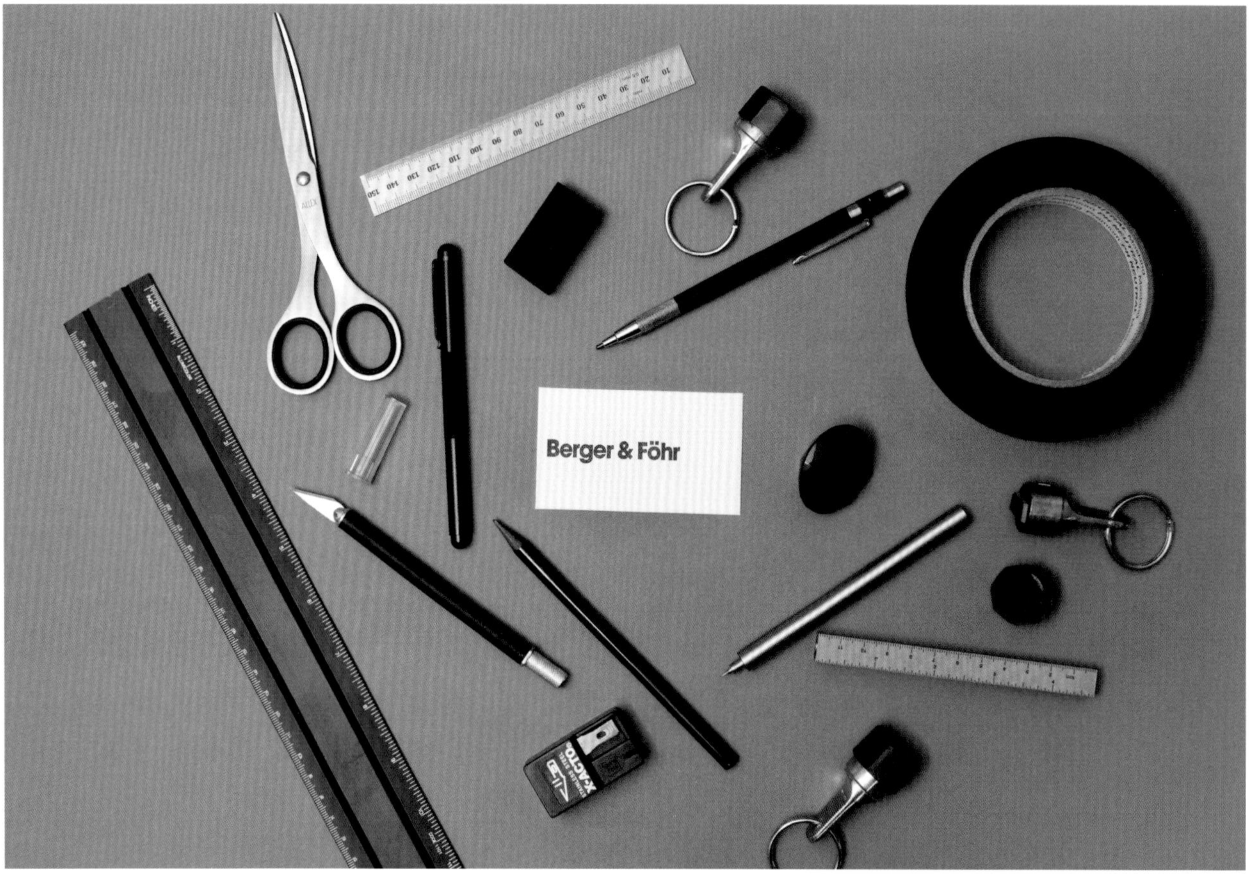

Berger & Föhr Identity

The Berger & Föhr (B&F) identity system is based on the rule of thirds. The B&F logotype and all affiliated collateral copy is set in Avant Garde Gothic Bold. The B&F symbol represents Berger on the left and Föhr on the right. The B&F communication collateral (business cards, letterhead, envelopes, bookmarks, etc.) employs a consistent grid and uniform type size while staying true to the identity system's use of the rule of thirds.
Photography by Jamie Kripke.

B&F
Berger & Föhr
$1.75
IRST-CLASS MAIL
INTERNATIONAL
EMIL OLSSON
SWEDEN
Berger & Föhr
IRST-CLASS MAIL
INTERNATIONAL
UNITED KINGDOM

Berger & Föhr
Berger & Föhr
Berger & Föhr
Berger & Föhr
Berger & Föhr
Berger & Föhr
Berger & Föhr
Berger & Föhr
Berger & Föhr

Karl Gerstner
Designing
Programmes
Designing Programmes
Paul Rand
Berger &

B&F
Berger & Föhr

Wendela van Dijk

Wendela van Dijk's two fashion stores in the centre of Rotterdam offer a large number of exclusive brands.

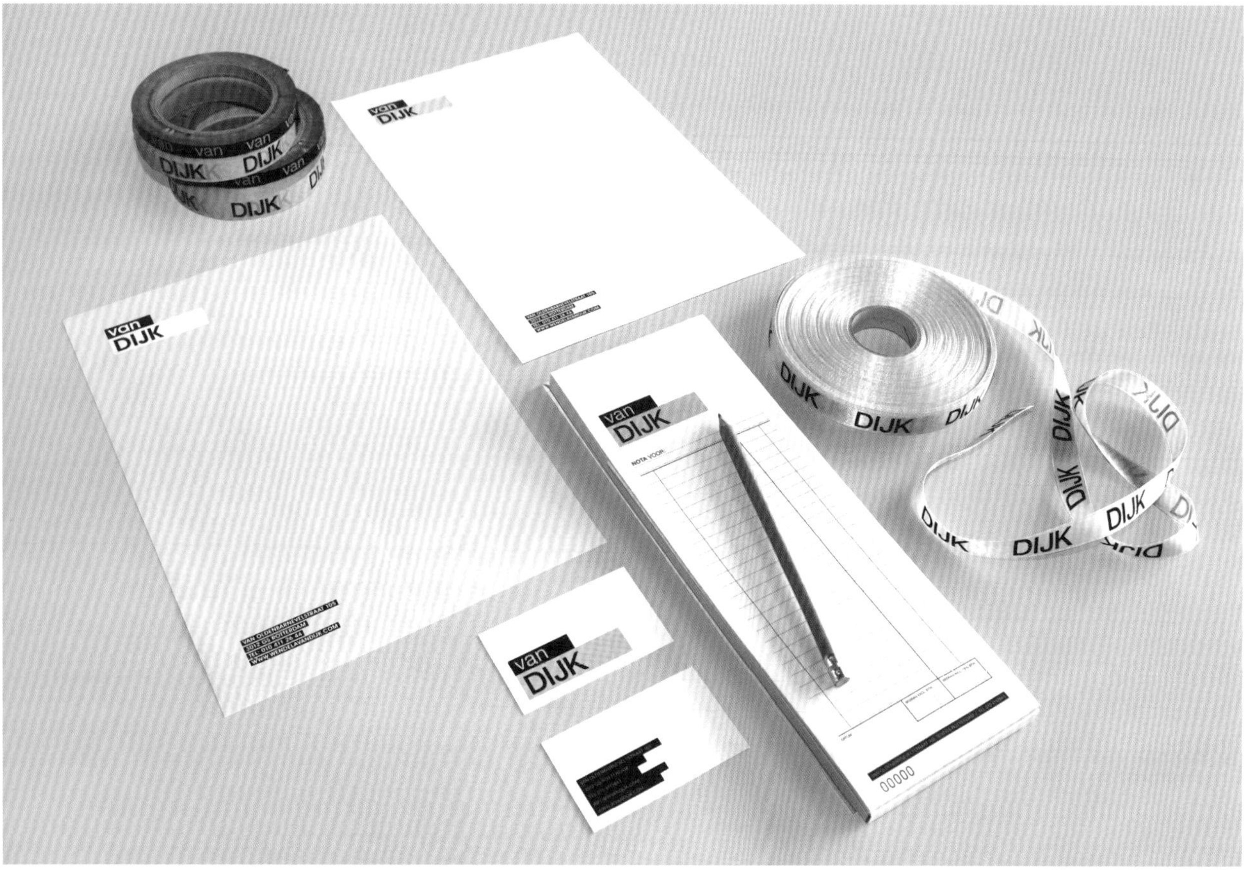

Blank Card

Blank's business card is sharp, elegant, and winks at all potential clients. Completed with UV varnish finishing and a sticker, it has the standard measures of a business card. But the special die-cut shape will tell you to get in line and acquire Blank services and tailored projects only!

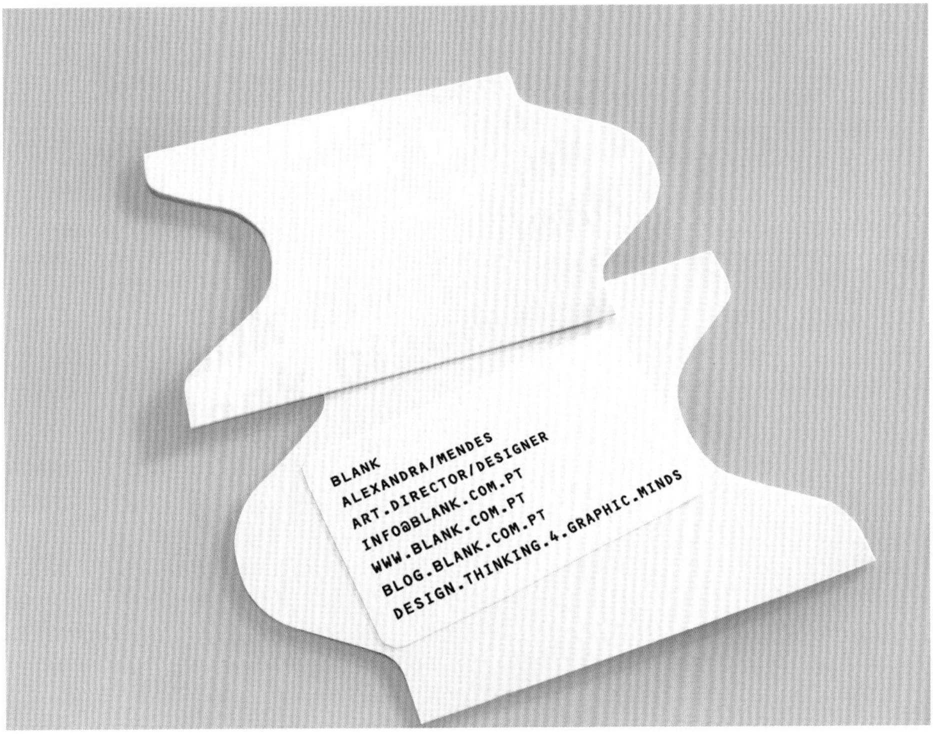

Maru Identity

Maru is a showroom and online boutique selling high-end Japanese design objects ranging from delicate porcelain to handmade stationery. Lundgren+Lindqvist were approached by Maru to design the boutique's identity, ranging from logotype, stationery, packaging and signage to the design and development of the online shop.
Maru means “circle” or “correct” in Japanese. In Japanese schools, teachers indicate that an answer is correct by drawing a circle next to it. We used this in the identity by placing the products in the webshop in circles of different colours (indicating which group of products they belong to) proclaiming that the product is approved by Maru.
With the logotype we wanted to visualize the story of Maru and illustrate the act of setting up a Japanese boutique in the capital of Norway. We found a quite literal way of doing this by integrating the Kanji symbol for Maru in the middle of the wordmark, replacing the A and R.
Photography by Kalle Sanner.

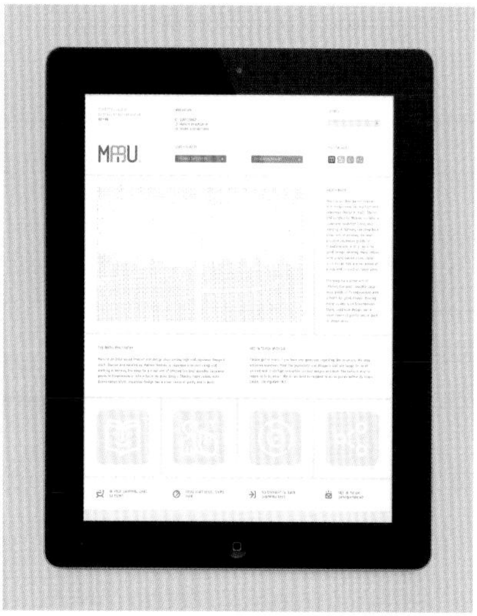

日本のデザインと工芸
ADRESSE: FORNEBURINGEN 13
NO-1360 FORNEBU, NORWAY
SHOP@MARU.NO – +47 48065271
WEBSHOP: MARU.NO
MOTOKO YOSHIDA
CEO/SIVILARKITEKT

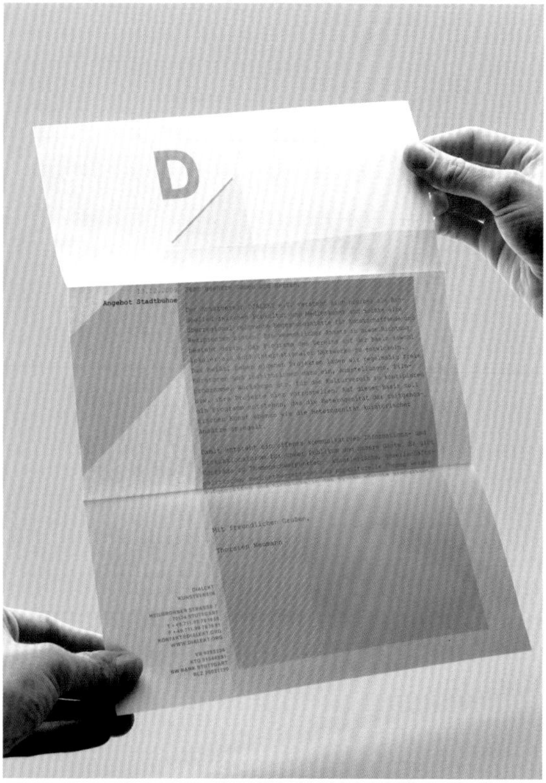

Dialekt Kunstverein Corporate Design

Gold & Wirtschaftswunder developed the corporate design for the Art Institution "Dialekt Kunstverein". This institution promotes young artists from all over Europe and organizes exhibitions and art events. The main components of the corporate design are the logo – the "D", which stands for "Dialect" and the "/" that reflects the collaborative character of the projects, bringing together artists from different national and artistic backgrounds. Also very visible in all Dialekt Kunstvereins stationery is a unique colour range and layered design elements.

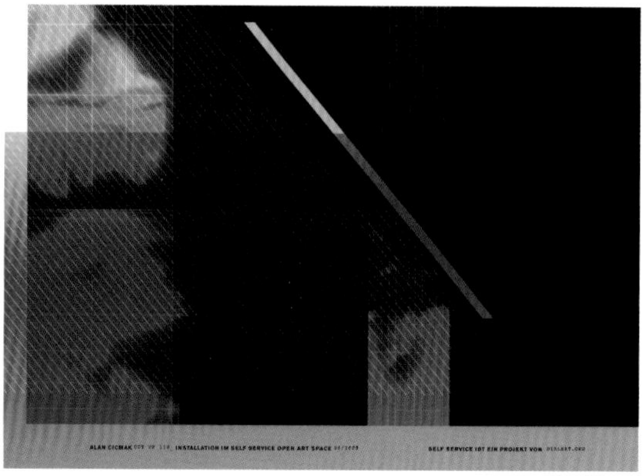

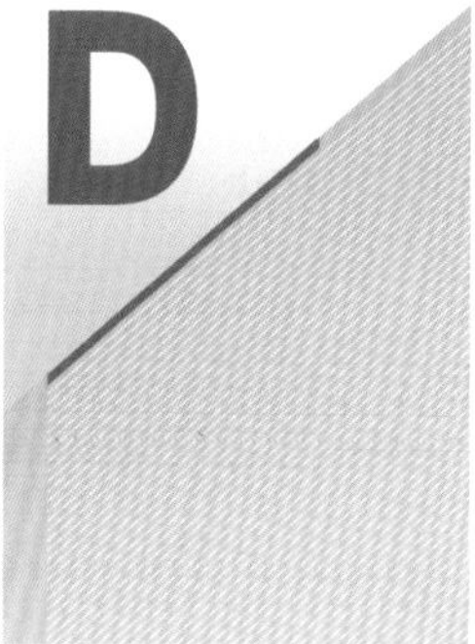

DIALEKT KUNSTVEREIN
HEILBRONNER STRASSE 7
70174 STUTTGART
KUNSTVEREIN DIALEKT MITGLIEDSKARTE
2010
CHRISTIAN SCHILLER

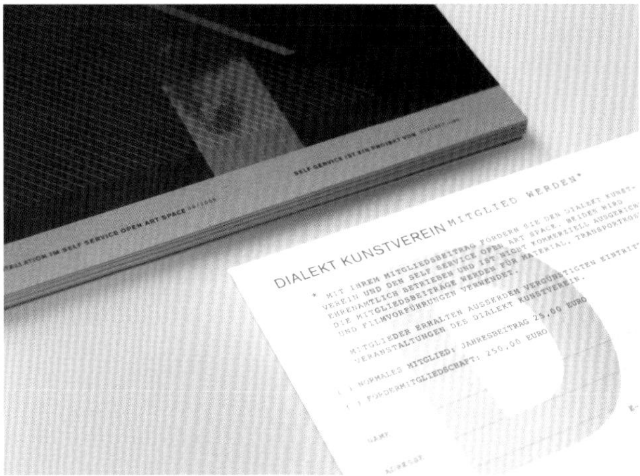
DIALEKT KUNSTVEREIN MITGLIED WERDEN*

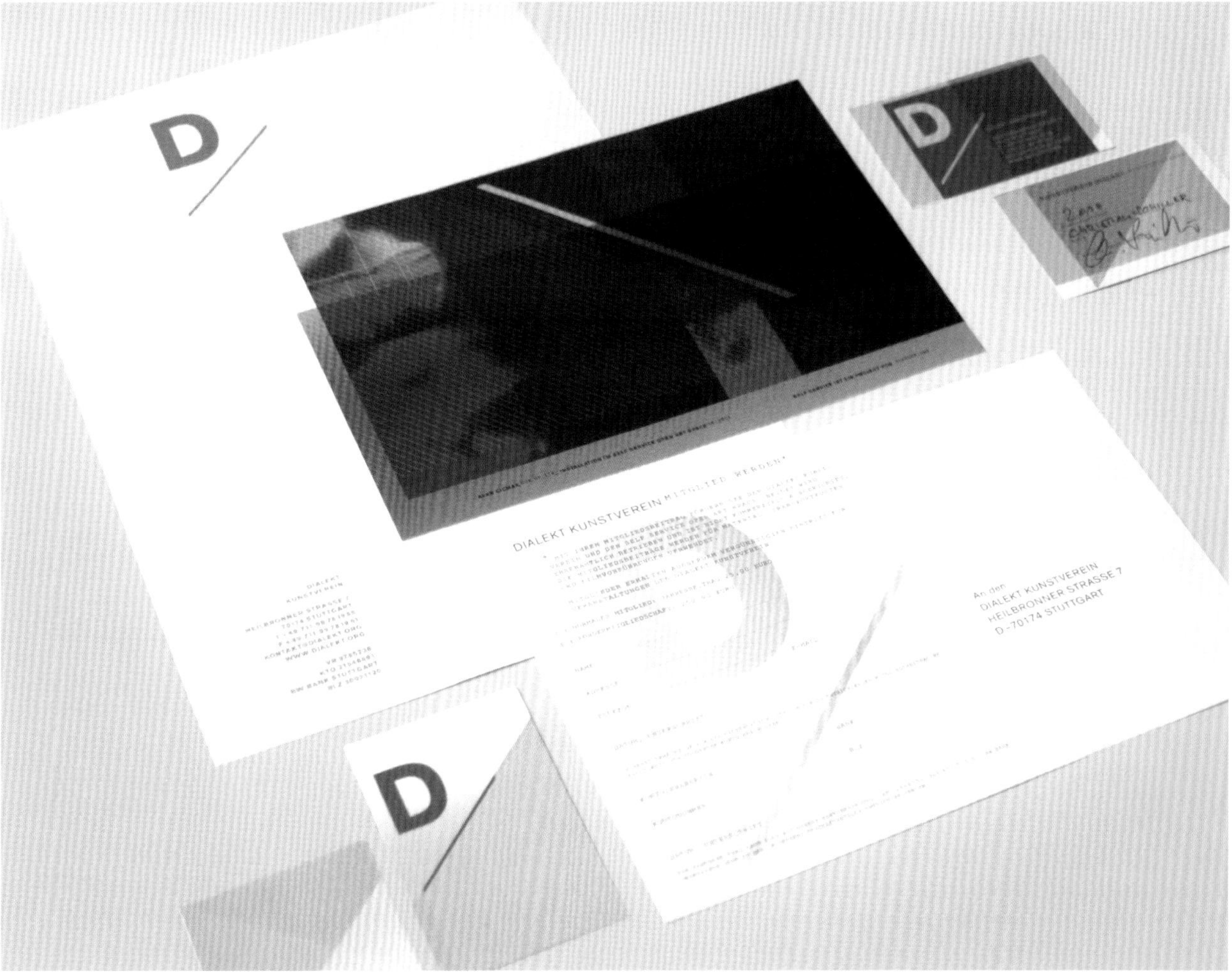
DIALEKT KUNSTVEREIN MITGLIED WERDEN*
An den
DIALEKT KUNSTVEREIN
HEILBRONNER STRASSE 7
D-70174 STUTTGART

SHE

SHE (Sustainable Health Enterprises) is a New York-based organization whose mission is to improve the quality of life for women and girls in developing countries by challenging current thinking, and by investing in people and ideas. Their first initiative, SHE/28, addresses the lack of affordable menstruation supplies in Rwanda. The identity needed to capture the heart and soul of a brand that empowers women and girls to stand tall and proud. Thus the wordmark itself "stands tall", emphasized by the bold underscore and colour palette. The text creates an empowering dialogue that strengthens the brand's values. The deliberate space beneath "SHE" allows initiatives to find their place within the parent brand, as in SHE/28.

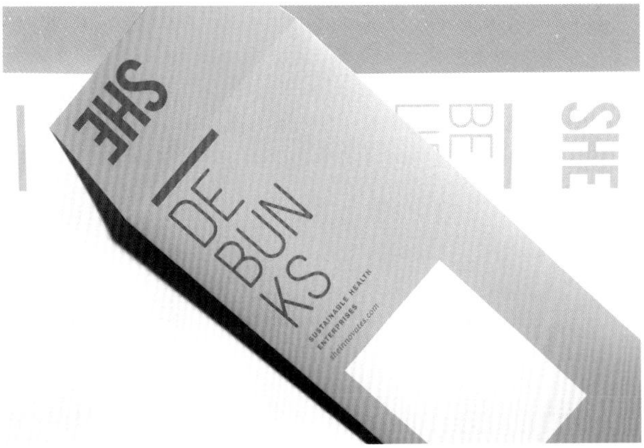
SHE
DE
BUN
KS
SUSTAINABLE HEALTH
ENTERPRISES
sheinnovates.com

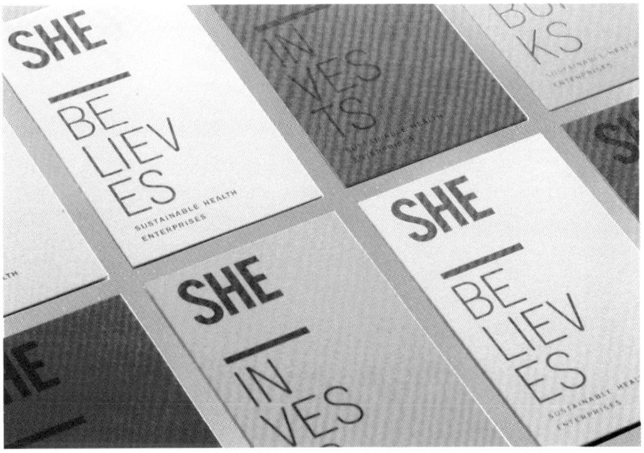
SHE
BE
LIEV
ES
SUSTAINABLE HEALTH
ENTERPRISES
SHE
IN
VES
SHE
BE
LIEV
ES

SUSTAINABLE HEALTH
ENTERPRISES
SHE
IN
VES
TS
SHE
28
SHE
SHE

ems@sheinnovates.com
917 538 5445
+250 (0)7 8343 6564

SHE
BE
LIEV
ES
SUSTAINABLE HEALTH
ENTERPRISES
SHE
DE
BUN
KS

SHE
BE
LIEV
ES
SUSTAINABLE HEALTH
ENTERPRISES
SHE
IN
VES
TS

COMMIT

Commit is a network of scientists, knowledge institutes, businesspeople and the Dutch government who try to solve social problems with IT technology, for example, user friendly technologies for healthcare. Lava started with a strategic plan for how to communicate these abstract concepts to the different stakeholders. The identity is based on the origins of typography and computer language; logic and syntax. Lava created a custom fixed-width typeface to be used for all communication. In every message Lava try to emphasize the instructional and poetic power of language and typography by referring to concrete poetry as well as programming language. In this way, the communication itself becomes the identity. The simplicity of the identity is in its elements, which consist of a typeface, and simple colored paper. As a result of this simplicity, all members of the community are able to implement and adopt its elements.

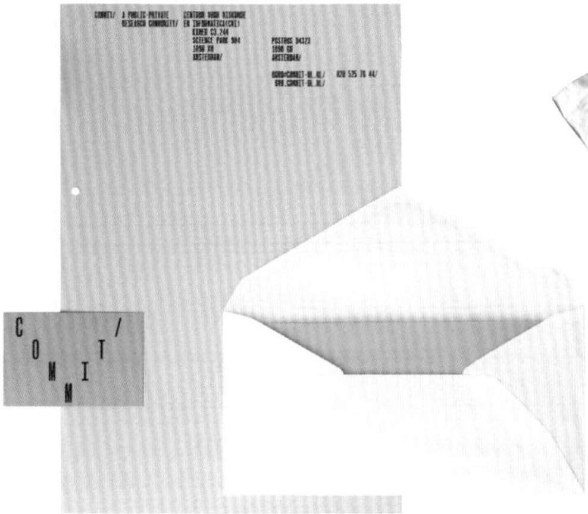

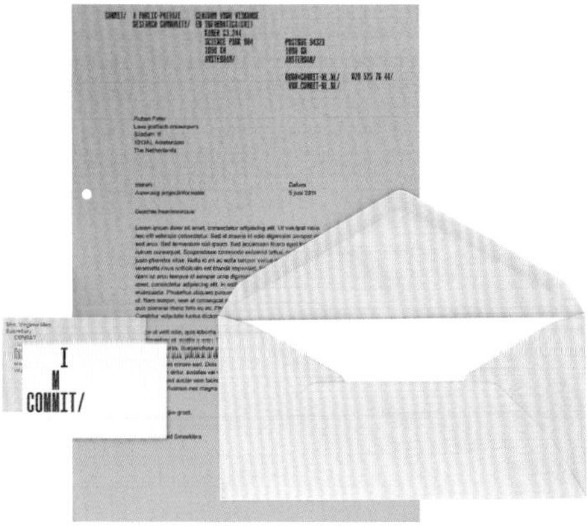

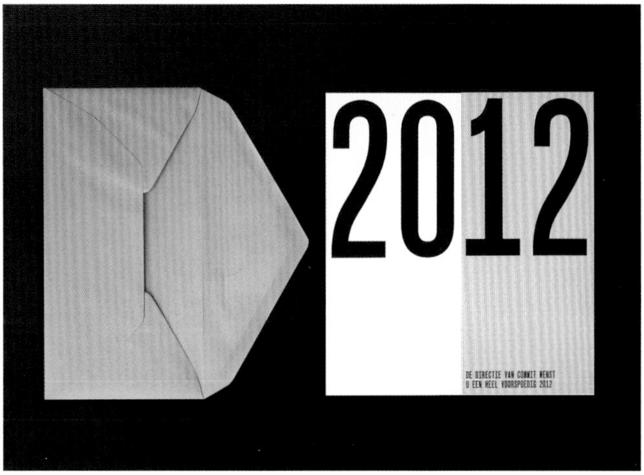
2012
DE DIRECTIE VAN COMMIT WENST
U EEN HEEL VOORSPOEDIG 2012

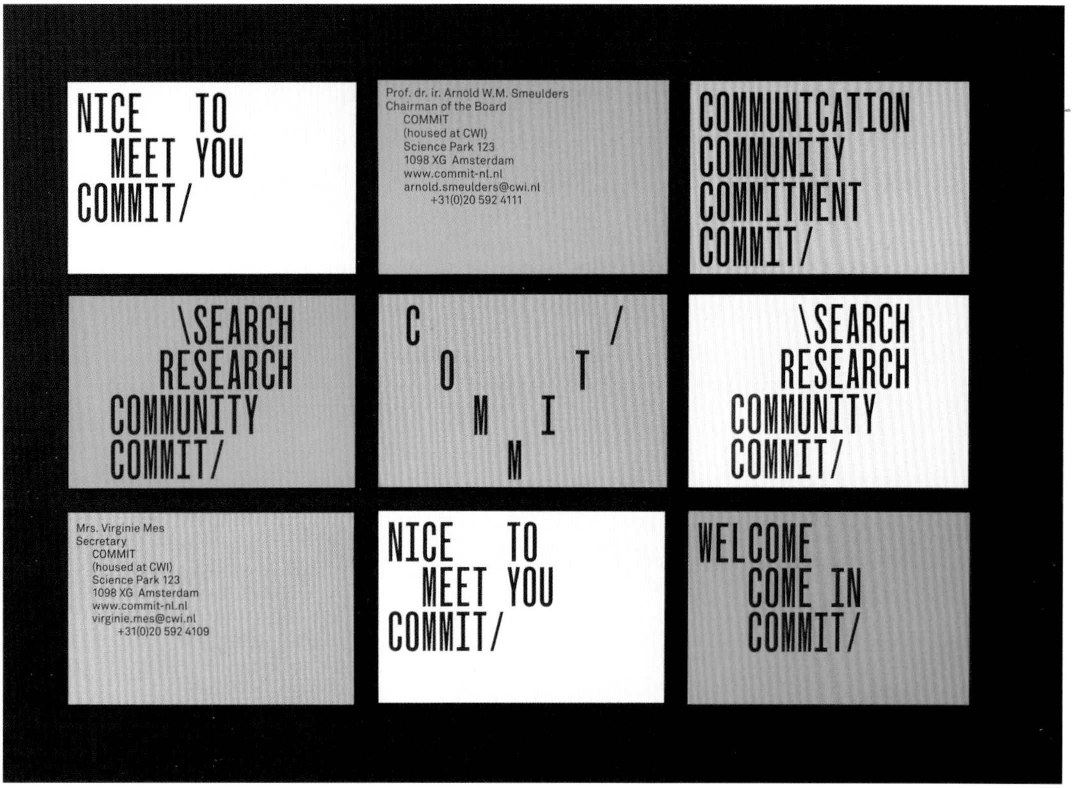
NICE TO
MEET YOU
COMMIT/
Prof. dr. ir. Arnold W.M. Smeulders
Chairman of the Board
COMMIT
(housed at CWI)
Science Park 123
1098 XG Amsterdam
www.commit-nl.nl
arnold.smeulders@cwi.nl
+31(0)20 592 4111
COMMUNICATION
COMMUNITY
COMMITMENT
COMMIT/
\SEARCH
RESEARCH
COMMUNITY
COMMIT/
C O M M I T /
\SEARCH
RESEARCH
COMMUNITY
COMMIT/
Mrs. Virginie Mes
Secretary
COMMIT
(housed at CWI)
Science Park 123
1098 XG Amsterdam
www.commit-nl.nl
virginie.mes@cwi.nl
+31(0)20 592 4109
NICE TO
MEET YOU
COMMIT/
WELCOME
COME IN
COMMIT/

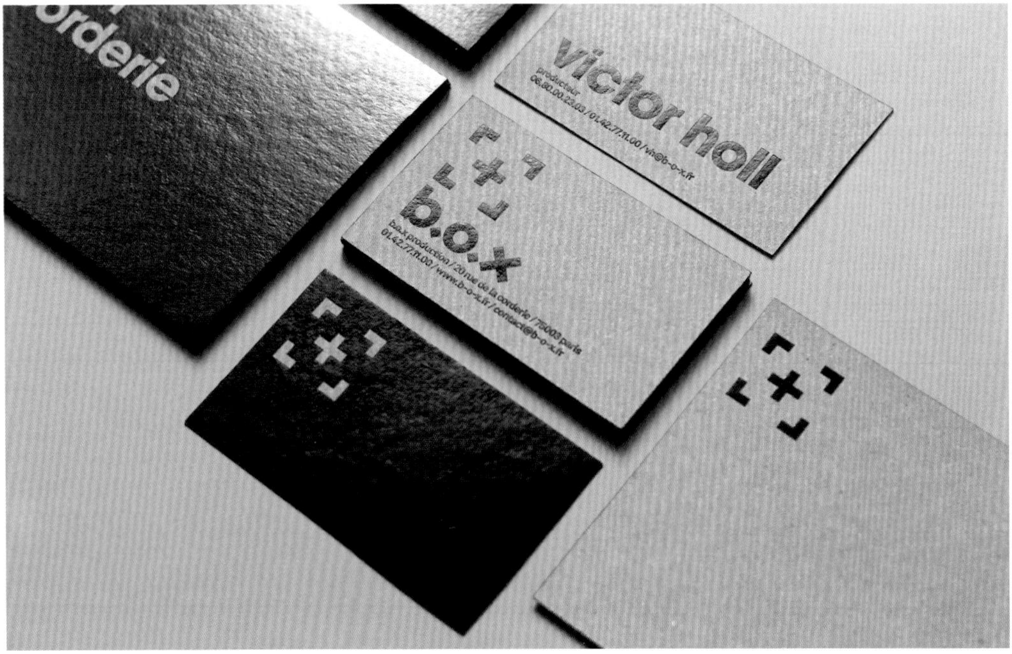

B.O.X Production

B.O.X Production is a video production company based in Paris. It needed a strong and visible identity to communicate both to big corporate companies and small independent music labels. We wanted to create an identity that would be both basic and sophisticated. The idea was to speak as loud as possible using the most discreet voice.
By using a big heavy Avant-Garde typeface, always at the same size and position across all the stationery, the text block containing the contact details became a defining element.
The tricky thing in the creation of the b.o.x identity was to use economic materials in a luxurious way. We used the same recycled cardboard to create business cards, compliment slips, and on DVD packaging (which wasn't part of the initial brief). The thickness of the cardboard allowed us to incorporate some fine details such as a black foil block on all the pieces.

b.o.x production
20 rue de la corderie
75003 paris
01.42.77.11.00
contact@b-o-x.fr
devis
b.o.x production
20 rue de la corderie
75003 paris
01.42.77.11.00
contact@b-o-x.fr
client
project
notes
notes
note
de
produ-
ction

b.o.x
victor holl
b.o.x
b.o.x production
20 rue de la corderie
75003 paris
01.42.77.11.00
contact@b-o-x.fr
b.o.x production
20 rue de la corderie
75003 paris
01.42.77.11.00
contact@b-o-x.fr
note
de
produ-
ction
client
project
director
version n°
date
length
format type
notes
client
project
notes
b.o.x production
20 rue de la corderie
75003 paris
01.42.77.11.00
contact@b-o-x.fr

Rebranding New Museum

Respected for the audacity and global scope of its curatorial program, New Museum is a leading destination for new art and new ideas. Conceived as a sculptural stack of rectilinear boxes shifted off-axis, its architecture features a variety of open, light-filled spaces clad in a seamless aluminum mesh. The elegantly bold structure suits both the museum's character as well as its neighborhood. Using typography and a restrained color palette, the proposed identity embraces the off-axis, shifting personality of the museum, allowing the identity to expand easily into various applications. Along with the stationery, cutouts and asymmetric secondary typography are used to further enhance the brand.

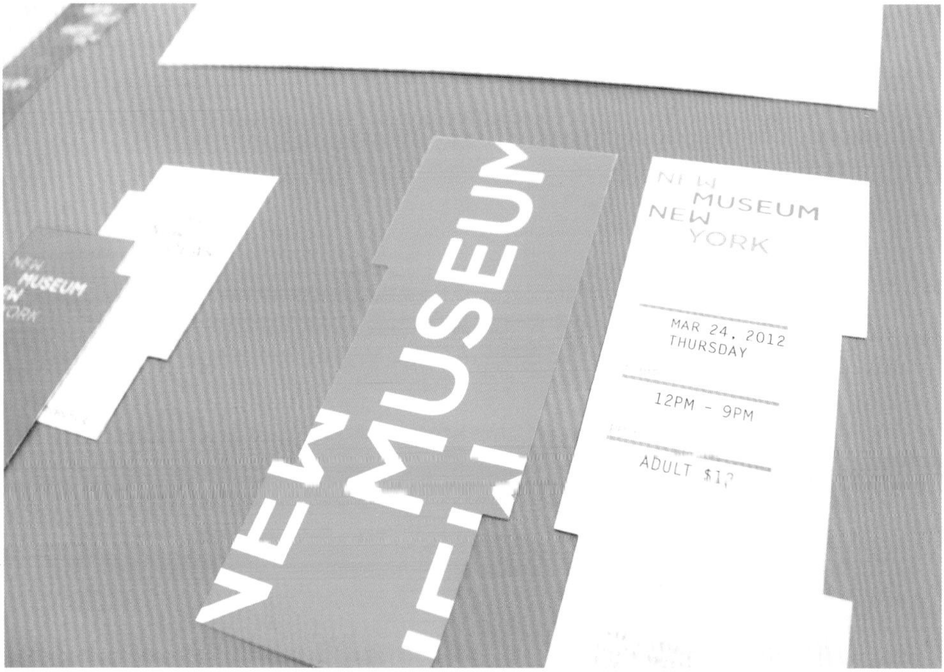

NEW
MUSEUM
NEW
YORK
NEW
ART

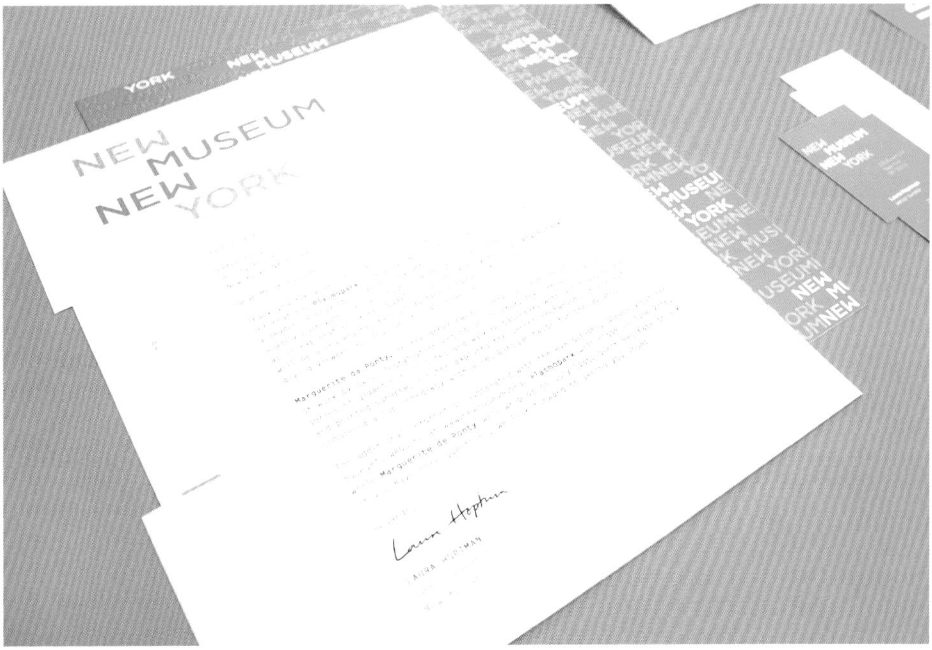
NEW
MUSEUM
NEW
YORK

The NoMad Hotel

be-pôles worked with The NoMad to produce its global brand identity and visual identity. The studio also developed The NoMad Hotel's art program based on the idea of the "voyage" at large, inspired both by The NoMad's Parisian influenced style and by be-pôles' collection of photographic books, the Portraits de Villes, in which a selected photographer has carte blanche to present his or her own vision of a city.

NoMad
02183
1170 BROADWAY
WELCOME TO NEW YORK.
SAFE TRAVELS. DON'T BE A STRANGER.
WE SHOULD DO THIS MORE OFTEN.
WE GO TOGETHER LIKE CHICKEN AND BEER.
WHERE HAVE YOU BEEN ALL OUR LIVES?
IT MUST BE LOVE. HAPPY ANNIVERSARY!
STAY COOL...
SWEET DREAMS...
IT MUST BE LOVE. HAPPY ANNIVERSARY!
LET'S DO THIS AGAIN SOMETIME.
NoMad

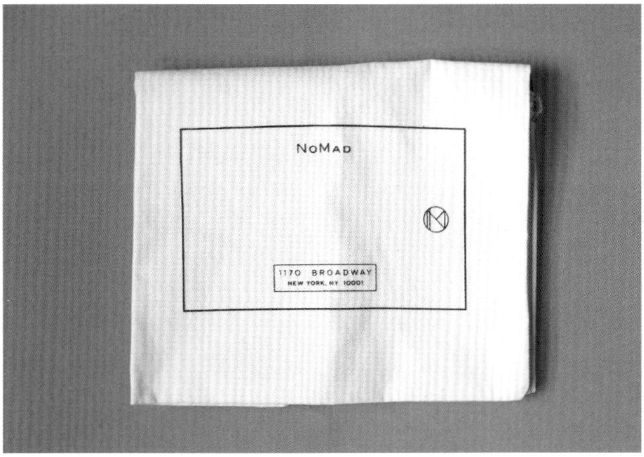
NoMad
1170 BROADWAY
NEW YORK, NY 10001

Daedal Architecture

The "d" of Daedal is a made of two elements, a line and a circle. This simple construction was inspired by the idea of puzzles and basic geometry. These two simple elements create a more complex form when combined. From this simple system other letterforms, symbols and patterns are constructed providing a visual language for the brand that is distinct, elegant and sophisticated.

This idea of taking two simple elements and combining them to create complex, yet elegant forms is what Daedal's philosophy and their approach to architecture is grounded in.

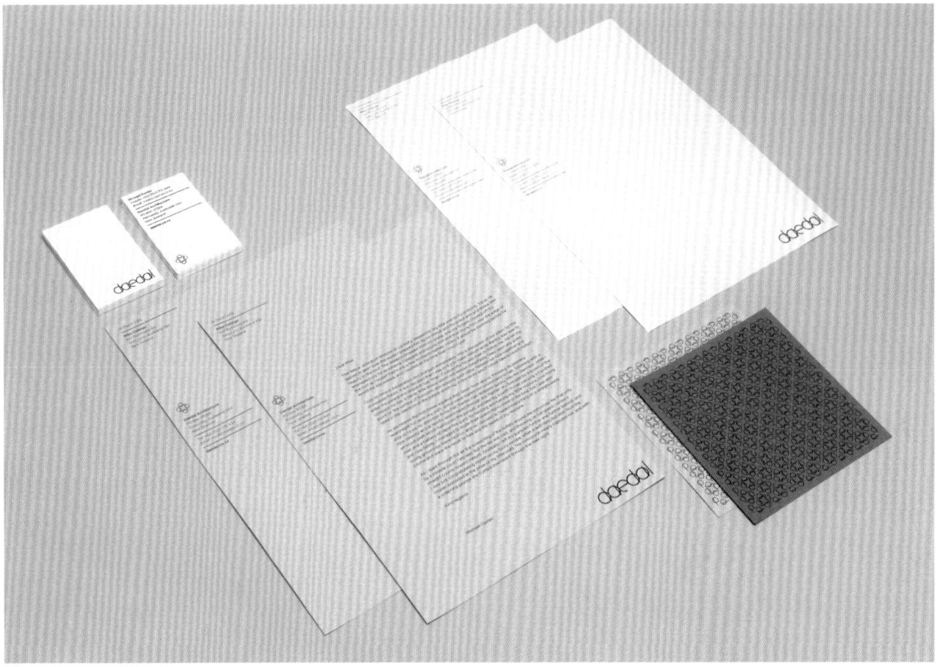
daedal
daedal
daedal

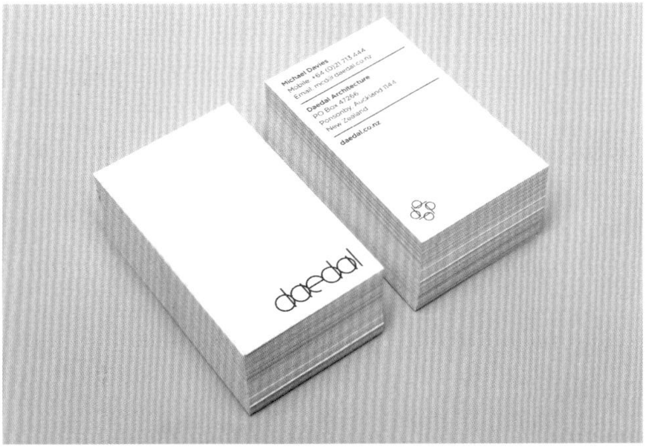
Michael Davies
Mobile: +64 (0)21 713 444
Email: md@daedal.co.nz
Daedal Architecture
PO Box 47266
Ponsonby, Auckland 1144
New Zealand
daedal.co.nz
daedal

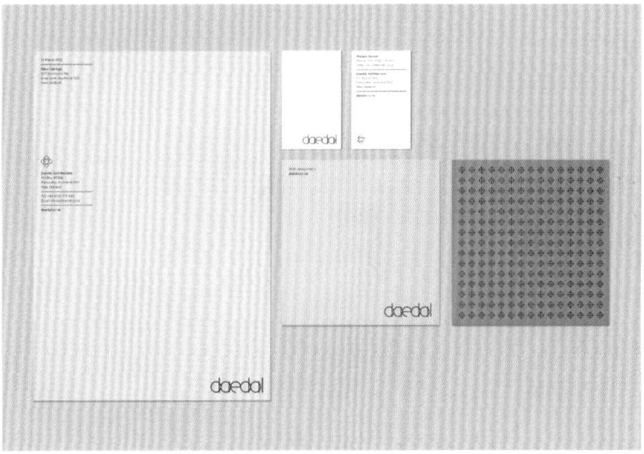
daedal
daedal
daedal

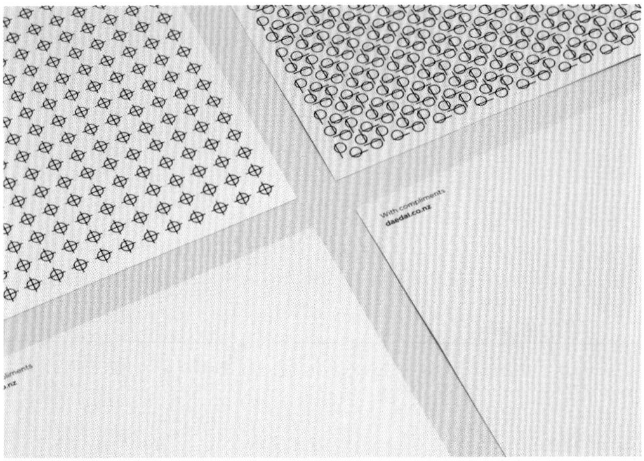
With compliments
daedal.co.nz

Summit

The logo and identity was created for Summit restaurant at The Broadmoor hotel (Colorado Springs), which was established in 1918 and is one of the oldest hotels in the United States. The hotel is also in close proximity to the summit of Pikes Peak. It is located near the famous annual Pikes Peak International Hill Climb, the second oldest motor sports race in America and a long standing Colorado Springs tradition.
This logo was designed with this significant event in mind, and the design incorporates elements of the nearby summit. The graphic element of the "S" represents the serpentine ascent to the mountain peak. Summit restaurant is also known to display winning cars of this annual race in their establishment. Photography by Andrea Martiradonna.

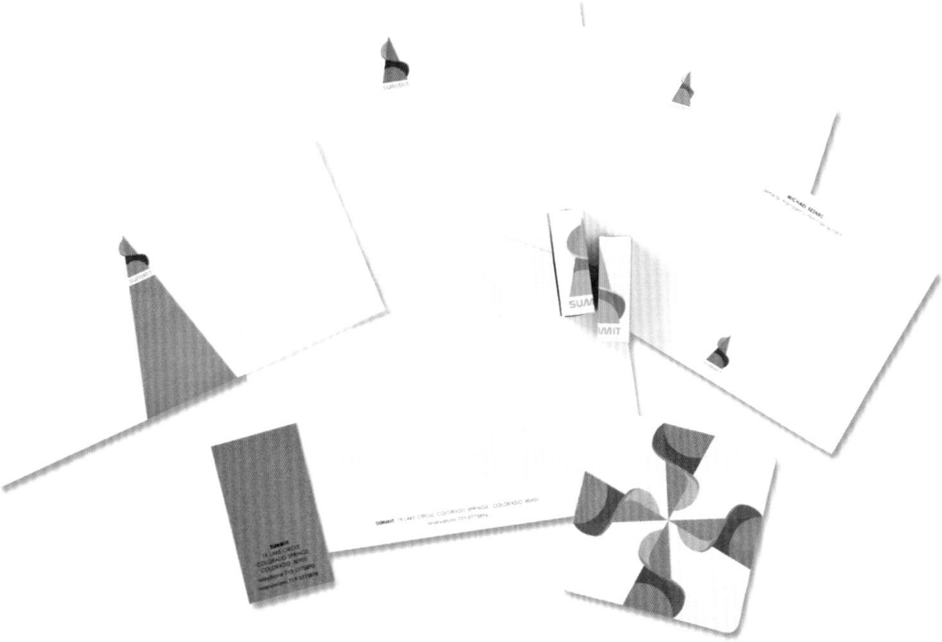

Southeastern Center for Contemporary Art

Located in Winston-Salem, North Carolina, the Southeastern Center for Contemporary Art (SECCA) reopened in 2012 following an extensive renovation. As a non-collecting institution, SECCA places value on its space, which is always evolving and changing with each visiting exhibition or production. Pentagram's Luke Hayman and team designed a new identity for SECCA that emphasizes the institution's commitment to change. "Flux" became an important key word during design explorations, and the final identity conveys a continuing flow; the logo literally moves and fluctuates, echoing the constant change of SECCA's galleries and community programs. The idea of motion is even found in the print materials of SECCA's identity. Though the presentation is static, the logo imparts the constant movement of the animated mark by appearing in different configurations in each application. These varied stills suggest movement across stationery, collateral materials, banners and signage. The color palette employs a spectrum of greens inspired by the wooded property and lush foliage surrounding the center.

Corporate Design IAT

We built a design in which the monastery of Traunkirchen / Austria as a scientific centre and the integration of the different sciences are inseparable. Through the reduced application of form, color and material we tried to cautiously approach the town Traunkirchen as a scientific focus.
It was important to create a symbol which represents all of the scientific areas like formal/logic sciences, arts, natural sciences and social sciences. These sciences each got a symbol, which we combined together as the logo of the Academy. The logo symbolizes the view out of a vaulted window in the monastery, where the academy is located, on the mountain (Traunstein) and the lake (Traunsee) in Traunkirchen / Austria.

INTER
NATIONALE
AKADEMIE
TRAUN
KIRCHEN

DIE INTER
NATIONALE
AKADEMIE
TRAUN
KIRCHEN

INTER
NATIONALE
AKADEMIE
TRAUN
KIRCHEN

Hatch Shaped Identity

For the visual communications of this architectual office we developed a package containing different shapes. These shapes can be combined in an infinite number of ways. The result is a big diversity of hatch shaped objects that illustrate the diverse areas of expertise the office has. By changing the scale of the shapes we emphasize all the levels the architect office operates on. Finally, we gave the identity a flexible character so the visual communications of the office can grow with their future ambitions.

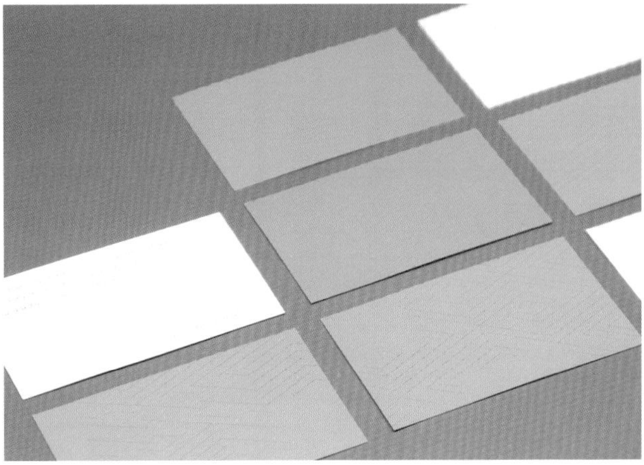

Millar Merrigan Stationery Refresh

Land development consultants Millar Merrigan commissioned Studio Constantine with the task of refreshing their core communications materials. Studio Constantine were keen to free up usable real estate from a previous treatment that was ink and space hungry. We opened out the design to let the structure of the content area define the scale and distribution of elements. A simple asymmetrical hanging alignment referenced the logotype and defined the right hand page margin on the letterhead. In order to broaden the expression of the Millar Merrigan brand, we used the compliment slips as a vehicle to highlight the secondary brand colour palette. Functionally, this adds a range of formality, context and differentiation for Millar Merrigan when liaising with a diverse client base.
Across the suite, Studio Constantine introduced a new uncoated, toothier paper stock; we were keen on increasing the tactility of the correspondence, making it feel weightier in the hand and stepping away from the arbitrary corporate letter.
Photography by Andrew Schweitzer.

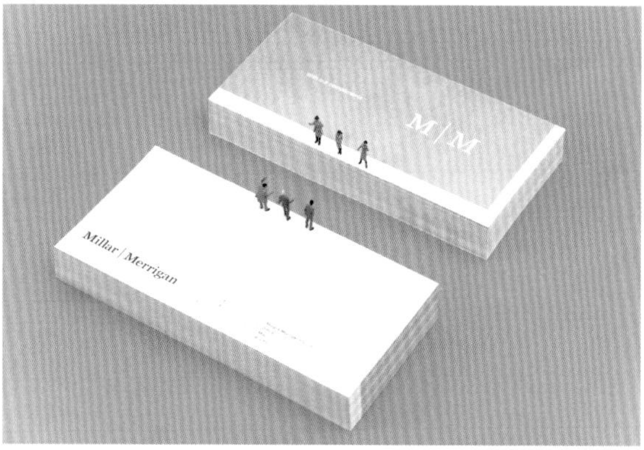

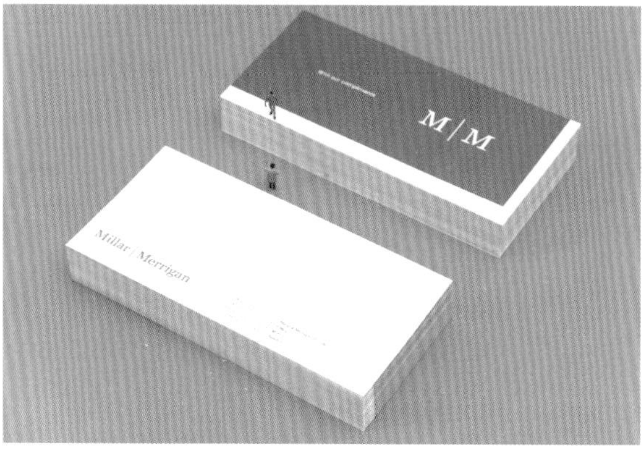

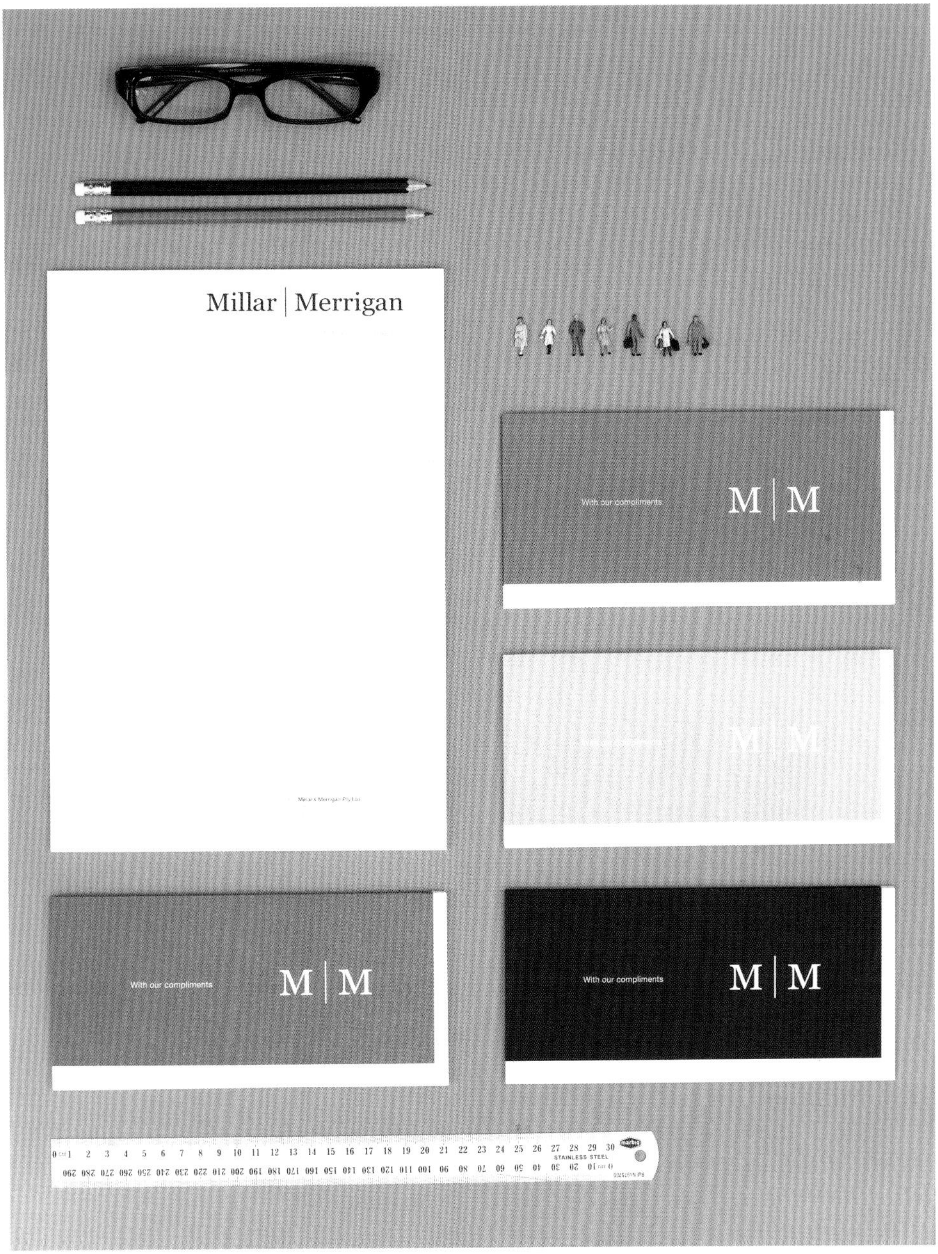
Millar | Merrigan
With our compliments
M | M
With our compliments
M | M
With our compliments
M | M
M | M

Turnstyle Stationery 2012

The Turnstyle stationery system is letterpressed on natural-colored art paper. The extraordinarily thick edges of the business card are gilded with traditional gold leaf, complemented by gold foil stamps elsewhere in the business cabinet. The red strokes on the face of the business card correspond to the diagonals within the "R" and "N" of the logo on the reverse. These strokes act as "cross-outs," negating all but the one bit of contact information that's really necessary in our digital world—the email address. Additional red strokes on the letterhead and mailing label function as salutation and addressee prompts. A sketch journal with corresponding pencil invites clients to take part in the creative process and conveys an appreciation for all things analog.

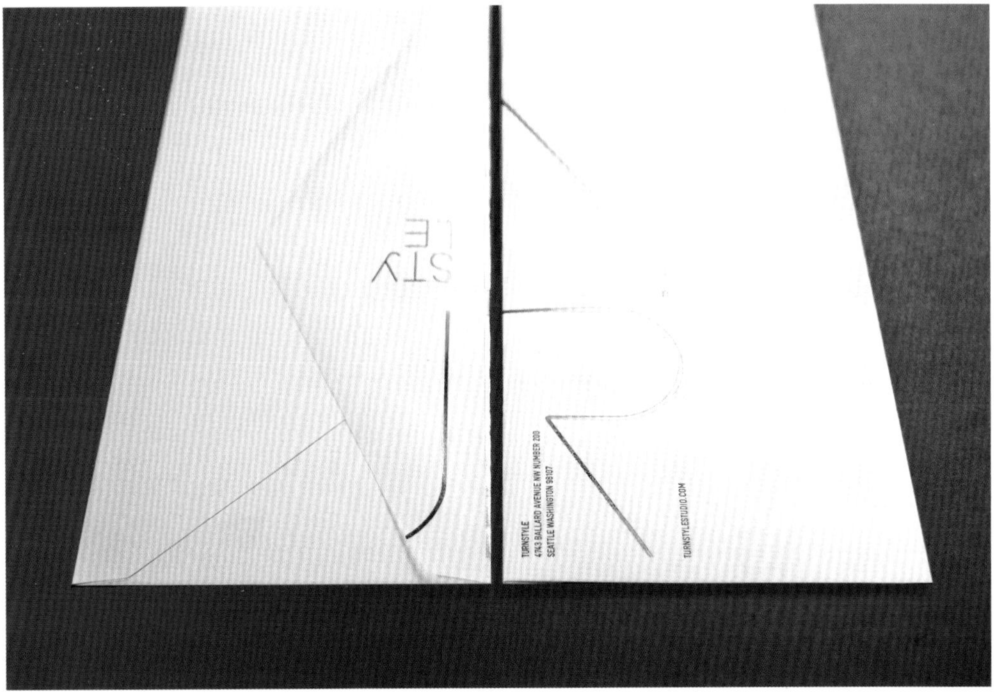
TURNSTYLE
4743 BALLARD AVENUE NW NUMBER 200
SEATTLE WASHINGTON 98107
TURNSTYLESTUDIO.COM

Montreux Café Identity

Full identity system developed for Montreux Café, with the aim to increase its brand awareness. We have also incorporated a set of brand colours to help improve the brand recognition of Montreux Café. A similar typeface is used to help bridge the transition of the rebrand, as well as keeping elements like the wheat symbol (as requested by the client), which was used to subtly frame the wordmark. By varying the thickness of the condensed typeface we are able to compact the wordmark as much as possible, but still maximize legibility. Photography by Kevin Lim.

online store
info@montreuxcafe.com
Shimei East Kitchen #05-10
3015 Bedok North Street 5
Singapore 486350
o + 65 6445 5798
montreuxcafe.com

X-MA C.I. &V.I. Design

X-MA Inc. is an all-around production company mainly dealing with lighting systems, filming and sound effects. I created "blank" space between figures to express a statement X-MA embodies: "Connecting people by making unknown spaces". This explains X-MA's will to create a variety of spaces or environments using something that is shapeless, like lighting.

Lopes Brenna Architetti Business Card

Like architecture, these laser-cut business cards blend differently according to their surroundings.

MEMOMA Visual Identity

Contemplation / Supposition / Thought
If every sound/image carries a wrap of known and used feelings that predispose the recipient to boredom despite the best efforts of every innovation, a break in the restricted circle of pure images manages to conquer the infinite variety of creation.
Under this parameter, (we) worked on a way to synthesize the ideas and ideals that represent us as a studio, such as "Noise", "TV Interference", "Breakdown", "Fracture", "Honesty", "Dynamic" and at the same time reinvented elements from the previous logo, such as the diagonals of the letter "M" which form three-sixths of our names. Within the process and as a final goal, (we) wanted a (really) different, solid and timeless logo that breaks with established rules of our environment, using only two colors and pure substrates for stationery. At the end we believe that all the above concepts are what we are.

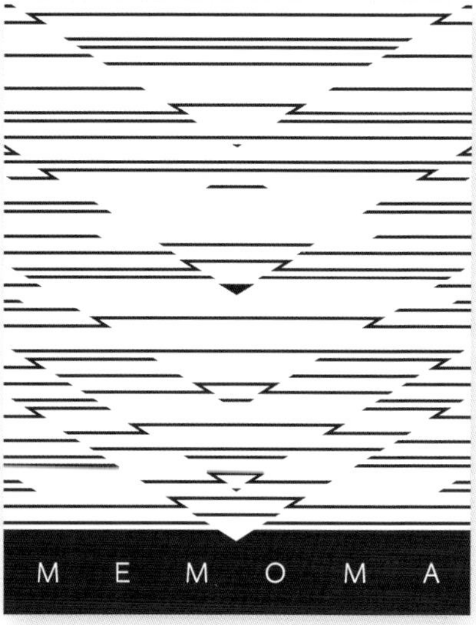

M E M O M A
memoma.tv w. www.memoma.tv
colonia Juárez

Macheete Corporate Identity

We created the corporate identity for Mareen Wordoff and her Communication and Public Relations Company MACHEETE. The logo, as well as the rest of the design, is designed to appear as if it has been cut by a machete. The blacks in the designs are rather distressed and dirty looking. For her stationery, the back side is printed in black while the logo image is mirrored in white so that when viewing the paper from the front side, the logo is shining through from the back!

MACHEETE
MACHEETE
MACHEETE
MACHEETE IS MAREEN WORDOFF
PAULSTRASSE 34 | 10557 BERLIN
MOBILE +49 (0) 163 73 65 296
WWW MACHEETE COM
MAIL@MACHEETE COM
MACHEETE
MACHEETE

MERRY X-MAS
TANNEN LAMETTA KUGELN
UND LICHTER
BRATAPFELDUFT UND FROHE GESICHTER
FREUDE AM SCHENKEN
DAS HERZ WIRD WEICH
MACHEETE WÜNSCHT
EINE FRÖHLICHE WEIHNACHTSZEIT!
MACHEETE

MACHEETE
MACHEETE

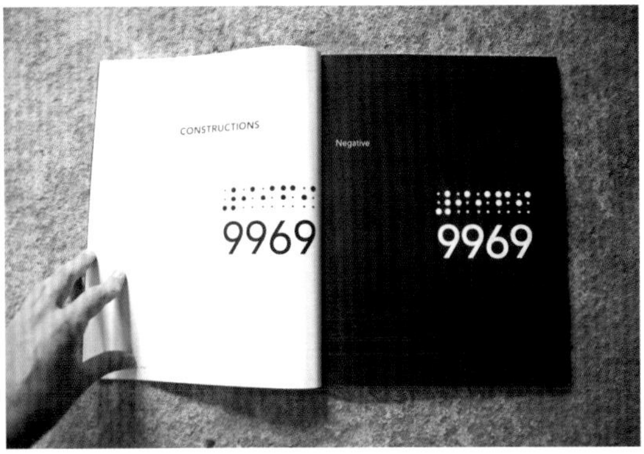

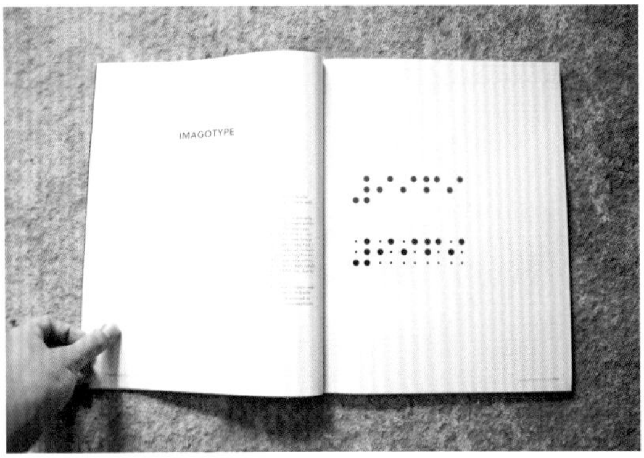

Brand Design 9969

9969 is an enterprise that works with visually impaired people. We wanted to generate a corporate image related to their objectives and beliefs and to link their identity with what they do, what they create and how they communicate through this invisible language. The project transmits this "blind exploration" to those who can see. Besides, this corporate image had to be functional both visually and haptically, connecting traditional and Braille writing. Combining those two writing systems was the main idea and the basis of this project. After all, we reconciled through design two languages that don't have to live apart.

9969
John Stanford

Don't look, feel.

9969
Don't look, feel.

SWITCH

We were asked to create the identity for a lighting design and consultancy firm. Avoiding overtly mechanical connotations, we focused on the designer's thinking process. A semi-colon mark is incorporated into the letter "H" to denote a "deliberate pause" in considering all aspects of a project before a solution is proposed. One can also interpret the lower part of the semi-colon as an actual switch, or as a doorway to possibilities. The folder is designed to be self-contained and formed from a single scored sheet of heavy white card. Slots were pre-cut to allow the inclusion of a name card and CD-ROM along with standard documents.

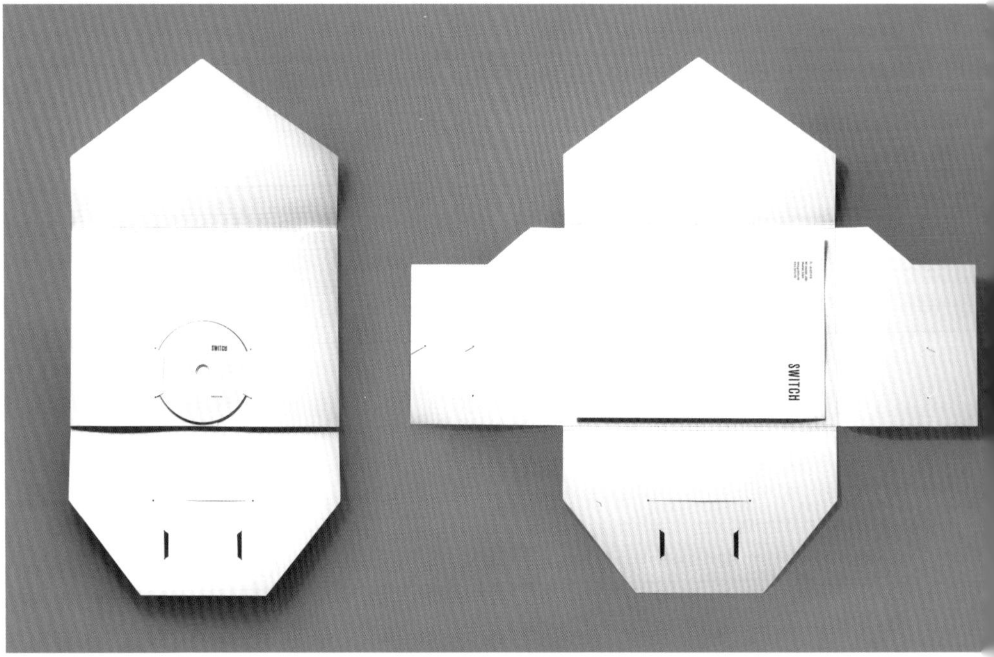

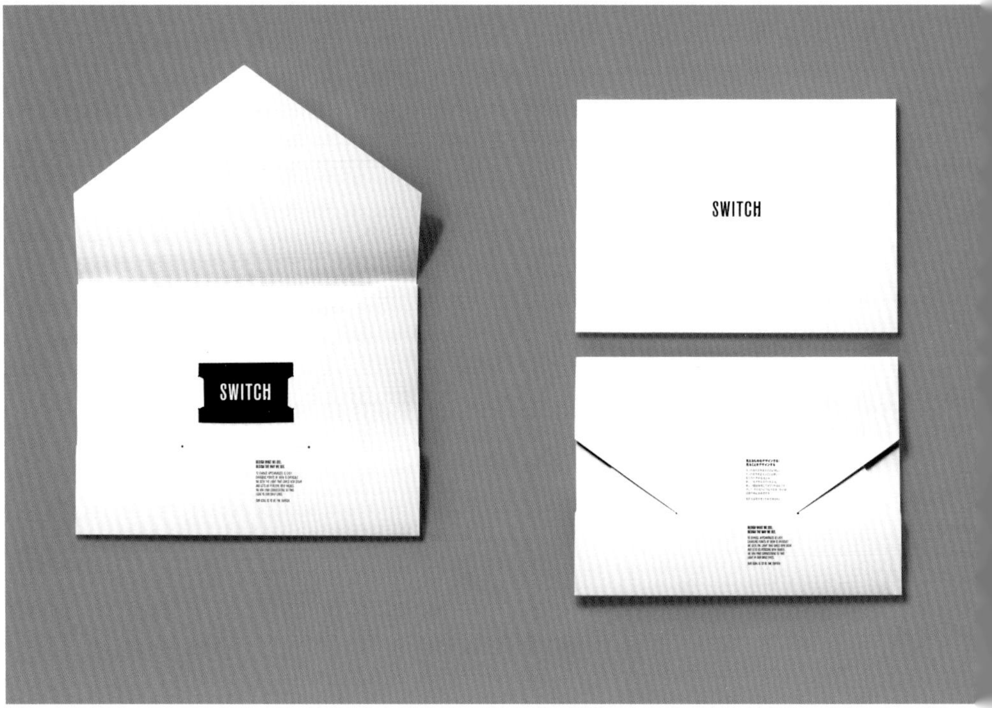

TEL +65-8123-6716
40C HONGKONG STREET
SINGAPORE 059679
TAKEO@SWITCH.PRO
WWW.SWITCH.PRO
SWITCH
SWITCH
SWITCH
TAKEO SUGAMATA
LIGHTING DESIGNER
TEL +65-8123-6716
40C HONGKONG STREET
SINGAPORE 059679
TAKEO@SWITCH.PRO
WWW.SWITCH.PRO

Le Cintré & Co.

Le Cintré & Co. is a boutique hotel that offers an atmosphere revolving around arts and urban culture, to an open minded, intellectual, non-conformist and creative target clientele. The hotel hosts conferences, exhibits, workshops and cultural activities. Le Cintré & Co. collaborates with artists from around the globe, working in various creative spheres, to promote and contribute to its constant development. Le Cintré & Co. is made up of multiple departments, sub brands and signature events, which all have specific names, functions and a logotype that support the main brand.

lecintrē+co

18 26 37

46 52 62

85 98

3285 rue
Saint-Ambroise
Griffintown
Montréal
QC Canada
H6B2A8
T. +1 514
845 4267
F. +1 514
845 4268
www.
lecintre.com
lecintrē+co
lecintrē+co
lecintrē+co
3285 rue
Saint-Ambroise
Griffintown
Montréal
QC Canada
H6B2A8
T. +1 514
845 4267
F. +1 514
845 4268
www.
lecintre.com

18
lecintrē+co

FEB Design Stationery

For our own stationery, we aimed to show the communicative quality of each one of the stationery elements, so the medium becomes the message and the central character of this assignment. The tone of the selected sentences reflects the close relationship that we daily nourish with our customers.

HELLO
OLÁ
NICE TO MEET YOU
FEB DESIGN
FROM FEB TO YOU
FEB
FROM FEB TO YOU
HELLO

BY FEB TO YOU
YOU'VE GOT MAIL
NICE TO MEET YOU
WE ARE FEB
FROM FEB
HELLO

RKNL Identity

RKNL furniture studio designs and produces furniture with its very own signature. The designs are based on a style which combines sharp outlines with soft forms. SMEL developed a new identity and name for Ronald Knol's furniture studio. The logo consists of letters designed by SMEL, inspired by the design language of the furniture.

RKNL
RKNL MEUBELSTUDIO - SYMBIOSE VAN VORM EN FUNDAMENT
HOOGHIEMSTRAPLEIN 59 3514 AX UTRECHT NEDERLAND

RKNL
RKNL MEUBELSTUDIO - SYMBIOSE VAN VORM EN FUNDAMENT
RONALD KNOL - KOVELAARSTRAAT 7 NL-3582 GN UTRECHT
TEL 06-21264203 WEB WWW.RKNL.NL E-MAIL INFO@RKNL.NL
RKNL
RKNL
RKNL
RKNL
RKNL

De Verre Bergen

The Verre Bergen Foundation initiates and realizes programs which invigorate and empower Rotterdam and her citizens. This straightforward and powerful approach is reflected in the design of the visual identity of the Foundation.

Fuse Design Stationery

All the Fuse Design stationery items are printed on GF Smith Colorplan cool grey stock in various weights. The business cards are a 540gsm card, with clear and black hot foil printing. The letterheads have also been foil and litho printed in one color. The envelopes have been hot foiled in black.

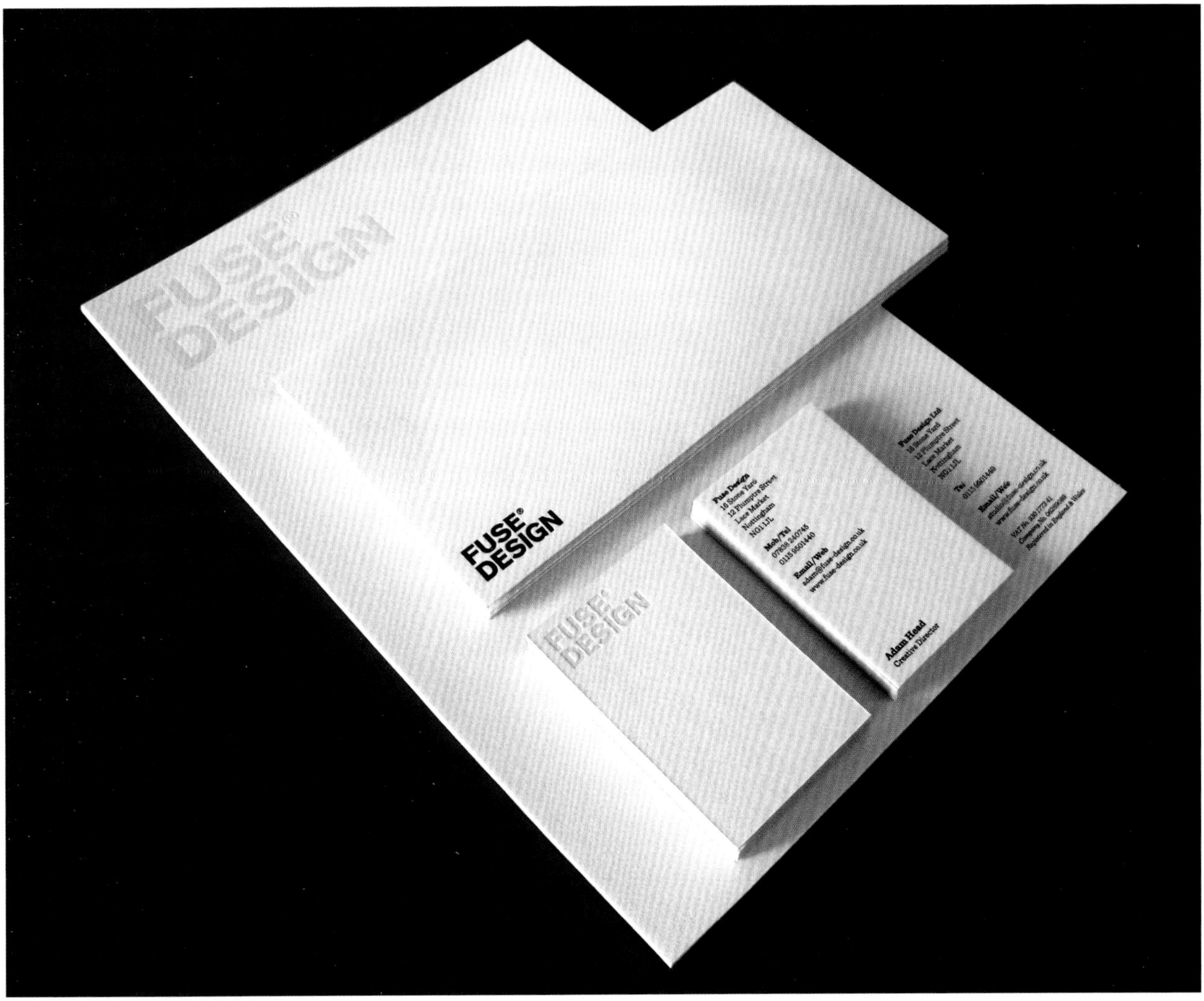

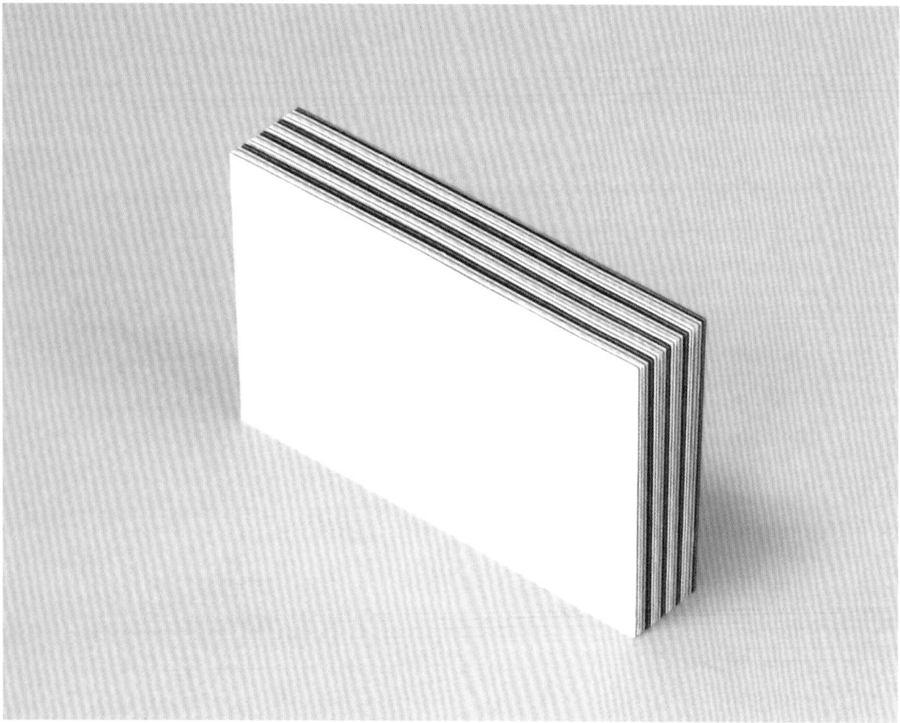

Claydon Reeves

Yacht and transportation design company Claydon Reeves gave us the task of creating a new brand identity and website for them, which had to reflect the outstanding quality and high end nature of their work, whilst developing a distinctive style that would set them apart from their competitors.
The finished marque draws inspiration from the shape of a wave and elegantly uses one carefully crafted line to create the partnership's initials CR. Influenced by the pair's technical drawings, the brand colours are comprised of classic black, blue and grey tones with warm yellow and orange highlights.
From a spot varnished logo on their business cards to foiled titles and premium papers in their handbound books, we used premium materials and processes in all areas of their communication. A bespoke content managed website provides a striking online showcase for their work alongside more traditional hardback portfolio books to be sent to their clients.

MOAR

MOAR was created with the intention of moving away from the limited concept and ideals of a traditional architecture company. Spaces play an important role in representing the force behind the message because they are effective communication tools for brands. MOAR takes particular interest in global perspectives to undertake all projects, focusing on an open vision of architecture, strategy, marketing, design and visual communication. Biquini has designed an identity that not only confers seriousness, but also has utility and the confidence that an architecture company requires. The image created is based on the essence of space, typography and colour to convey a charming feel. Music is the silence between the notes; silence creates the rhythm and constitutes the melodies. In that sense, empty space between forms defines the typographic letters, just as the empty space between walls defines architectural space. With this in mind, we developed a flexible visual identity constructed on the basis of a geometric screen in which shapes of the brand are drawn. Each type is geometrically fragmented, acquires remodeled shapes, and creates spaces simultaneously open and closed. Therefore we create a dialogue between outside and inside, paralleling the concept of full and empty.

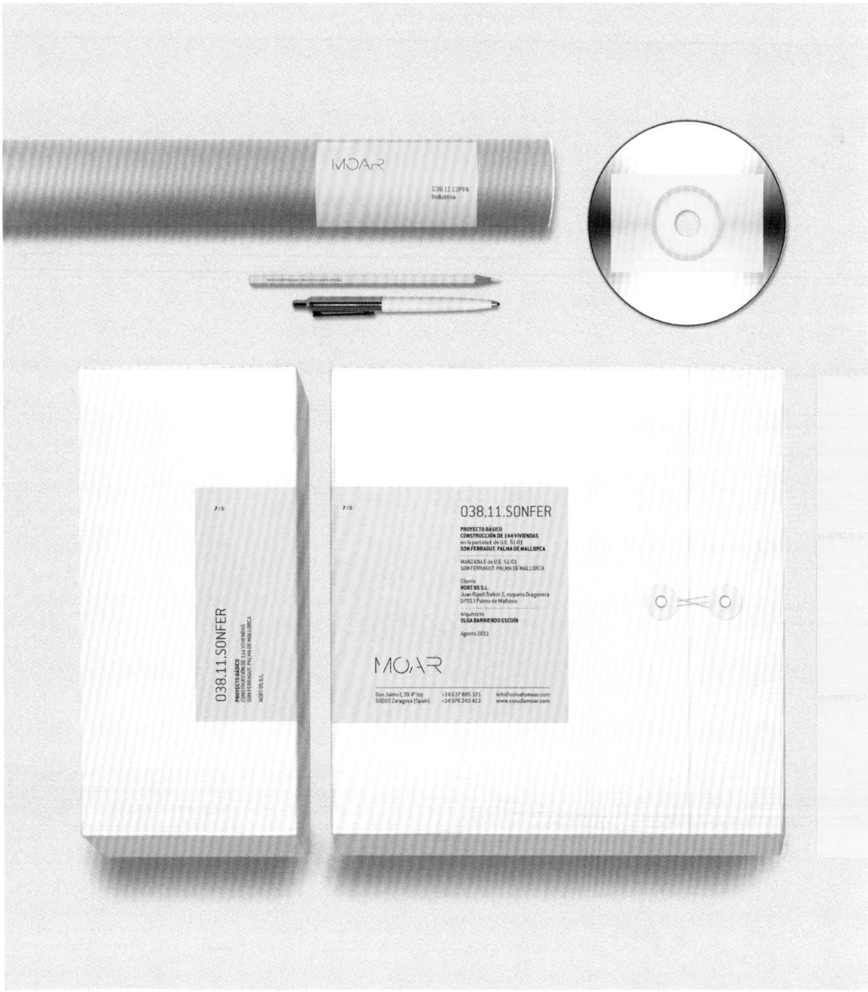

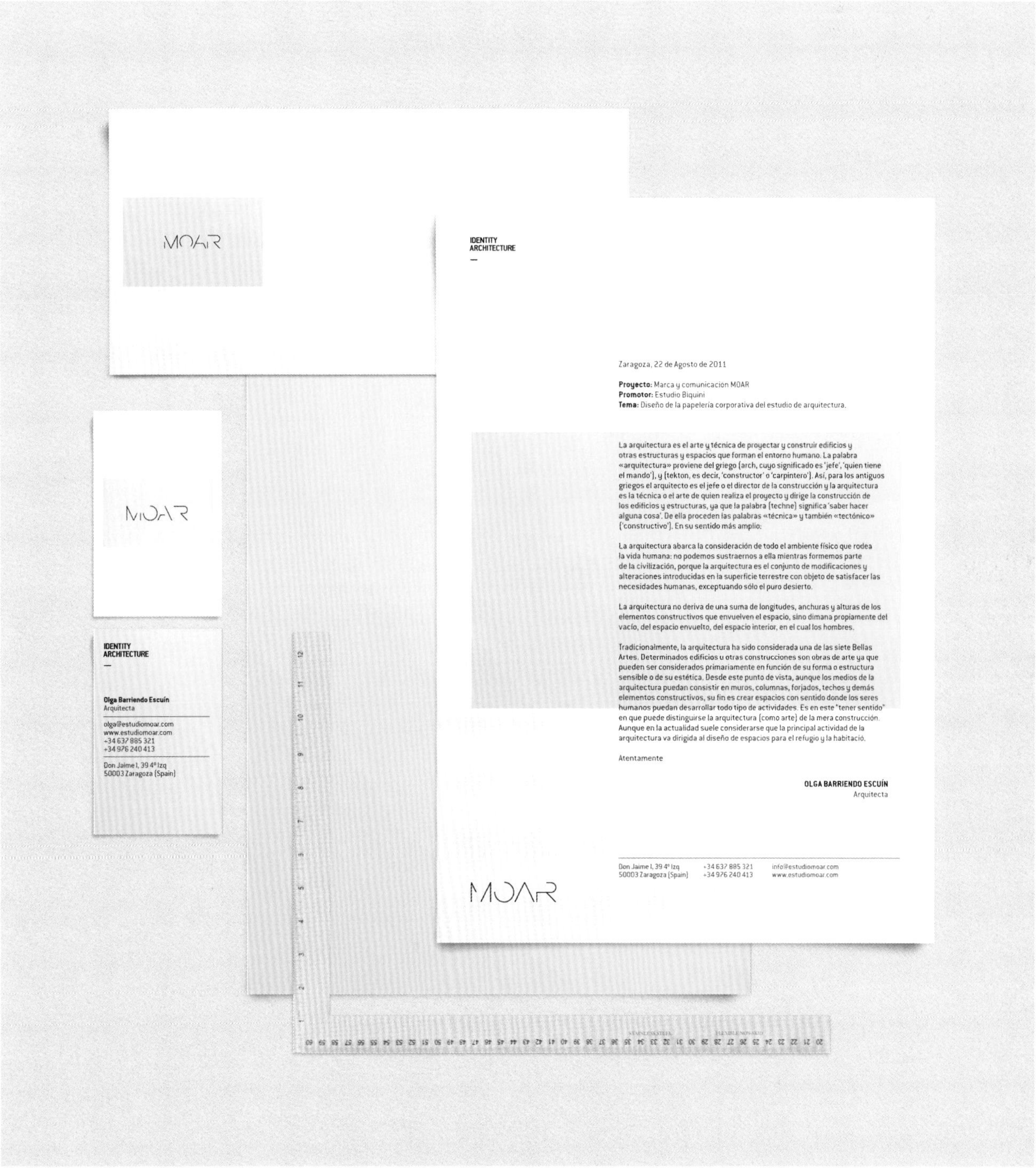
MOAR
MOAR
IDENTITY
ARCHITECTURE
Olga Barriendo Escuín
Arquitecta
olga@estudiomoar.com
www.estudiomoar.com
+34 637 885 321
+34 976 240 413
Don Jaime I, 39 4º Izq
50003 Zaragoza (Spain)
IDENTITY
ARCHITECTURE
Zaragoza, 22 de Agosto de 2011
Proyecto: Marca y comunicación MOAR
Promotor: Estudio Biquini
Tema: Diseño de la papelería corporativa del estudio de arquitectura.
La arquitectura es el arte y técnica de proyectar y construir edificios y otras estructuras y espacios que forman el entorno humano. La palabra «arquitectura» proviene del griego (arch, cuyo significado es 'jefe', 'quien tiene el mando'), y (tekton, es decir, 'constructor' o 'carpintero'). Así, para los antiguos griegos el arquitecto es el jefe o el director de la construcción y la arquitectura es la técnica o el arte de quien realiza el proyecto y dirige la construcción de los edificios y estructuras, ya que la palabra (techne) significa 'saber hacer alguna cosa'. De ella proceden las palabras «técnica» y también «tectónico» ('constructivo'). En su sentido más amplio:
La arquitectura abarca la consideración de todo el ambiente físico que rodea la vida humana: no podemos sustraernos a ella mientras formemos parte de la civilización, porque la arquitectura es el conjunto de modificaciones y alteraciones introducidas en la superficie terrestre con objeto de satisfacer las necesidades humanas, exceptuando sólo el puro desierto.
La arquitectura no deriva de una suma de longitudes, anchuras y alturas de los elementos constructivos que envuelven el espacio, sino dimana propiamente del vacío, del espacio envuelto, del espacio interior, en el cual los hombres.
Tradicionalmente, la arquitectura ha sido considerada una de las siete Bellas Artes. Determinados edificios u otras construcciones son obras de arte ya que pueden ser considerados primariamente en función de su forma o estructura sensible o de su estética. Desde este punto de vista, aunque los medios de la arquitectura puedan consistir en muros, columnas, forjados, techos y demás elementos constructivos, su fin es crear espacios con sentido donde los seres humanos puedan desarrollar todo tipo de actividades. Es en este "tener sentido" en que puede distinguirse la arquitectura (como arte) de la mera construcción. Aunque en la actualidad suele considerarse que la principal actividad de la arquitectura va dirigida al diseño de espacios para el refugio y la habitació.
Atentamente
OLGA BARRIENDO ESCUÍN
Arquitecta
Don Jaime I, 39 4º Izq
50003 Zaragoza (Spain)
+34 637 885 321
+34 976 240 413
info@estudiomoar.com
www.estudiomoar.com
MOAR

Studio Beige Stationery

Visual identity for Studio Beige design studio.

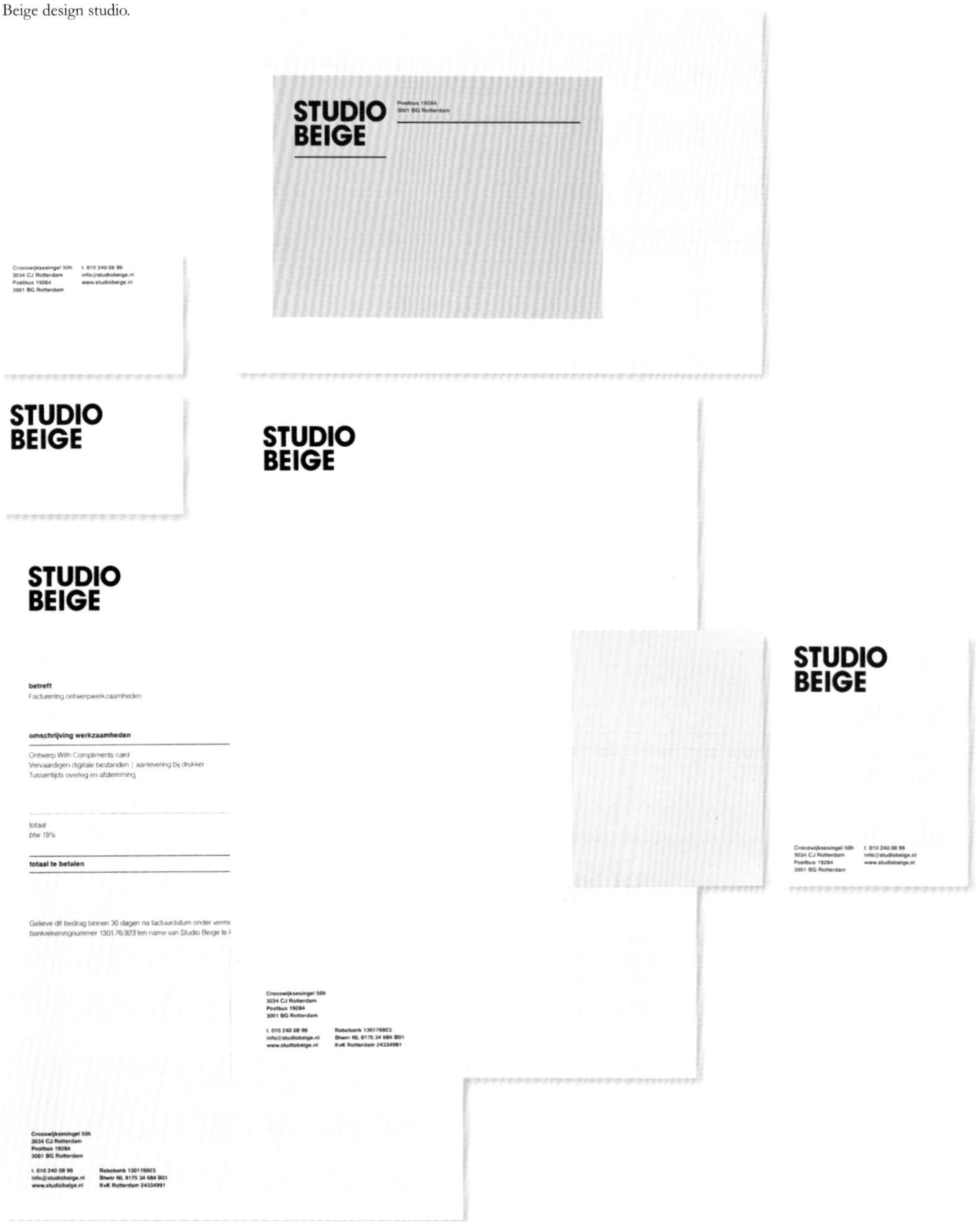

STUDIO
BEIGE
NICE TO
MEET YOU

STUDIO
BEIGE
Crooswijksesingel 50h
3034 CJ Rotterdam
Postbus 19284
3001 BG Rotterdam
t. 010 240 08 99
info@studiobeige.nl
www.studiobeige.nl

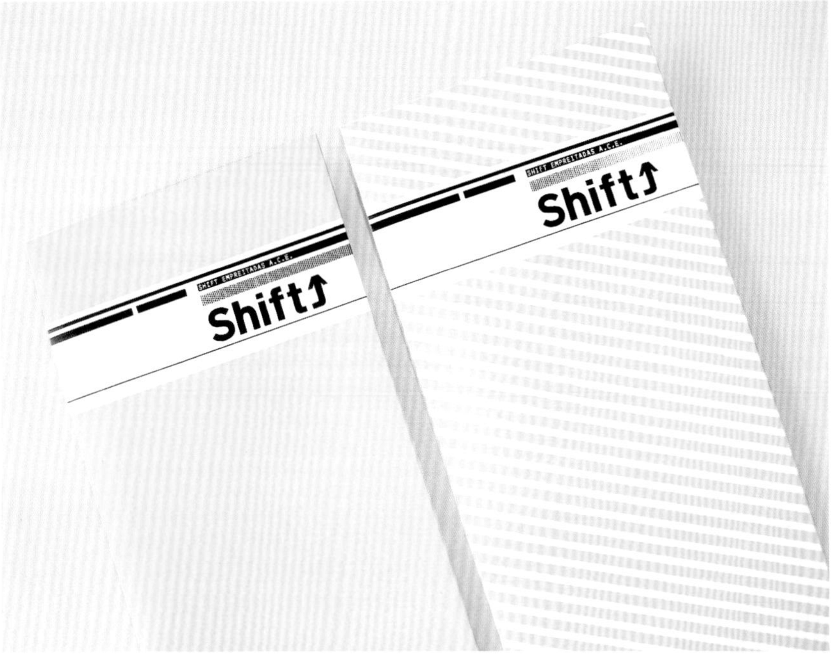

Shift

Shift is a construction company working as a hub, uniting efforts from business partners to develop its projects. Shift stands for "Exchange, move or transfer from one place to another". When talking about construction work, heavy machinery and loud noise, one would expect immediate awareness of something that would not pass unnoticed. Simplicity added to consistency translates into bold action. Clean, clear, bold action. This was Blank's motto when developing Shift's brand identity.

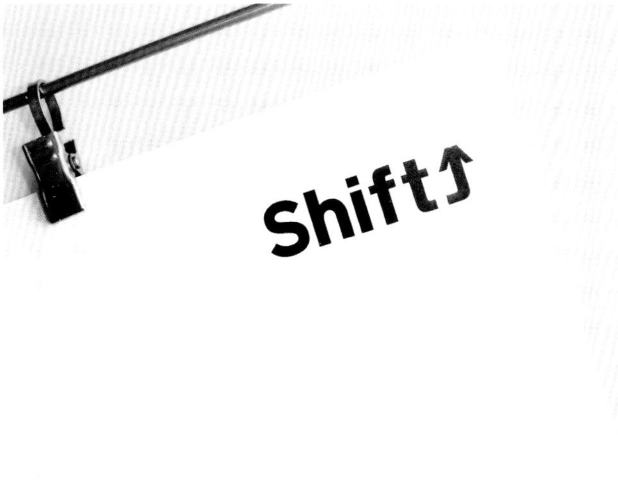
Shift

Shift
OUTPUT
INPUT

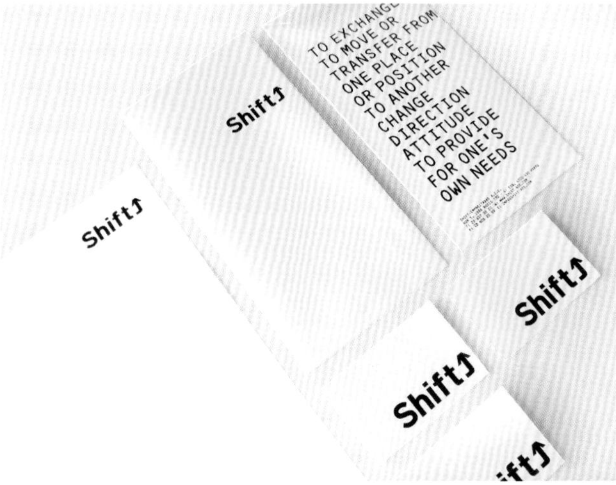
Shift
TO MOVE OR
TRANSFER FROM
ONE PLACE
OR POSITION
TO ANOTHER
CHANGE
DIRECTION
ATTITUDE
TO PROVIDE
FOR ONE'S
OWN NEEDS
Shift
Shift
Shift

Shift
Shift
Shift
Shift
Shift

Shift

Shift
SHIFT-EMPREITADAS A.C.E
SEDE: AV. D. AFONSO HENRIQUES 537
4450-014 MATOSINHOS
T: 22 609 23 45
F: 22 609 23 46
E: INFO@SHIFT-ACE.COM
W: WWW.SHIFT-ACE.COM

Ray Lemon

To create a communication concept for the bar "Ray Lemon" in Heilbronn, we generated two constants: the colour yellow (in combination with the grey of the visible exposed concrete) and the fictional Character "Ray". He now appears in every dialogue and even established his own friends, which are easily recognizable by the laser marks they wear. The invitation to the event "Menu in Gelb" is furnished with spices used in the current menu, while the origami folding technique creates a valuable and individual character.

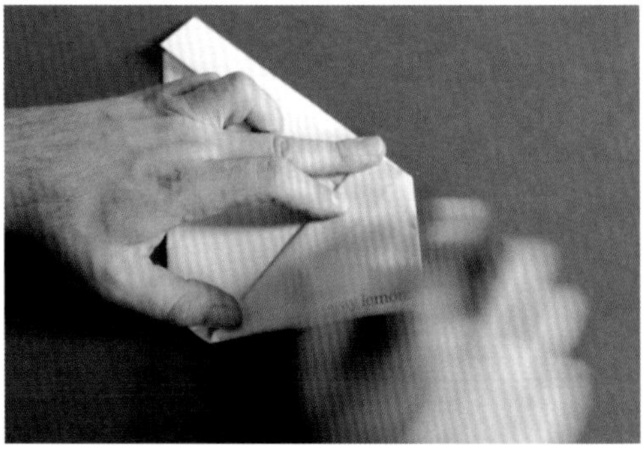

ray lemon.
ray lemon.
ray lemon.
CLIQUE

ray lemon.
ray lemon.
ray lemon.
RAY
MAHSA HOSSEINI
ray lemon.

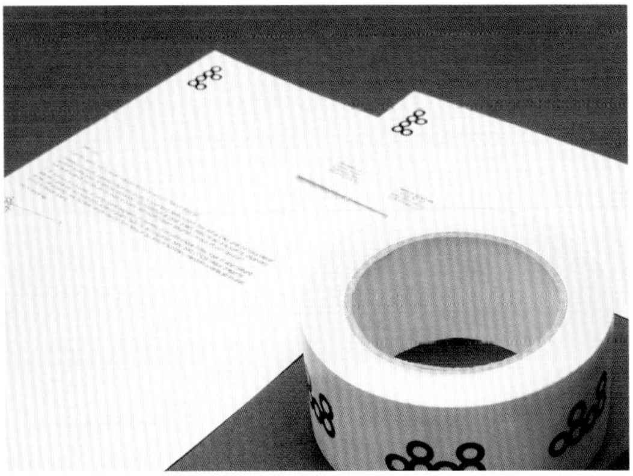

Terralec

Terralec has a well-established reputation for selling high quality stage lighting and audio equipment to the entertainment industry. I was approached to create a new identity for them to help reflect this increased reputation, as well as maintain their continued ambitions for growth and quality. The idea was to create something that would make them stand out from the crowd, whilst also signifying what the company does. As a result, the whole stationery range was printed on bright Pop'Set ® Citrus Yellow paper to create maximum visual impact that, along with the new logo, represents the company's expertise in lighting in a clean, modern way. Business card details were laser cut into 2mm Perspex® Fluorescent Yellow, a light gathering material that glows around the edges when in daylight. Continuing on from the new identity, there are now plans to redesign the website, along with motion graphics that make great use of the new logo.

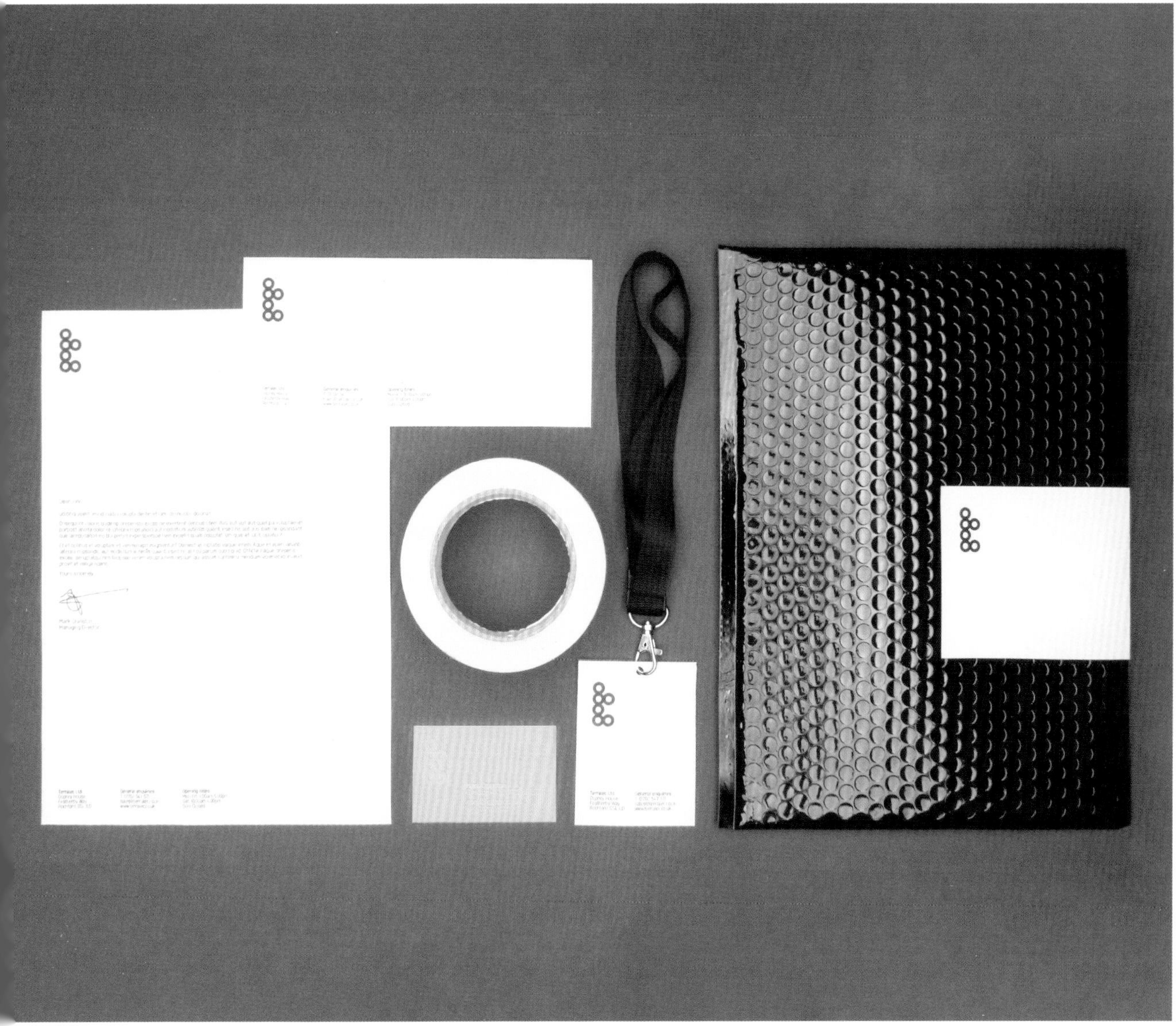

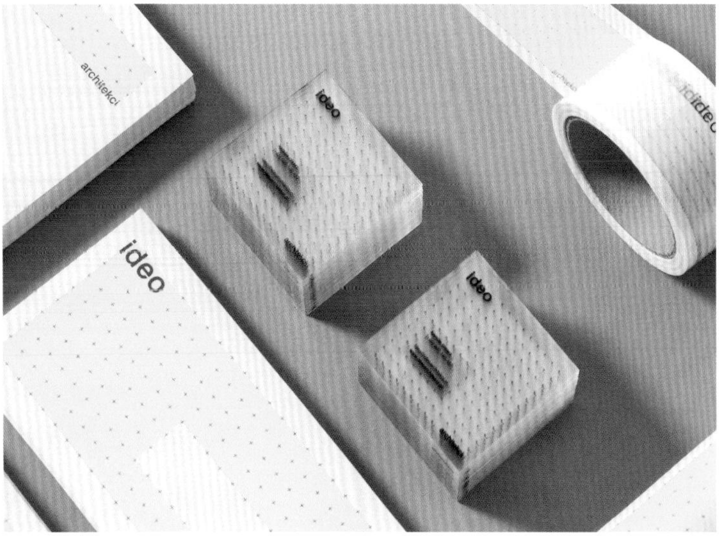

ideo architekci

Branding of "ideo architekci" studio from Wroclaw. The idea behind the logo is "maximum flexibility" with an adjustable logo size and shape based on the "Cross Grid" system. The basic logo shape expands on different media. The logo becomes a living form, filling out the space and adjusting itself to the ID area. The "Cross Grid" system allows the possibility to create a "text field" inside the logo ID structure. It can be used on a variety of promotional materials for the identity. On the basis of the new flexible logo system, we have designed all necessary corporate materials plus extra elements such as tape, marking spray and yellow markers. The most characteristic element of the new identity is the design of business cards. They're made of 3mm transparent material in which the refracting light creates interesting logo reflections depending on the angle of looking at their edges.
The whole branding process was complemented by a web design and brand manual standardizing the use of the new identity.

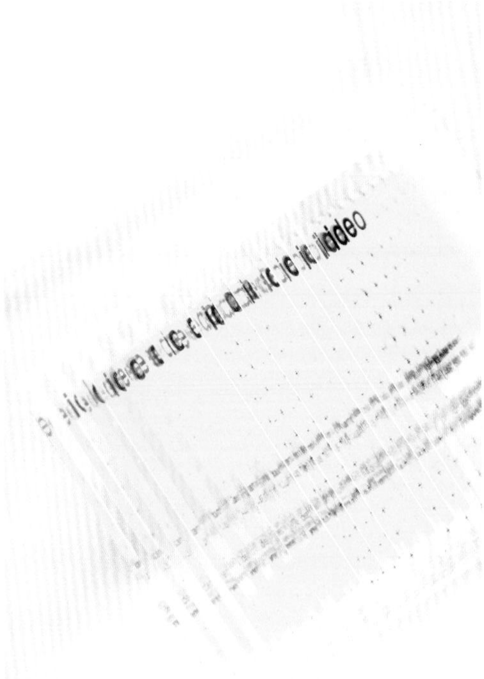

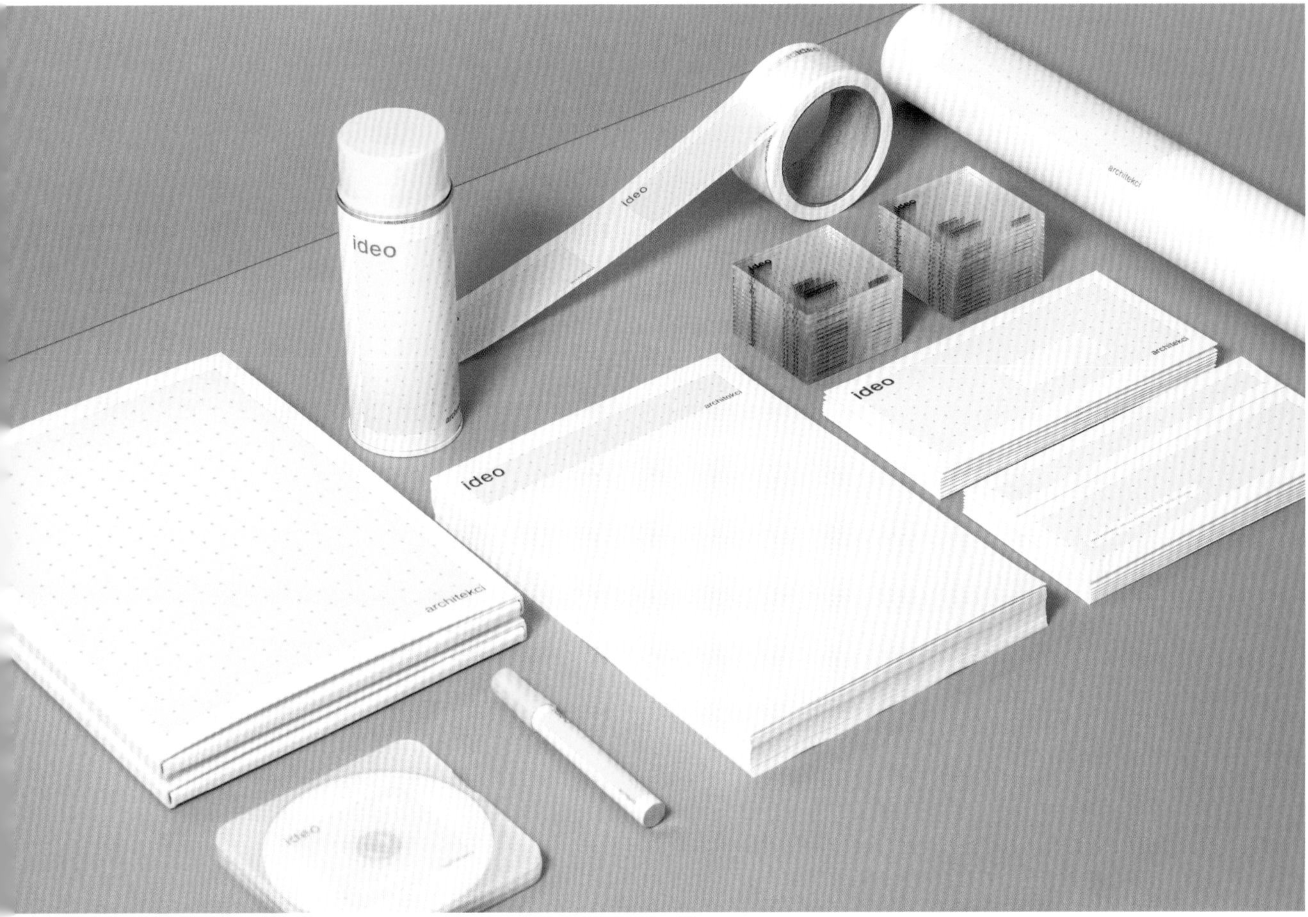
ideo
ideo
ideo
ideo
architekci
architekci
architekci
ideo

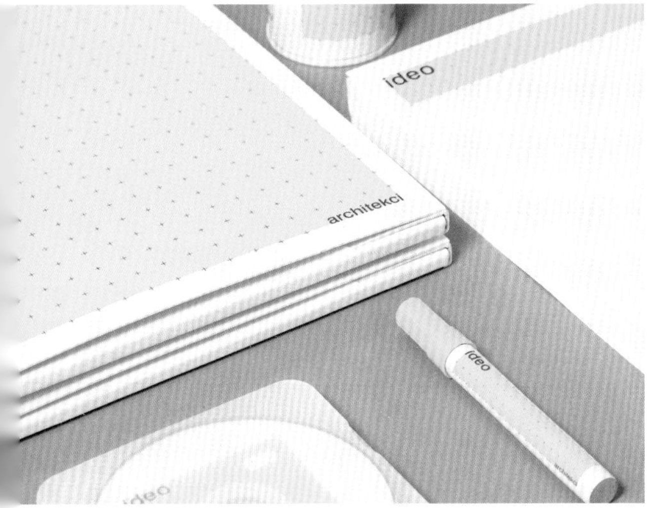
ideo
architekci
ideo

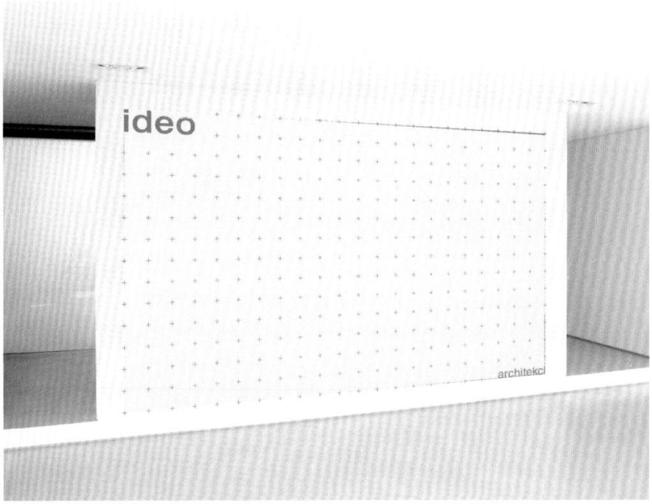
ideo
architekci

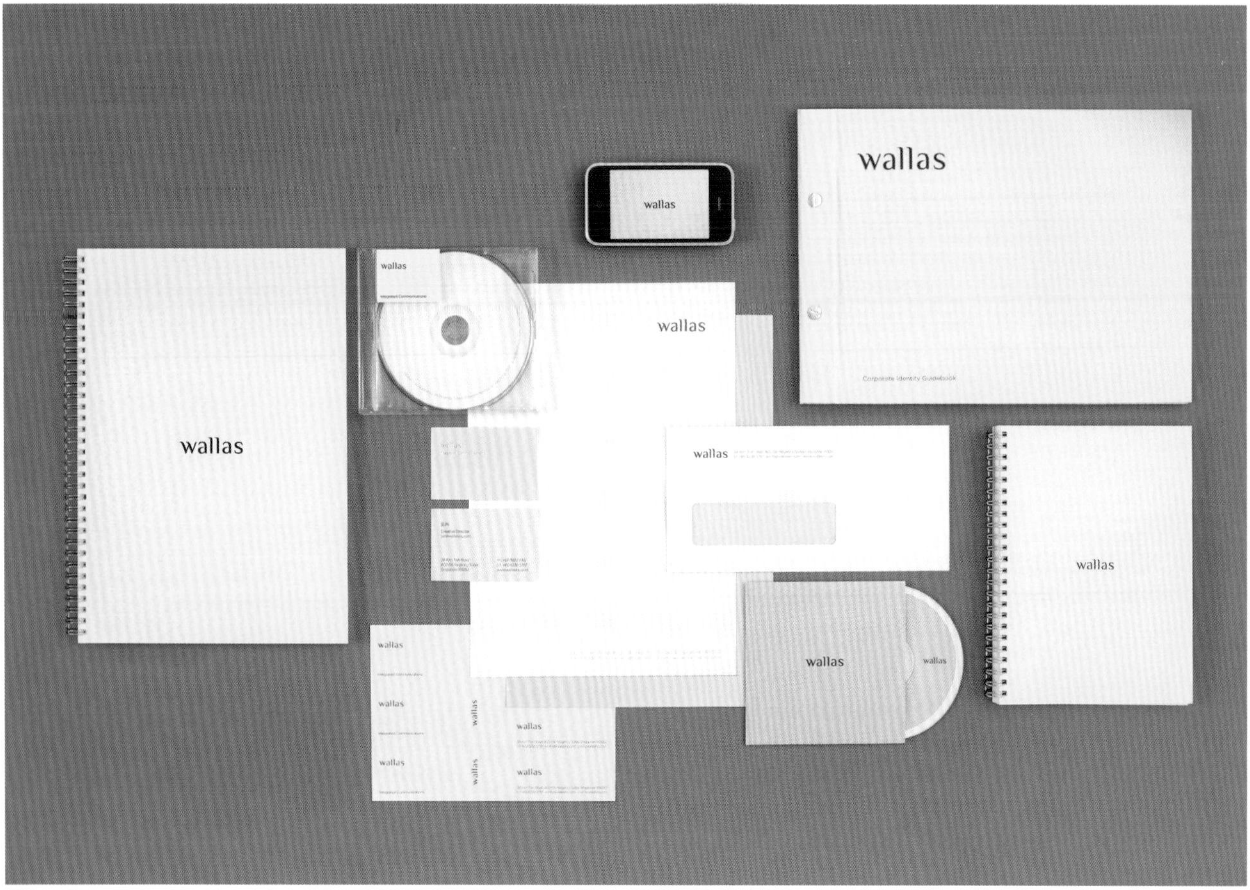

Wallas Inc Identity

We developed an identity for Wallas Inc, a start-up integrated communications agency. We were responsible for the creation of the wordmark, complete with a corporate identity guidebook, and the design of all other communication devices. The wordmark on the name card is printed with foil-blocking onto the PMS 116 320gsm uncoated stock. Photography by Jeremy Lee.

Kina

Visual identity and stationery for the communication agency: Kina. Typographic visual identity that plays with the different planes and geometry of the letter K.

Kinetica

Kinetica is an ingenious industrial design bureau based in Santa Catarina, Mexico, offering custom solutions for non-standard architectural challenges. The studio works with top-level international, national and local architecture firms to develop the most obsessive and mind blowing industrial projects. Face redesigned the brand from head to toe, from their manifesto, their DNA and their communication through words and images. Kinetica's identity is based on the simple concept of modular grids with movement. The only generic geometric shape we use is a circle. Modern design, bright color, Swiss typography and the gridded space create an industrial yet classy atmosphere.

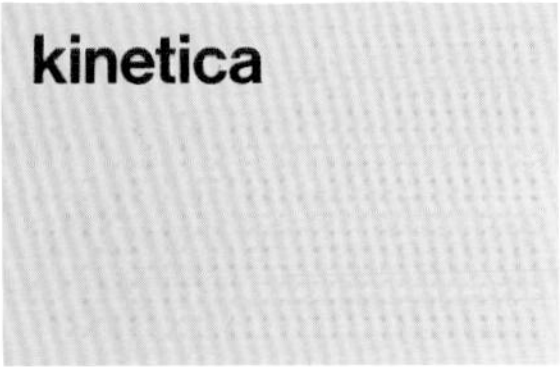

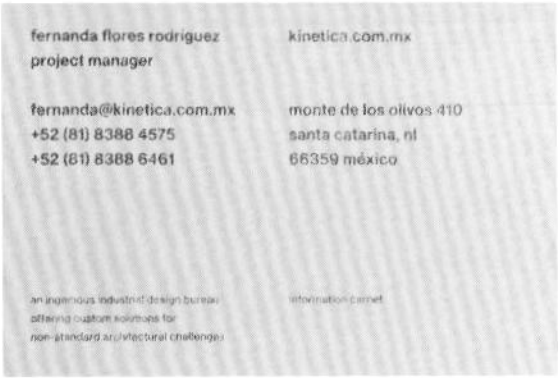

kinetica

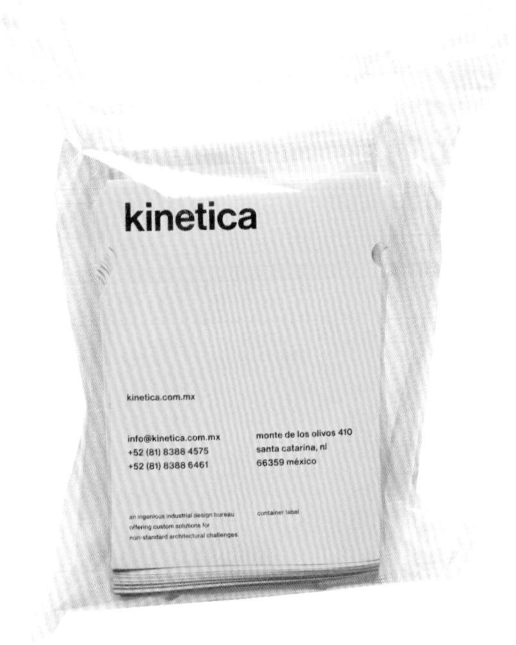

kinetica
kinetica.com.mx

kinetica

kinetica
kinetica.com.mx
info@kinetica.com.mx
+52 (81) 8388 4575
+52 (81) 8388 6461
monte de los olivos 410
santa catarina, nl
66359 méxico
an ingenious industrial design bureau
offering custom solutions for
non-standard architectural challenges
container label

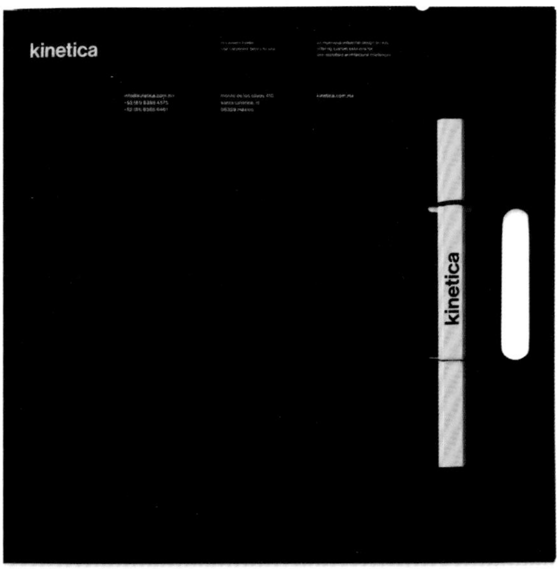
kinetica
kinetica

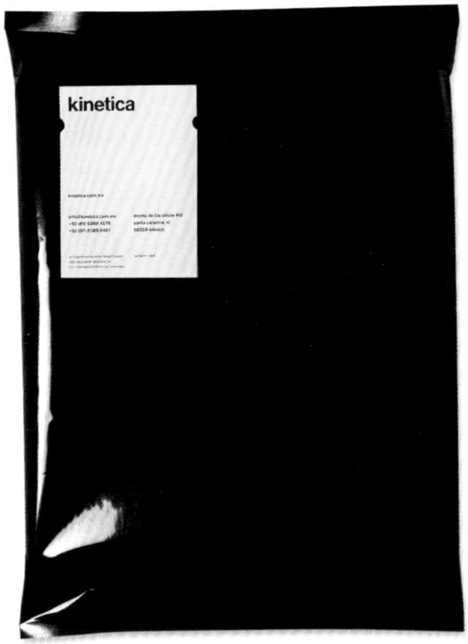
kinetica

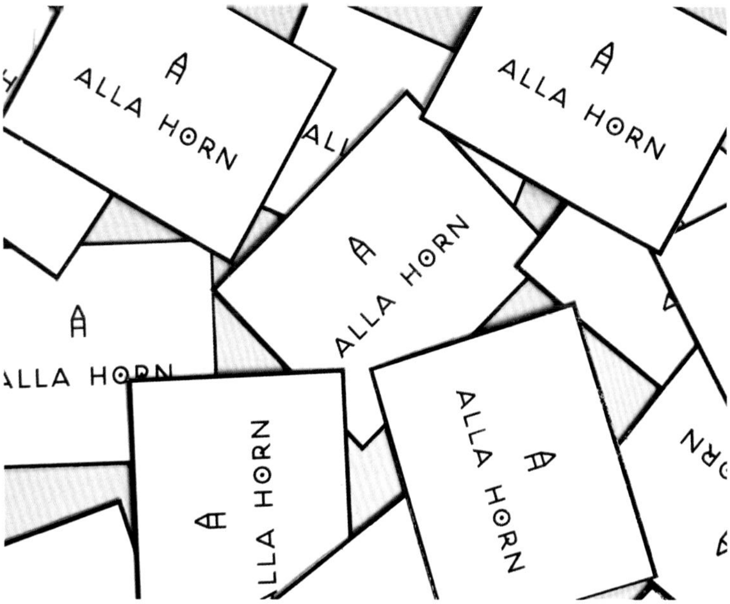

Alla Horn

Alla Horn is an interior design company which prides itself on the functionality of their solutions. The identity for the company is a reflection of their unique motives where function is the foundation for the visual solution. The logo captures the crucial planning and considerations made in sketches during Alla Horn's analogue before digital design process. As Alla Horn regard function over form as their single minded proposition, the typeface GT Haptik by Grilli is a typeface which has been specially optimized to be read blindfolded. This is a reflection of function over form where optical criteria become secondary.

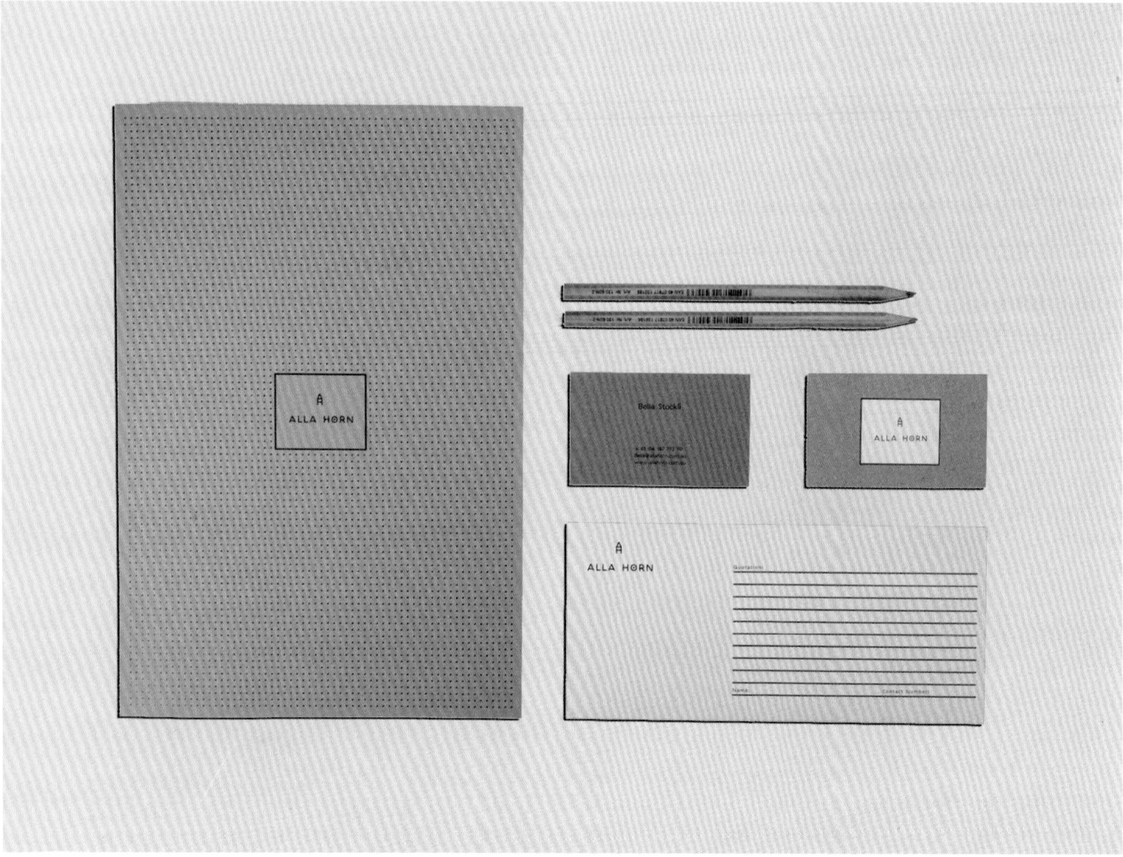

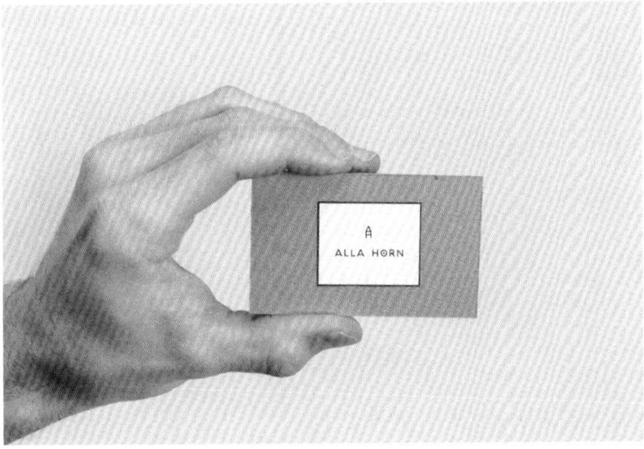
ALLA HORN

ALLA HORN
Annita Seifert
ALLA HORN

Central Magazine's Identity

Central Magazine's identity concept is based on two principal ideas: the name of the publication and the location of the main offices.

Central is one of the biggest traditional markets in Las Palmas de Gran Canaria city (Canary Islands, Spain). Years back, when editor in chief John López started to run the project, he placed Central's first office a few meters away from the market. Situated in the middle of the city, traffic was continuous, which caused the whole identity to be formed by the use of typography in different ways, like the traffic movement on a city map. Every element in the identity is applied with different kind of rubber stamps into recycled cardboard or paper, in order to resemble antique stationery used in the market and create different compositions for each new inspired piece. Materials play an important role, representing the rudeness of the streets and the purity of the content.

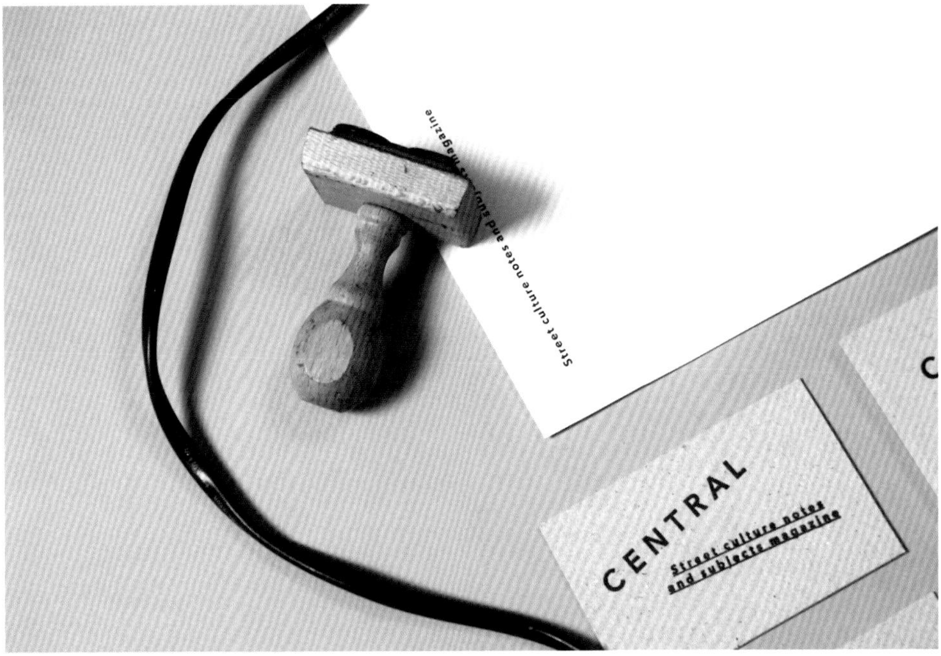
CENTRAL
Street culture notes
and subjects magazine

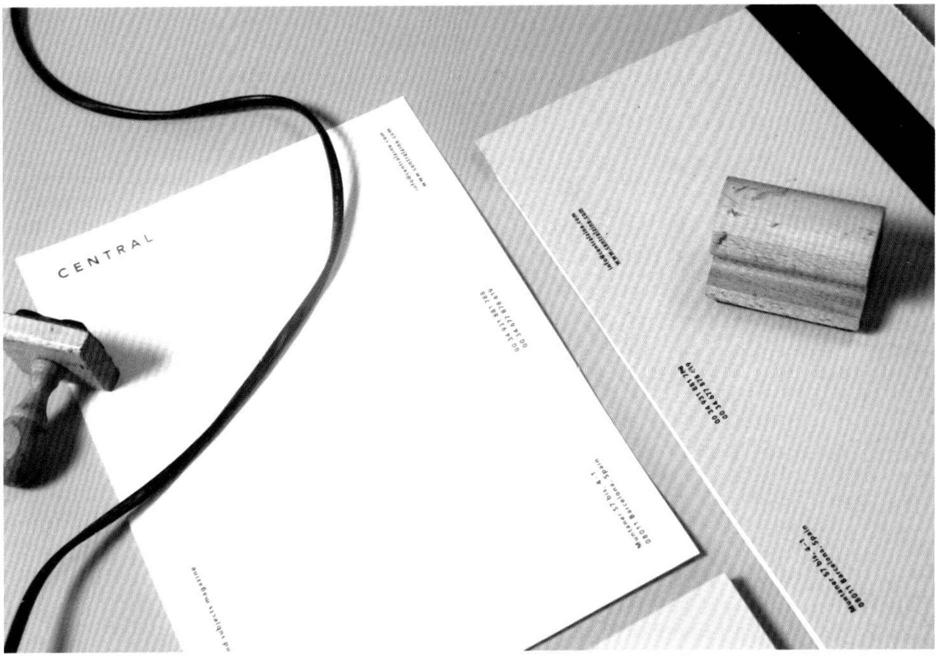
CENTRAL

MADE Visual Identity

Complete visual identity for design and communication agency MADE. MADE is a communication unit, focusing on custom publishing for Scandinavian lifestyle brands. Besides the logo and visual identity the work includes stationery and promotional material.

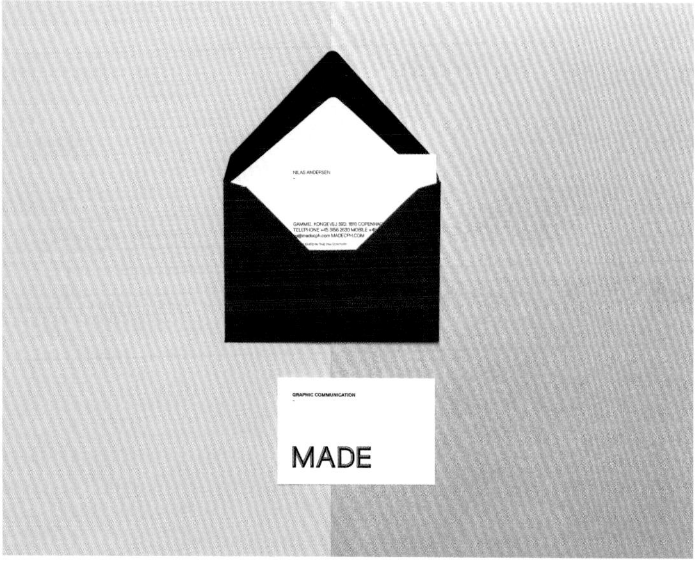

MADE

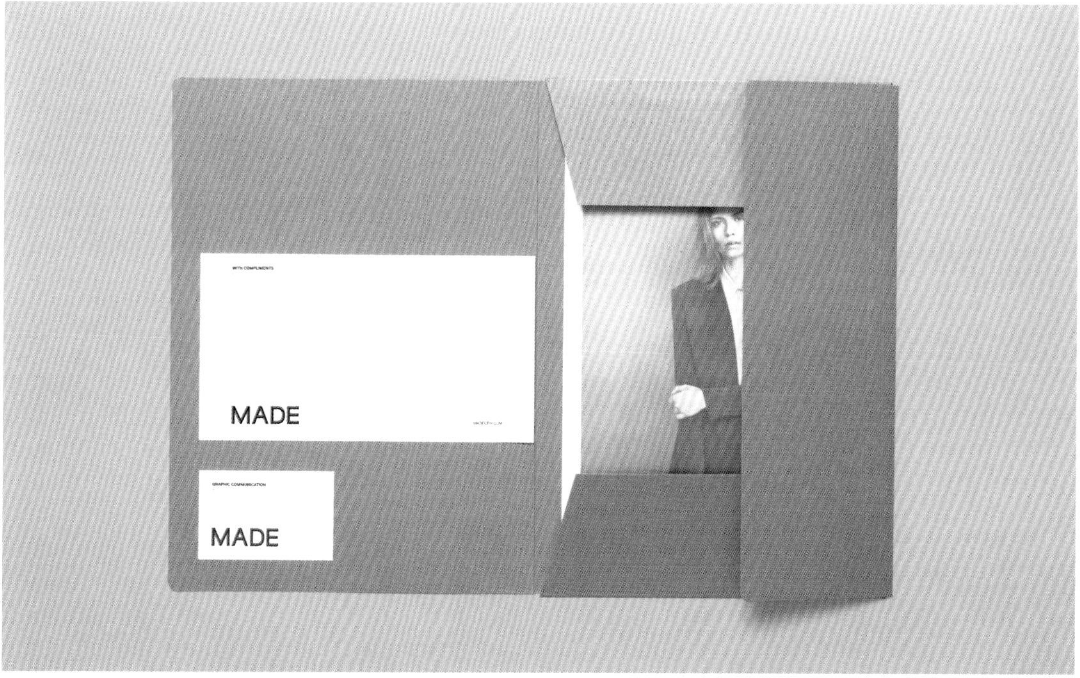
WITH COMPLIMENTS
MADE
GRAPHIC COMMUNICATION
MADE

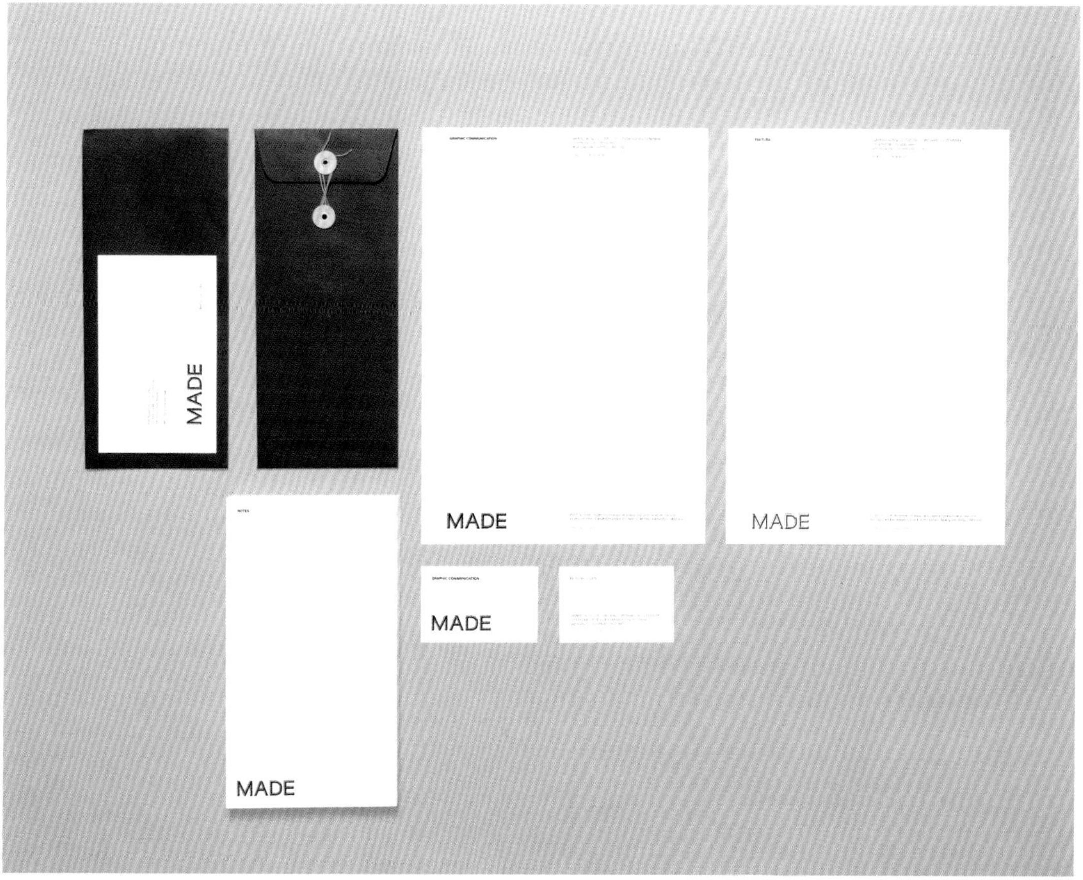
MADE
NOTES
MADE
GRAPHIC COMMUNICATION
MADE
MADE
GRAPHIC COMMUNICATION
MADE

Eskimo Identity

Eskimo is a design studio based in Murmansk (Russia). In the Russian language ЭСКИМО (Eskimo) means choc-ice (chocolate ice cream). The design is minimal with much attention paid to materials and production technologies. The colors were chosen to match the colors of choc-ice.
Photography by Andrey Pleshkov.

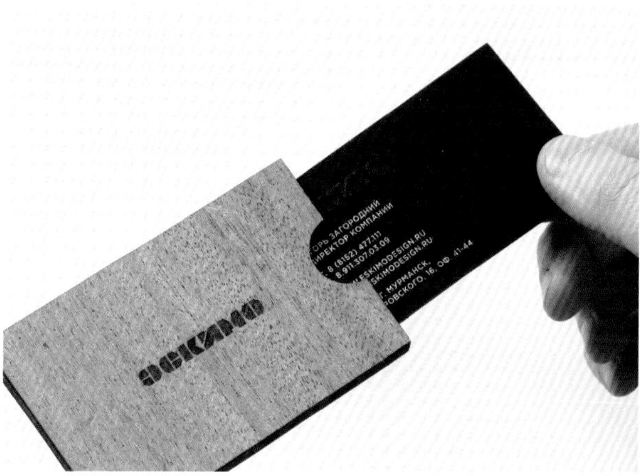

Adam and Eve Law Firm Branding

The brief was to create a law firm identity hat pushed the creative boundaries of branding and marketing with a slightly controversial approach using religious influences to drive the design. The identity plays off the idea of God's creation being protected by the Ten Commandments, as intellectual property protects people's ideas. Traditional biblical ideas are utilized in order to communicate Adam and Eve's values as an Intellectual Property Law Firm. The name "Adam & Eve" sets an obvious tone and Ten "Commandments" were created to illustrate the company's values. These commandments/ values influenced the design solutions, for example one value was "Adam and Eve law firm is a friend to nature", which inspired the eco materials and stocks. The design direction led to mixing old, traditional styles with modern techniques, such as the scroll wax sealed invitation in a modern day mailing tube.

ADAM&EVE
INTELLECTUAL PROPERTY
SEVEN O'CLOCK - THE FIRST OF JUNE
TWO THOUSAND AND TWELVE
ADAM&EVE
INTELLECTUAL PROPERTY
ADAM&EVE
INTELLECTUAL PROPERTY

ADAM&EVE

ADAM&EVE

SEAM

SEAM is a design consultancy specializing in mostly architectural lighting design. They work with teams like FOA, Zaha Hadid, and Amanda Levete. They focus on the architectural side of lighting. The word SEAM literally came from a play of the directors' initials (Amarasri Songcharoen, Emory Smith). Metaphorically, SEAM is the entity that brings things together. This can be through design collaboration, materials, cross disciplines, etc.

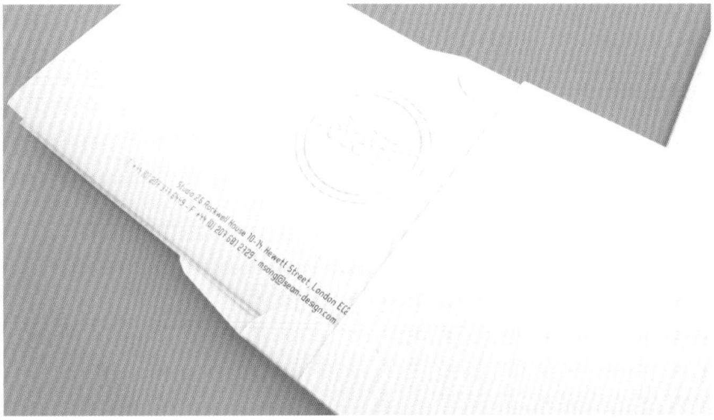

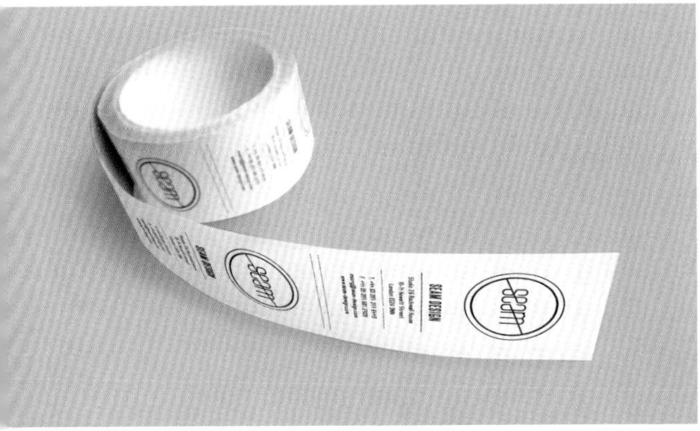

Studio 2.6 Rockwell House 10-14 Hewett Street, London EC2A 3NN
T: +44 (0) 207 377 6449 - F: +44 (0) 207 681 2129 - msong@seam-design.com - www.seam-design.com

AMARASRI SONGCHAROEN
Director
Studio 2.6 Rockwell House
10-14 Hewett Street
London EC2A 3NN
T: +44 (0) 207 377 6449
F: +44 (0) 207 681 2129
msong@seam-design.com
www.seam-design.com

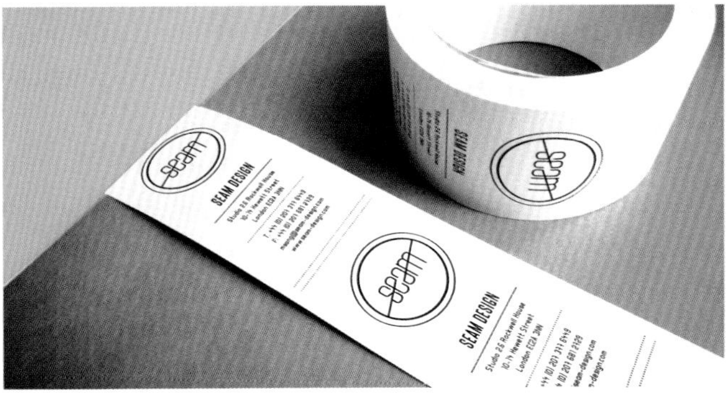
SEAM DESIGN

SEAM DESIGN
Studio 2.6 Rockwell House
10-14 Hewett Street
London EC2A 3NN

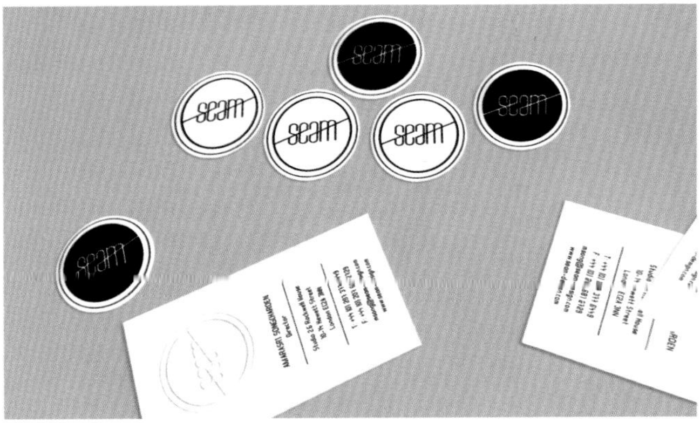

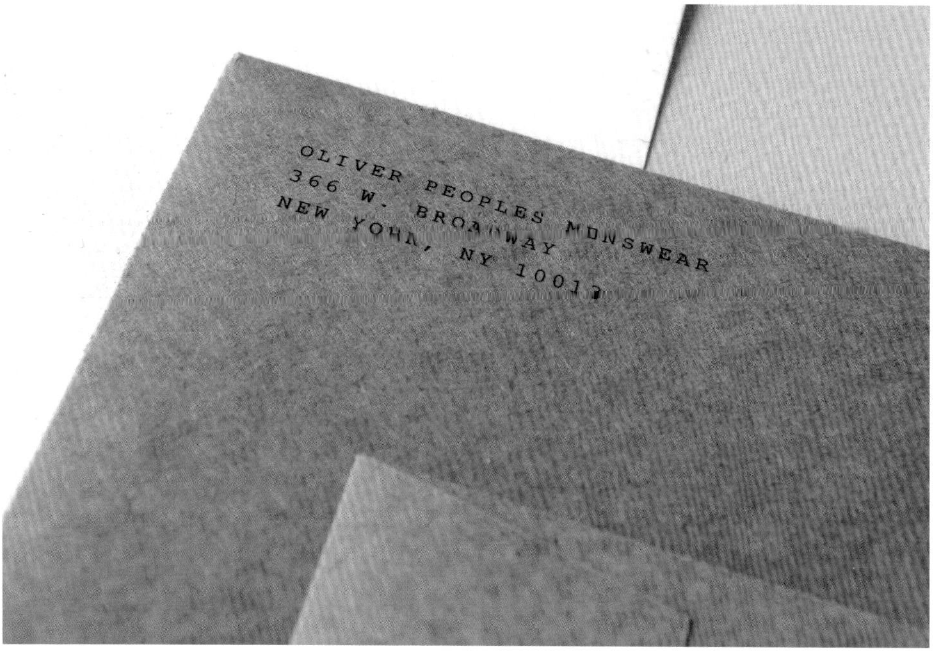

Oliver Peoples Menswear

This proposal functions as a complementary brand extension of Oliver Peoples, the eyewear manufacturer. Extending from the established Oliver Peoples' American vintage aesthetic, I envisioned the clothing line to be equally classic, refined, and utilitarian with a slight rugged edge—all of these qualities are reinforced with the use of papers with rough textures to mirror the tactile quality of the clothing. I also chose to work with a palette of neutrals to reinforce the line's general color scheme. For the logotype, I created letterforms from basic geometric shapes as a typographic interpretation of Oliver People's existing logo, which is also very geometric in nature. I opted to use Courier New as the brand's typeface because it is unadorned and utilitarian, contrasting with the graphic logotype.

OLIVER PEOPLES MENSWEAR
366 W. BROADWAY
NEW YORK, NY 10013

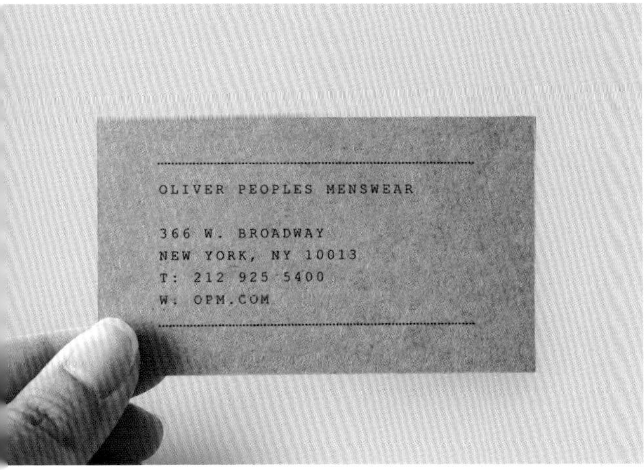
OLIVER PEOPLES MENSWEAR
366 W. BROADWAY
NEW YORK, NY 10013
T: 212 925 5400
W: OPM.COM

A-P Identity

Ari Prasetya's identity was approached as a direct solution to create a bespoke logo and identity that would complement the refined nature of his furniture. The logo was based heavily on the angles and the unique broken up "imperfections"of his design, allowing the logo to take on these principles and adopt a solid presence without overpowering the simplicity of the concept.

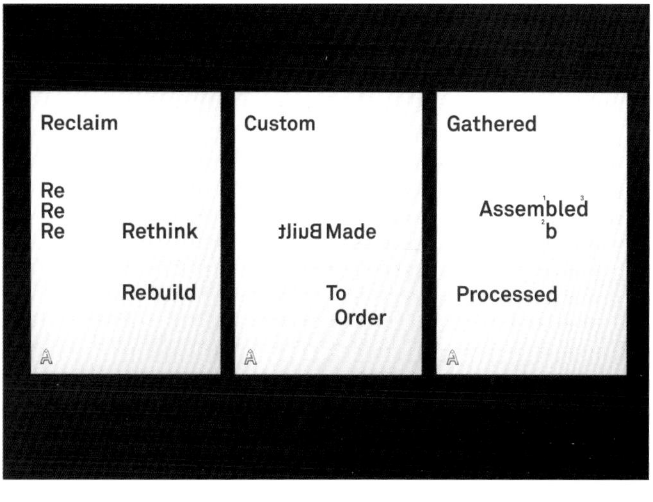

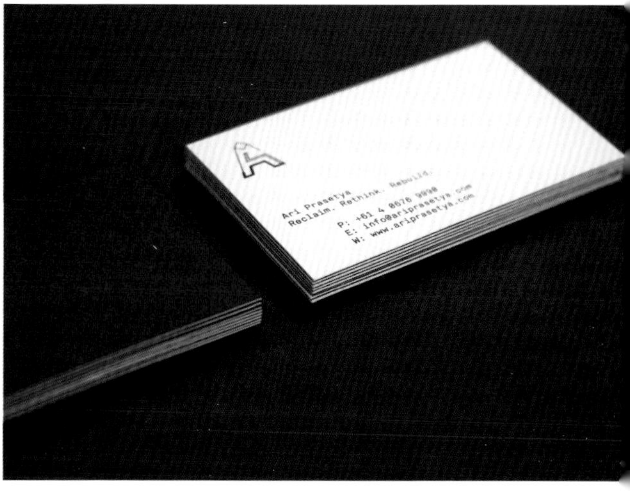

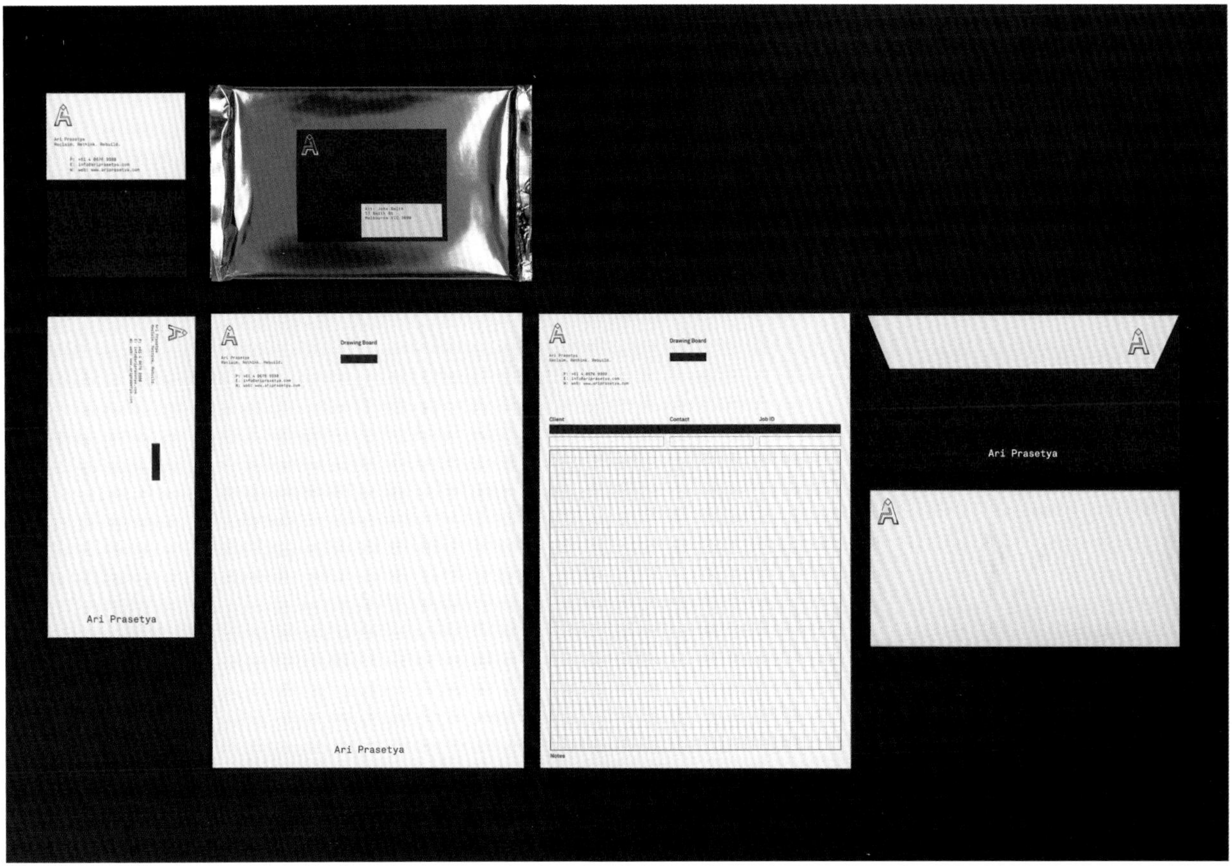
Ari Prasetya
Drawing Board
Drawing Board
Client
Contact
Job ID
Notes
Ari Prasetya
Ari Prasetya

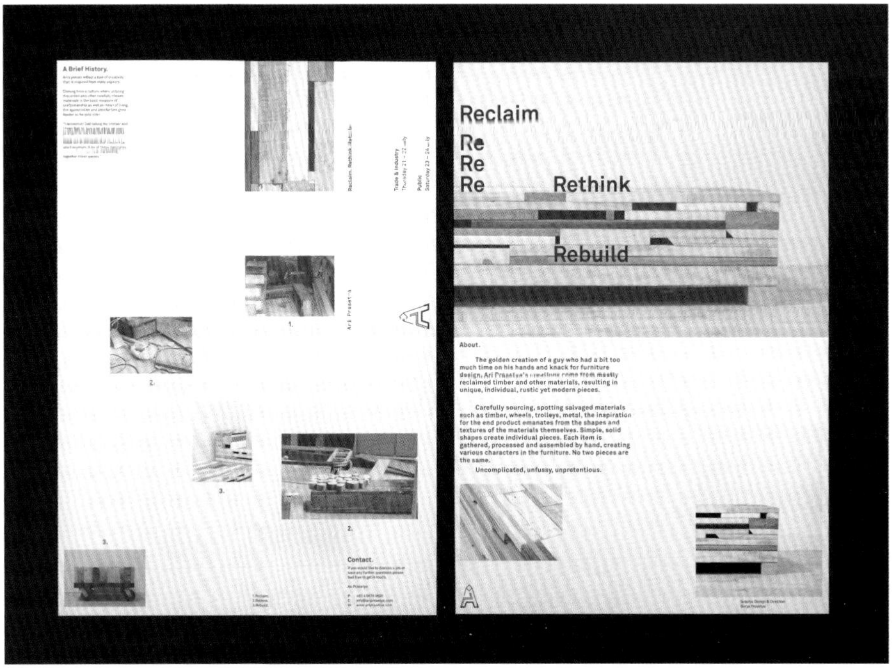
A Brief History.
Reclaim
Re
Re
Re
Rethink
Rebuild
About.
The golden creation of a guy who had a bit too much time on his hands and knack for furniture design. Ari Prasetya's creations come from mostly reclaimed timber and other materials, resulting in unique, individual, rustic yet modern pieces.
Carefully sourcing, spotting salvaged materials such as timber, wheels, trolleys, metal, the inspiration for the end product emanates from the shapes and textures of the materials themselves. Simple, solid shapes create individual pieces. Each item is gathered, processed and assembled by hand, creating various characters in the furniture. No two pieces are the same.
Uncomplicated, unfussy, unpretentious.
Contact.

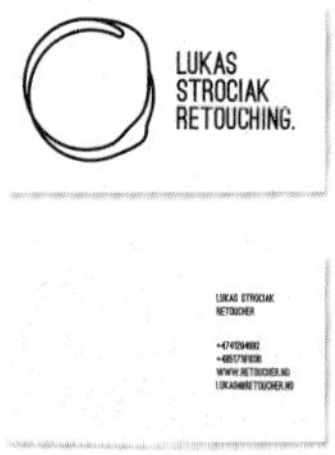

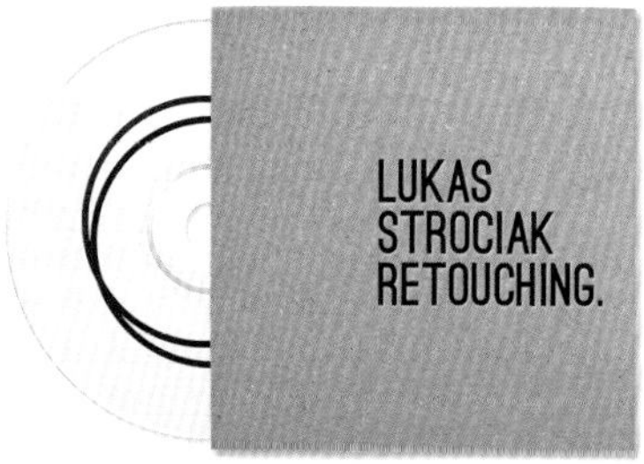

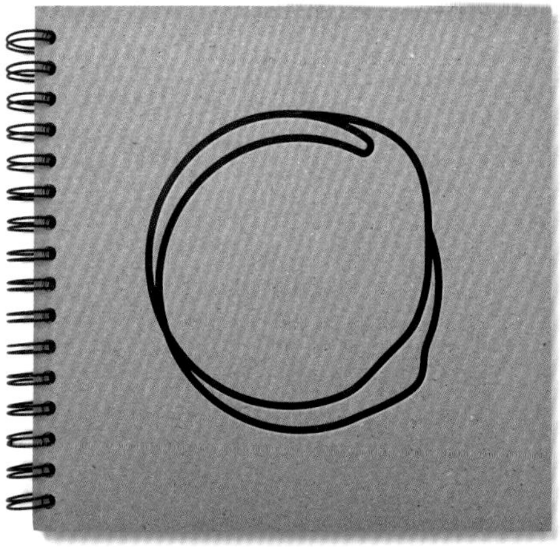

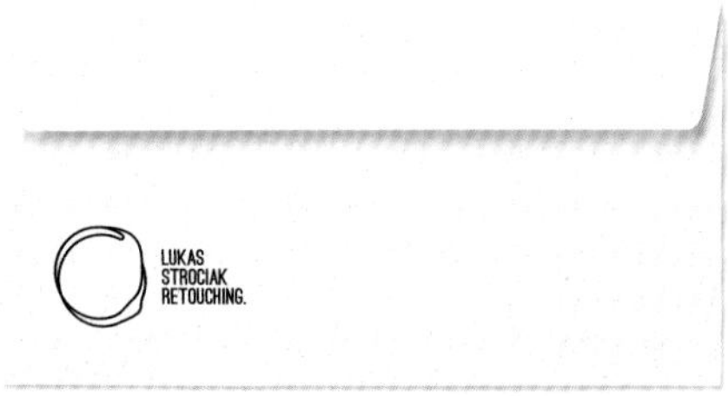

Lukas Strociak Retouching

Lukas Strociak Retouching is a small photography post-production studio based in Sandnes, Norway. Most of their clients are photographers working in the fashion industry and that's also where their main focus is. They set out to bring perfection to every image they process while still keeping its soul and the photographers' original vision.

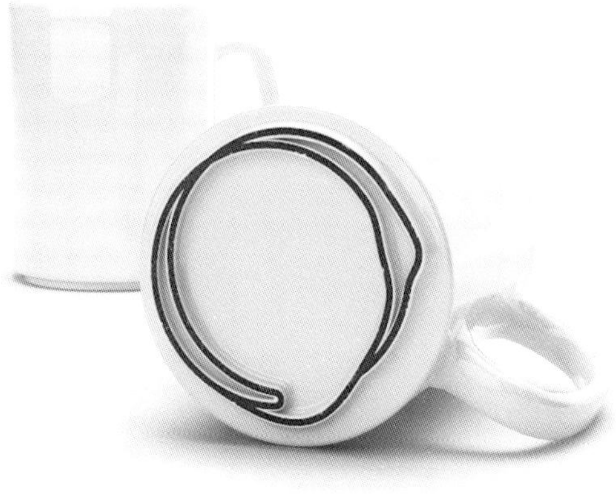

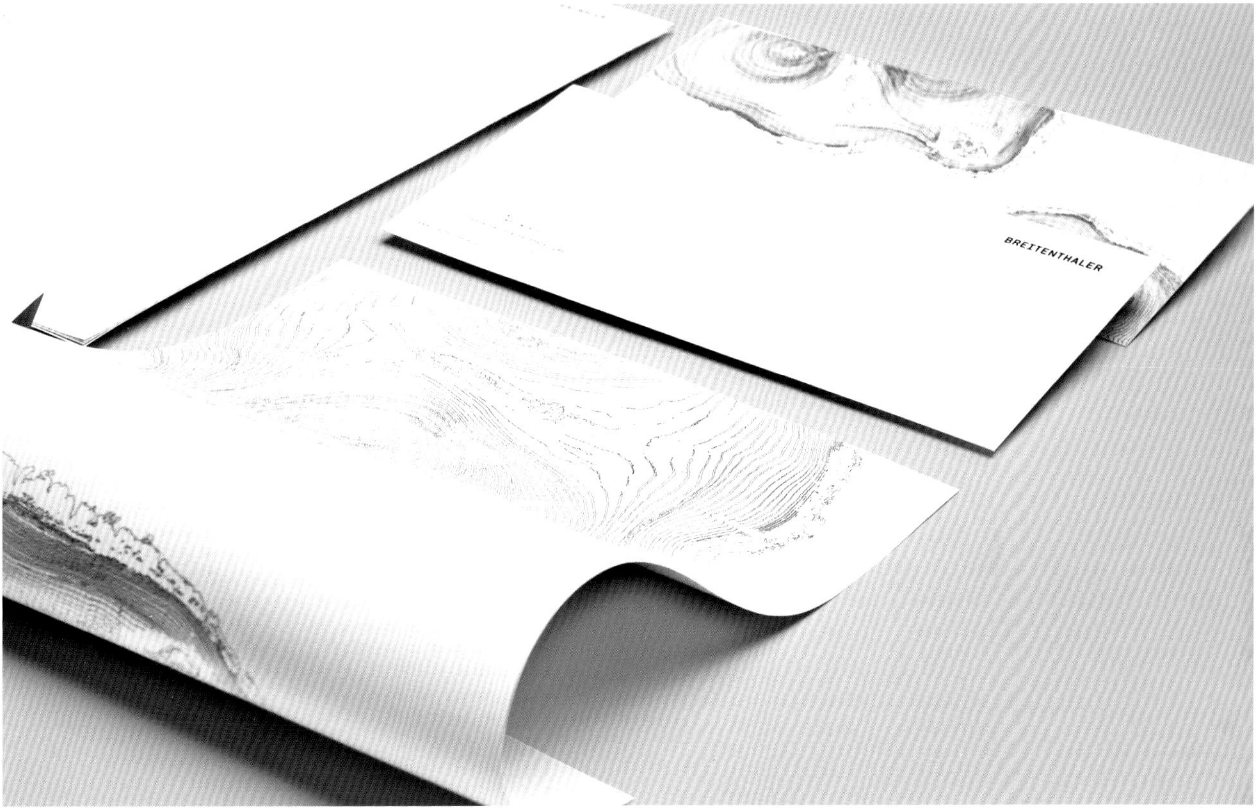

Breitenthaler

Excellent furniture design can be born only if you devote time to the personality and the wishes of your clients, to your own vision, and to the perfect construction of the piece. It's necessary that you continually find a new approach but stay true to yourself. The Austrian company "Möbelbau Breitenthaler" stands for creative design combined with craftsmanship, for extreme aesthetic appeal and a true passion for materials, forms and colors. The result is timeless, beautiful furniture with a consistent focus on the material - wood. Moodley brand identity has set up a monument to this timeless material, which unifies all of the above values that the company stands for.
Photography by Wolfgang Croce and Marion Luttenberger.

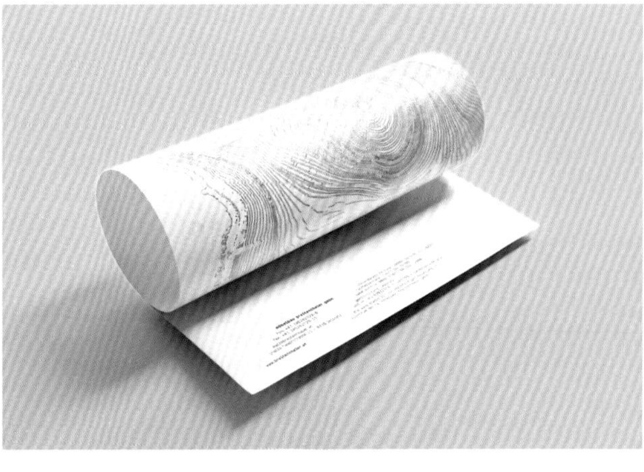

Estelle Dévé

Luke Brown was asked to design the identity, the collateral and packaging for Estelle Dévé Jewellery.

Estelle Dévé.
Estelle Dévé.

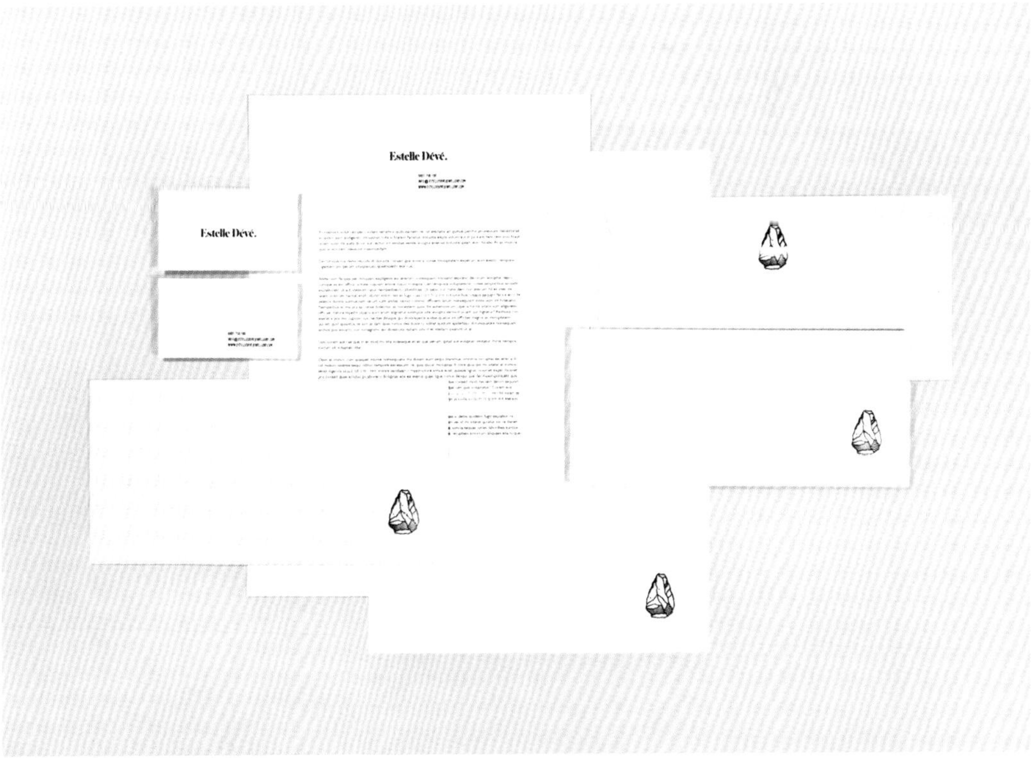
Estelle Dévé.
Estelle Dévé.

FINI

With a client list including NGV, NGA, National Library of Australia, State Library of Victoria, Art Gallery of NSW, and many regional Galleries, FINI Frames offers high-end framing service for artists and galleries across Australia. Maythorpe executed a stylish and sophisticated identity that brings them in line with the high-end clientele they serve. The identity features a bespoke logotype and simple palette of black on white — expertly letter pressed by Taylord Press.

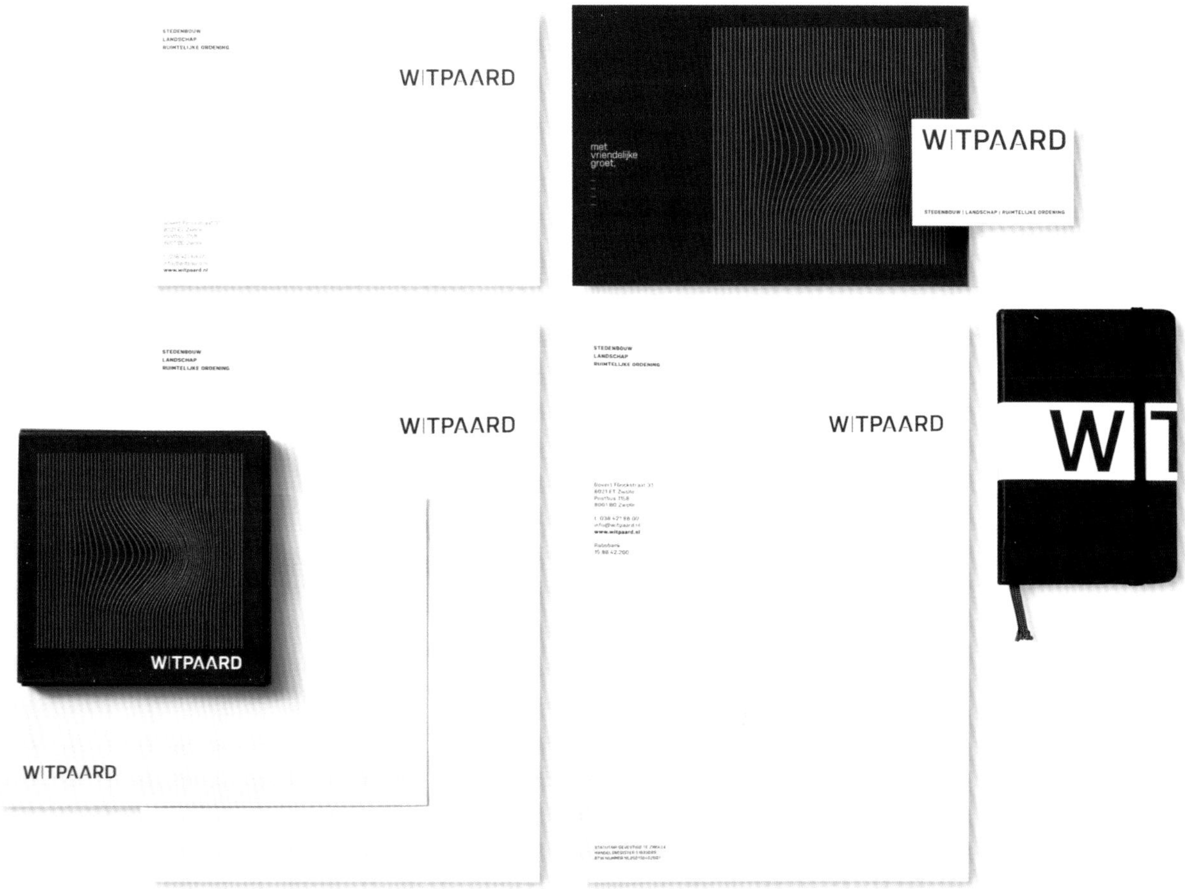

Witpaard

Urban design agency Witpaard develops landscapes and surroundings, both for residential areas and industrial estates. Their aim is to optimize spatial quality, facilitating human life in all its aspects. For this client Studio Beige designed a new logo and restyled their existing visual identity. Moreover we developed a stationery set and a brochure. The newly designed website was realized at the end of 2011.

Andfold Studio Stationery

This stationery design and promotional mailer were produced as part of Andfold's 2010 identity update. The design highlights the studio's minimalist approach through both the identity generation and the choice of specialist printing enhancements. The uppercase logotype was chosen to focus on geometry, using both a two stroke and solid logotype to address different needs. The items were sent to existing and prospective clients across the UK. The promotional mailer was printed on 700gsm GF Smith Smoke Colorplan featuring gloss black foil embossed detailing on both sides. The business cards used GF Smith Duplexed Colorplan consisting of 270gsm Real Grey combined with 270gsm Dark Grey and feature a diffusion foil emboss on the front with embossed white detailing on the reverse.

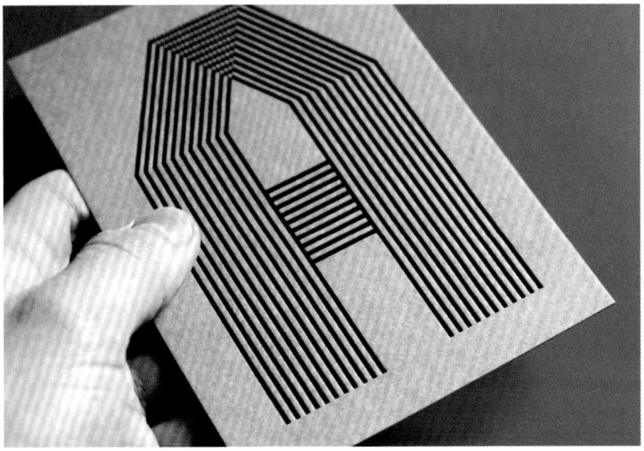

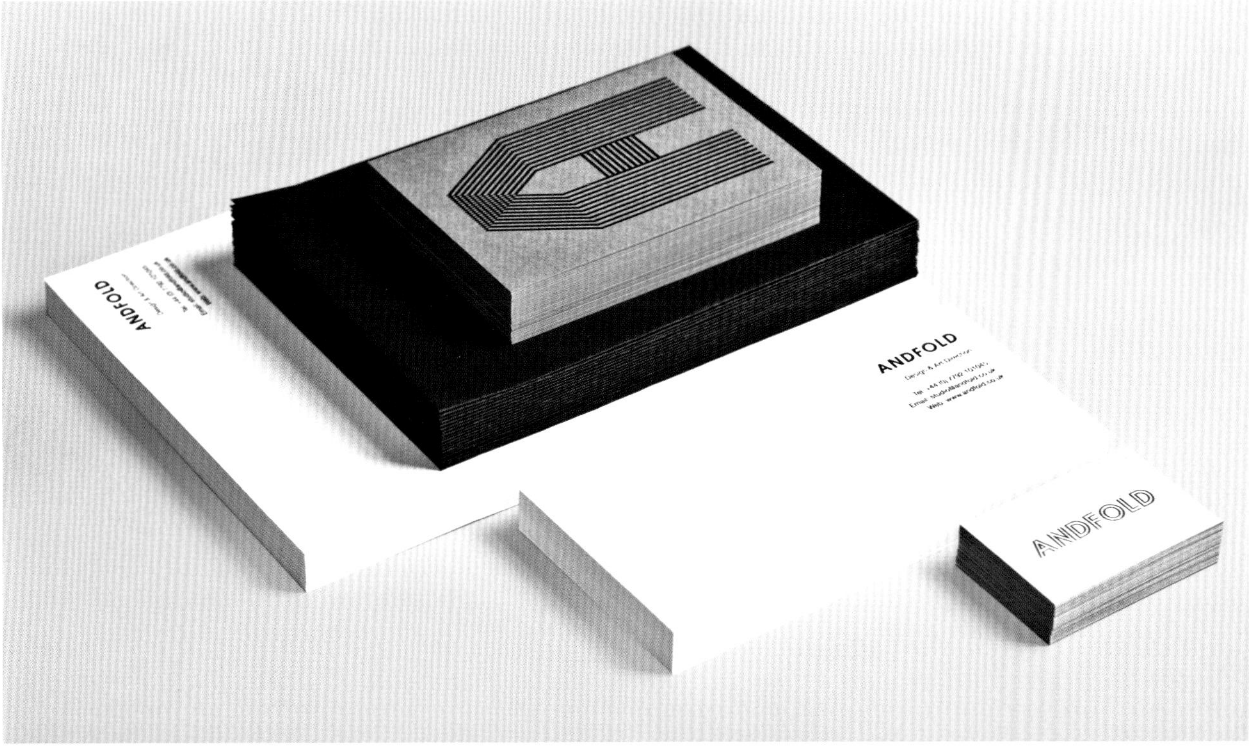
ANDFOLD
ANDFOLD
ANDFOLD

ANDFOLD

ANDFOLD

Lesley Lucano Photography

This project consisted of the development of a new brand identity, web design, stationery, logo and all the collateral material for Lesley Lucano Photography. The client required a simple and elegant logo to reflect the photography work they do. Gill Sans was selected as the typeface for this project because of its elegance and simplicity. The typeface was the most important component because the entire logo is made out of letters. The double "L" in the logo reflects the name of Lesley Lucano, and it also resembles a picture frame. There were two colors selected, black and light orange, which combine and contrast nicely.

LESLEY LUCANO
PHOTOGRAPHY

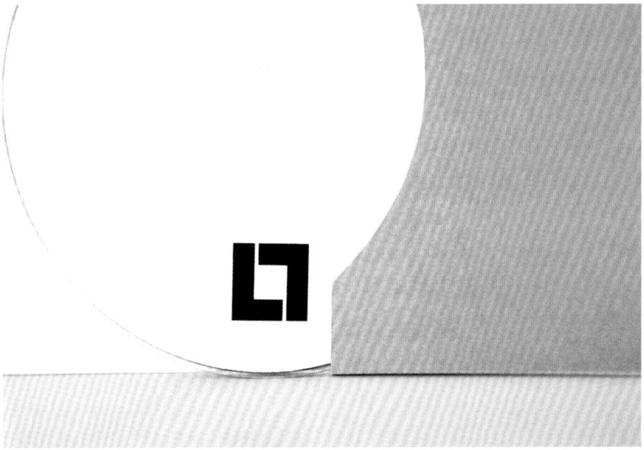

Five Franklin Place Marketing Material

Pentagram's Luke Hayman and team created the marketing materials for Five Franklin Place, an innovative 20-story residential tower that was to be built in Tribeca, New York. The designers created an elegant graphics program that included a hardcover book, stationery, press materials, floor plans, direct mail pieces, and sales center environmental graphics, advertising and event invitations.
The graphics reference the building's distinctive architecture in the form of a customized version of the font Odile Upright Italic, the letterforms of which mimic the horizontal bands of the building. A juxtaposition of matte and high-gloss finishes suggests the rough and smooth mix of building materials. The hardcover book resembled a high-end art or design publication more than a typical marketing brochure.

Five Franklin Place

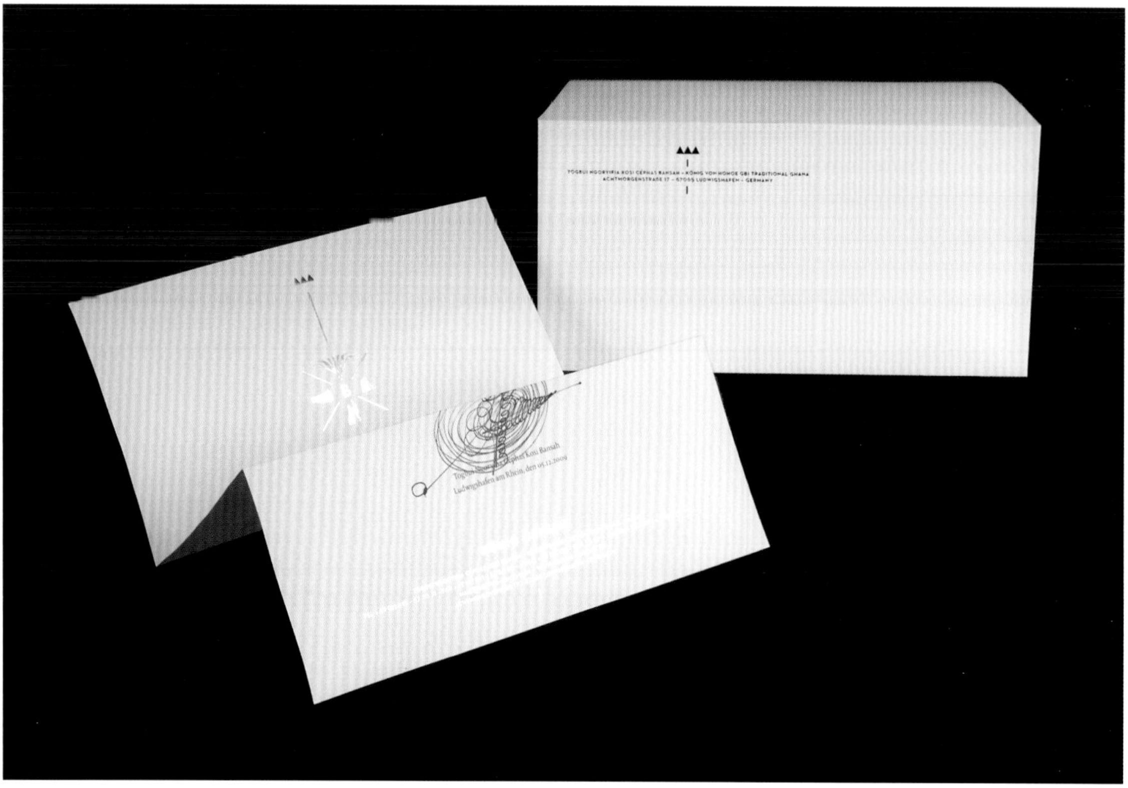

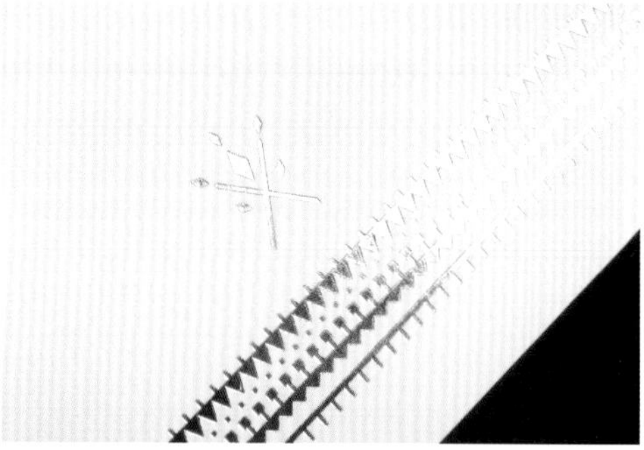

King Bansah

King Bansah is an African King. He lives and works in Ludwigshafen, Germany as a car mechanic and governs his people from there. King Bansah does a lot of activities and performances in order to collect money for his aid projects. He sings, is a guest on TV shows, and appears at many events, but he is also a real King with serious concerns. The new corporate design underlines the authenticity and lordliness of the King, as an essential visual statement making his many activities possible. They combine the royal and exotic to form a distinct impression. One example of his engagement is his own royal beer AKOSOMBO. All benefit from the beer is passed to the King's aid projects in Ghana.
Photography by Mirka Laura Severa.

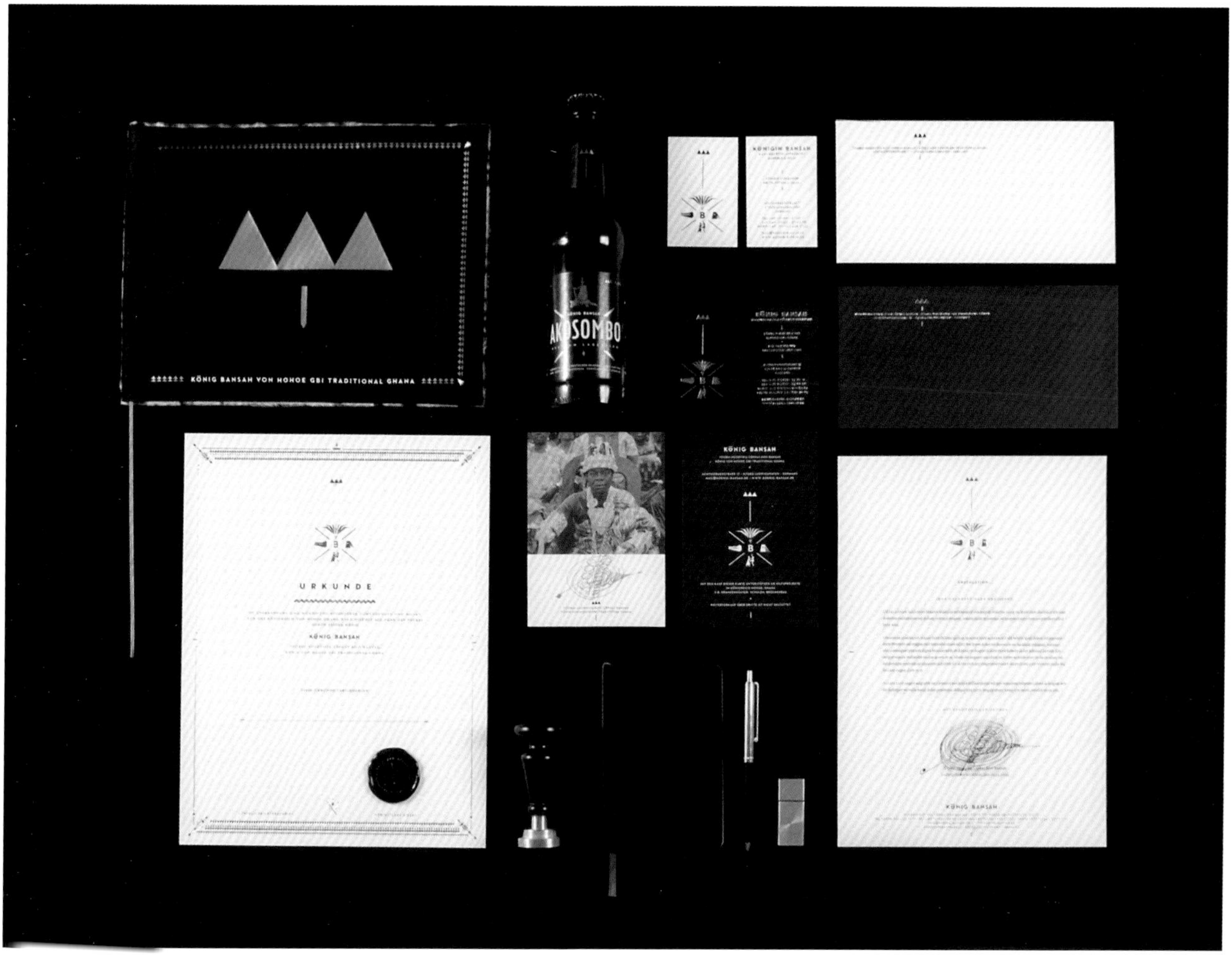
KÖNIG BANSAH VON HOHOE GBI TRADITIONAL GHANA
AKOSOMBO
URKUNDE
KÖNIG BANSAH

KÖNIG BANSAH
TOGBUI NGORYIFIA CÉPHAS KOSI BANSAH
KÖNIG VON HOHOE GBI
TRADITIONAL GHANA
KFZ-MEISTER UND
LANDMASCHINENMEISTER

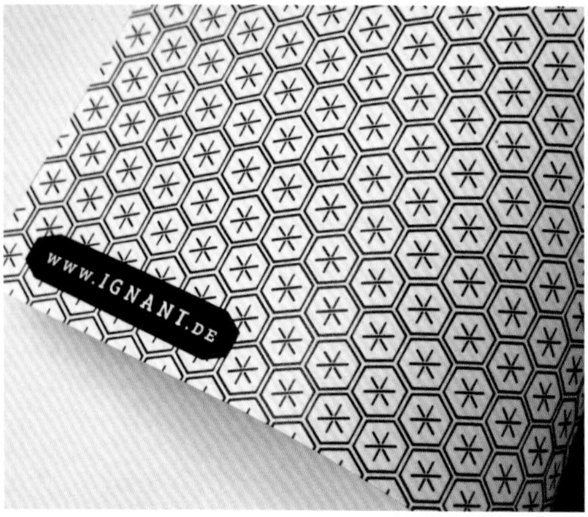

IGNANT

The interdisciplinary blog IGNANT launched a complete makeover. We happily contributed to its new appearance and developed an iconography, refined the emblem, and created supplementary printed material.

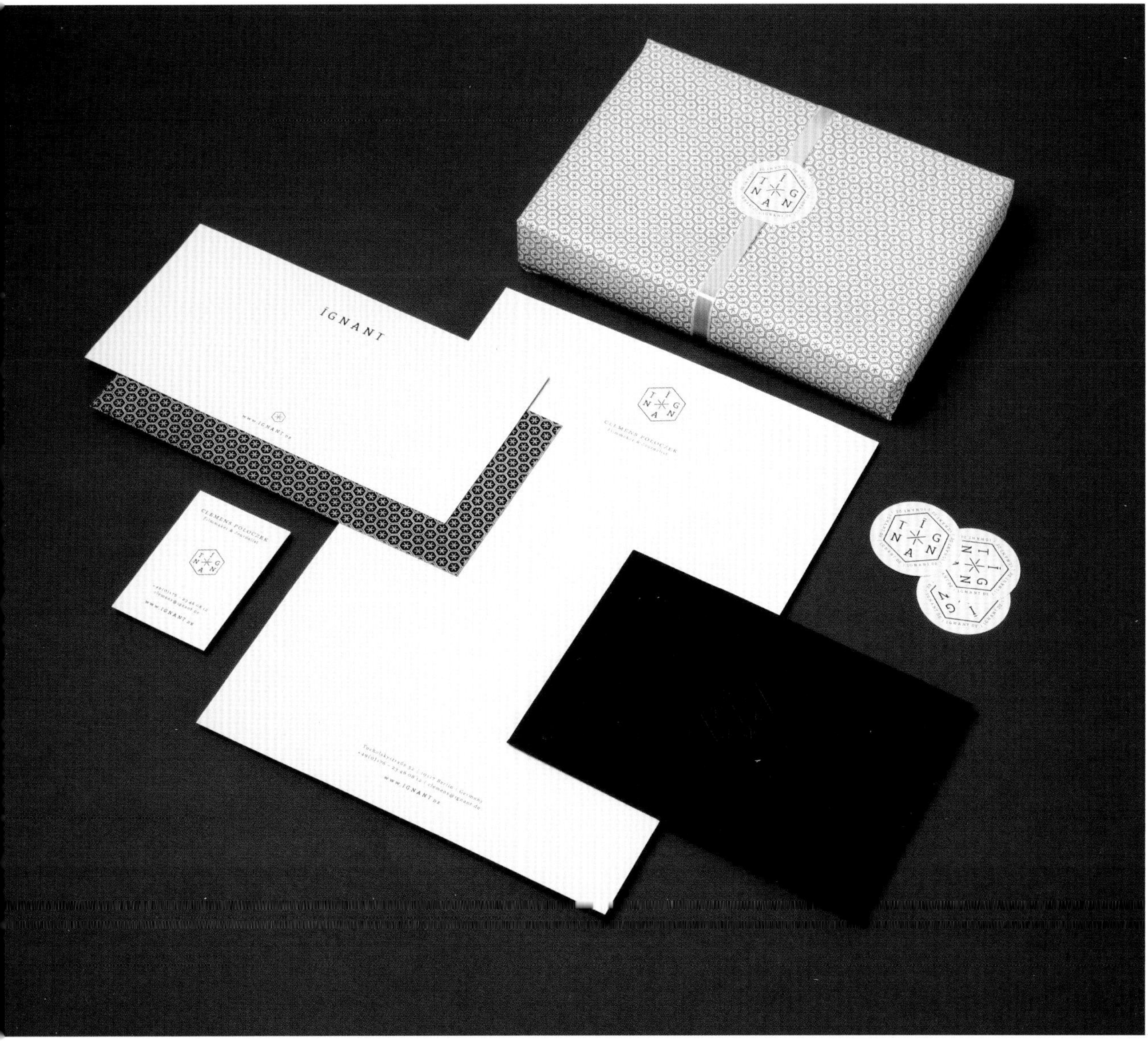
ĪGNANT

Marco Oggian Identity

The idea behind the logo is to represent Marco Oggian's personality and his traits. The two half circles that divide "M" represent his glasses while the overall vision of the logo depicts a reader. The branding identity was realized giving much importance to the paper, and using natural paper. Everything was created in a very simple way with a minimalist approach.

MARCO OGGIAN

DVD

who is HUE Branding

who is HUE is Australia's newest handbag and accessories retailer. The branding and application reflect the overall aesthetic of the product, where price meets quality. Aimed at the mid-high end of the market, the logo interprets these values to create a simple, playful and functional brand.

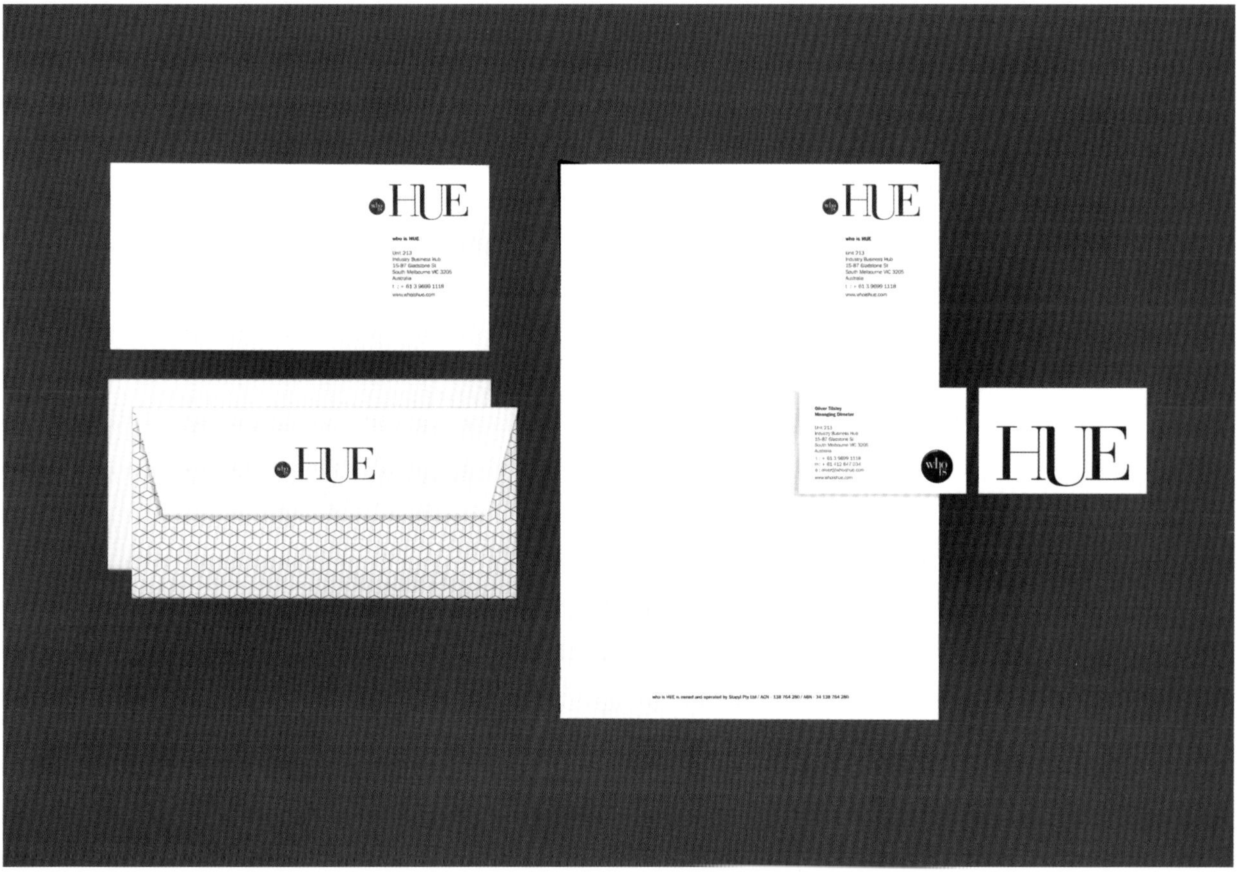
HUE
who is HUE
Unit 213
Industry Business Hub
South Melbourne VIC 3205
Australia
HUE
Oliver Tilsley
HUE
HUE

whoishue.com

HUE
HUE

10 Jahre Suite212

Theme of the 10th anniversary of the famous Stuttgart Bar "Suite212" was "Jail Hotel". We created an identity by alienating the baden-württemberg national emblem. (As the summons is pink here, we had no choice about the colour.) The invitation was sealed with wax and shows the number "10", a key visual for our reverse-graffiti guerilla campaign "watch out for the 10". The invitation was printed on pink paper, wrapped by natron kraft paper and sealed by wax. Inside a map of the location.

SUITE
212

LAD
UNG
SUITE
212

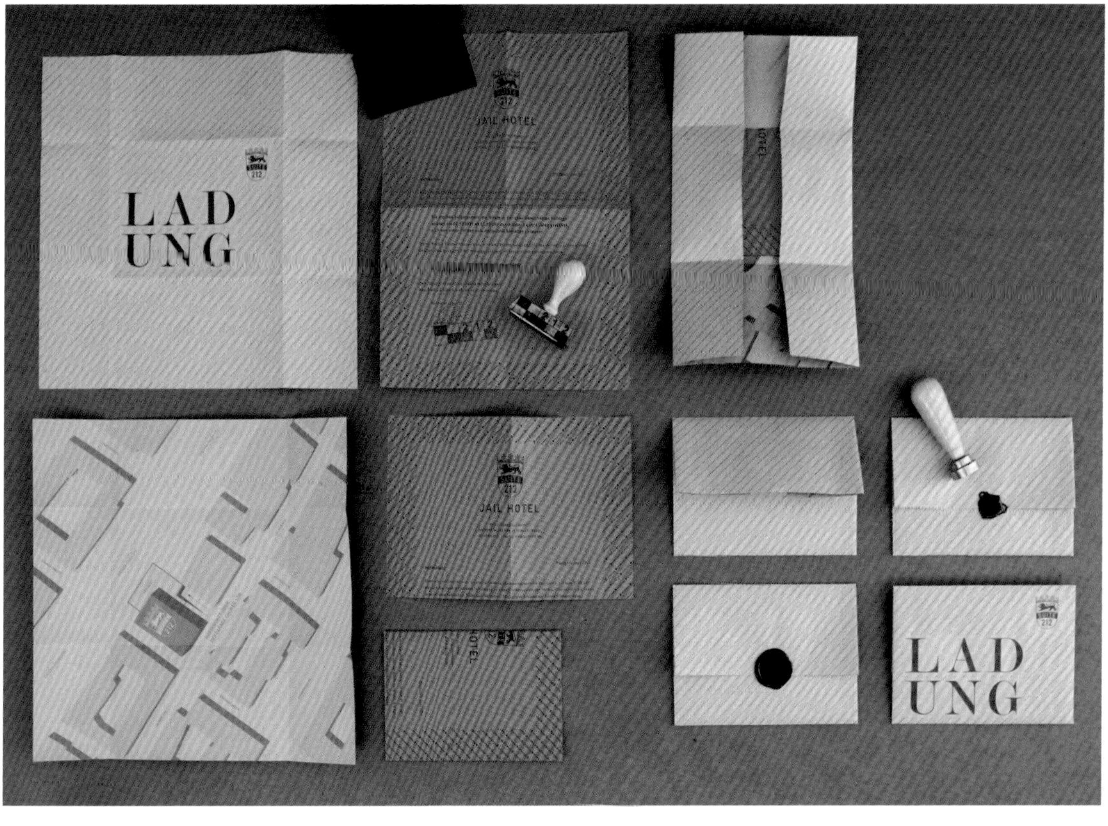
LAD
UNG
JAIL HOTEL
JAIL HOTEL
LAD
UNG

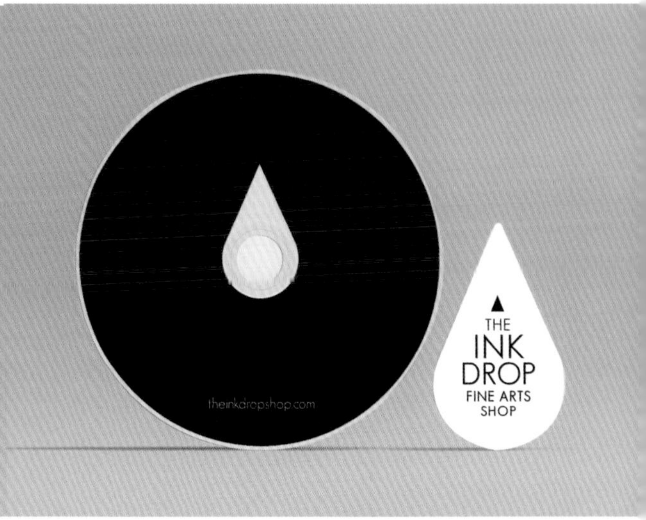

The Ink Drop Fine Arts Shop

Since the store sells handmade goods, we decided to depict a moment when the process of creation is just being started. Literally when a brush is ready to touch paper, when an ink drop is just about to fall down and…! The image of an ink drop being ready to drip down became a key visual element. The simple and recognizable shape was used on every element of the brand identity. The store also acquired the name Ink Drop Fine Arts Shop.

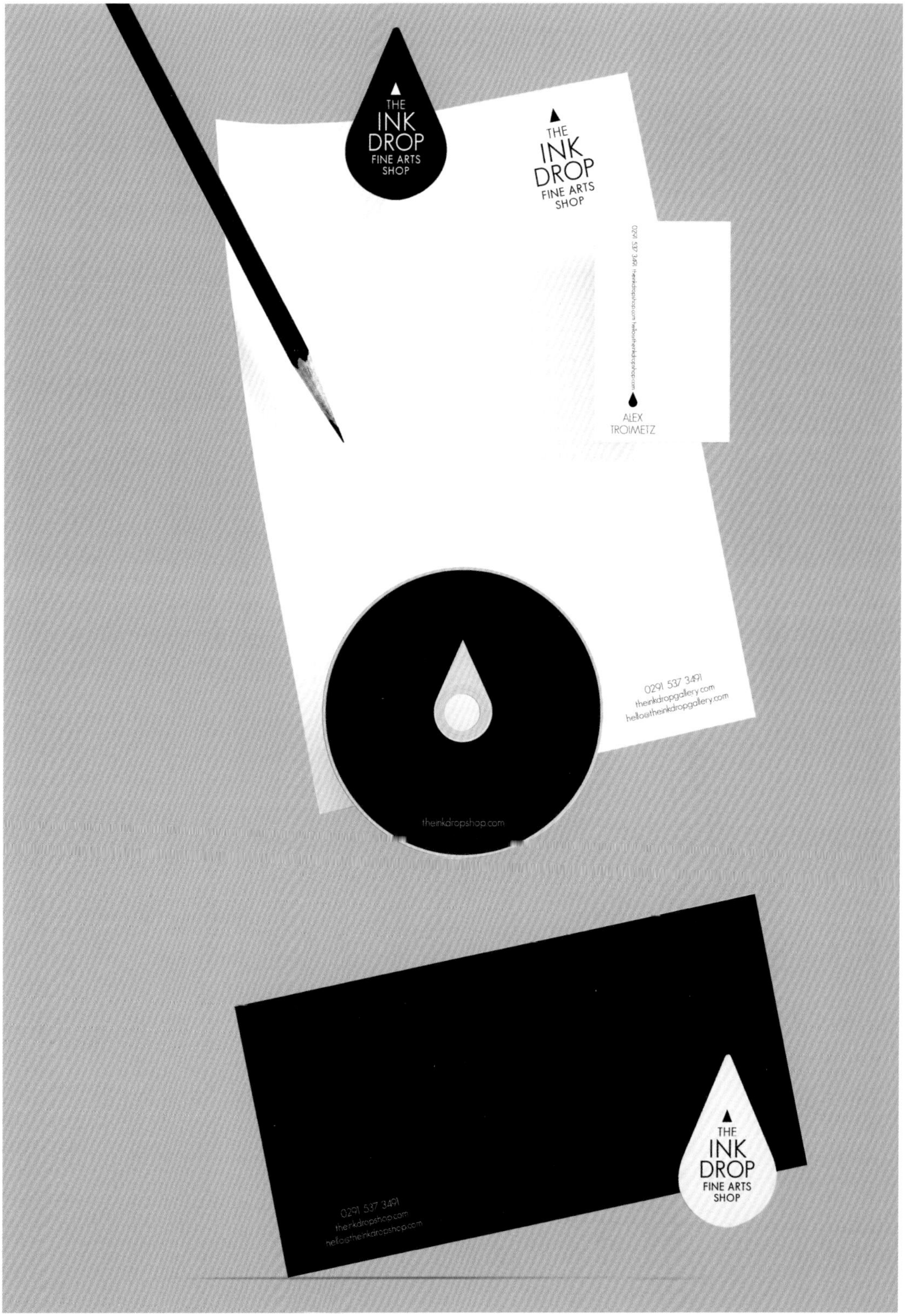
THE
INK
DROP
FINE ARTS
SHOP
THE
INK
DROP
FINE ARTS
SHOP
ALEX
TROIMETZ
0291 537 3491
theinkdropgallery.com
hello@theinkdropgallery.com
theinkdropshop.com
THE
INK
DROP
FINE ARTS
SHOP
0291 537 3491
theinkdropshop.com
hello@theinkdropshop.com

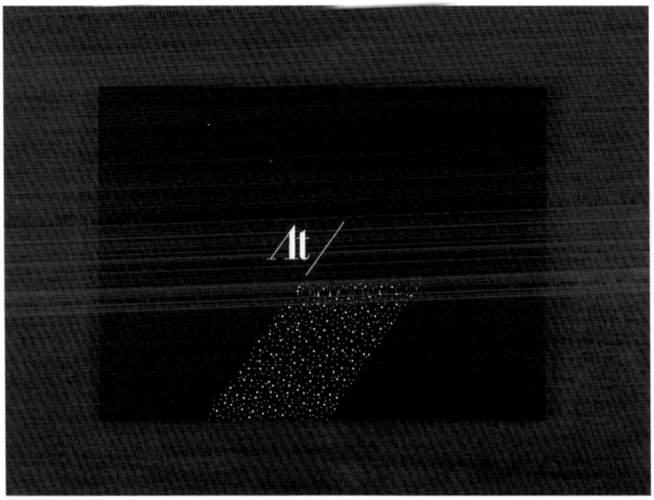
At

Atelier
VISUAL ARTS DESIGN & LIFE
HÉCTOR AYUSO
HECTOR@LAWEBDELATELIER.COM
+34 936 763 633 · GLEVA, 24 BAJOS
08006 BARCELONA, SPAIN
AIMÉE CAMPOS
AIMEE@LAWEBDELATELIER.COM
+34 936 763 633 · GLEVA, 24 BAJOS
08006 BARCELONA, SPAIN
A PLACE TO DESIGN YOUR FUTURE
HOLA@LAWEBDELATELIER.COM
+34 936 763 633 · GLEVA, 24 BAJOS
08006 BARCELONA, SPAIN

Atelier
VISUAL ARTS DESIGN & LIFE
2009 2010
Francisco López
Creación y Producción de Proyectos
Multidisciplinares en el Área de Diseño

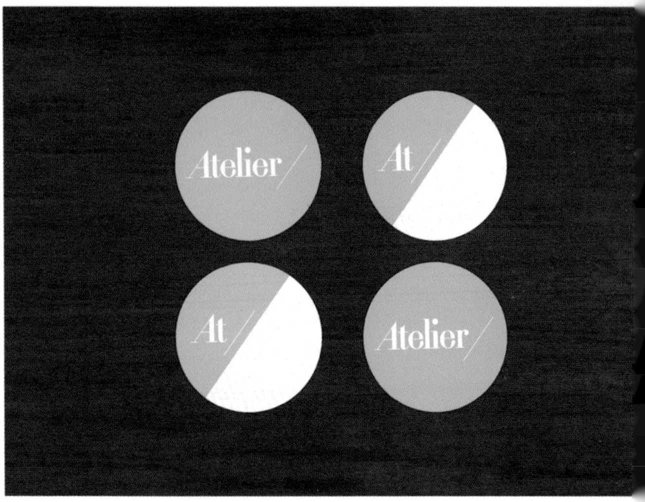
Atelier
At
At
Atelier

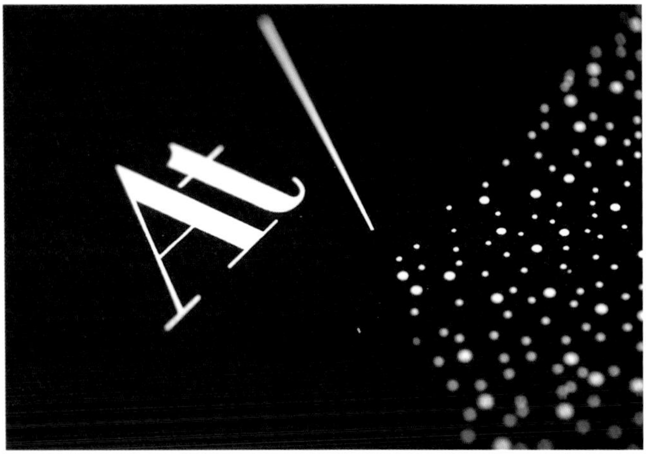
At

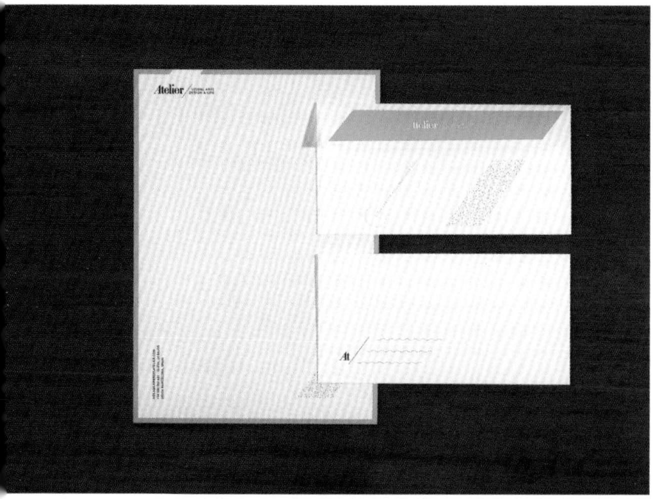

Atelier Identity

Rebranding the identity of the Visual Arts and Design School Atelier from Barcelona. The identity is based on the juxtaposition of geometric and organic elements flowing across the different pieces. The pure conceptual shapes overlay the natural elements that give context to the ideas. The vibrant orange color was chosen as representative of the vitality of the young creative mind, and the deep blue as a link to the knowledge and experience of professors.

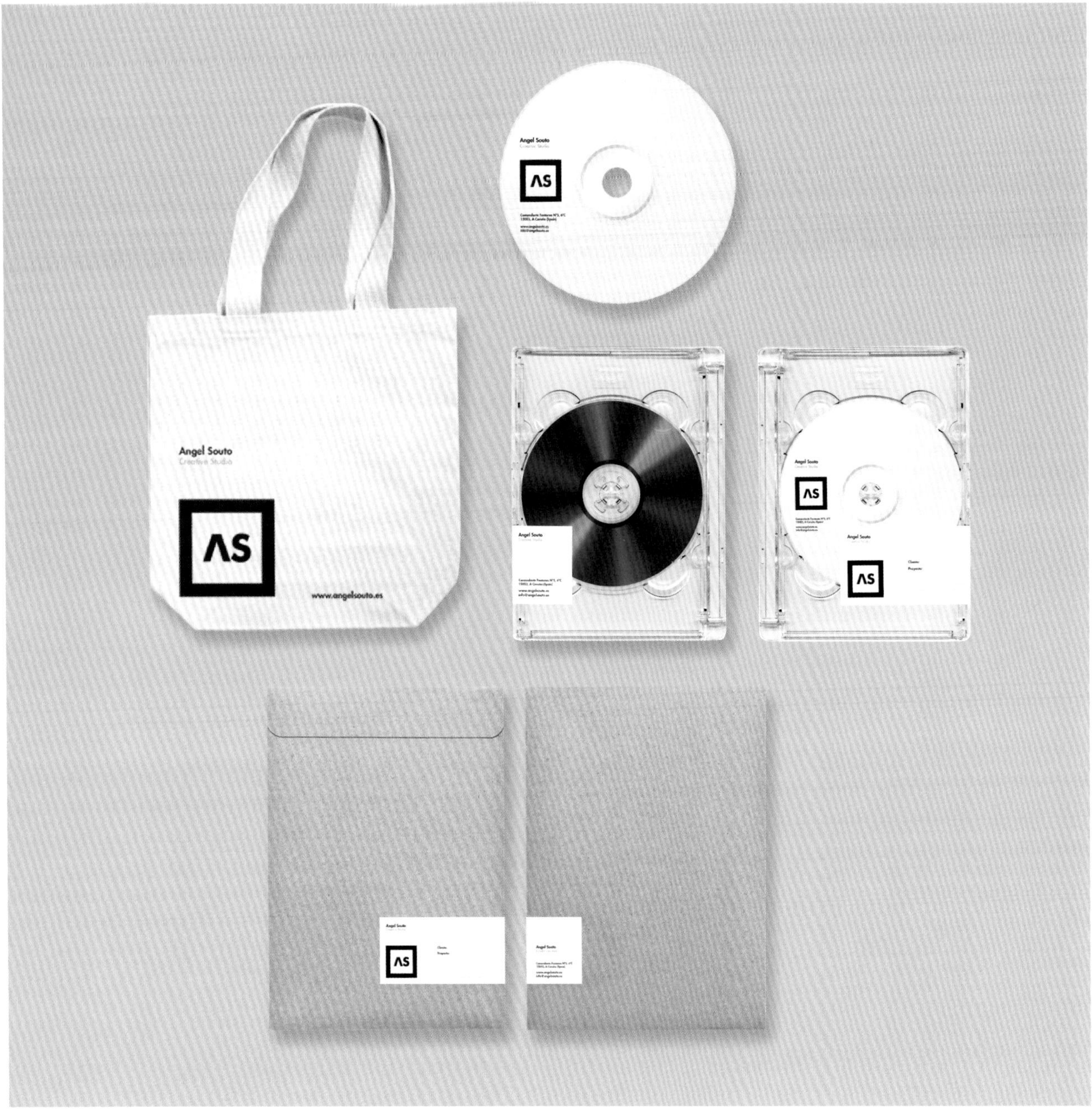

Angel Souto Creative Studio Stationery

We have updated the identity of our Studio to transmit the new direction of Angel Souto Creative Studio. Our work has always been noted for its cleanliness and sobriety, but our previous identity could not reflect this line, so we decided to completely change the visual identity. We think the design now reflects what we wanted- it is timeless, clean, and it has strength and personality.

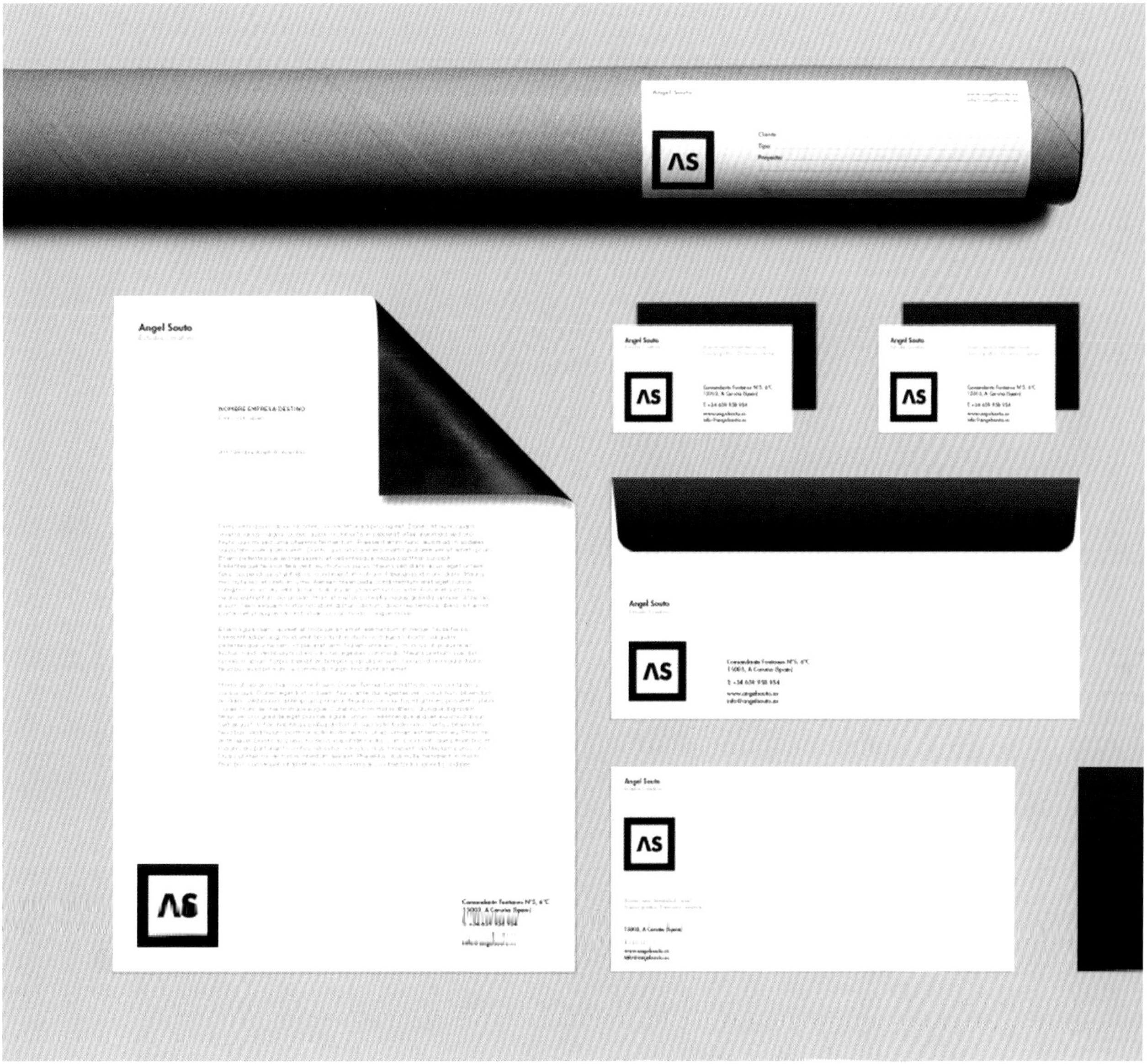
Angel Souto
Cliente
Tipo
Proyecto
NOMBRE EMPRESA DESTINO

We Saw: Open Lab

We Saw is a cross-disciplinary collective of professionals including architects, decorators, and web developers who work from the design of building spaces to create theatre costumes. A univocal logo, along with low-budget materials for the production of their corporate identity in combination with specially designed perforations, to represent a team with creative views on each project.
Photography by Dimitris Poupalos.

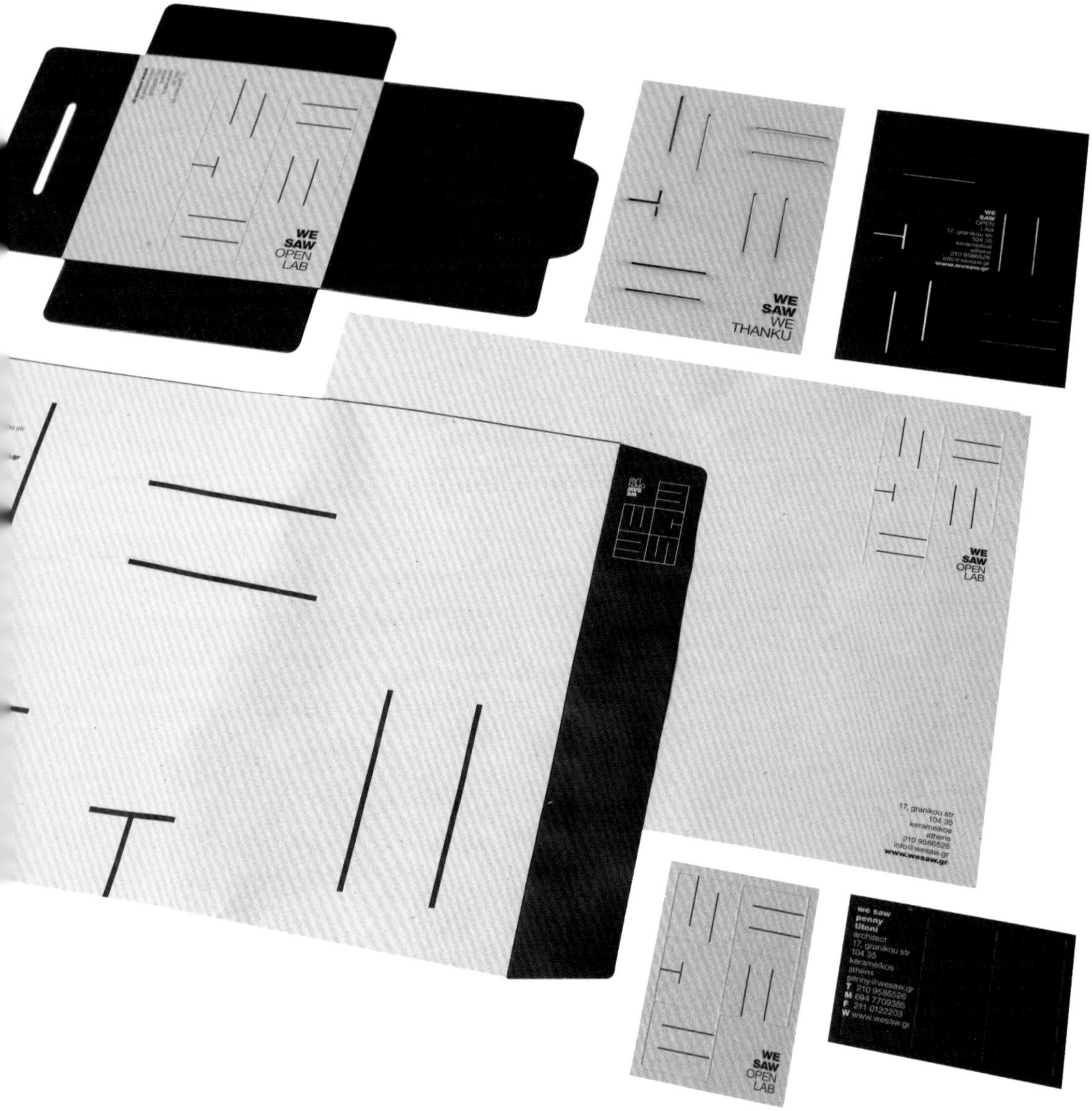

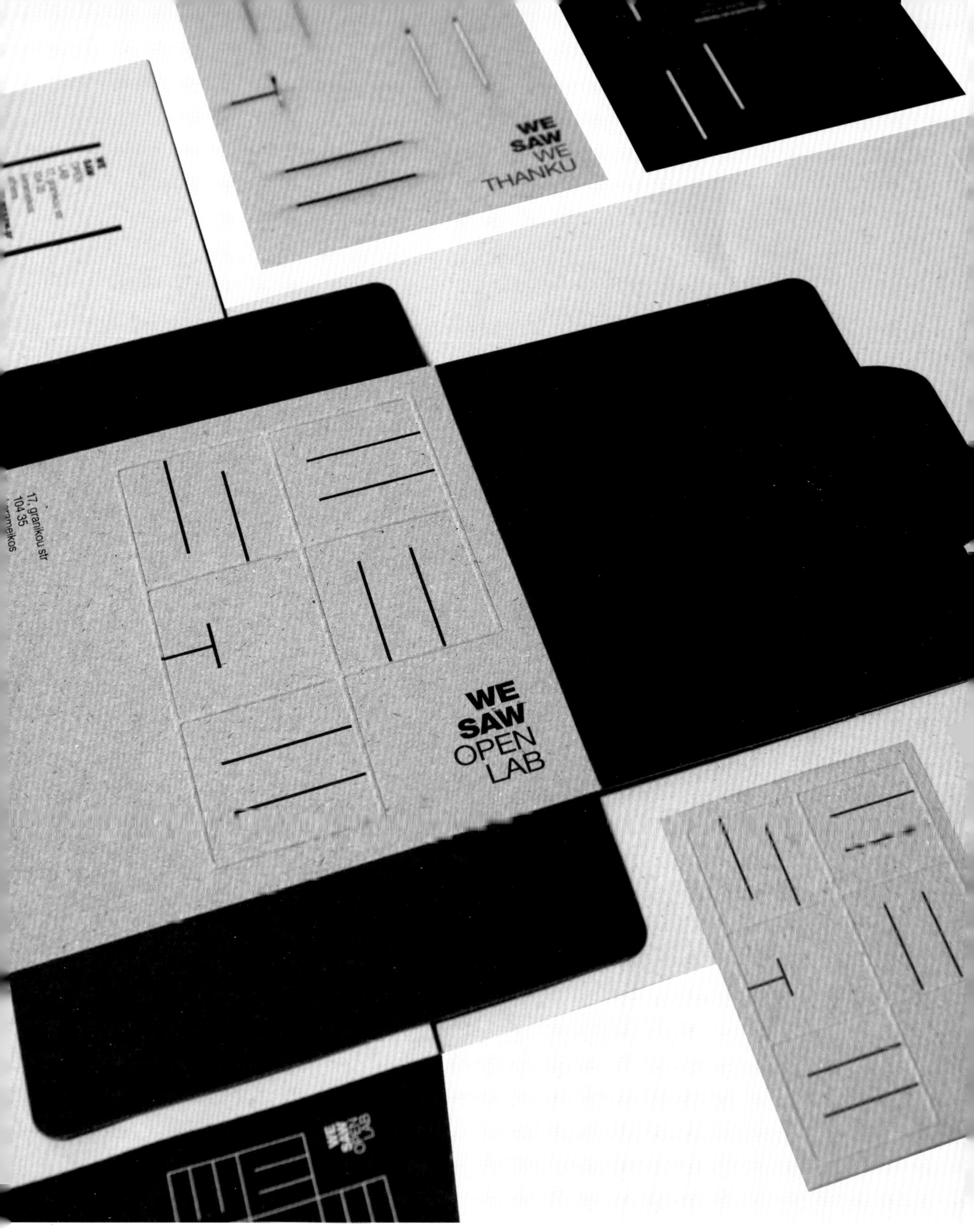
WE
SAW
WE
THANKU
17, granikou str
104 35
WE
SAW
OPEN
LAB

White Cover

White Cover is a publishing house presenting small-scale, carbon-neutral books and magazines, addressing subject matter related to the microeconomies of local communities from various part of Greece. The main elements of the logotype and corporate identity are the use of simple monochromatic typography and white papers. The idea is to convey the concept of starting anew, from a white paper.

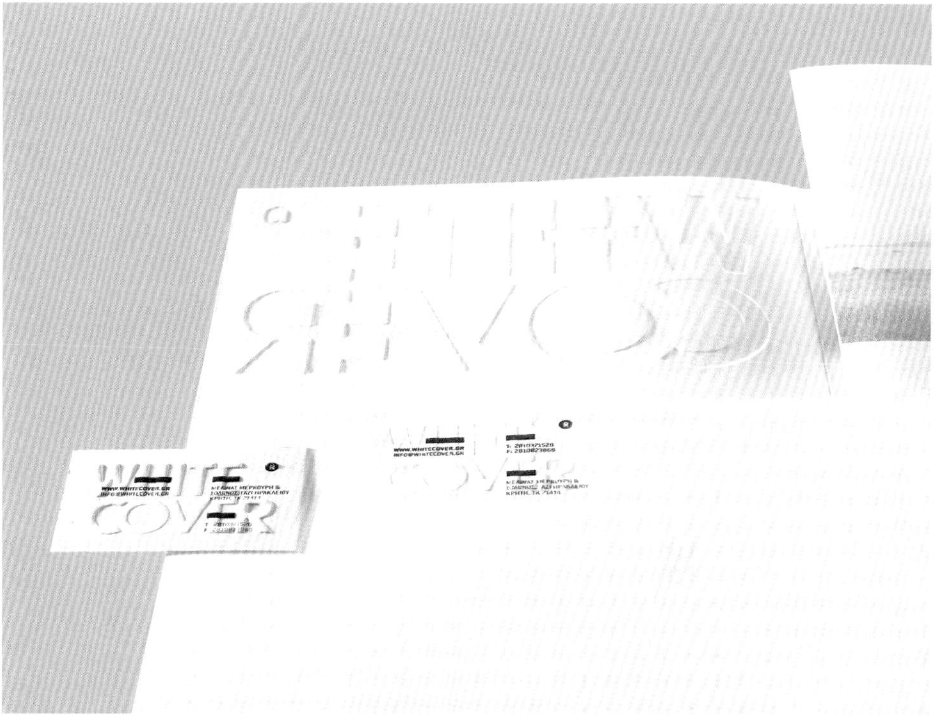
WWW.WHITECOVER.GR
INFO@WHITECOVER.GR

WHITE
COVER

Loft 37 Visual Identity

"Minimalism, plus some great details" was the brief from the award winning web agency Loft 37 when they asked for a rejuvenation of their visual identity. BRUNSWICKER delivered a simple design with high-end production to meet the company's needs.

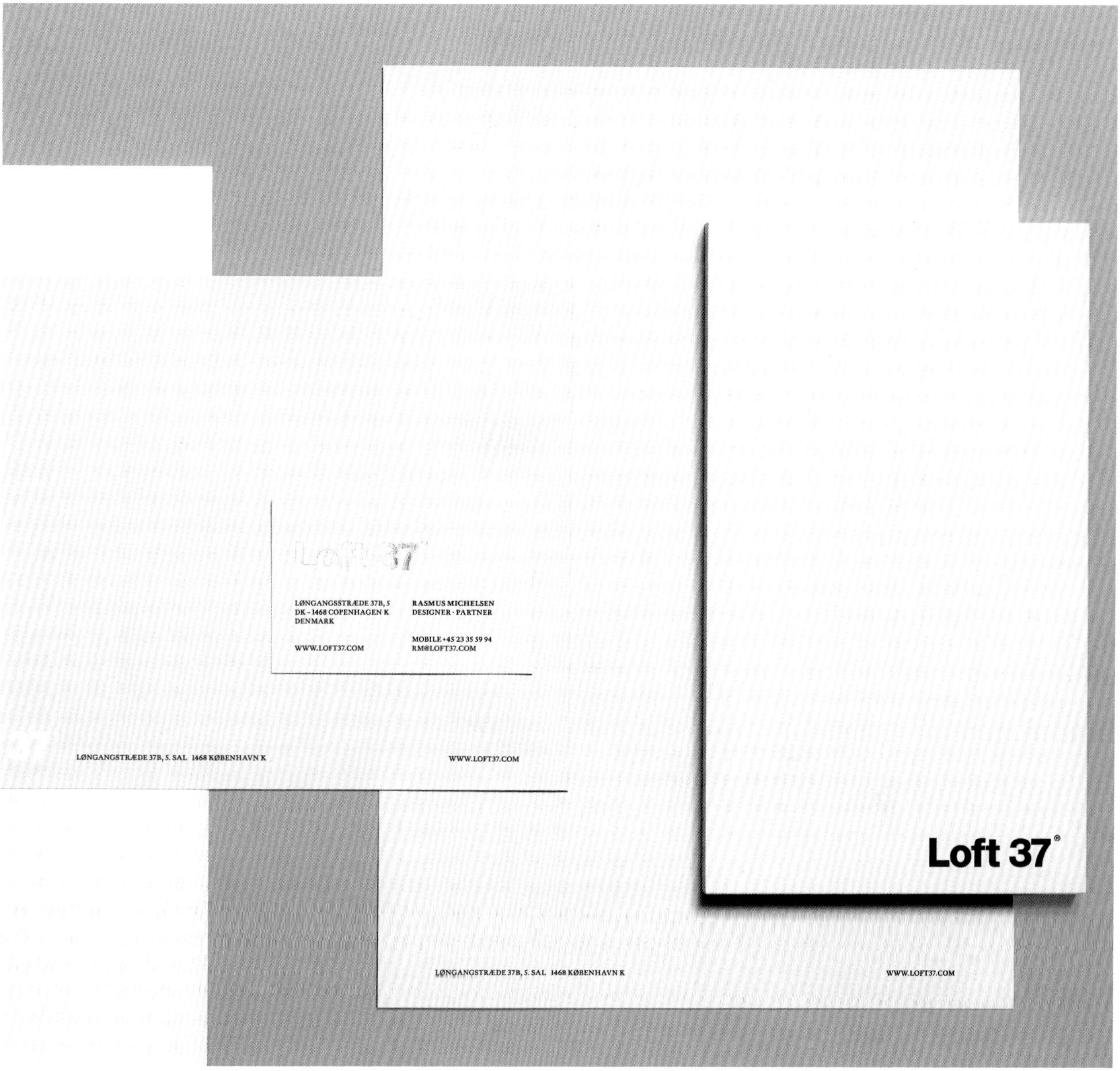
LØNGANGSSTRÆDE 37B, 5
DK - 1468 COPENHAGEN K
DENMARK
WWW.LOFT37.COM
RASMUS MICHELSEN
DESIGNER · PARTNER
MOBILE +45 23 35 59 94
RM@LOFT37.COM
LØNGANGSTRÆDE 37B, 5. SAL 1468 KØBENHAVN K
WWW.LOFT37.COM
Loft 37®
LØNGANGSTRÆDE 37B, 5. SAL 1468 KØBENHAVN K
WWW.LOFT37.COM

Loft 37®

Black Umbrella

Black Umbrella builds practical, efficient disaster plans for individuals, couples and families. The client chose the name umbrella for its symbolism of protection. We wanted to build upon the idea. As most of their services are for an individual's or family's home, we used the outer shape of an umbrella as a shield for the house. The logo can be used on its own or can be combined with a complex grid which represents the intricate network of connections and services.

Catherine Hooper
president
590 Madison Avenue
21st Floor
New York, NY 10022
catherine@blackumbrella.com
blackumbrella.com
black umbrella

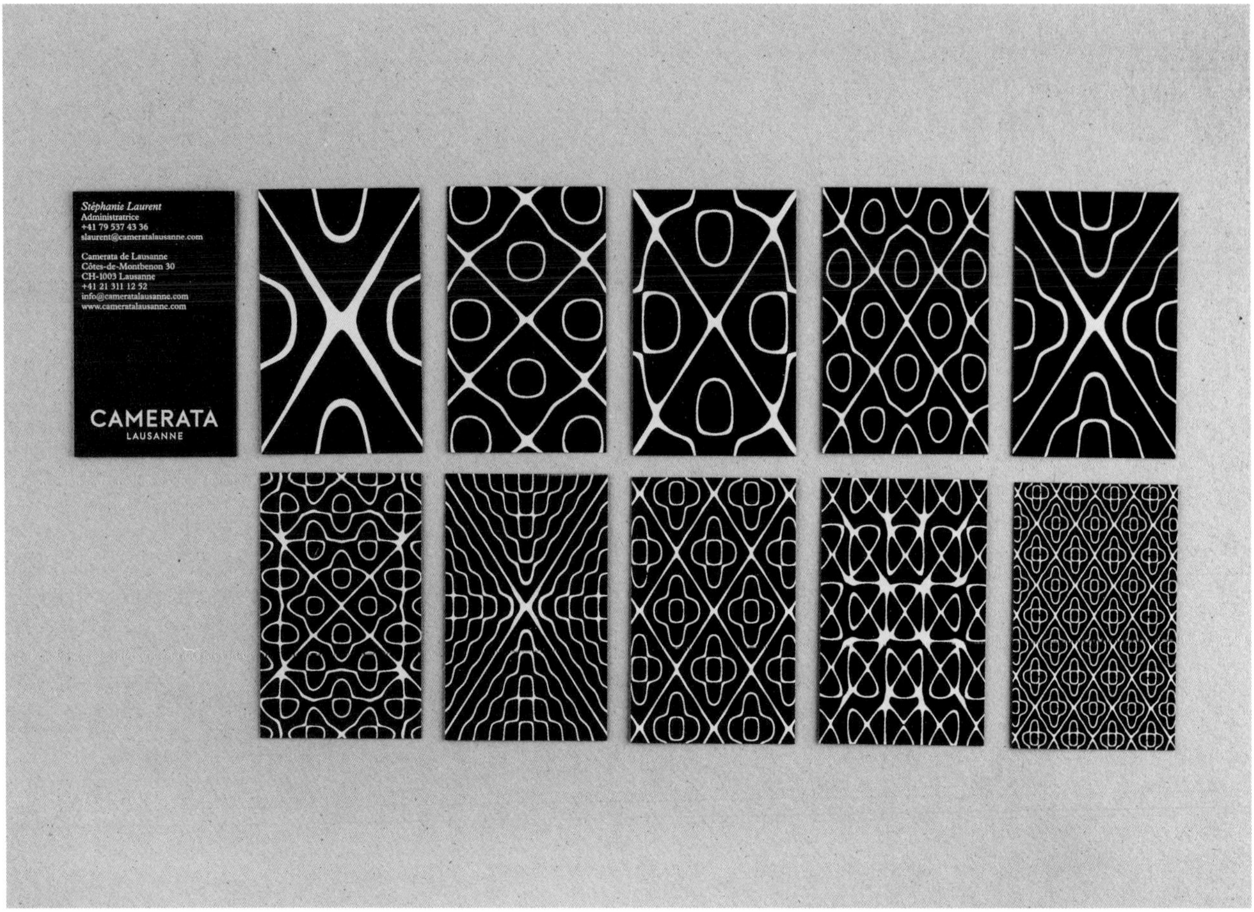

Camerata de Lausanne

My research led me to the work of Ernst Chladni, a German physicist and the father of modern acoustics. Chladni had discovered that by taking a copper disc sprinkled with sand and rubbing it with a bow, he could obtain geometrical figures. This fact demonstrates that music also has a physical effect on matter. So I followed the geometrical thread discovered by Chladni and used it on all communication media for the Camerata de Lausanne. To give it a more contemporary feel and make it more manageable, I had software written by Mathieu Rudaz which allows us to generate images directly on the computer using a specific frequency.

Camerata de Lausanne
CAMERATA
LAUSANNE
CAMERATA
LAUSANNE
CAMERATA
LAUSANNE

CAMERATA
LAUSANNE

Belmacz Identity

Belmacz is a London based jewelry company which opened its first shop and gallery in London Mayfair. The identity takes our original logo (which has been in use for about 8 years) but adds a variety of thicker, "raw" letter shapes. Those shapes relate to the process in which raw minerals and diamonds are more and more refined until they become a piece of jewelry. The visual references start with the mines, go to the raw materials, then to raw letter shapes and finally to the refined letters of the original logo. On their journey from the mine to the jewelry shop the materials go through many hands and constantly change location. It was important to visualize this idea of dislocation and constant travel. The new Belmacz identity is a complex system of connections and works across may different items and media. Every shape that has been cut out on one item of communication re-appears on another. For example a shape missing on a business card can re-appear on a carrier bag.

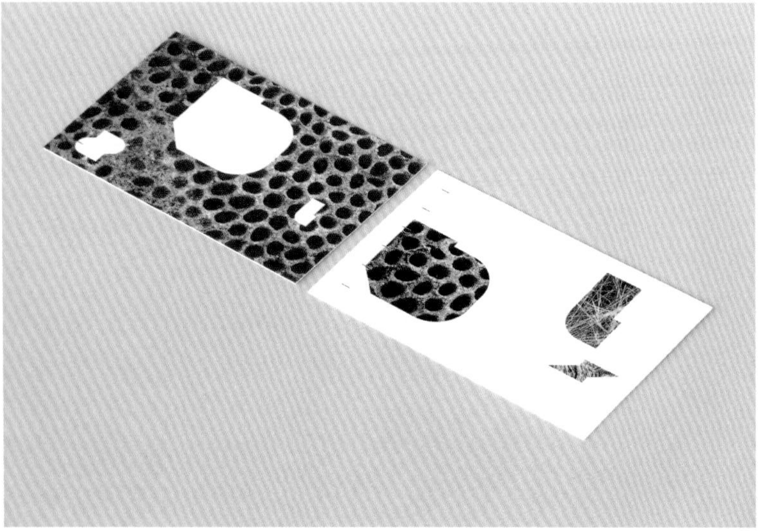

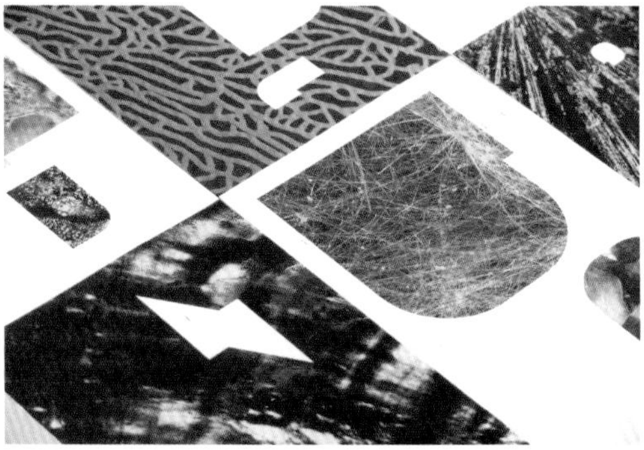

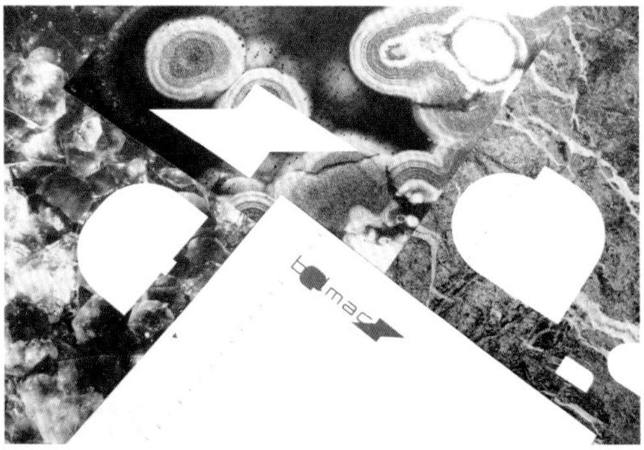

Art
Objects of Virtu

Customer Details

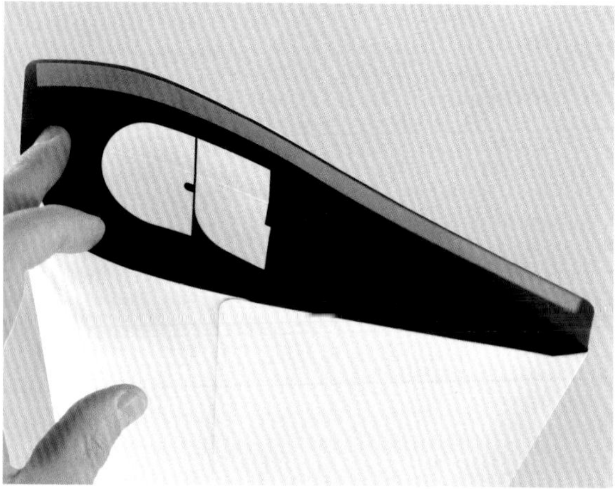

Cosmoslac

Although Cosmoslac is a company that produces paints, its new brand (company and product) identity is black and white, in order to stand out from the colorful competition. This approach has made Cosmoslac a unique case and has been awarded Greek and European Awards (packaging of emulsion paints and Ral sprays).

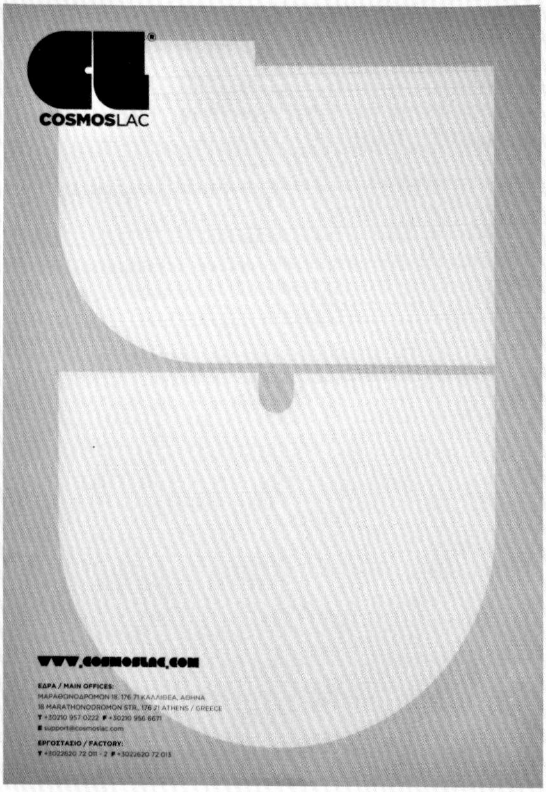

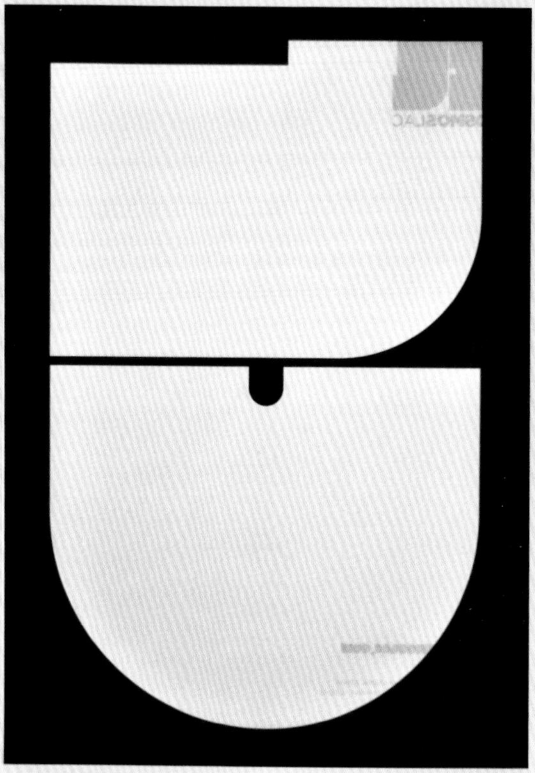

COSMOSLAC
Τάσος Σένκος
M 694 549 1194 E home@cosmoslac.com
ΕΔΡΑ ΜΑΡΑΘΩΝΟΔΡΟΜΩΝ 18, 17671 ΚΑΛΛΙΘΕΑ

COSMOSLAC

Right Now

Right Now is a volunteer, nonprofit media organization led by young people focusing on human rights issues in Australia. They are committed to covering human rights issues through free, accessible, creative and engaging online, print and radio media. When they won a grant to develop their new website, Right Now engaged BTP. After developing a strong typographic logo, BTP worked with local Melbourne illustrator Luci Everett to design a series of abstract collages. The solid circular mark became an interchangeable space for the collages — allowing the final logo to take on ever evolving moods and aesthetics. The logo and collages were used together over a range of stationery including business cards, drink coasters and bookmarks.

RIGHT
NOW

HUMAN RIGHTS
in AUSTRALIA

Noguera & Vintró

Gifts and stationery distributor.

Turnstyle Stationery 2007

Turnstyle, a Seattle-based graphic design firm, designed a set of stationery. The letterhead, envelope, note cards and business cards pack a one-two emboss/deboss punch. The business cards are three-ply and ridiculously thick—thicker than a credit card. In addition to being a vehicle for introductions and sharing contact information, you can use the cards for a wide range of activities such as scraping ice off your windshield, salsa dipping, breaking and entering, etc.

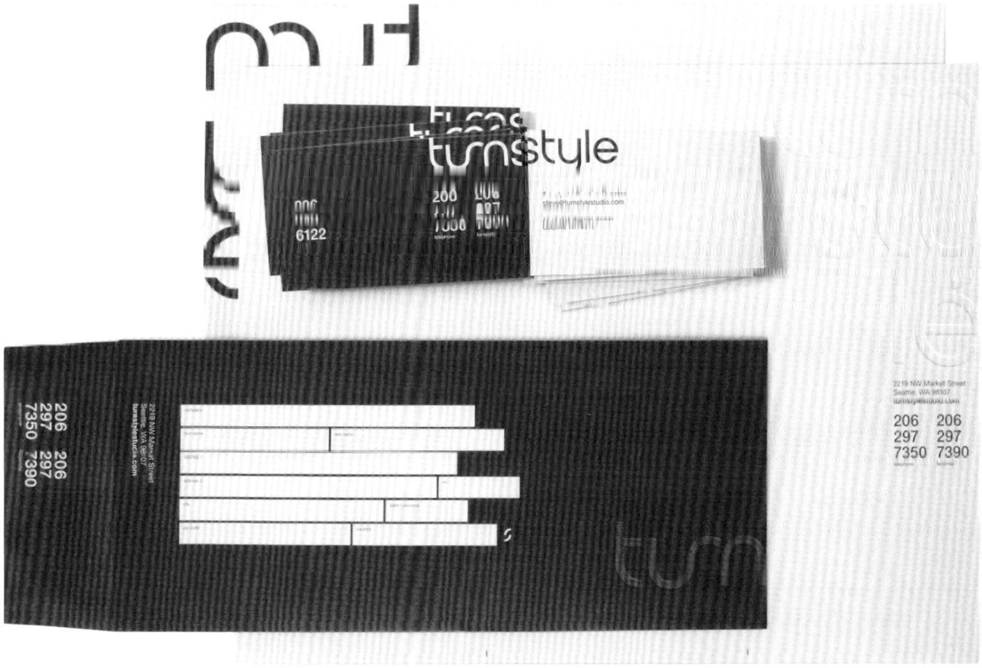

Fat Cow

Fat Cow is a specialty beef restaurant that uses the Japanese way of picking, cooking and serving beef. Drawing inspiration largely from the Japanese aesthetic of Wabi Sabi with traits that include simplicity, economy, austerity, modesty and the appreciation of the ingenuous integrity of natural objects and processes, wood is used primarily as the platform of this brand communication. The non-uniformity and texture suggests the Wabi Sabi beauty of imperfection. The mark and the searing on the wood are also reminiscent of the branding of cattle.

CAMDEN MEDICAL CENTRE
SINGAPORE 248649
F: +65 6735 7808
WWW.FAT-COW.COM.SG

BEVERAGE
WHILE YOU WAIT
PREPARED FOR YOU
SOURCED FOR YOUR TABLE
SOMETHING SWEET

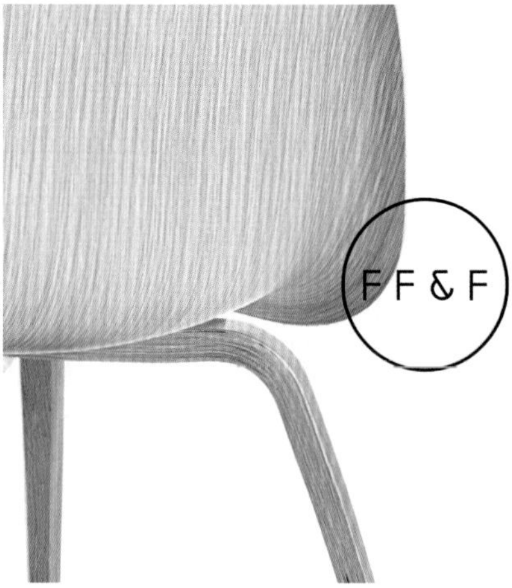

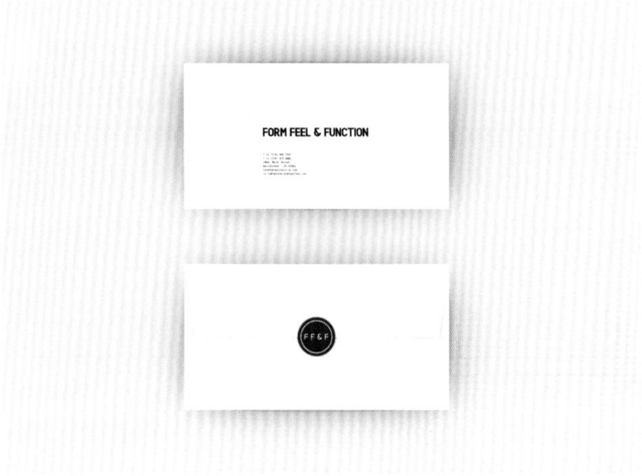

FF&F

FF&F is a branding identity created for a start up company based in Los Angeles which is committed to promoting young talented designers. The goal was to design a minimalistic and modern identity so it can be easily used with a wide range of different projects.

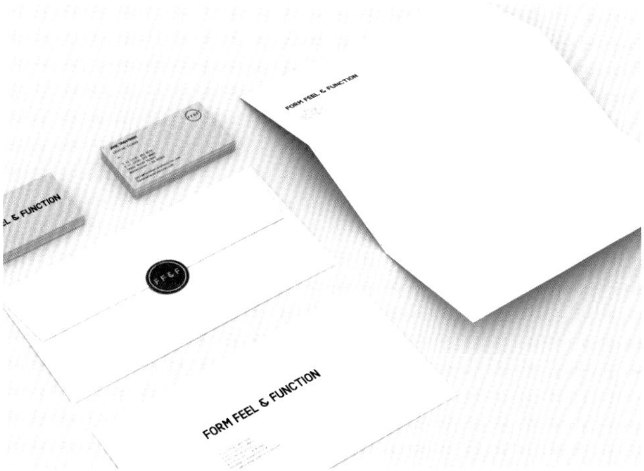
FORM FEEL & FUNCTION
FF&F
FORM FEEL & FUNCTION

FORM FEEL & FUNCTION
JANIE TRAN-TRINH
CREATIVE THINKER
T +1 (714) 651 9172
F +1 (714) 373 8883
14941 Moran Street
Westminster CA 92683
janie@formfeelandfunction.com
formfeelandfunction.com
FF&F

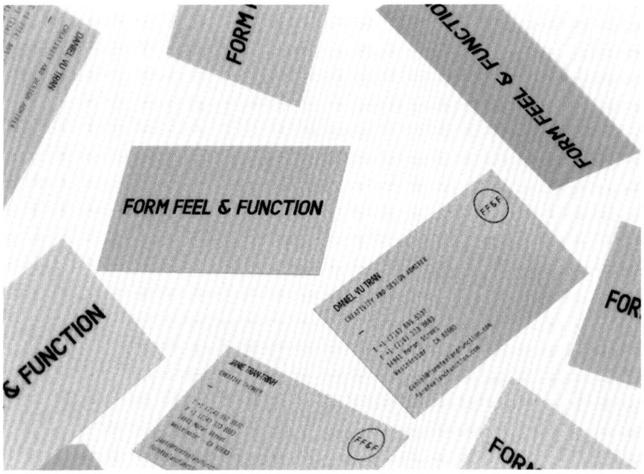
FORM FEEL & FUNCTION
FORM FEEL & FUNCTION
DANIEL VU TRAN
FF&F
JANIE TRAN-TRINH

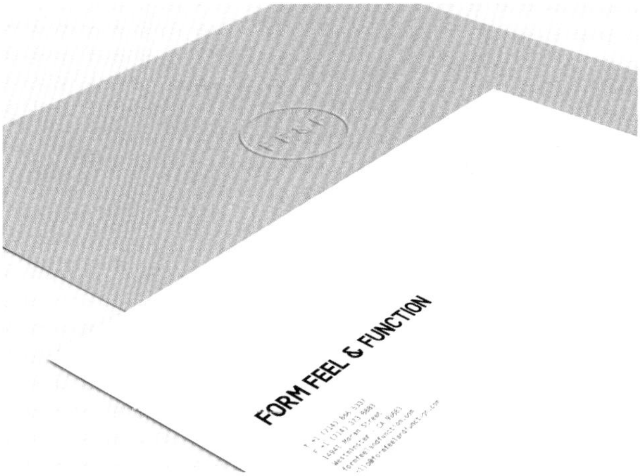
FORM FEEL & FUNCTION

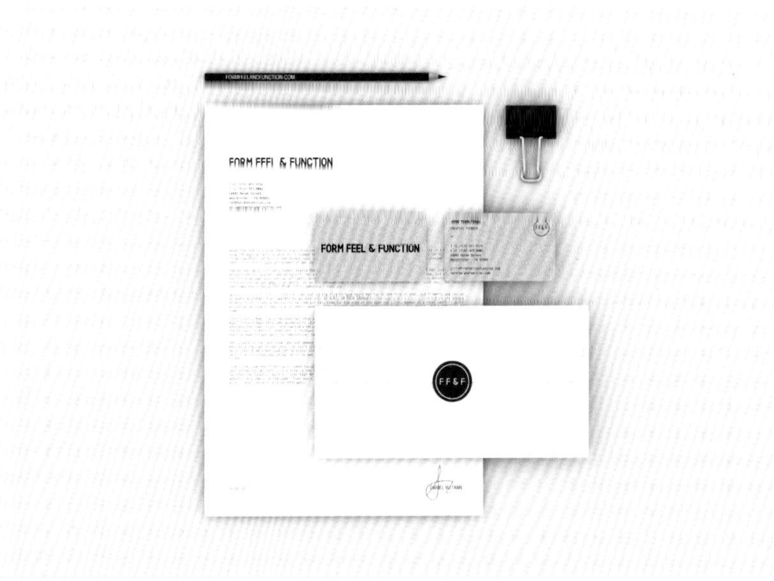
FORM FEEL & FUNCTION
FORM FEEL & FUNCTION
FF&F

Museumall

Museumall is a collection of different shoes and also the shopping hall of a national chain brand for taste, fashion, lifestyle and value. For the naming of the brand, we added "mall" in English and "Wu (物)" in Chinese, which directly echoes the characteristics of diverse products and imbues personality and humor. There's a little bit of fun involved. From dinosaur bones and bone shoes to office supplies, promotional materials, and advertising, the core brand philosophy of Museumall is to form a well-built, complete brand image that leaves a lasting impression.

博物物馆

博物物馆

Visual Identity Vibeke Skar

Vibeke Skar needed a simple web site for her work, as well as business cards and hang tags for showcasing her products at fairs worldwide. By combining the latter, we saved money, time and materials, and designed a business card with a picture of the product. This way, not only is the designer remembered, but the contact information and an image of the product are all in one place. We also designed correspondence cards to follow up with manufacturers. The business cards will also function as advertisements for her products, independent of fairs and exhibitions.
Photography by Henrik Beck Cæmpe.

Studio
Vibeke
Skar
Vibeke Skar
Product Designer
E: info@vibekeskar.com
W: vibekeskar.com

Studio
Vibeke
Skar

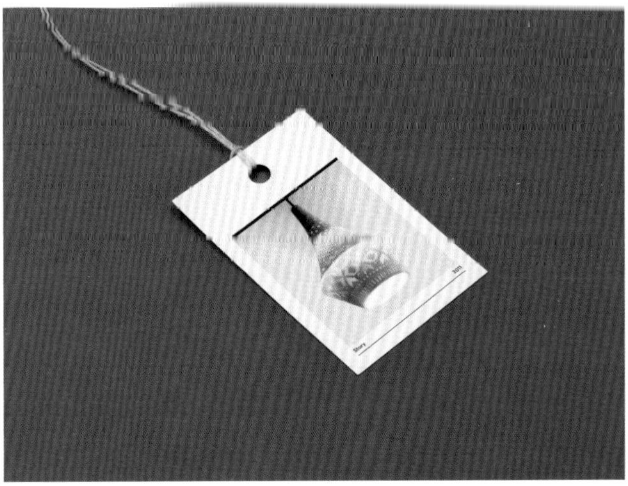

Madult Stationery

To show the partnership and connection between the two founders of the stationery line of Madult, we chose the image of 3D glasses. Blue is for Kevin, and red for Tam. The name card, envelope and letter head are over printed with each founder's information. If you wish to see Kevin's contact information, it can only be viewed through the colored PVC printed with Tam's contact information - expressing the idea of teamwork and brotherhood.

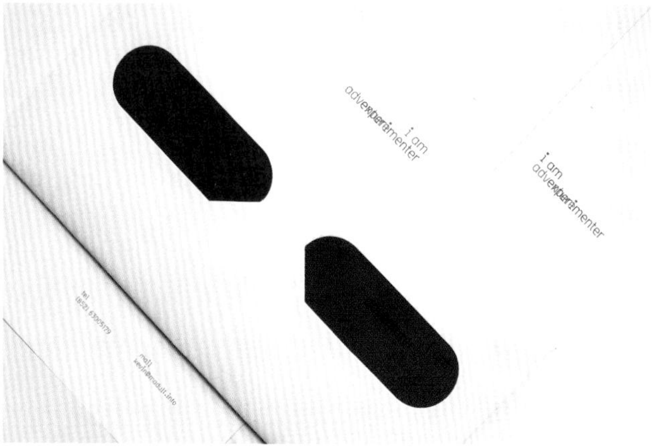

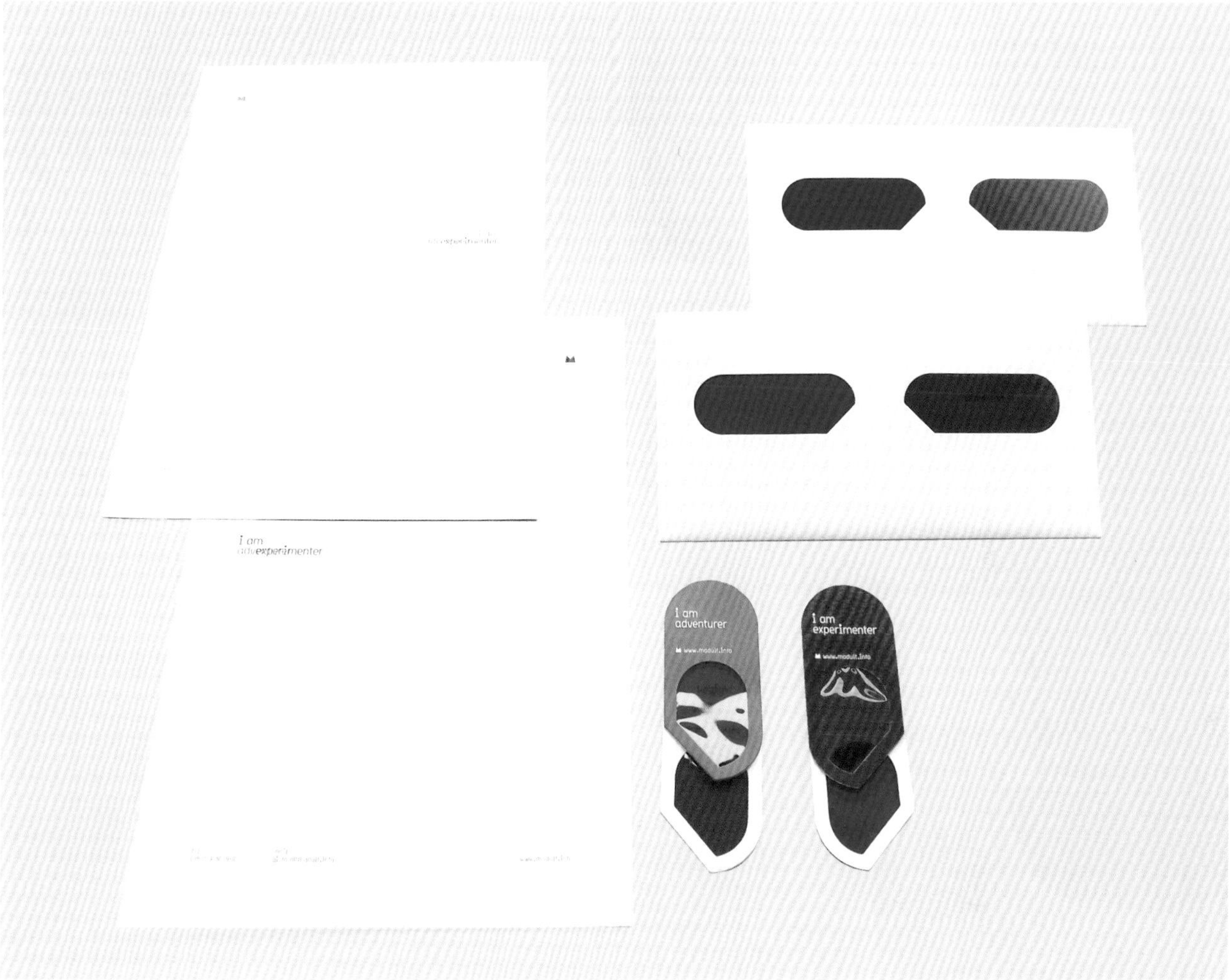
I am
adventurer
www.moduit.info
I am
experimenter
www.moduit.info

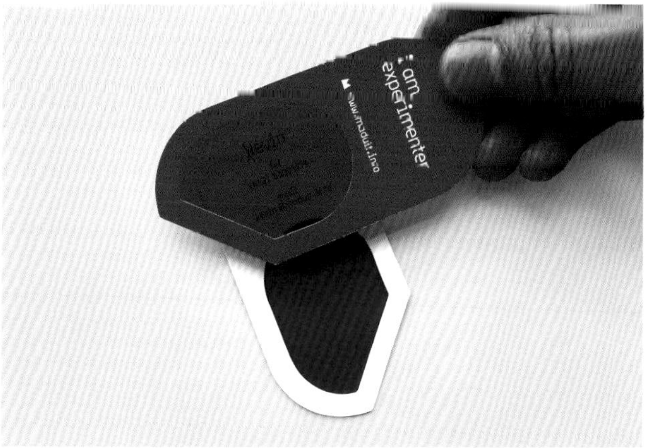
i am
experimenter
www.moduit.info

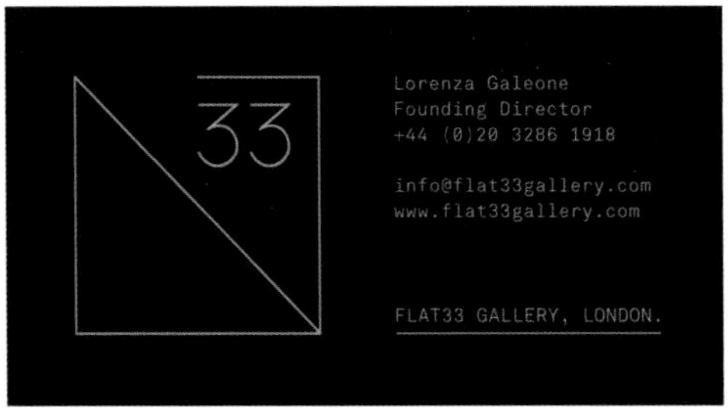

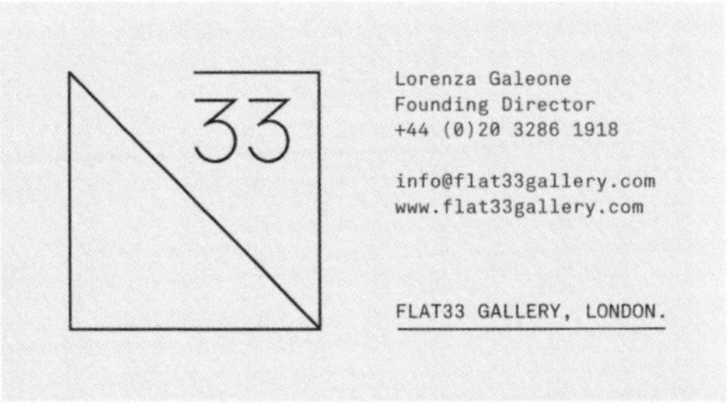

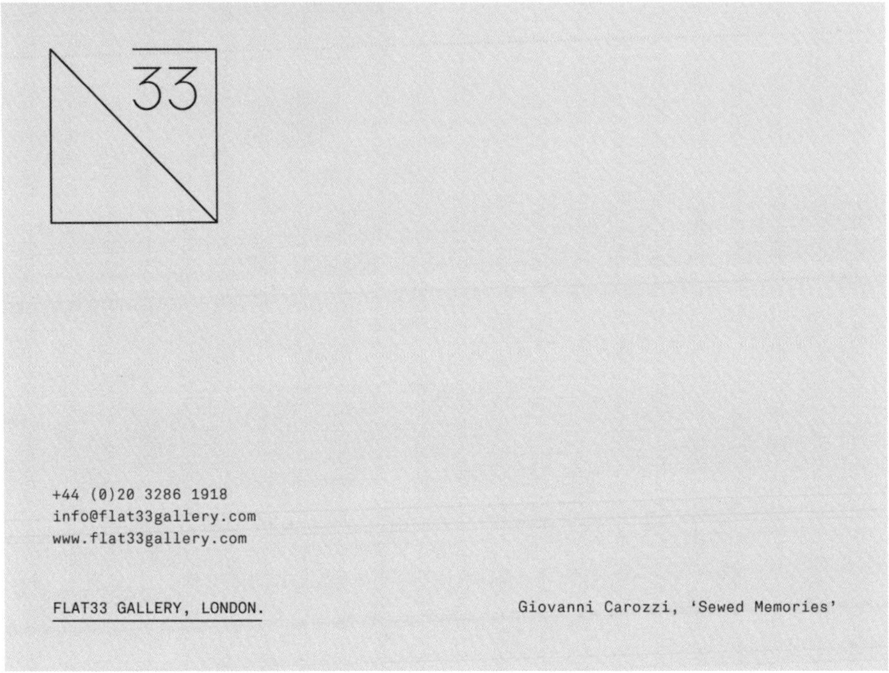

Flat33 Gallery Identity

Flat33 Gallery is a gallery exhibiting contemporary art in the heart of East London's arts community. The identity design is minimal yet meaningful, combining a symbolic, streamlined logo (the diagonal is a reference to the staircase of the gallery's high-rise location) with pared-down typography and a colourless palette. The challenge was to strip away ornamentation while giving the gallery a distinctive personality.

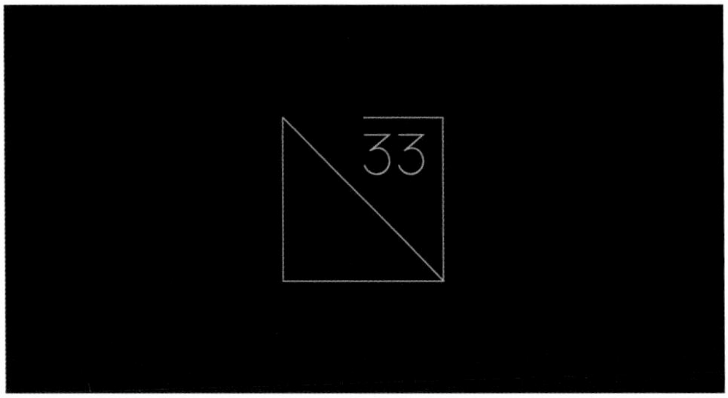

KODANSHA

This logotype is meant to function as the publisher's [illegible]. What is important in the client's [illegible] dealings and [illegible] of contents and translations is the stance that is presented at the bargaining [illegible] this project we strove to create a font that was well balanced, being both highly readable and highly original. We developed the Japanese logotype in conjunction with the English logotype. The [illegible] of the stroke ends is unique, and the characters for Kodansha, [illegible], with their high stroke count, are impressive and memorable.

講
談
社

KODANSHA
2-12-21 otowa, bunkyo-ku
tokyo 112-8001 japan
telephone: 03-3945-1111

TAKEO

Takeo supplies paper, and with it, a sense of well being. It offers the magnificence of paper as a thing that brings happiness in the very brushing of fiber against fingertip, not just paper as a medium. Takeo makes good paper, wonderful and accessible sample books, and collaborates conceptually with customers on the best ways to use paper.

Paper has a life span as well. Takeo conceives paper, creates paper and improves upon paper, whether for the purpose of materially making the first pronouncement of a new era or materially preserving the traditions of the past.

A sample book is an information highway connecting Takeo with its customers, the designers who decide how paper will be used. What is the best way to get a high quality sample book to the designer's workspace? We are designing samples that show the papers' appeal and introduce their treatment, while illustrating the breadth and variety of both.

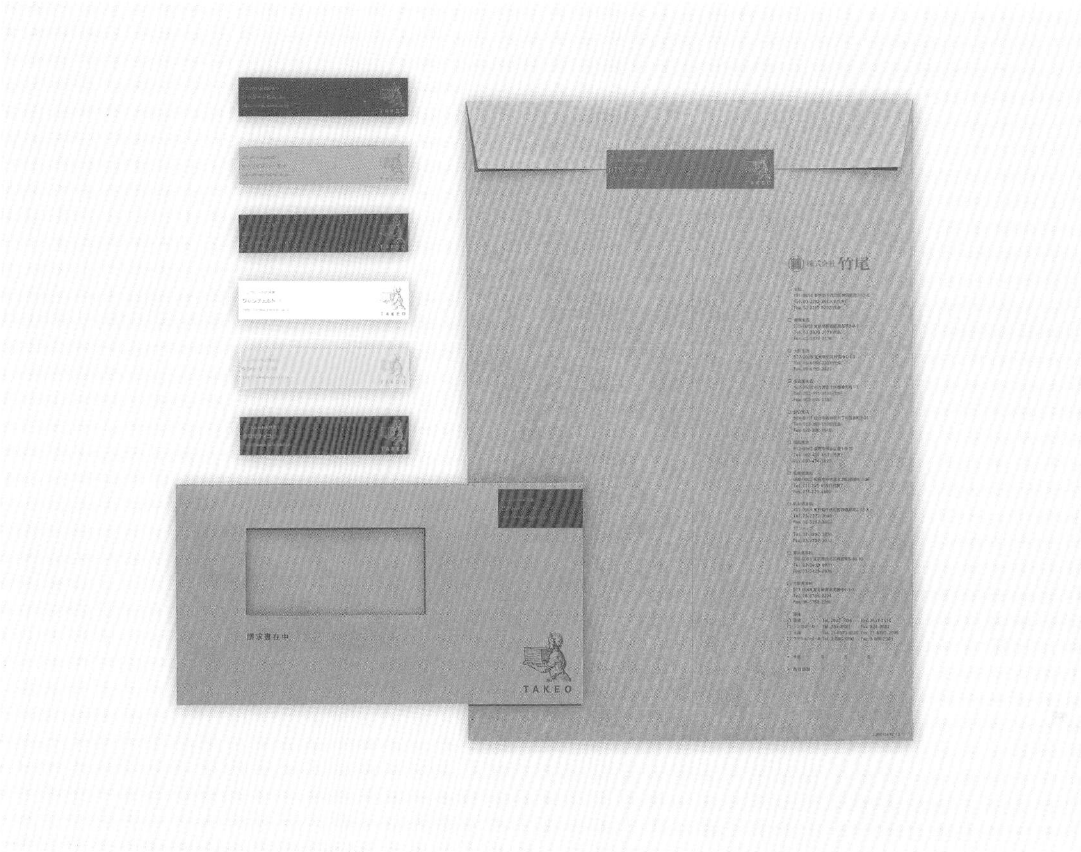
株式会社 竹尾
請求書在中
TAKEO

宣伝企画部 企画課
部長
竹尾 太郎
株式会社 竹尾
101-0054 東京都千代田区神田錦町3-12-6
TEL:03-3292-3619 FAX:03-3219-9060
MOBILE:090-6024-7850 www.takeo.co.jp
E-MAIL:cmpd@takeo.co.jp

UNIQUE
ENVIRONMENTAL
SPACES
STSTYLE.COM.AU
4/1A
WINDSOR PL
WINDSOR 3182
MELBOURNE
AUSTRALIA
0406 535 100
STEVE@STSTYLE.COM.AU
4/1A WINDSOR PLACE
WINDSOR 3182
MELBOURNE AUSTRALIA
UNIQUE
ENVIRONMENTAL
SPACES
0419 291 272
TRAVIS@STSTYLE.COM.AU
4/1A WINDSOR PLACE
WINDSOR 3182
MELBOURNE AUSTRALIA
UNIQUE
ENVIRONMENTAL
SPACES

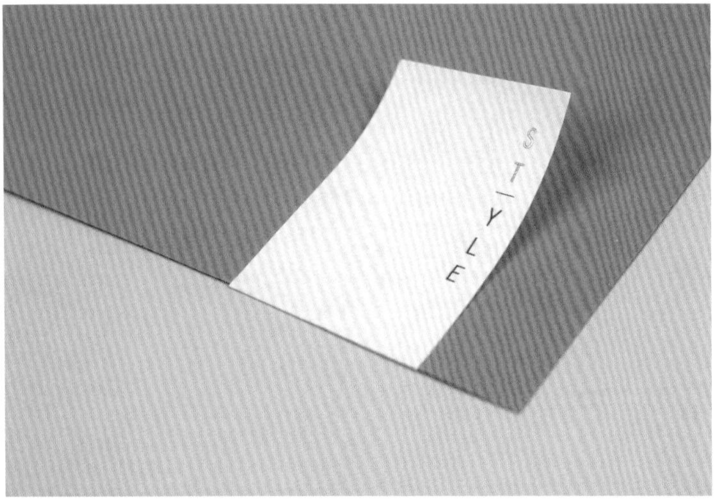
STYLE

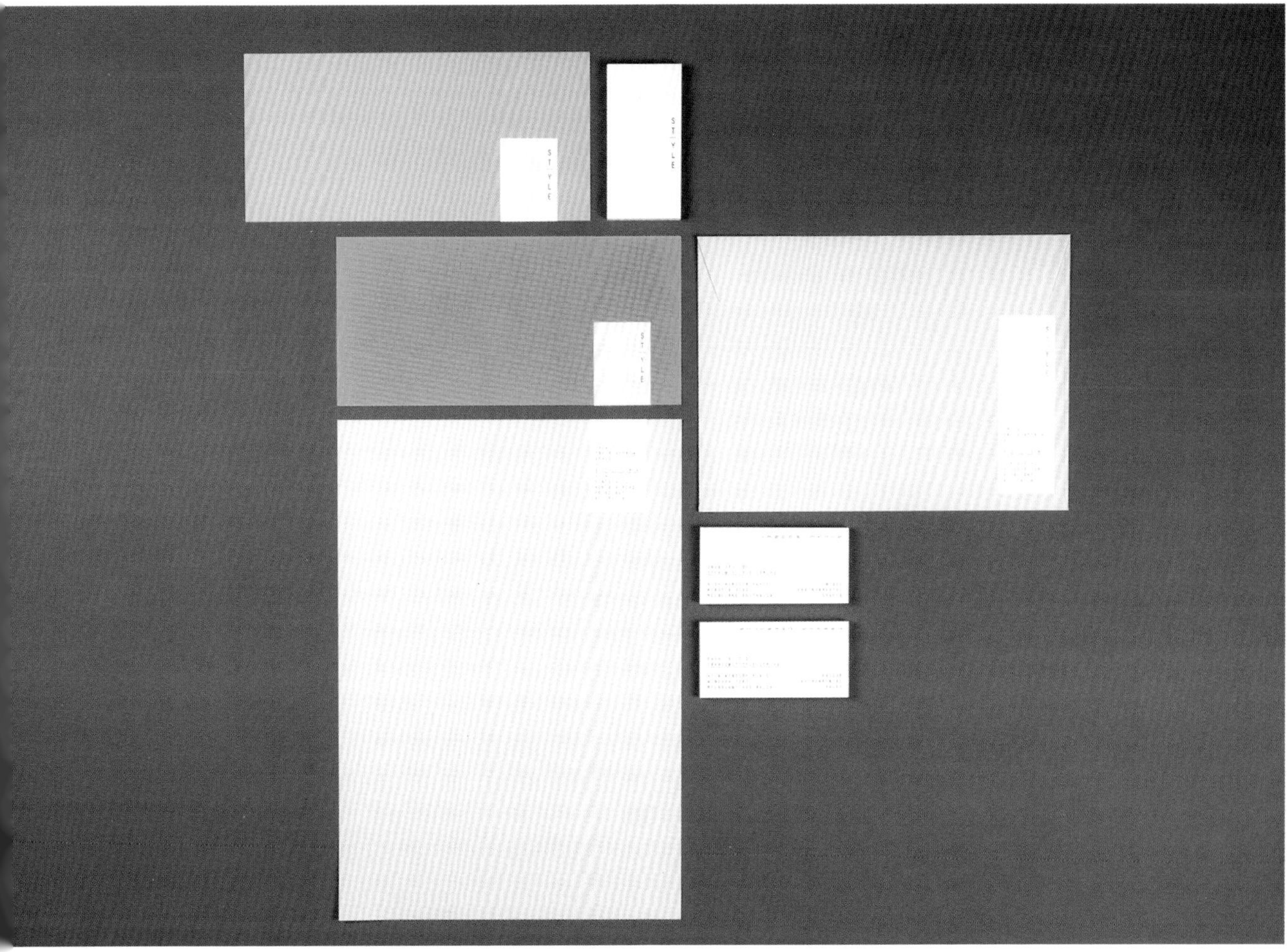

ST Style

ST Style is an interior design firm specializing in retail spaces. Being adept at creating solutions within tight budgets and timeframes, ST Style's designs are unique, functional and memorable. BTP were commissioned to rebrand their existing image with an up to date aesthetic that represented a leading design industry member. The ST Style name was originally born from the names of its founders, Steve and Travis, and had already developed strong brand equity.

We began by consolidating the stuttering "ST Style" name to appear as "STyle". As the word "style" adequately claimed what it embodied, the solution resulted in a type marque offering restrained use of stylized form. This simplistic type marque was applied across a diverse range of coloured stocks in reflection of the business' practice – also enabling a simple brand refresh by the implementation of a fresh stock palette. Copper foiling was used as a finish on the business cards and stickers. The copper foil complements the interchangeable range of stocks creating an elegant and fresh stationery suite.

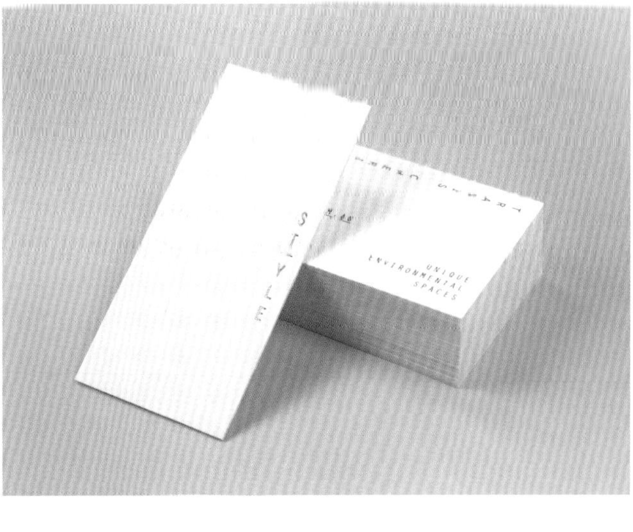

Jackie Smith

Jackie Smith is a shoe and handbag brand that has managed to position itself as one of Argentina's most important brands in the accessible luxury market. Valeria Smith, creative director, and Julian Lozzia, CEO of the company, came to FBDI in 2007 to make them a part of the brand's gestation and to help build the Jackie universe. Taking the brand's name and its position in the market as starting points, FBDI defined an identity that reflects the essence of a feminine world: classic, international, romantic, timeless and sophisticated. Inside this conceptual world we defined and designed Jackie's visual identity, logo, color palette, packaging and advertising campaigns. As a result of the brand's construction, Jackie Smith became, in only two collections, a top brand within the handbags category.

JACKIE SMITH
JACKIE SMITH
JACKIE SMITH

JACKIE SMITH

JACKIE SMITH

Fórmula P Comunicação Identidade

Fórmula P has been in the advertising field for around 20 years, and to celebrate the anniversary, the agency decided to change its visual identity. The design, care and insight in the choice of materials set the tone for the new line of the agency which is based on tradition and evolution. For the new visual identity of Fórmula P, we created a very modern design, consistent with the agency always thinking ahead. But we can't look to the future without rescuing the past and the pioneering company history of 20 years. That's why we decided to create a contemporary design and apply it on paper with a retro finish.

PAULINHO diretor presidente
MÔNIKA DE SOUZA diretora executiva

PAULINHO diretor presidente
FORMULA℗.COM.BR

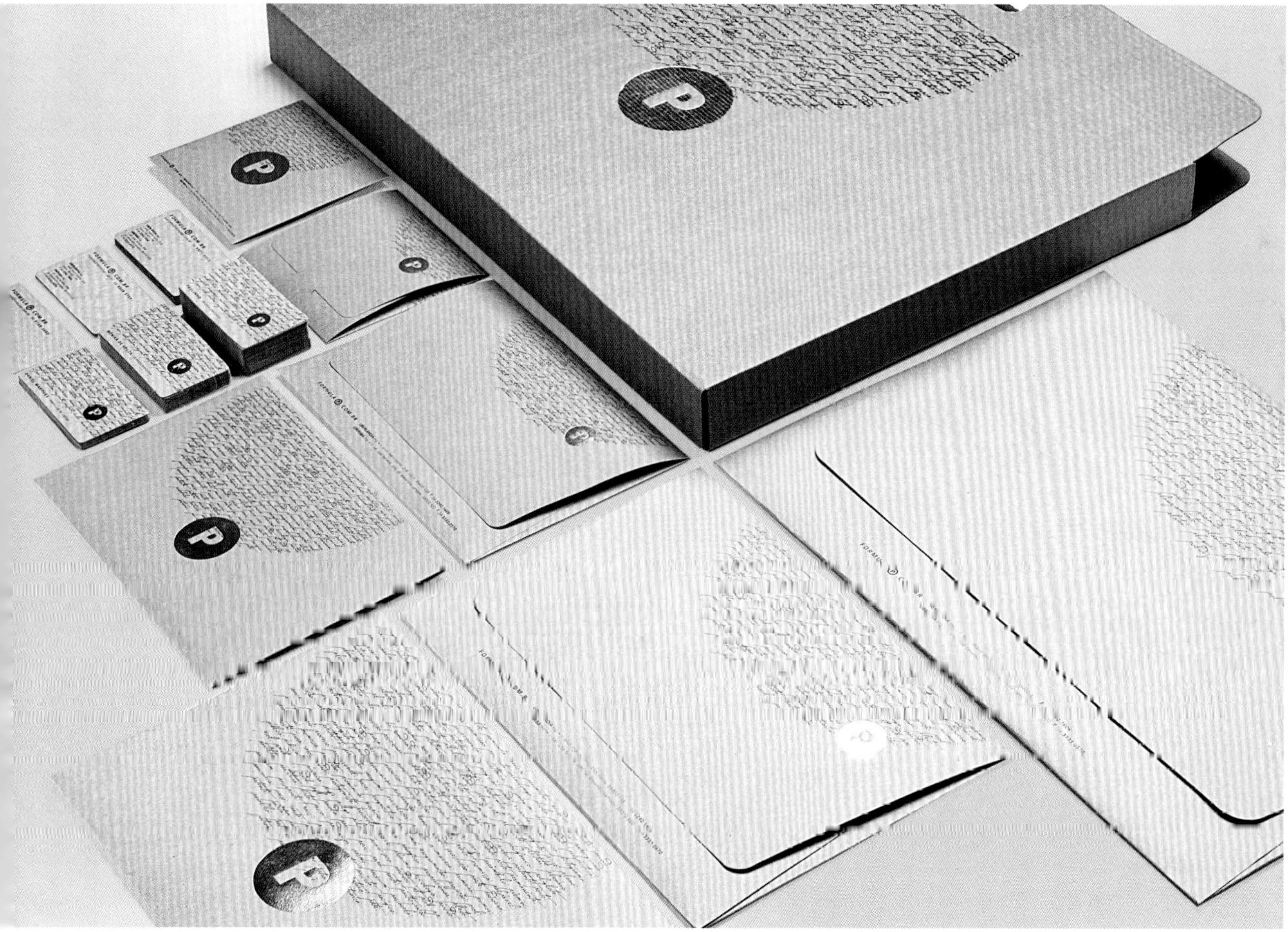

BEC Visual Identity Design Proposal

Visual Identity for a Chinese state-owned company "BEC-Beijing Electronics Holding". We combine the elements of electrons and seeds, which have an energy core, meaning carrying and heritage. We mix the 3 letters "B E C" in the core, designed to have the feel of a circuit. "B," "E," and "C" spin off one by one in different speeds and directions to become a dynamic logo. No matter which position they stop in, they always look like electrons with an energy core.

BEIJING ELECTRONICS HOLDING

BEIJING ELECTRONICS HOLDING

Mijnen Pieper Bicycle Parts

The company Pieper Industrie Vertretungen was founded in 1911, in the German town of Haan. For over a hundred years, they have been supplying retailers across Europe. In 2012 the company entered a new phase when Wilfried Mijnen became the new owner and the name changed to Mijnen Pieper Bicycle Parts.
The company commissioned Urform to create a new brand identity including rethinking the product color and branding. The goal of implementing the new identity was to create more consistency in the product range and more recognition in communication. In 2012 and 2013 we will integrate the new style in all packaging and product branding. We were inspired by the identity the company used 60 years ago.

MIJNEN PIEPER
BICYCLE PARTS

Paul Hutchison
paul@hypetype.co.uk
Hype Type Studio
Graphic Design
& Art Direction
www.hypetype.co.uk

HYPE
TYPE
STUDIO

Paul Hutchison
paul@hypetype.co.uk
Hype Type Studio
Graphic Design
& Art Direction
www.hypetype.co.uk
HYPE
TYPE
STUDIO

Hype Type Stationery

Like our clients we have a need for tactile communication which connects. From our stationery to our latest book, materials, printing and application all play an important role in articulating the brand. Careful consideration was given when selecting materials and print techniques, with the aim to promote continuity in a creative way.

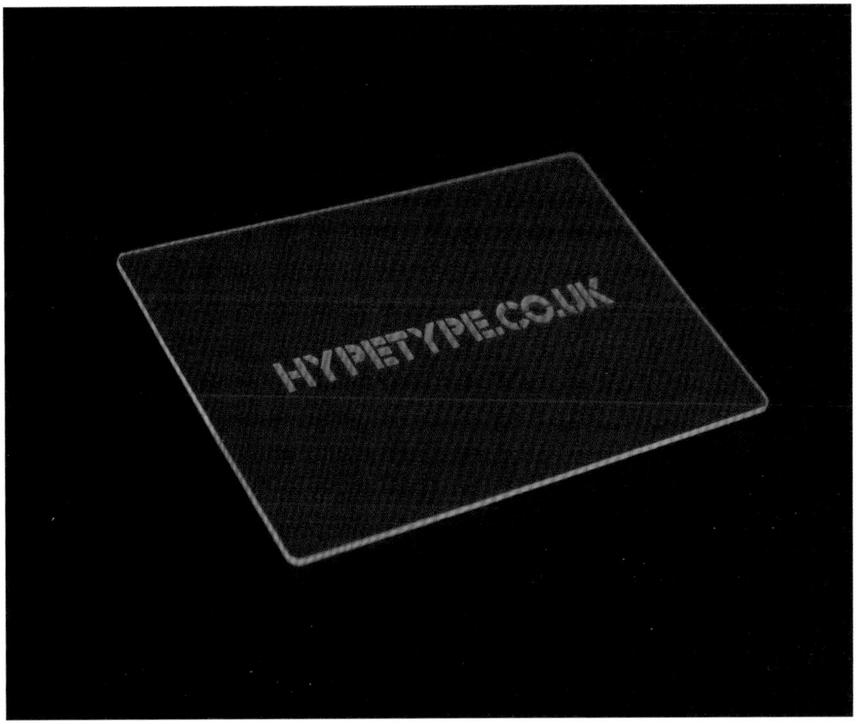

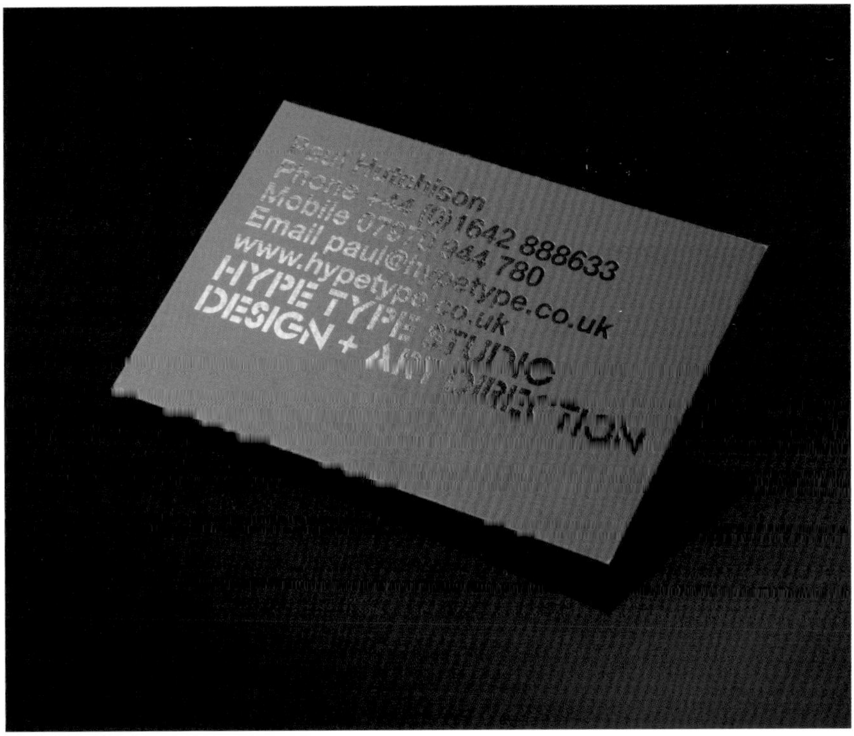

Pickle Pictures Brand Identity

Mike from Pickle Pictures came to Liquorice Studio with a big personality and even bigger ambition. The studio helped him to develop a bold and memorable brand identity, which works across print and the web and comes to life in motion. Key to the strategy was developing a logo that embodies Mike's bright, friendly and personable approach when animated whilst acting as a crisp and corporate mark of trust when printed. A palette of greens creates a clean and memorable atmosphere while rounded "pickle inspired" typography from Linetto lends a refined sense of fun to the brand.
The resulting Pickle Pictures branding translates seamlessly across digital and print formats whilst maintaining a strong clarity of the brand's vision. The approach ensured every dollar spent by Pickle on their brand would be a worthwhile investment for the future.

info@pickle-pictures.com
pickle-pictures.com

PICKLE
PICTURES

pickle-pictures.com
pickle-pictures.com
Pickle Pictures is a full service video production
company formed in 2012. Drawing on a finely tuned
network of industry professionals, including outstanding
writers, animators, directors and cinematographers,
and with experience across internal communications,
training videos, advertising, music and promotional videos,
Pickle Pictures can tailor a team to suit any job.
Michael
0437 958 830

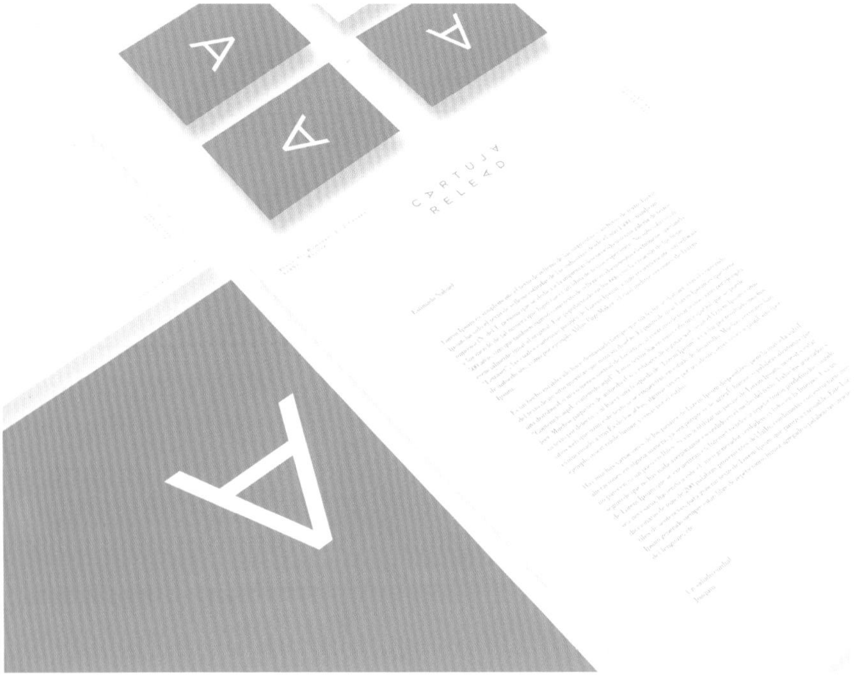

Cartuja Relead

Cartuja Relead is a recycling company focused on car waste. In order to create their logo, we started from the graphic concept of the arrows that compose the recycling symbol but we choose a more subtle option: to refer to the idea just by modifying the inclination of the "A" letter, whose shape is geometrically similar to an arrowhead. Thus, we get a simple, legible logo with a brand weight that will be positioned over time.

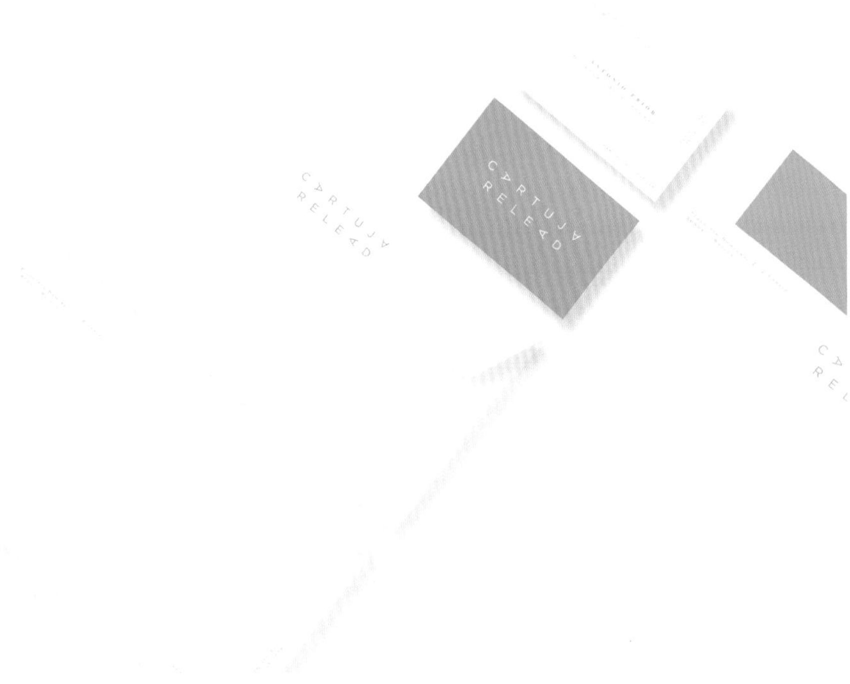

CARTUJA
RELEAD

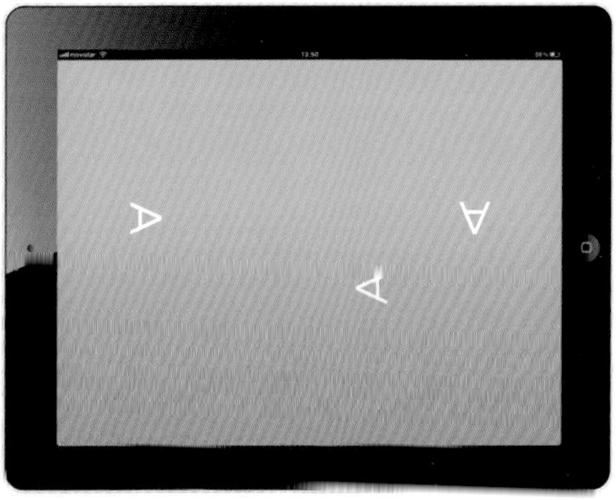

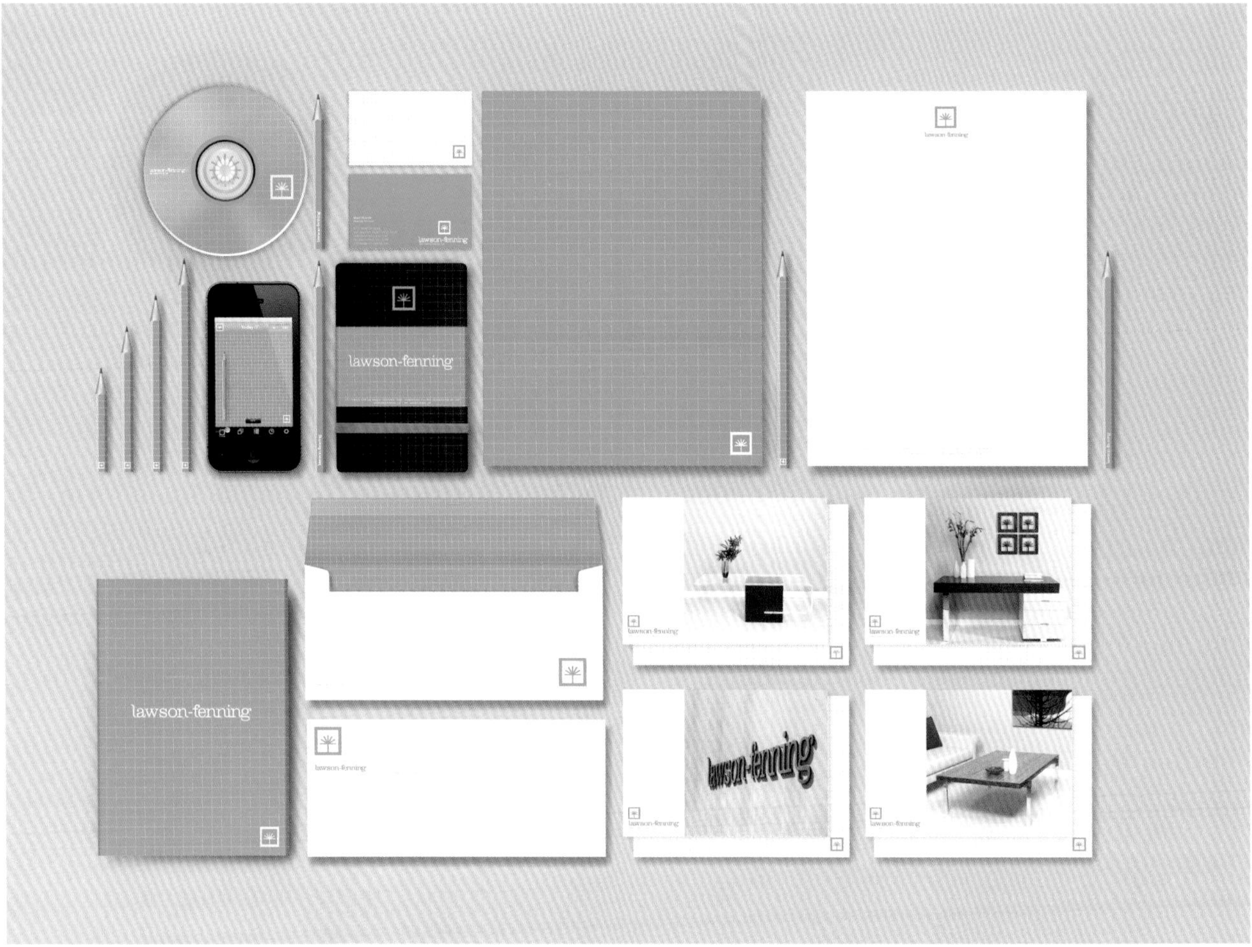
lawson-fenning
lawson-fenning

lawson-fenning

lawson-fenning

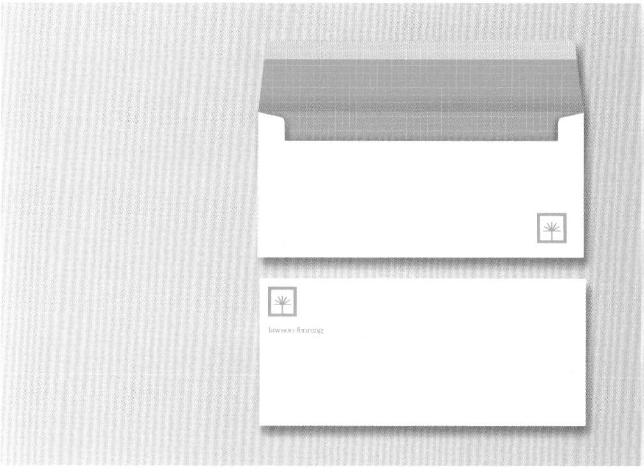

Lawson & Fenning Identity

Tom Tor Studio was commissioned to rebrand Lawson & Fenning Identity System's marketing campaign. Lawson-Fenning is a furniture [illegible] and often contradictory aspects of the Los Angeles area. The shop's line of furniture and accessories borrows the glam of Hollywood Regency, the playful forms and materials of Mid-century [illegible] and the visual efficiency of Dutch Modernism. Furthermore, a well [illegible] curated selection of vintage furniture and accessories from the '40s '50s and '60s is available. ID, Logo, Stationery, website, packaging, catalogs, storefront singage, dvd pack, promotional media were all created. Photography by Zachary [illegible]

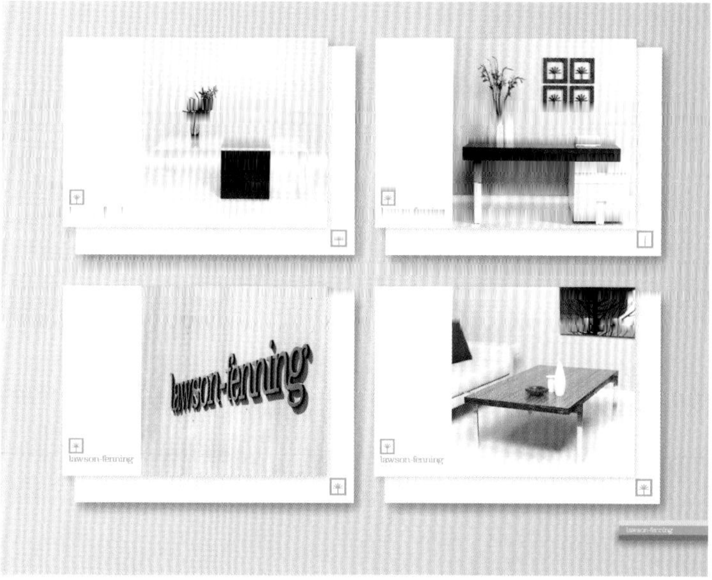

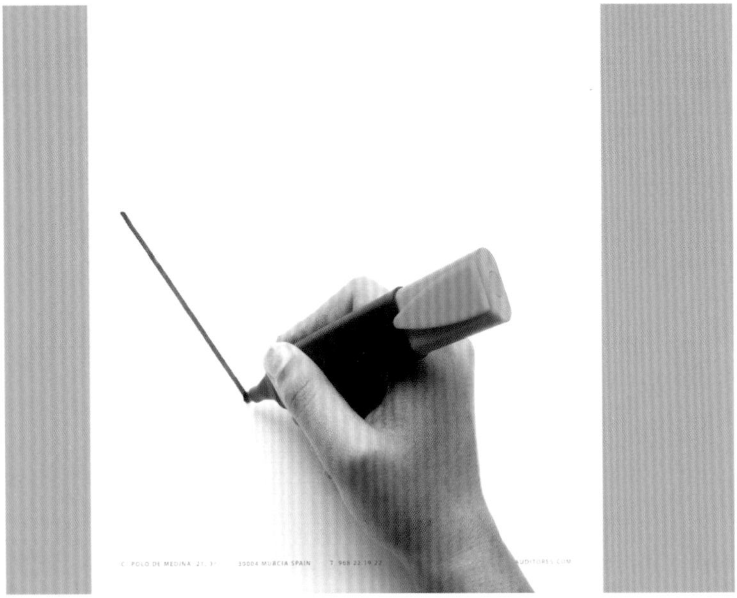

Luis Economista

Identity design and stationery which play with the graph analysis in economics. Each of these pieces also works as material for notes and sketches.

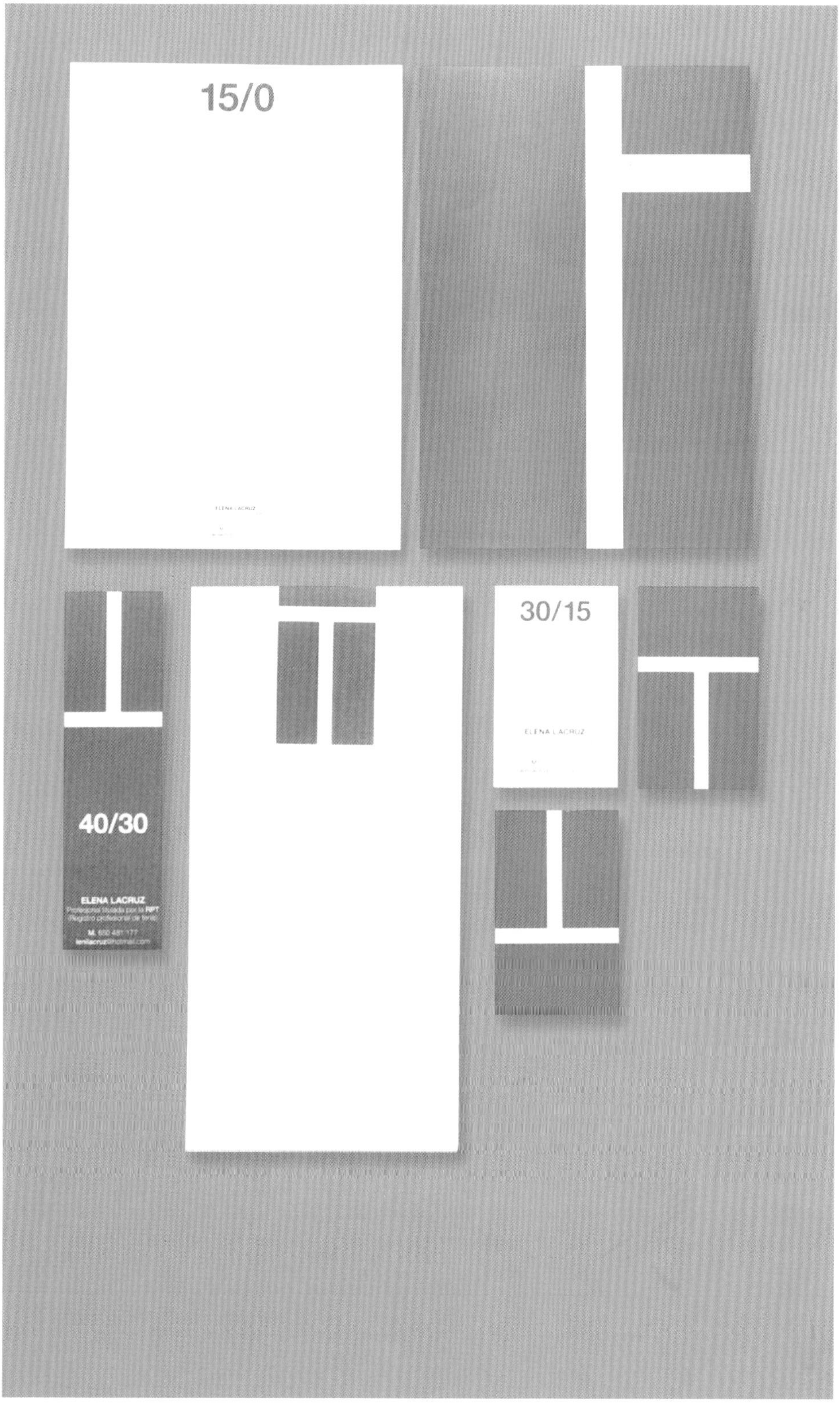

Elena Lacruz

Corporate Identity for a professional tennis teacher based on the score system of the game itself, the original color of the tennis courts and its dividing lines. The stationery items have changing scores, giving it dynamism. A sober and strong typeface and a centered layout of data evokes the most classic face of the sport.

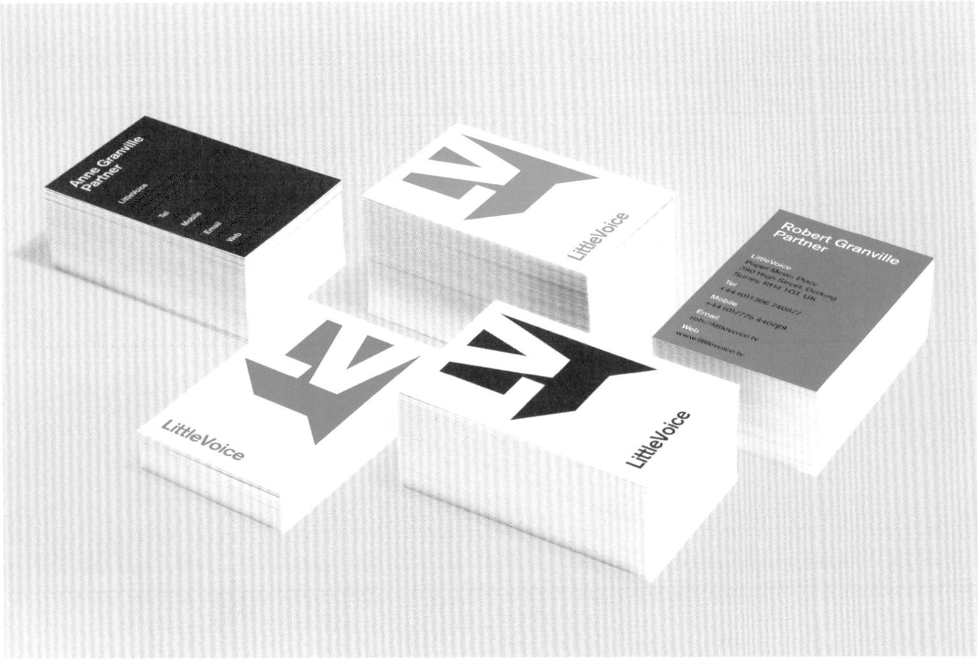

Little Voice Identity & Stationery

Little Voice Media provides audio and video communication to businesses and organizations in order to help them communicate their message more effectively. They were looking for a new identity that was vibrant, fresh, cutting edge, energetic, and simple. Importantly, it needed to work as a symbol as well as on all other communications. We created an identity that meets all those needs, which can also be used dynamically in motion graphics.

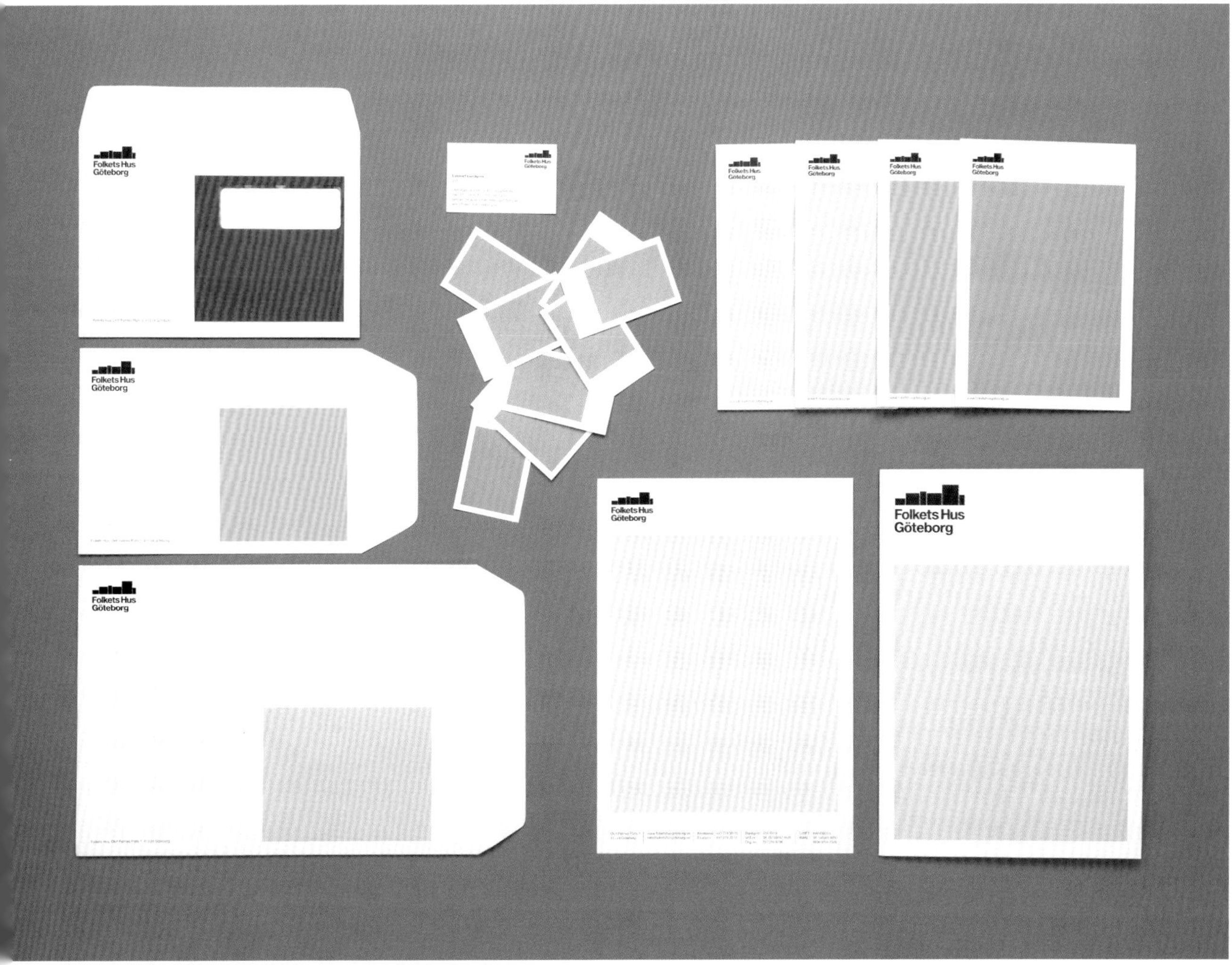

Folkets Hus Gothenburg

Folkets Hus is a [illegible] in Gothenburg on the west coast of Sweden. They have a long tradition of renting rooms out to both large companies and smaller groups of people. We did a set of stationery inspired of by rooms and buildings with a happy and [illegible]

Barker Helme Identity

Helen Barker Helme was looking for a unique and creative identity for her new interior design business. Her ability to choose the right colour and position of furnishings for her clients' interiors provided the inspiration. A series of different coloured stickers were created and a graph paper graphic was printed onto business cards, compliment slips and letterheads.
Helen chooses an individual colour and position for each personalized set of stationery, thus reflecting the bespoke and direct service she offers through her creative interior design.

Barker-Helme

Helen Barker-Helme

The Young Academy of Sweden

The Royal Swedish Academy of Sciences has established a new academy for young researchers within all disciplines working in Sweden. The aim is to create an interdisciplinary forum and research-political platform for elite researchers and scientists in Sweden. Ritator created an identity which communicates the ethos of The Young Academy, who represent new thinking as well as the tradition of The Royal Swedish Academy of Science. The logo is designed to resemble a conventional crest or emblem in which every element denotes a specific meaning, yet is made up entirely of abstract forms. This duality represents the integration of old and new. The symbol aims to encourage diverse interpretations, depicting the activity of the Academy itself. Photography by Matti Östling.

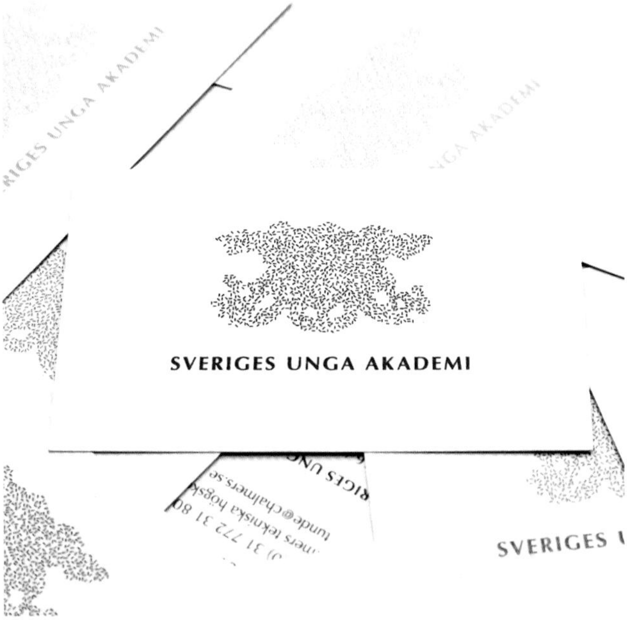

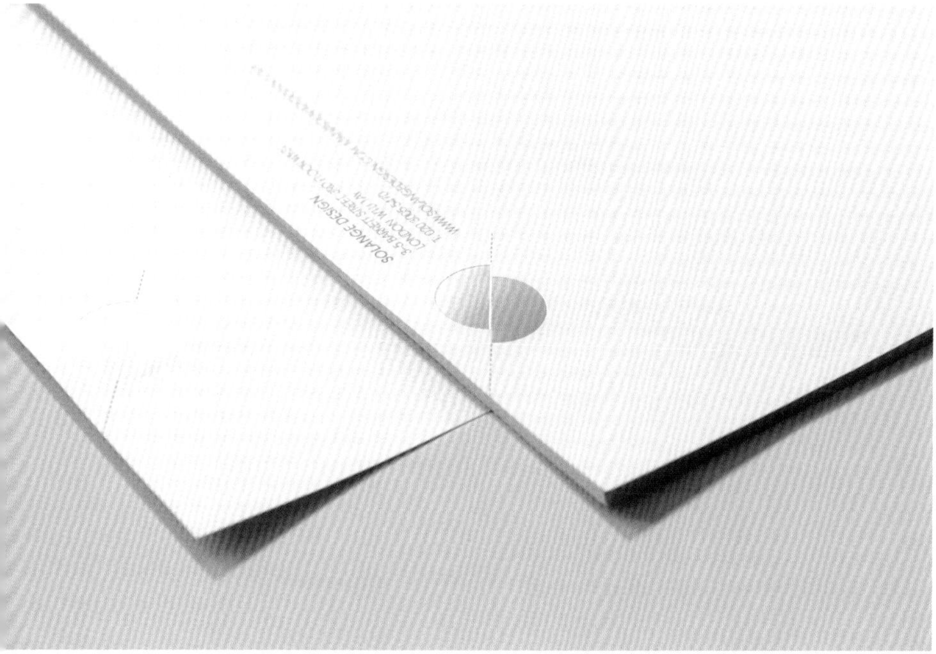

Solange Design Stationery

Identity and stationery to suit internationally celebrated interior conceptualist Emma Oldham, one of London's prominent and influential design figures. The gold marque, an off-set circle that, with subtlety, shows an 'S', was adapted from a favourite piece of her jewellery.
A simple yet striking mix of soft white, metallic gold and fluorescent orange gives a joyous, spacial identity and stationery collection to reflect her decadent yet confidently zen style.
Flood printing of the fluorescent orange on the reverse of the letterhead and continuation sheets continually reflects colourful light, giving an architectural feel to Emma's work and ensuring any correspondence really has desk shout!
Subtly textured, heavy stocks (achieved with GF Smith's Colorplan) give a soft, tactile feel that adds to the ambience of an individual, warm, elegant, trend leading home that Solange Design creates so beautifully.

Zaha Hadid Architects

As part of the Zaha Hadid Architects brand identity project we created a suite of stationery items that uses a variety of paper stocks, colours and textures. The aim was to reflect the myriad materials used in the buildings Zaha Hadid Architects create whilst providing an element of surprise. The new logotype is highlighted in a silver foil. The reverse of the letterhead and comp slip feature a pattern in foil.

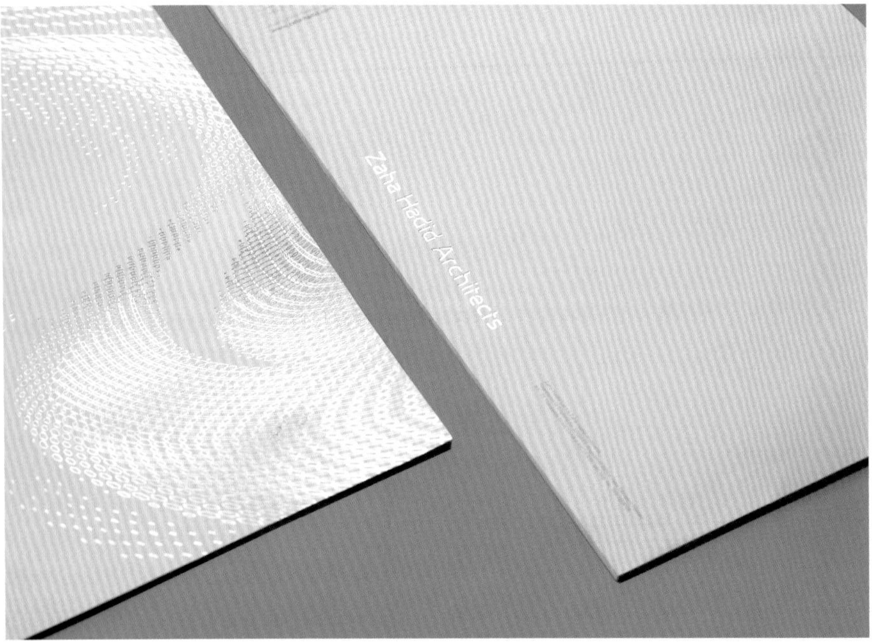

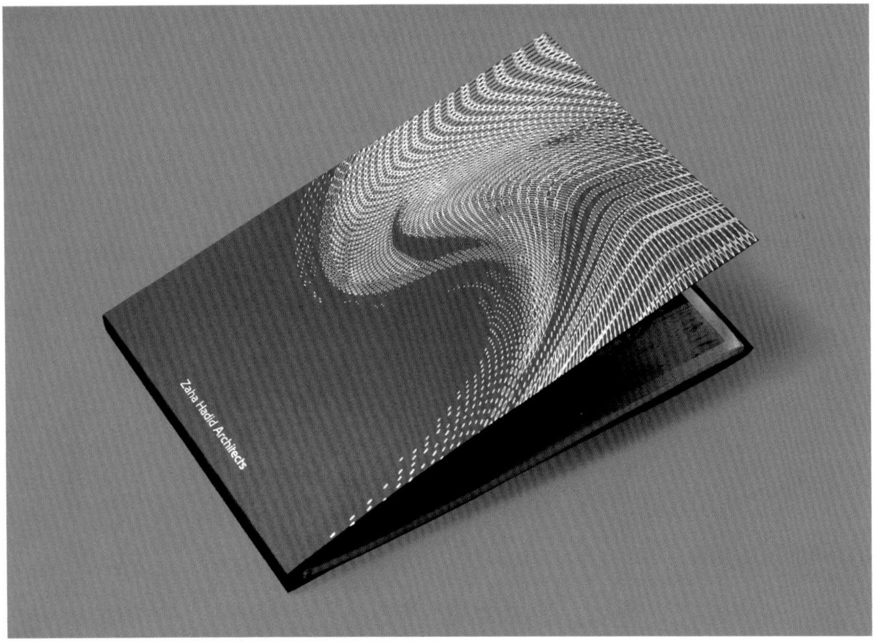

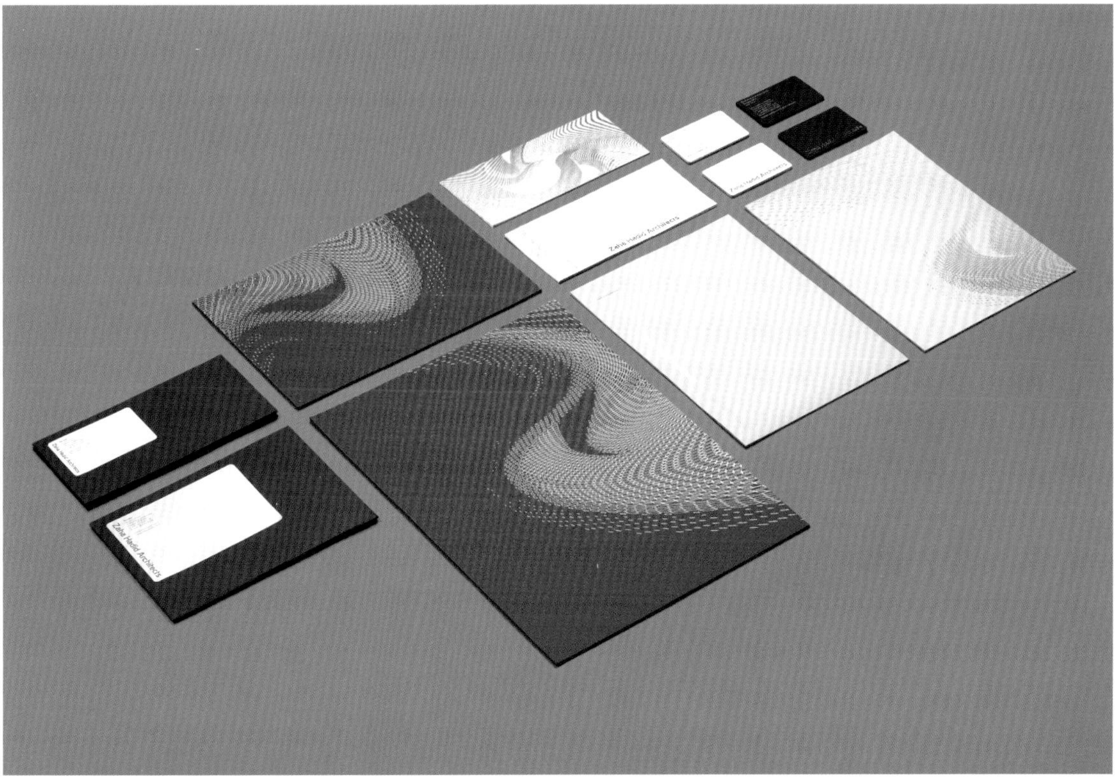
Zaha Hadid Architects

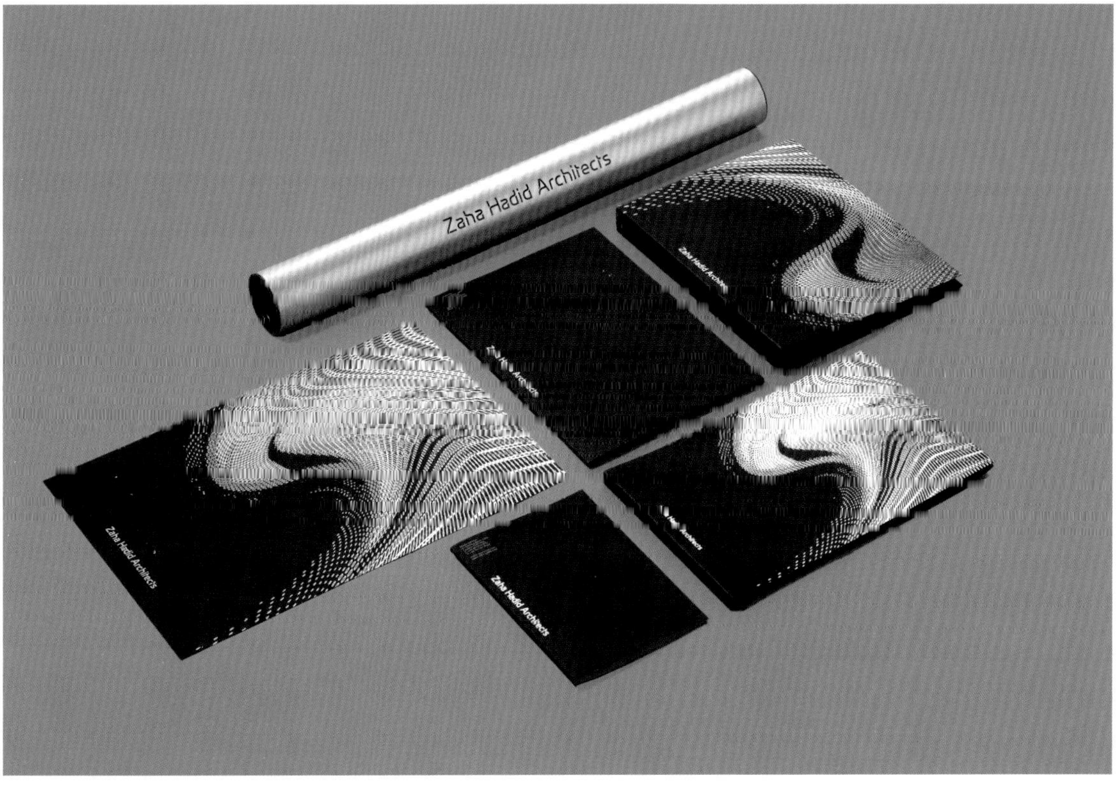
Zaha Hadid Architects
Zaha Hadid Architects
Zaha Hadid Architects

Union Latin

Visual identity project for the open competition organized by the international organization "Latin Union".
Founded in 1954, its aim is to promote and preserve Latin culture throughout the world. The institution brings together 36 Member States and represents the 6 Latin languages (Catalan, Spanish, French, Italian, Romanian, and Portuguese). The key issue to be resolved in order to implement successfully the project was to design a logotype that would work at the same time for the 6 languages mentioned above. The final solution is based on the concept of "common denominator" among the 6 languages for the words "Latin Union". The result is a simple and flexible visual system, in which color plays a key role.
Pictures by Fotolia.

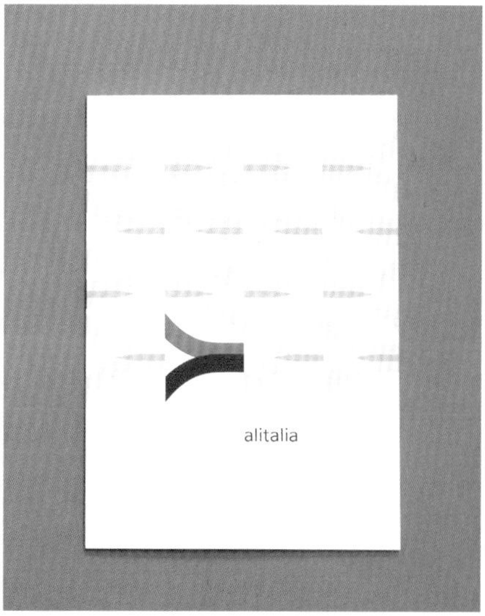

Rebranding Alitalia

At the start of this project, Alitalia, an Italian airline, had just merged with another Italian airline to become Italy's largest provider of passenger flight and freight services. The merger idea was used to create an identity that suggests speed and infinity. The horizontality of the graphic elements and typesetting in the applications further expand the brand concept. Color-wise, the green and red of the Italian flag merges to become a new color, blue, which is the color of the European Union flag, suggesting the new services Alitalia offers across Europe.

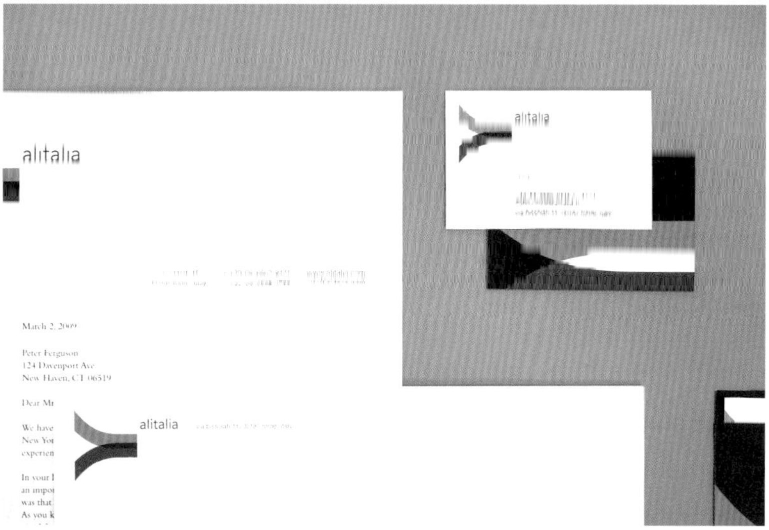

Nuevo Sur

Nuevo Sur is a real estate development in Mexico. It embraces the idea of a city within a city with residential, commercial and executive areas. For its comprehensive approach Nuevo Sur is the place to be, live, stay, work and play. Each area in the development has its own personality expressed through a family of names that shares the umbrella suffix "Sur". So we have Plaza Sur, Terraza Sur, Corredor Sur and Foro Sur.
Given these characteristics it was very important to achieve an identity system that resembles and communicates the flexible uses of this development. With this priority in mind, the foundation concepts for the identity were dynamism and flexibility; attributes that are expressed through geometrical and modular construction.
Nuevo Sur is a geometric-oriented graphic system that is not afraid to play.

NUEVO SUR
CORREDOR SUR
TERRAZA SUR
FORO SUR
PLAZA SUR

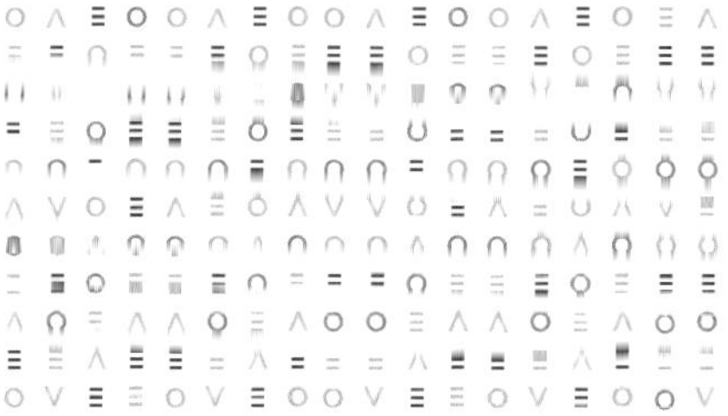

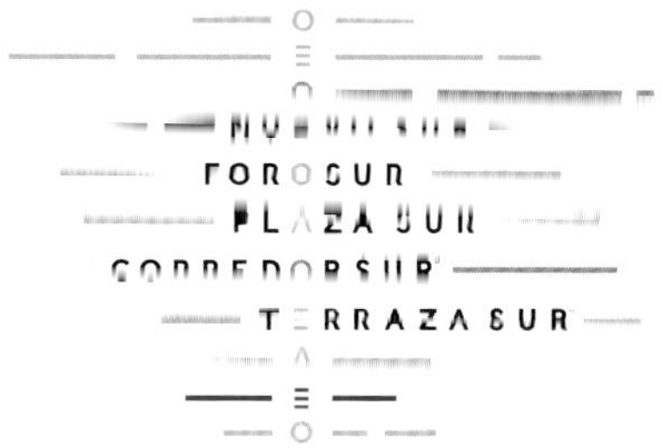

NUEVO SUR

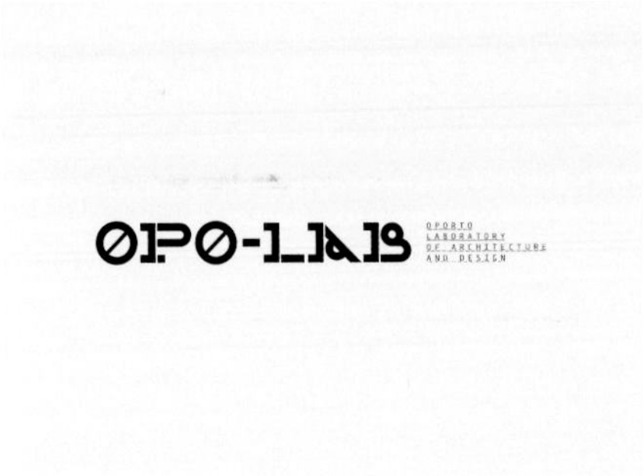

Opolab Identity

Opolab is a multi-disciplinary project in the heart of Oporto downtown dedicated to creative thinking and the use of new technologies in architecture, design and other artistic expressions. It offers a wide range of education courses, events, workshops and creative labs to local community. Bearing in mind that "the identity has to be really strong", I decided to draw letters and design a set of mono-spaced characters. There is no need to present the logo massively. These letters are exclusive enough to be a permanent identity for posters, websites, book covers, etc. Opolab is also a creativity cluster where a number of departments operate: opo-lab, fab-lab, edu-lab, id-lab, events, studio, and other still developing departments. Each logo can be set with various configurations: single lined or broken blocks with hyphens.

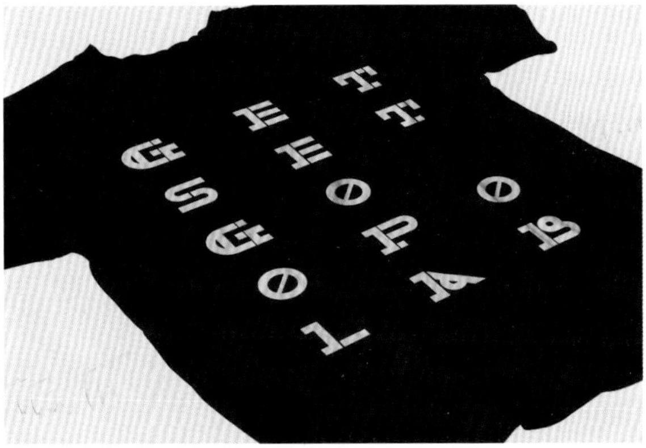

03out
GET SET FESTIVAL

LUÍS FERNANDES
CO-DIRECTOR – ARCHITECT
918 544 196
OPO-LAB
FAB-LAB
ID-LAB
EDU-LAB
EVENTS
STUDIO
Rua do Bolhão 151
Armazém B
4000-112
Porto
T +351 220 000 000
F +351 220 000 000
E info@opolab.com
www.opolab.com

Børk

For my final project at the Iceland Academy of the Arts I chose to create and brand a creative studio that makes gift wrapping paper. I wanted the company and the gift wrapping series to be Scandinavian in look and theme. The name I chose for the creative studio is Børk, short for Börkur or Bark, as in tree bark. Usage of the logo around corners in signage and in the stationery package is a reference to the initial meaning of the name- to cover or conceal something. I decided to use the line crossing the Ø as a graphical element, as a folding line for the identity. This is because the name refers to covering, concealing, or wrapping around something- so I thought the logo should reflect that. For the stationery, business cards, envelopes and CD envelope, the logo and the folding lines create the visual interpretation of concealing something in a simple way.

Børk.

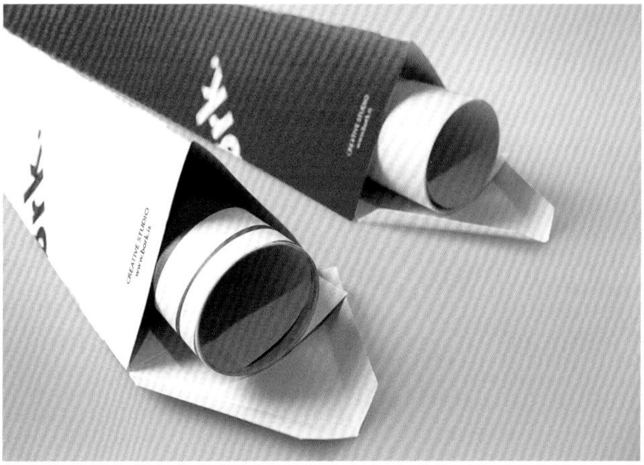

Børk.

BRBD - Breitbanddienste GmbH

This logotype and visual style was created for a young German businessman. The objective was to create a corporate design that will appeal to older and younger generations but will be very serious and modern at the same time. The main supporting element is a significant condensed font through which the design operates with dignity. An important element of this corporate design is a combination of horizontal and vertical shooting fonts and logotypes. The combination of black and white underlines the purity of graphic elaboration.

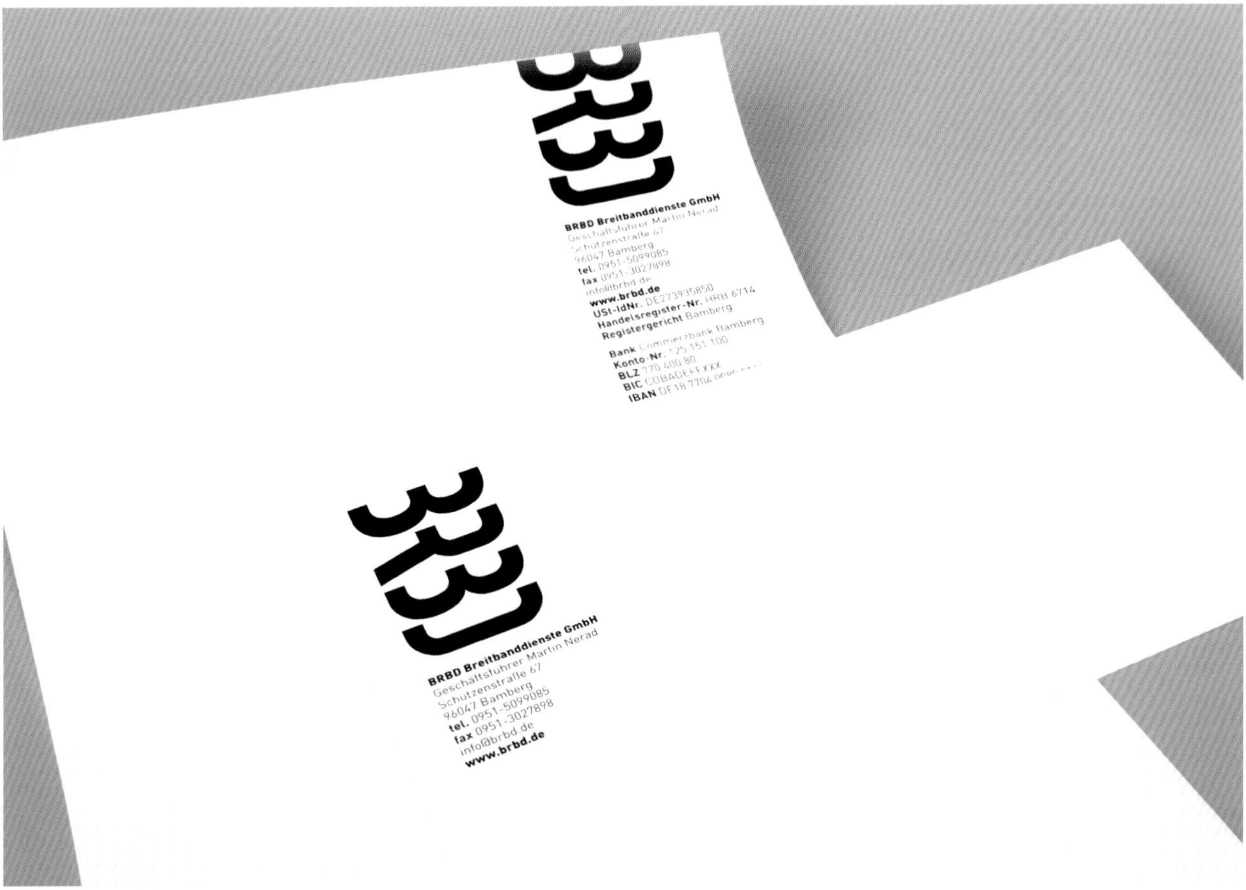
BRBD Breitbanddienste GmbH
Geschäftsführer Martin Nerad
Schützenstraße 67
96047 Bamberg
tel. 0951-5099085
fax 0951-3027898
info@brbd.de
www.brbd.de
USt-IdNr. DE273935850
Handelsregister-Nr. HRB 6714
Registergericht Bamberg
Bank Commerzbank Bamberg
Konto-Nr. 125 151 100
BLZ 770 400 80
BIC COBADEFFXXX
BRBD Breitbanddienste GmbH
Geschäftsführer Martin Nerad
Schützenstraße 67
96047 Bamberg
tel. 0951-5099085
fax 0951-3027898
info@brbd.de
www.brbd.de

MARTIN
NERAD
M.A.
BRBD
Breitbanddienste GmbH
Schützenstraße 67
96047 Bamberg
tel. 0951-3094120
fax 0951-3094121
mn@typopark.de
GmbH
Breitbanddienste
VOLARE
MAGNA FEUS
MMOLORE
MINEUM

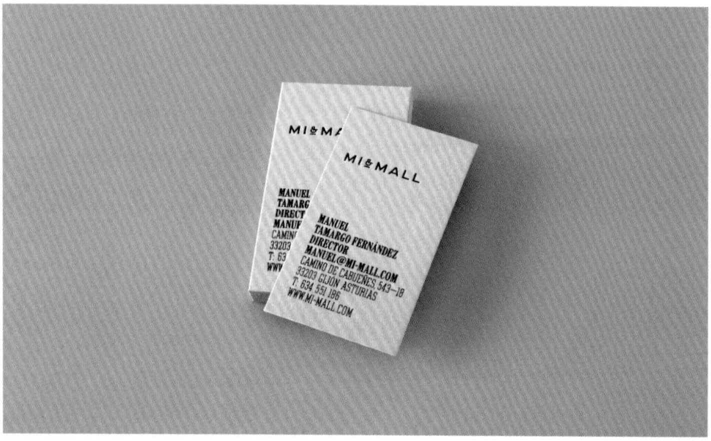

Mi & Mall

Mi & Mall is a new online shopping site that brings together and supports small to medium fashion shops for people interested in trends and exclusive collections. Based around a simple logo-type, ampersand detail, a pale colour palatte and a tactile print and material choice, their visual identity, mixes high fashion cues and craft aesthetics to deliver style and exclusivity with a sense of handmade quality and individuality.

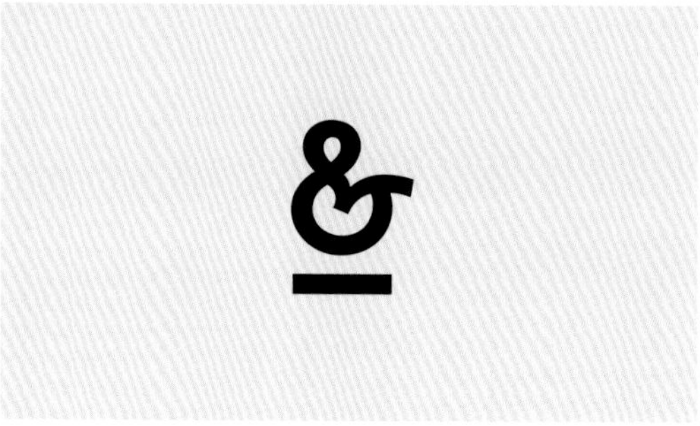

MI&MALL
MANUEL
TAMARGO FERNÁNDEZ
DIRECTOR
MANUEL@MI-MALL.COM
CAMINO DE CABUEÑES, 543–18
33203 GIJÓN ASTURIAS
T. 634 551 186
WWW.MI-MALL.COM
MI&MALL
CAMINO DE CABUEÑES, 543–18
33203 GIJÓN ASTURIAS
WWW.MI-MALL.COM

MI&

MI&
EXTREME
MI&MALL

Misc. Store & Office

Miscellaneous Store & Office is a web store and agency that sells and represents a collection of quality items ranging from stationery and paper wares to furniture. Every piece is as functional as it is outstanding. Working with business-to-business clients, brands and individual customers, the identity should be able to present itself in different situations and forms without losing its characteristics. We therefore created a distinctive palette of elements that can be used in a variety of combinations to create the right look and feel for any occasion.

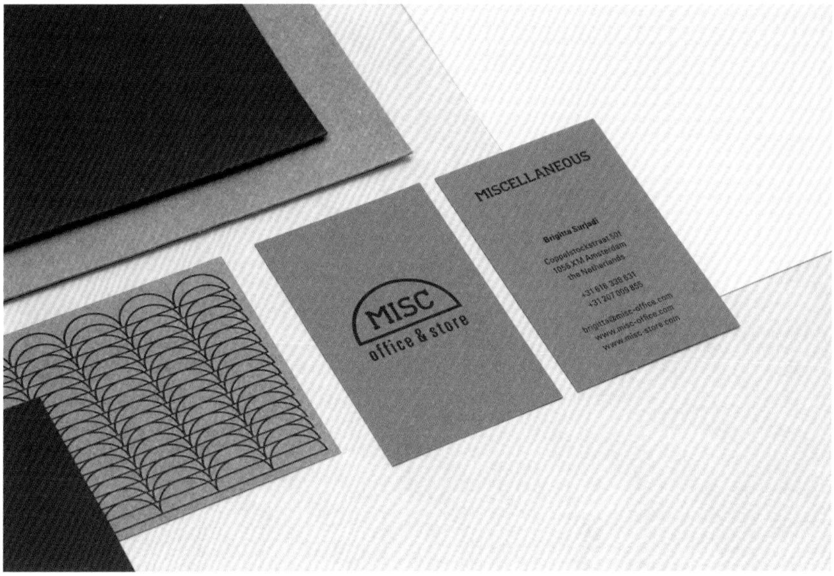
MISC
office & store
MISCELLANEOUS
Brigitta Surjadi
Coppelstockstraat 501
1056 XM Amsterdam
the Netherlands
+31 616 338 631
+31 207 009 855
brigitta@misc-office.com
www.misc-office.com
www.misc-store.com

MISC
office & store
MISCELLANEOUS

Pocklington Press "Twenty Five of One"

IYA were commissioned by Pocklington Press to create the branding and packaging for their first major project. Collaborating with 4 London based artists, a print maker, a photographer and us as a design studio, the project was to create a unique, cutting-edge portfolio of fine art prints which explores and expresses traditional print making techniques as a backlash reaction to the throw away print making trend of today. The brief to the artists was to create fine art prints reflecting the issues of "Unarchive the Archive". The result was a beautiful oversized folder which housed 25/1 archive prints that were sold as a complete package. The outcome we hope is to change society's thoughts about the importance of traditional crafts and the future of art in print.
Photography by Dylan Collard and David Sykes.

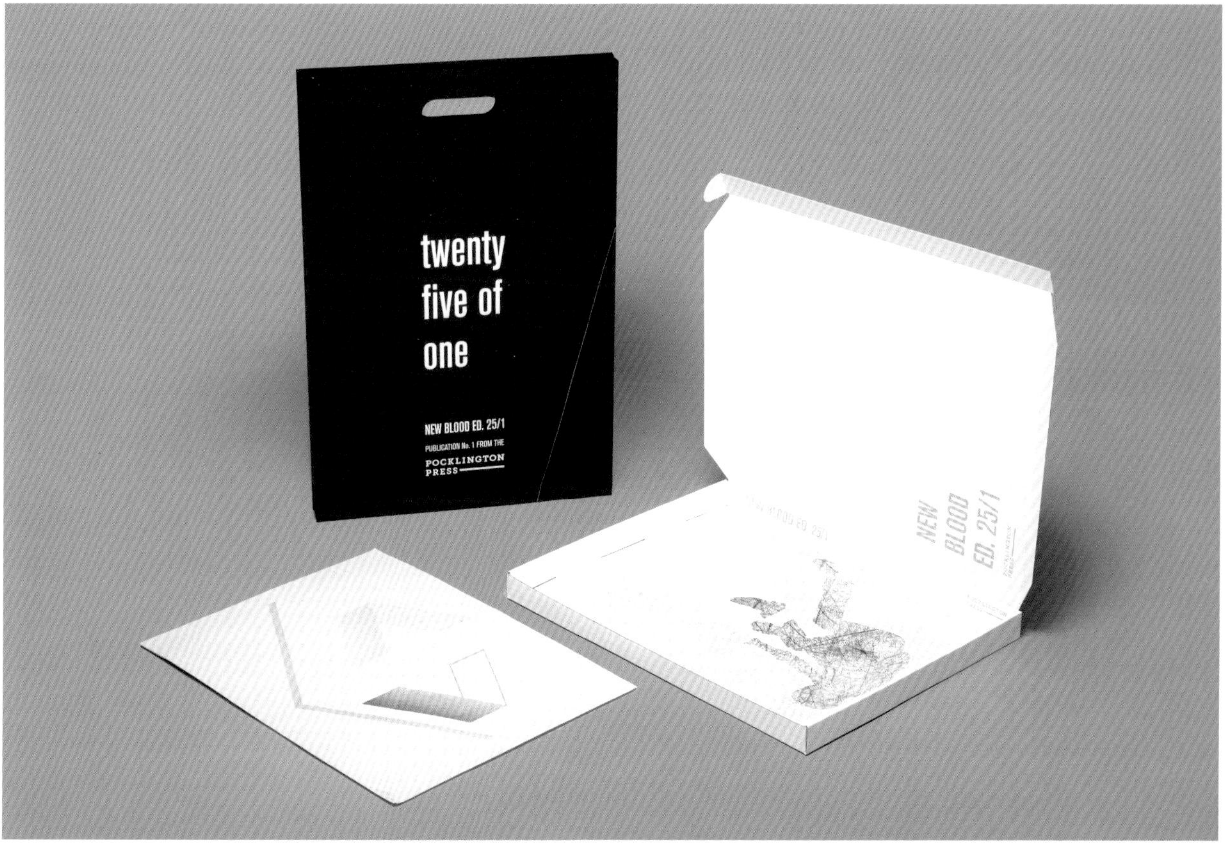
twenty
five of
one
NEW BLOOD ED. 25/1
PUBLICATION No. 1 FROM THE
POCKLINGTON
PRESS
NEW
BLOOD
ED. 25/1

NEW BLOOD ED. 25/1
PUBLICATION No. 1 FROM THE
POCKLINGTON
PRESS

POCKLINGTON
PRESS

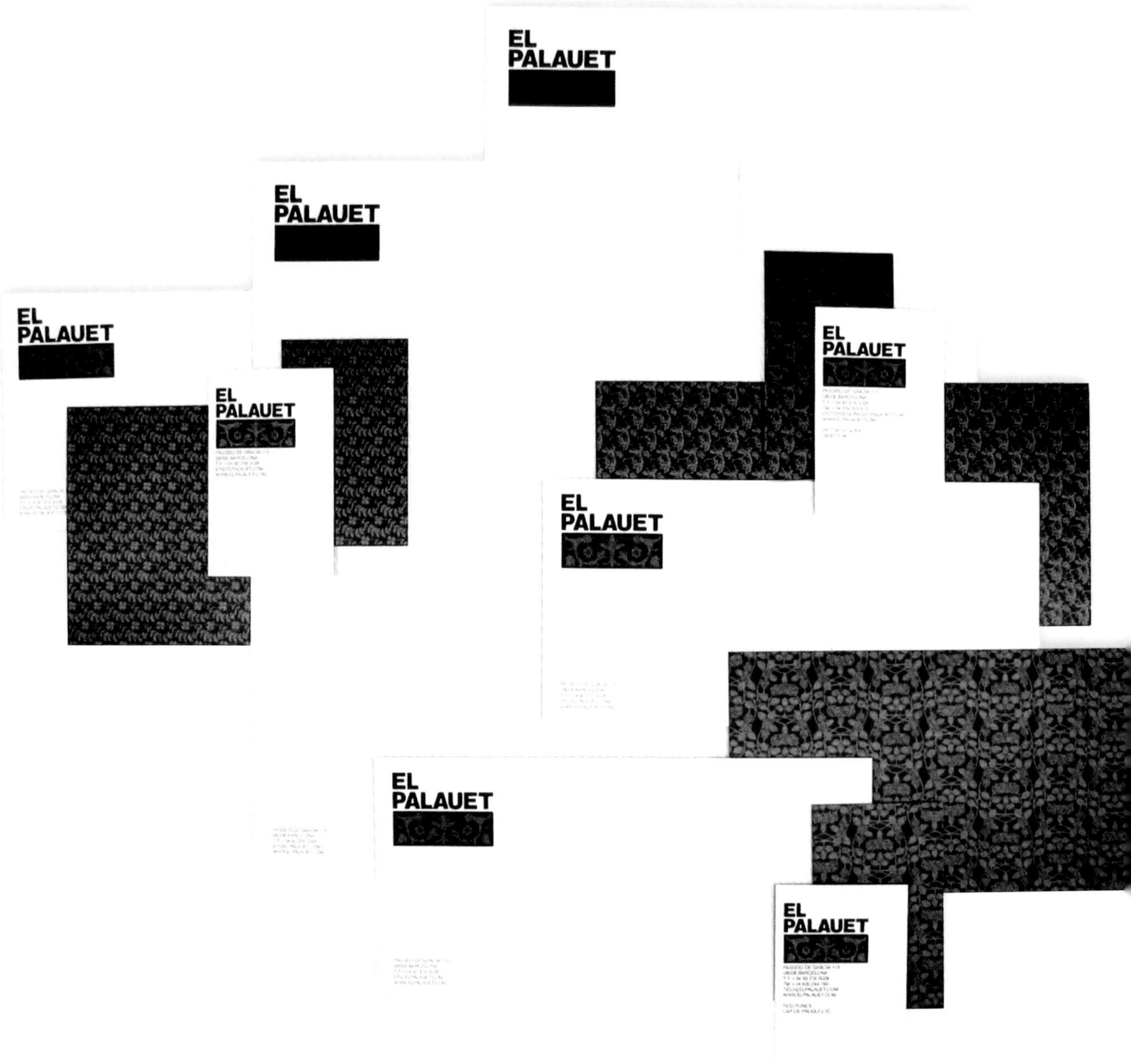
EL PALAUET
EL PALAUET
EL PALAUET
EL PALAUET
EL PALAUET
EL PALAUET
EL PALAUET
EL PALAUET

El Palauet

Corporate Identity for a XIX Century Events palace.

Michael Hsu Office of Architecture

Michael Hsu is considered to be one of the preeminent modernist architects in Austin. His prolific, award-winning portfolio is too numerous to list here. Clean-lined and modernist at its core, the work of his office appears to rely heavily on pitch-perfect texture and material decisions rather than grand geometric gestures. There is almost always an economy of form coupled with a sense of judgment about color that is geared to make a memorable impact every time.

The identity is as reductive as possible, indulging texture in a way we're rarely allowed. This was an opportunity to express the architect's name and mark in the same way Michael expresses his client's needs and desires. Double and triple letterpress, raised form and highly-structured typography rely on minute descriptive tags, allowing us to speak with his tone, but in a much smaller amount of space.

Michael Hsu Design Office
mhsudesign.com
Michael Hsu
Office Of Architecture
hsuoffice.com

Office

Michael Hsu
Office Of Architecture
3423 Guadalupe Street
Suite 200
Austin, Texas 78705
512 706 4303
hsuoffice.com

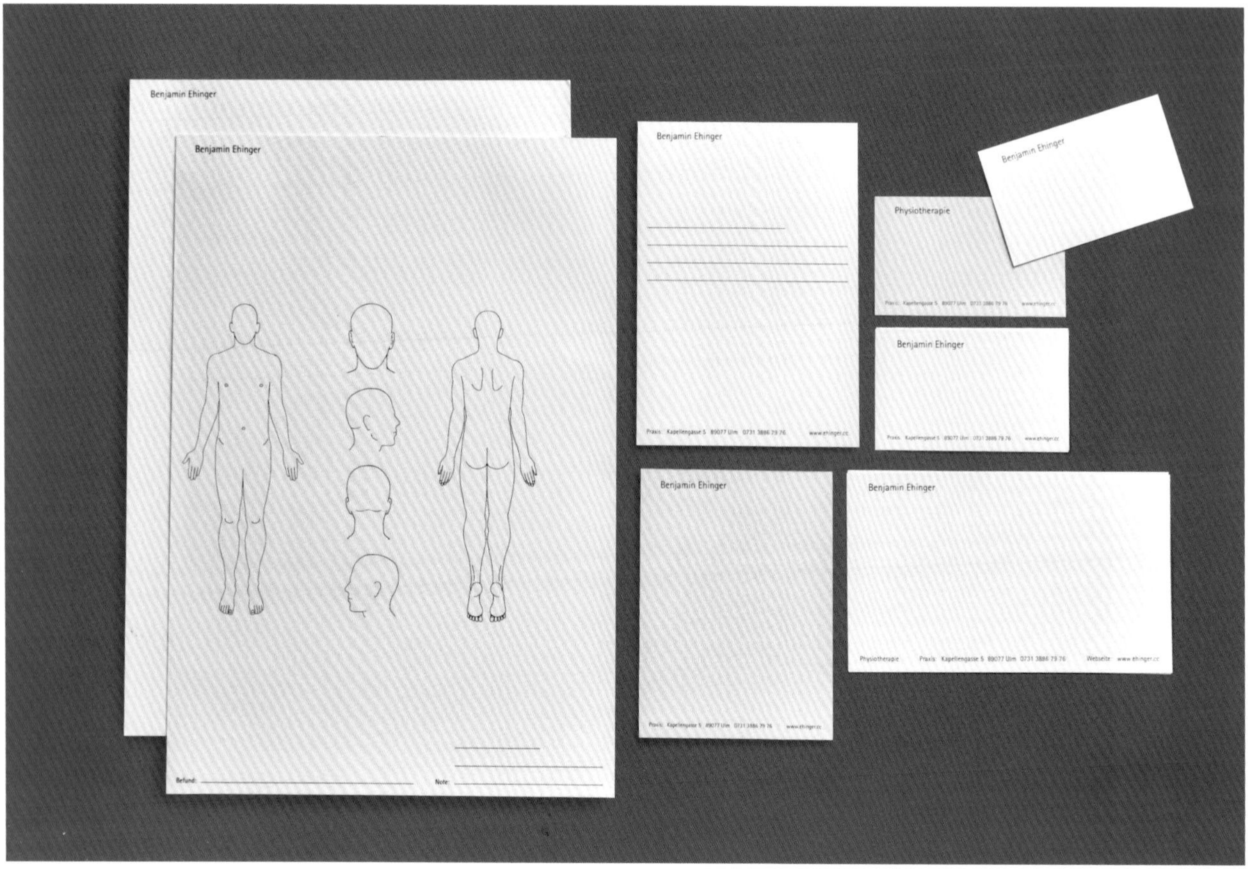

Benjamin Ehinger Identity

Benjamin Ehinger approached me to design an identity for his newly established physiotherapie practice. I based all my work on Otl Aicher's Rotis typeface because Aicher was born in Ulm, the German town where Benjamin established his clinic.
We used Naturalis paper for all collateral, both in Absolute White and Vanilla Smooth to create a beige & white color palette, less cold than the classic blue/ green & white palette used by medical businesses. The deliberately pared-down design was printed on business cards, letterheads, comp. slips, notebooks, stickers…using either black or clear foil stamping.

Norm

Norm approached me to design a new identity for their growing architecture and design studio. Working closely with Jonas Bjerre-Poulsen, I designed a simple, strong logotype, based on Frutiger's Avenir typeface, and used it on all collateral: website, newsletter, letterheads, business cards, labels…
While the logotype is systematically clear foil stamped, all information is printed with a gloss gunmetal foil on a 100% cotton paper, GF Smith's Crane Crest, creating a real tactile experience and expressing our common approach to design: simple forms paired with attention to details.

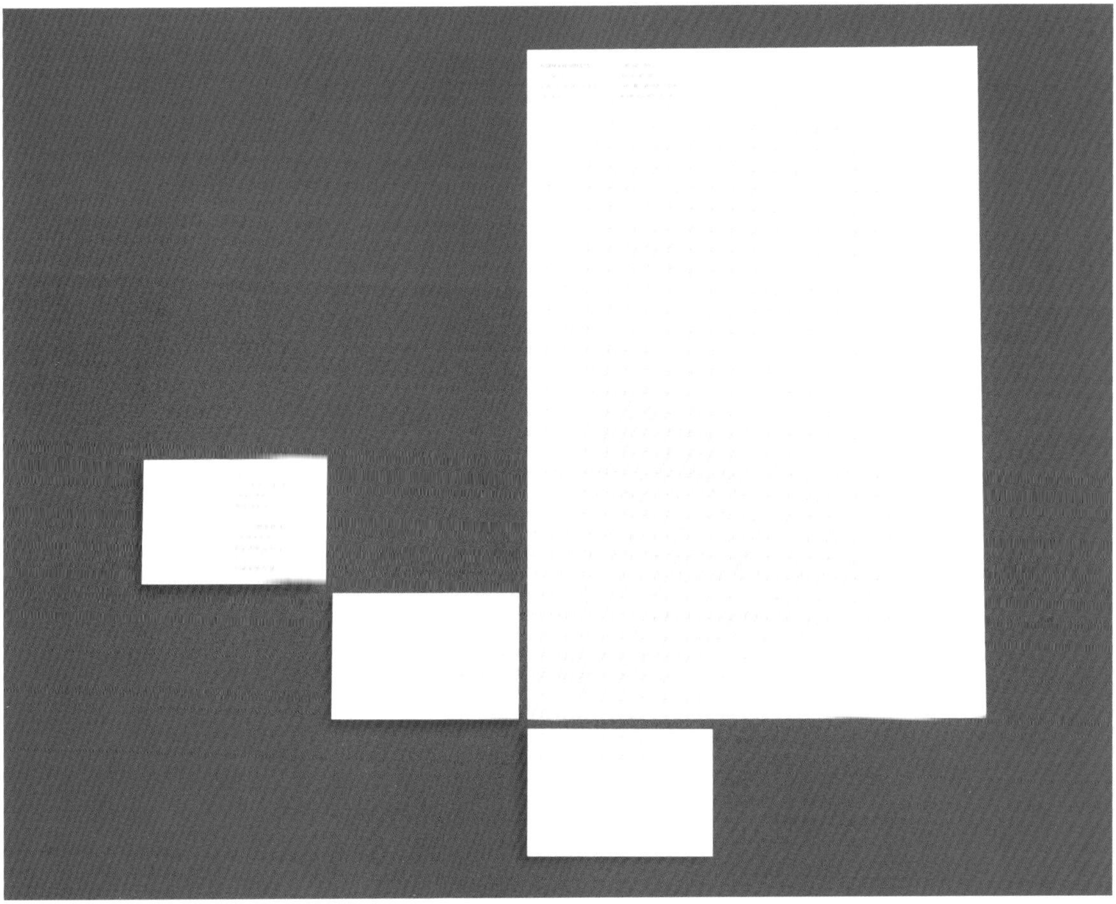

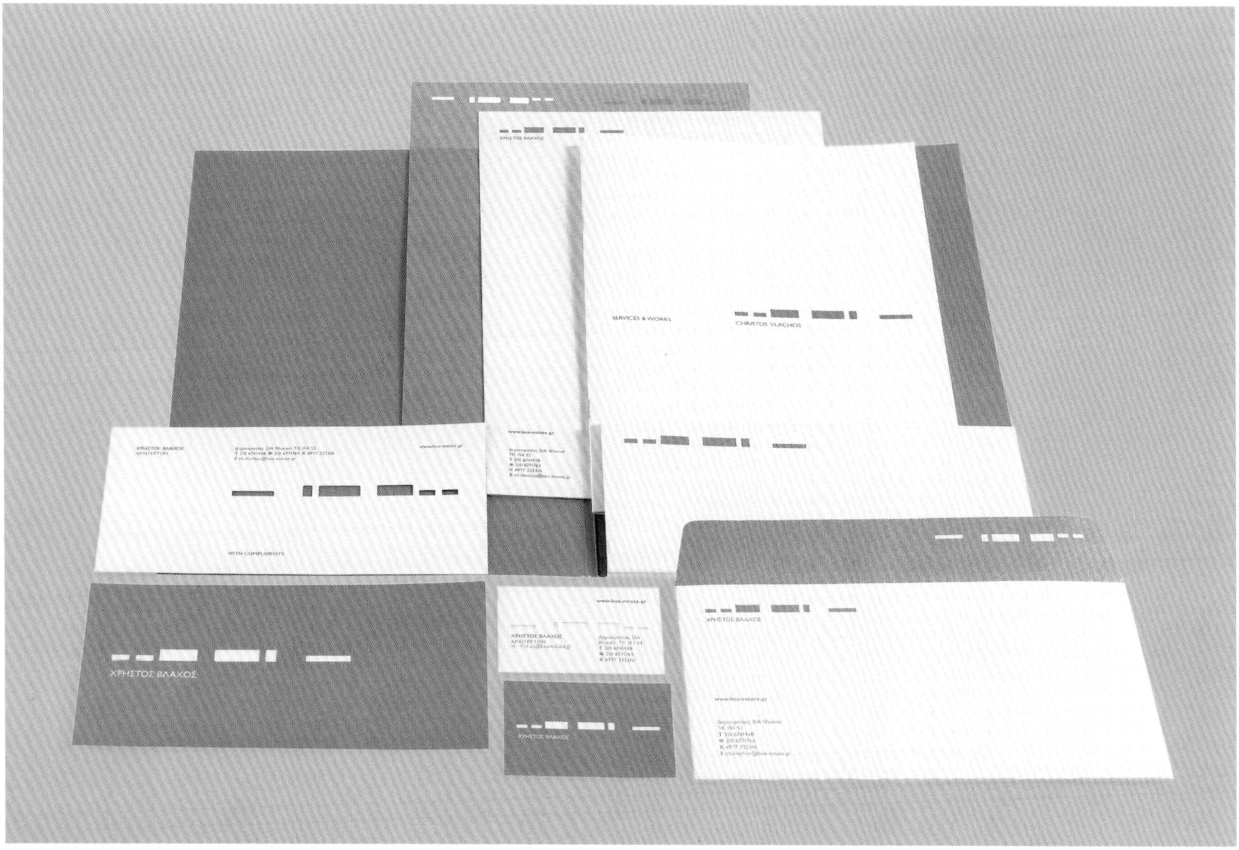

CHRISTOS VLACHOS

Christos Vlachos Architects

Logotype, visual identity and interface design for Christos Vlachos, an architect who designs and develops summer houses on the island of Kea which is evolving the idea of the "stone village". The design concept is based on Vlachos' architectural language emphasizing the use of panoramic forms, abstraction and large-scale geometrical openings towards the sea and the landscape. Photography by Dimitris Poupalos.

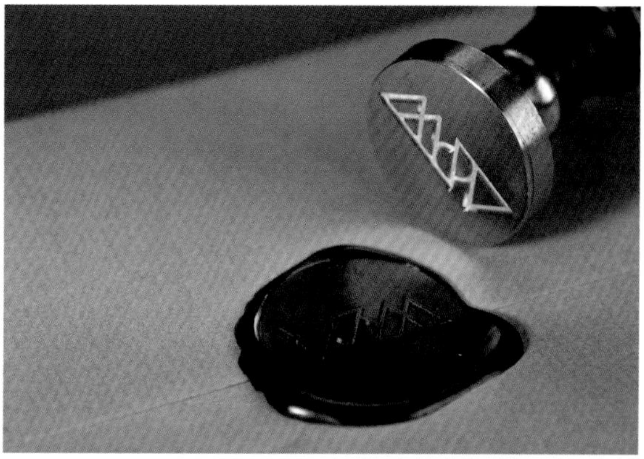

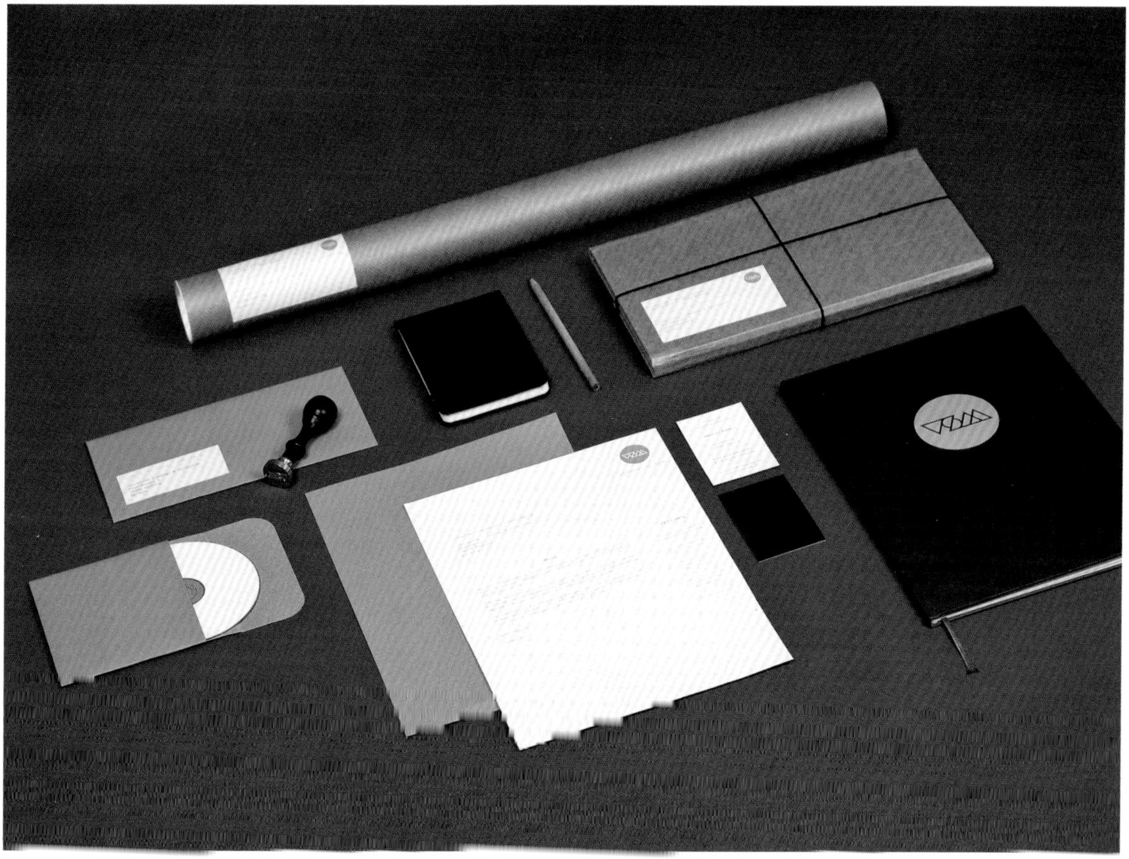

Visualism Corporate Design

We love simple geometric shapes and design with contrast; these used together with a strong concept is, for us, the foundation for timeless design. The Visualism corporate identity is based on constructed elements such as logo and typography, and, when combined with warm colors and organic materials, it results in a credible and friendly impression.

TEMPLE Brand Identity

Featuring striking black and white combinations that channel traditional elegance with an almost ghostly aura, London studio Temple's own brand identity and collateral reinforce their precise design methodology. Emphasizing purity and timelessness (in stark contrast to today's cluttered, ephemeral visual design culture), Temple typically eschews the emotional effects of colour and focuses on creating impact through form and contrast. Perhaps best embodied by the studio's stationery featuring both found and original objects including all-black pencils, obelisk-like mailing packages and handmade stamps, Temple's brand identity neatly echoes the studio's distinctive and achromatic vision of fine design.

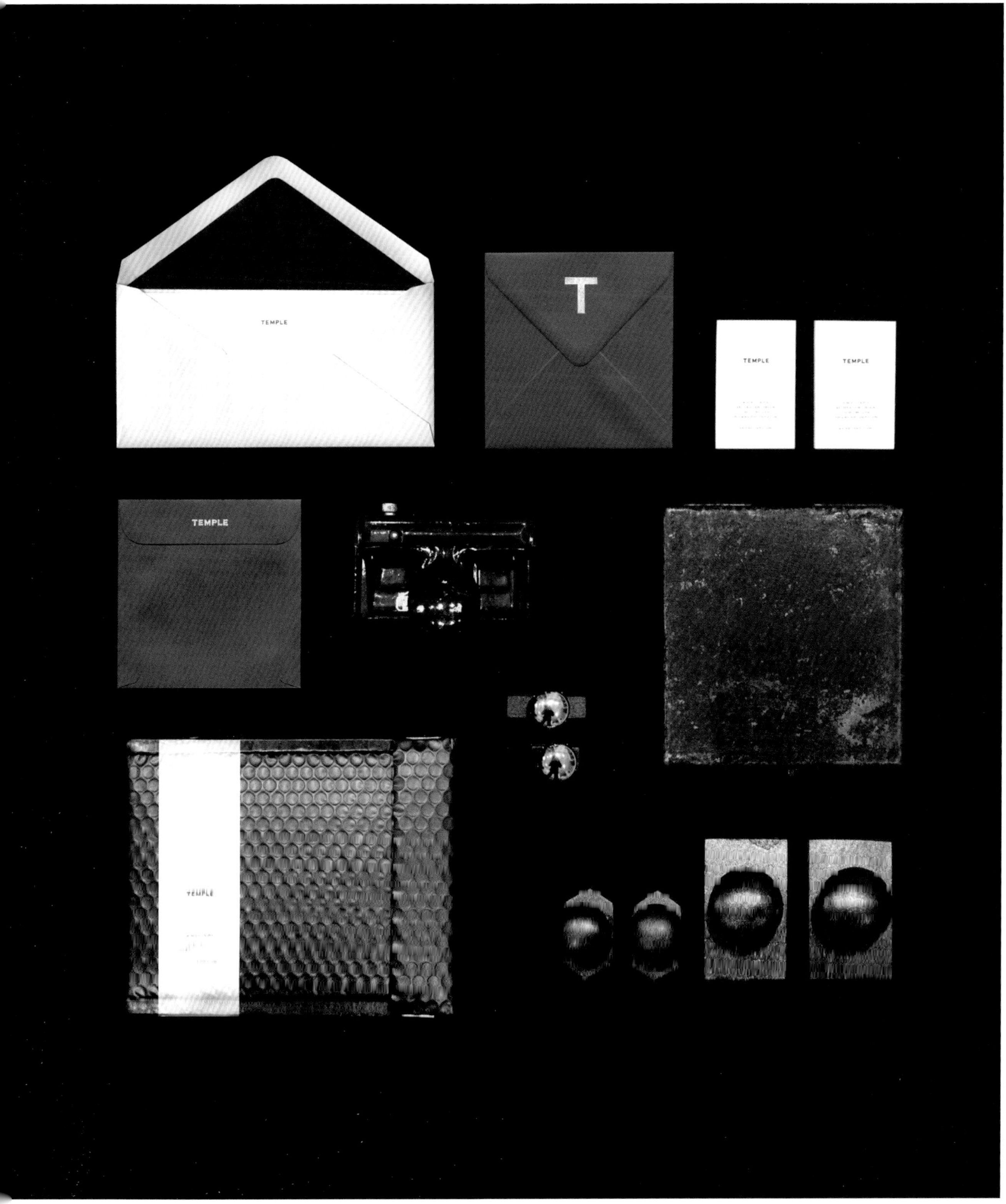
TEMPLE
T
TEMPLE
TEMPLE
TEMPLE
TEMPLE

RAAD

RAAD is an architecture and interior design studio. In order to create a visual universe which reflects this duality, Pacifica explored a hexagonal shape. This shape fills the space in a natural and perfect way. One natural example of this form is hexagonal basaltic columns formed of cooled lava from ancient volcanic activity in an island in Ireland. The central idea for the identity came from the concept of filling in the hexagonal shape. The design evolved from the outside to the inside, just as RAAD works from architecture to design. As an architecture project, we planned the exterior design and then we structured and filled the geometric shape. We developed the visual universe to the brand by using seven different stamps applied to the stationery.

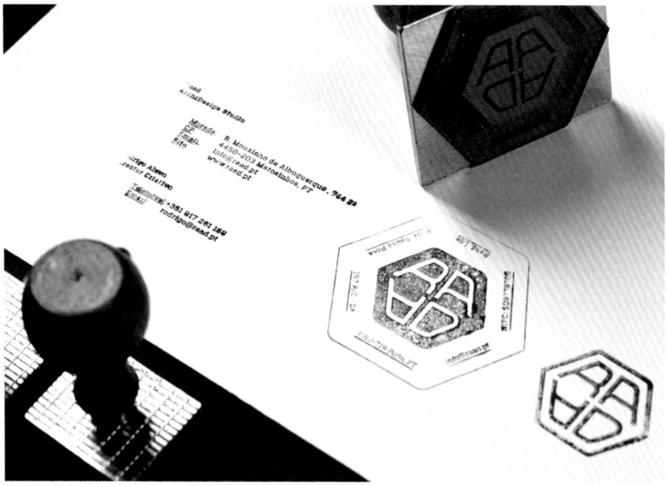

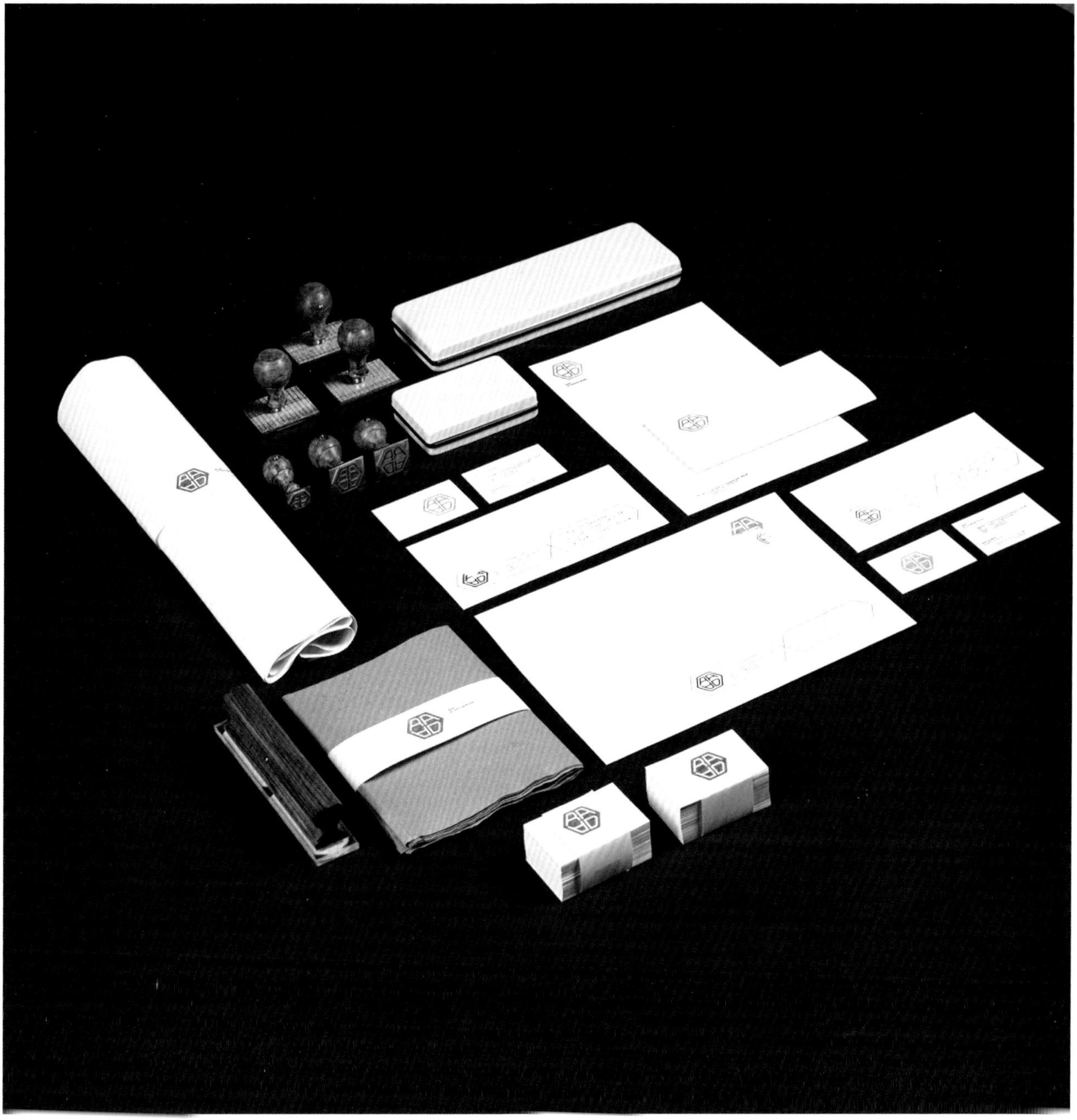

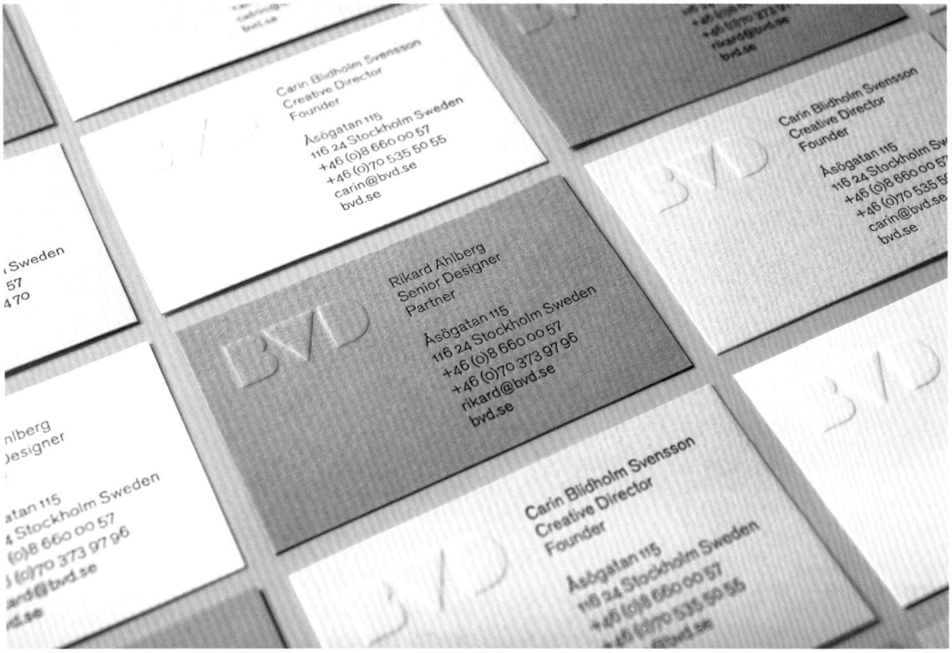

BVD New Identity

We have given ourselves a new design. BVD has appointed a new CEO, installed a new Chairman of the Board and welcomed a new Partner and in our minds an updated company requires an updated identity. Our new identity reflects our ambitions and represents our quality standards in all parts. Now we have a distinct logo with clean, geometrical lines. A logo that stands out, that is usable on all forms, and that is easy recognizable expresses our goal of clarity and simplification.

Rikard Ahlberg
Senior Designer
Partner
Åsögatan 115
116 24 Stockholm Sweden
+46 (0)8 660 00 57
+46 (0)70 373 97 96
rikard@bvd.se
bvd.se
Carin Blidholm Svensson
Creative Director
Founder
Åsögatan 115
116 24 Stockholm Sweden
+46 (0)8 660 00 57
+46 (0)70 535 50 55
carin@bvd.se
bvd.se
Bookmark the
new bvd.se

FRANK'S

Frank's is the first speakeasy bar of Buenos Aires, a secret bar available to only those who know how to get there. The term "speakeasy" originated in New York in the first decades of the 20th century. During this time, the city was under a period known as prohibition, a law that banned the manufacture, sale and consumption of alcohol. It is because of this restriction that speakeasy bars started to appear, establishing secret communities where clients were responsible for bringing in new customers using passwords and invitations. With materials and textures reminiscent of the rustic feel of 1920s decor, FBDI developed the brand image and the graphic system that composes the Frank's world.

JOIN US
!!
FAMILY
& FRIENDS
NIGHT
!!
4777 6541
OPEN BAR
YOU ARE
INVITED
FRANK'S
BUENOS AIRES
FRANK'S
MOMENTS & DRINKS Cº
Nº. 1445
FRANK'S
MOMENTS & DRINKS Cº
Nº. 1445

BUENOS AIRES
FRANK'S
MOMENTS & DRINKS Cº
Nº. 1445

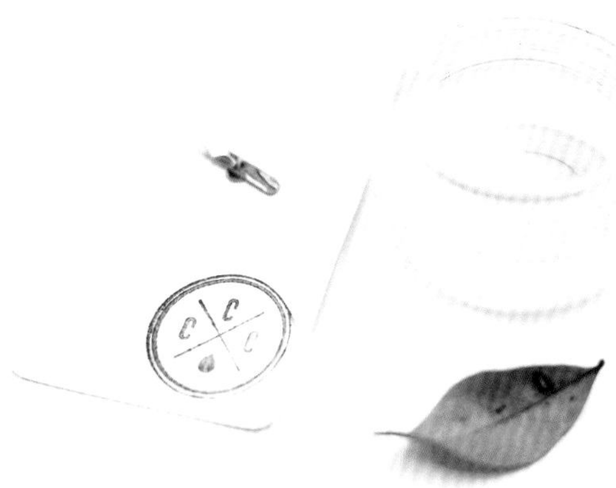

Come Closer Club

Every year the BASF Coatings GmbH invites important clients from the automotive industries to a presentation of the current Color Collection in the form of a Color Show. For this event a special theme has to be conceived that always adheres to the annual Global Trend Book Theme, which in 2011 was "COME CLOSER". For the annual Color Show 2011 all of the clients were invited to be members in the "Come Closer Club"– a fictional private club for honorary members. In this familial atmosphere the members had the great pleasure to see and know the recently developed Special Collection of Color Coatings. Based on this concept invitations and additional event accessories like pins were designed. Together with the invitation every member received a Club Box with different sized vessels and was asked to collect favorite items with great color hues to show and discuss at the workshop.

Place of discovery:
Color:
Structure:
Principle:
Special focus:

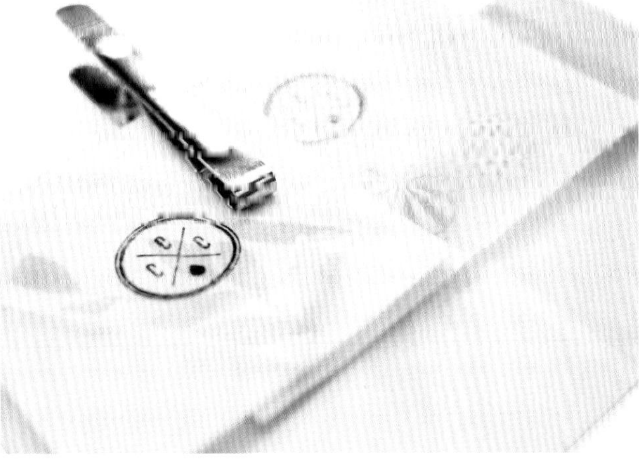

Vårdapoteket Identity

Vårdapoteket is a Swedish pharmacy chain with 24 pharmacies placed in care related locations. To distinguish themselves from the often very clinical and barren environments of hospitals, SDL developed a new identity inspired by the human body. With a strong and positive color palette and a pattern based on the internal organs of the human body, a strong base for their new identity was created. This graphic language is now used in all types of applications; from in-store wallpaper to all sorts of printed material, such as stationery, retail and POS materials. SDL provided Vårdapoteket with a simple and playful toolbox that creates an inspiring identity and much appreciated retail environment.
Photography by Felix Odell.

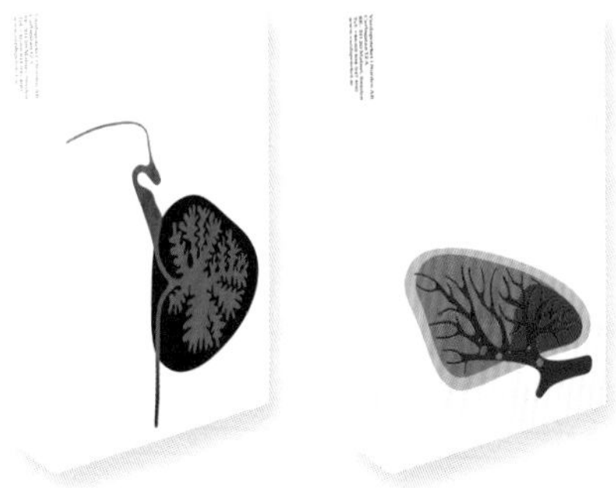

ned dig?
i medlem i vår kundklubb.

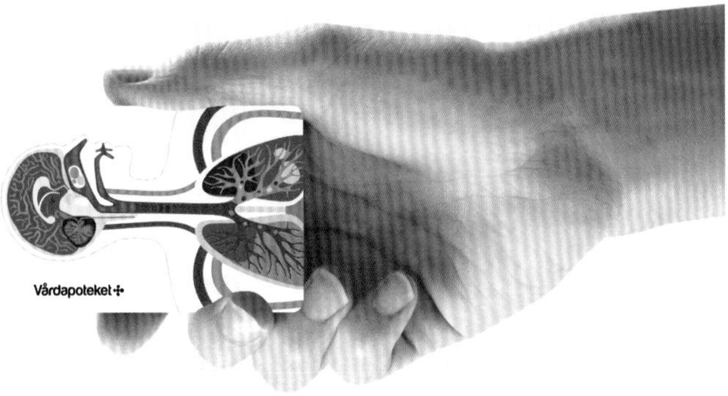
Vårdapoteket

Rítmia. Music Therapy

Atipus was asked to create an identity for social music therapist and educator Celia Castillo. The identity is based on rhythmic exercises that Celia develops; the basic aim is to provoke different moods in her patients.

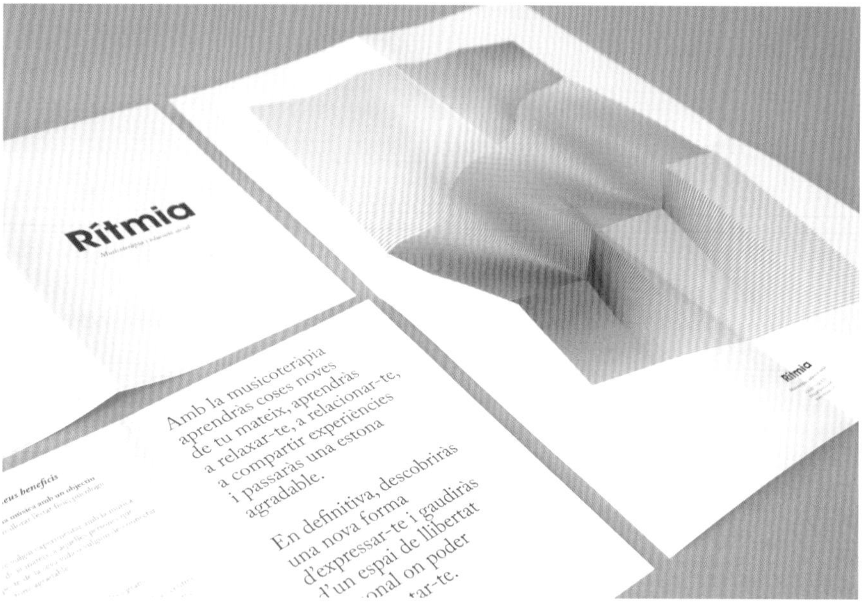

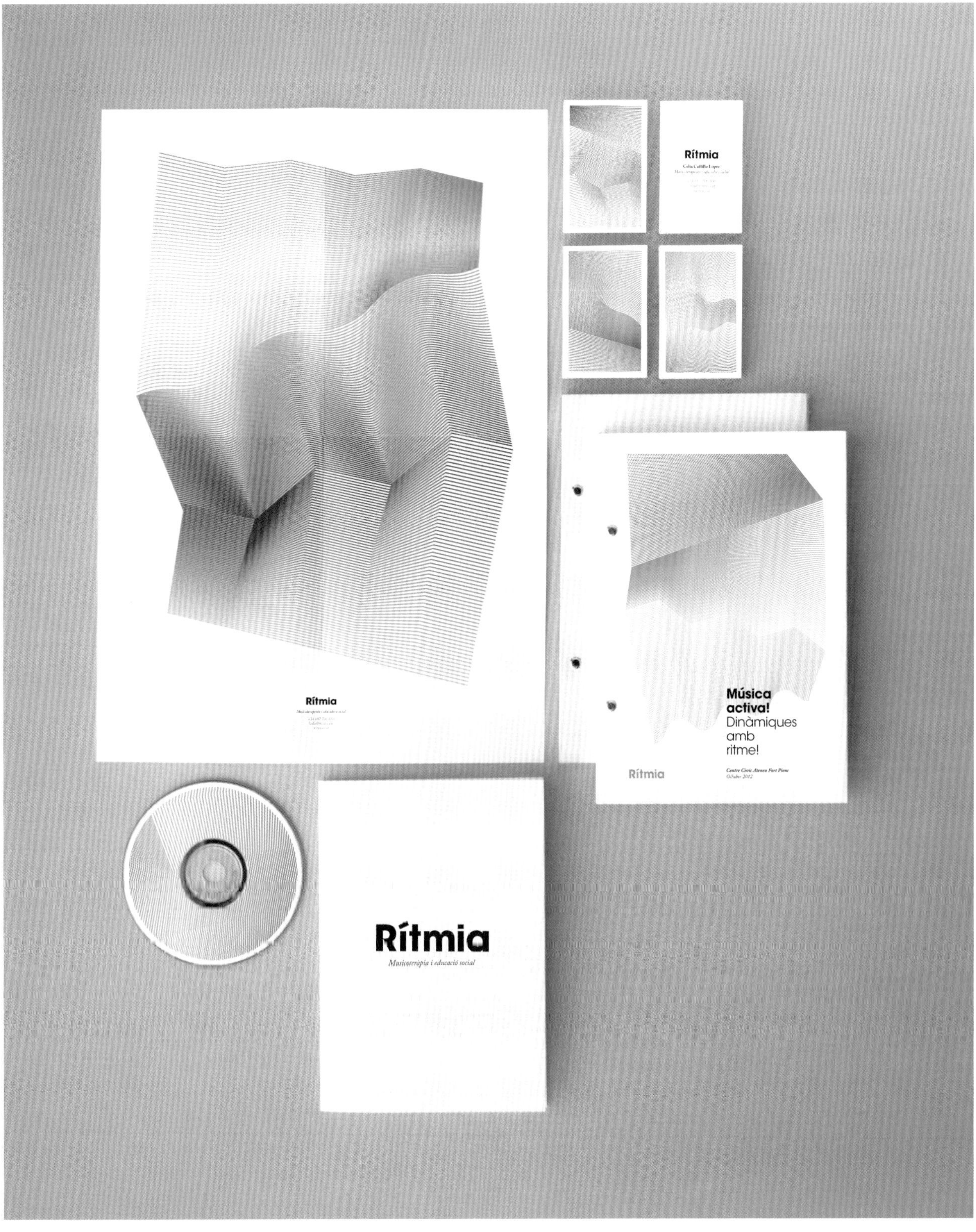
Rítmia
Rítmia
Música
activa!
Dinàmiques
amb
ritme!
Rítmia
Centre Civic Ateneu Fort Pienc
Octubre 2012
Rítmia
Musicoteràpia i educació social

Kissthedesign

A3 Collectif was commissioned to develop the new corporate identity of Kissthedesign Gallery. To complement its enhanced activity, Kissthedesign decided to get a new visual identity, based on the early logo's colours and rounded shape. A3 completely rethought and redesigned the visual identity of Kissthedesign. The font "Kiss rounded" was specially developed for the Gallery, a rounded typography that shows a bright and contemporary style. The logo consists of a polygonal shape with ten sides, which recalls a sophisticated diamond. On the business cards, the "diamond" has been highlighted with a silkscreen varnish to emphasize the exclusive facets of the Gallery's activities in high end design and fine art.

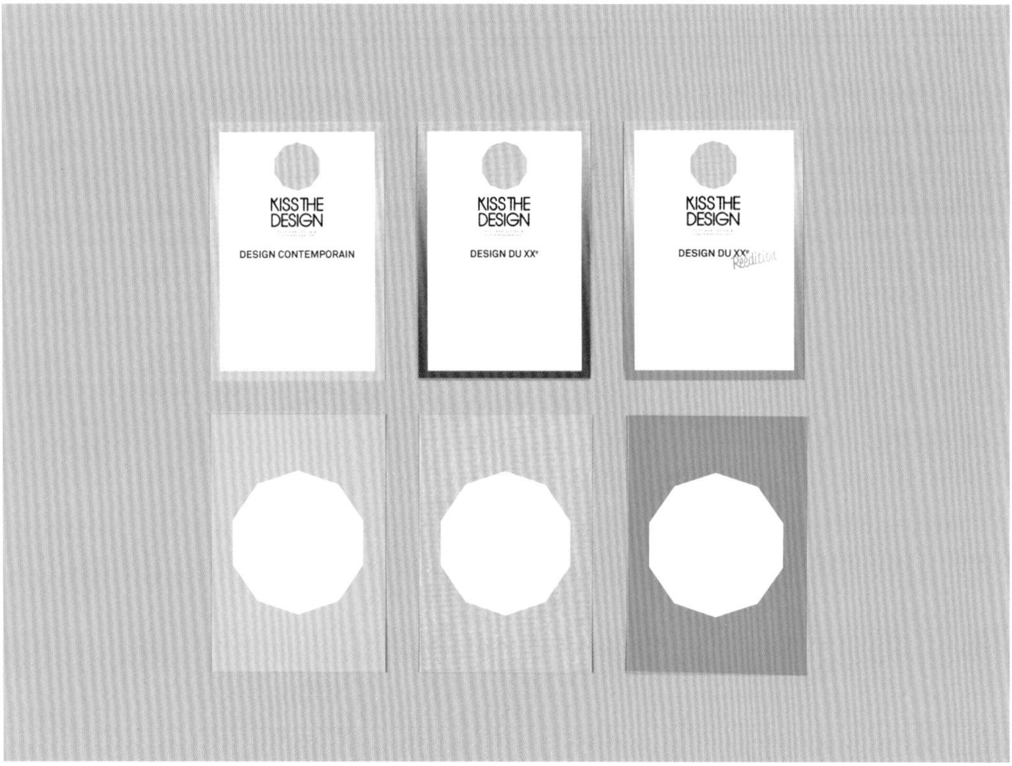

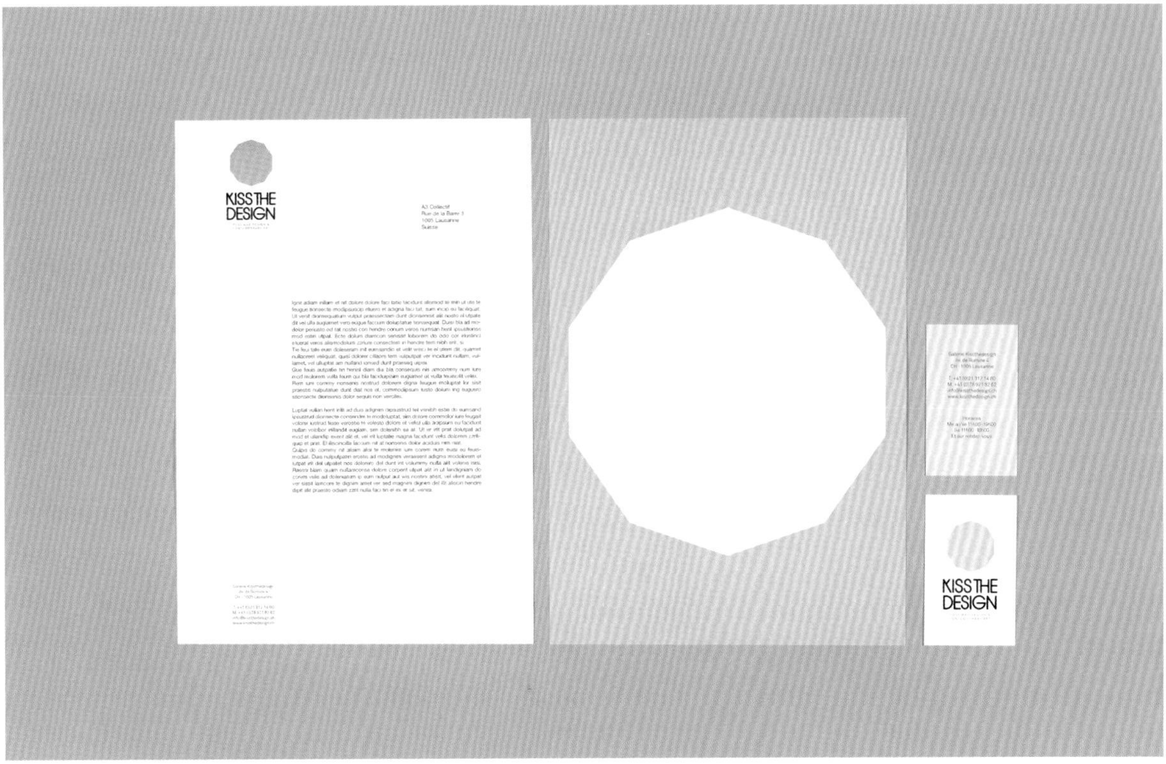
KISS THE DESIGN

KISS THE DESIGN
INAUGURATION
DU NOUVEL ESPACE
ET PRÉSENTATION
DE LA COLLECTION
SERGE MOUILLE
9 MARS DÈS 18H
www.kissthedesign.ch
YOUNG
DESIGNER
TOBIAS
SCHAFER
Exposition du 09.03
au 06.10.2012
Vernissage
le 08.03.2012
Dès 18h00
1005 Lausanne

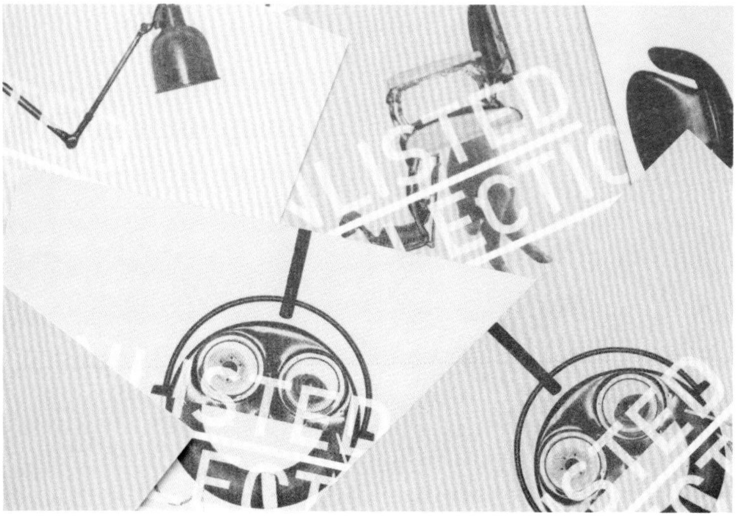

Unlisted Collection

The collection's whimsical and quirky take on each of their hotel inspired the use of Dadaism in the brand identity and collateral, where images are picked and paired with deliberate irrationality. The colon in the logotype allows room for imagination by the guests, leaving the image of the hotel open to their interpretation. The photography is by Ronald Leong and Jovian Lim.

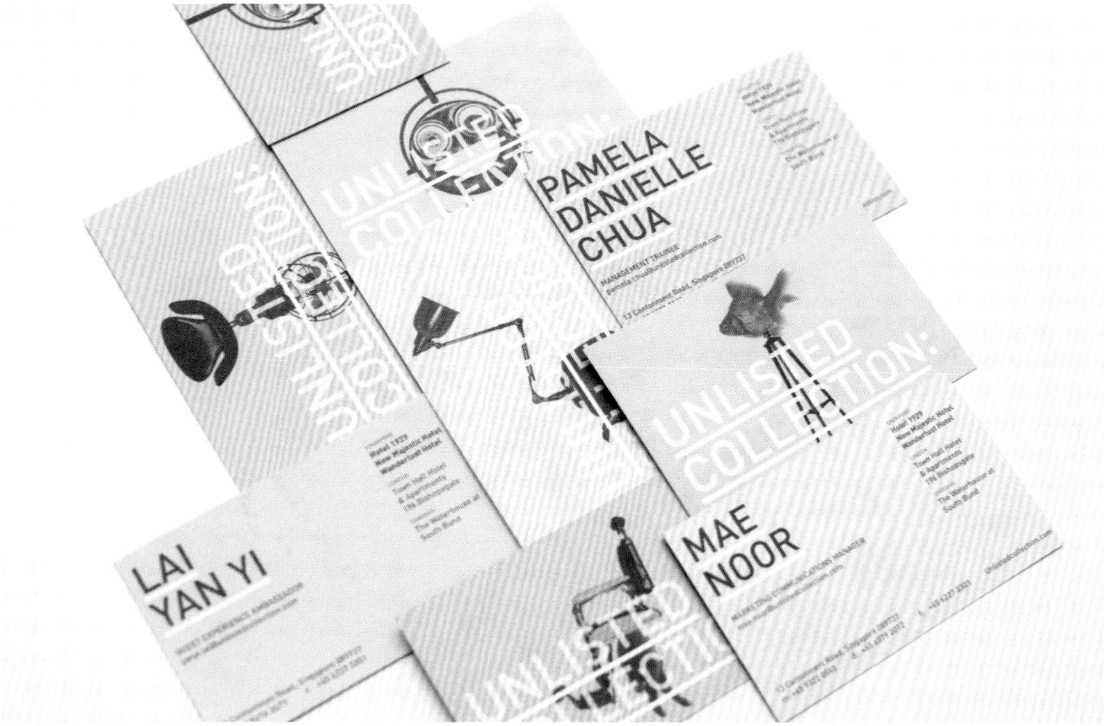
UNLISTED COLLECTION:
PAMELA DANIELLE CHUA
MANAGEMENT TRAINEE
Hotel 1929
New Majestic Hotel
Wanderlust Hotel
Town Hall Hotel & Apartments
196 Bishopsgate
The Waterhouse at South Bund
LAI YAN YI
MAE NOOR
MARKETING COMMUNICATIONS MANAGER

CHARMAINE WEE
Hotel 1929
New Majestic Hotel
Wanderlust Hotel
Town Hall Hotel & Apartments
196 Bishopsgate
SRI WAHIDAH MASTURI
SALES & MARKETING MANAGER

Darryl Jingwen Wee

"Trans" is a Latin noun or prefix, meaning "across" or "beyond". Designed for a translator and writer for the arts, these cards reflect the process of the vocation and personality of their owner. Published articles by the writer were taken and turned into handmade paper, imbuing the essence of his craft into his identity. Contact details were then hand-printed onto each individual card using a transfer marker. Just as a translator's role is that of bridging language boundaries, this process of transference from one medium to another is reiterated in how each card is made. Every card is handmade, and therefore beautifully idiosyncratic.

〒166-0001 東京都杉並区阿佐谷北3-3-20
3-3-20 Asagaya Kita, Suginami-ku,
Tokyo 166-0001
Japan +81 (0)80 6659 1741
Singapore +65 9435 0230
darryl.wee@gmail.com
Darryl Jingwen Wee
ダリル・ジングウェン・ウィー
黄景文
Writer • Translator • Interpreter
執筆・翻訳・通訳

〒166-0001 東京都杉並区阿佐谷北3-3-20
3-3-20 Asagaya Kita, Suginami-ku,
Tokyo 166-0001
Japan +81 (0)80 6659 1741
Singapore +65 9435 0230
darryl.wee@gmail.com
Darryl Jingwen Wee
ダリル・ジングウェン・ウィー
黄景文
Writer • Translator • Interpreter
執筆・翻訳・通訳

7GigaCloud

Identity, Branding & Web Design for an IT company based in Saudi Arabia. 7GigaCloud contacted Face to design a stylish, international-looking identity, and we created a very basic and very aesthetic concept: 7 lines to symbolize not only the brand, but the 7 billion people across the planet covered by their expertise. Typography, black, white and silver never looked this good.

Mal de Mar

An electronic journal where ideas and projects involving art, design, architecture, photography and the art of traveling all merge into one, in the name of Beauty.

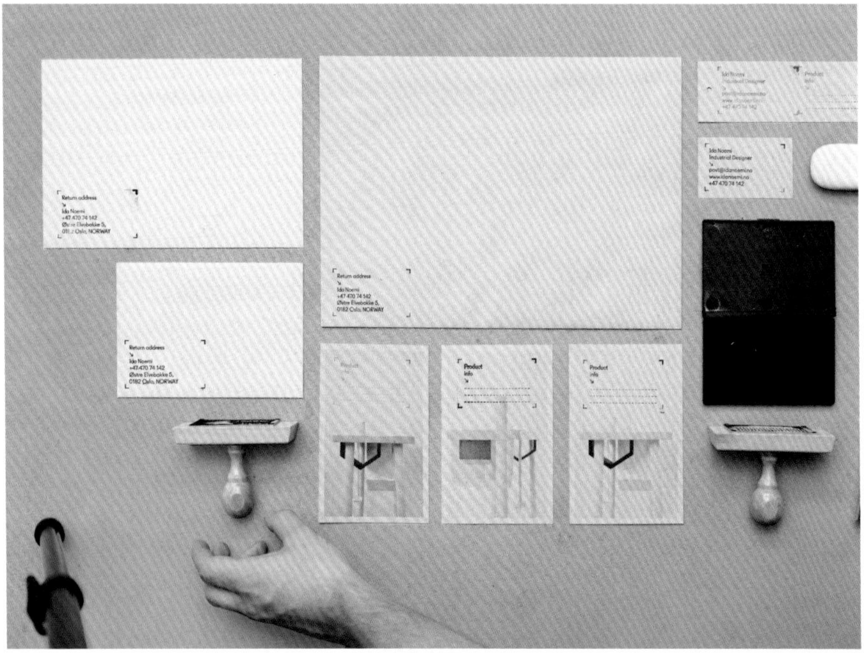

Visual Identity Ida Noemi

Ida Noemi is an industrial design graduate who needed a small-scale identity for herself as a freelance designer. The whole profile is designed for easy and low-cost production. Everything is kept low key, and is based on the use of stamps. Business cards, mailing labels, and hang tags for design or furniture fairs can all be created using only three stamps. No excess elements, simply information and photos.
Product photo by Kaja Bruskeland
Portfolio photo by Marius Nilsen

Product
info
Return address
Ida Noemi
+47 470 74 142
Østre Elvebakke 5,
0182 Oslo, NORWAY
Ida Noemi
Industrial Designer
post@idanoemi.no
www.idanoemi.no
+47 470 74 142

Ida Noemi
Industrial Designer
post@idanoemi.no
+47 470 74 142

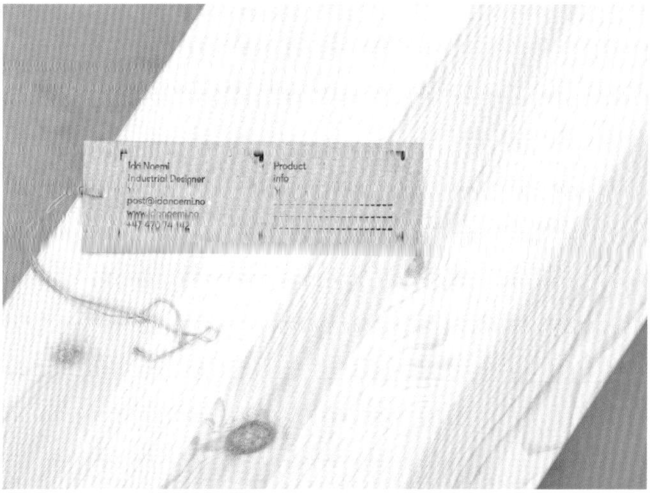
Ida Noemi
Industrial Designer
post@idanoemi.no
Product
info

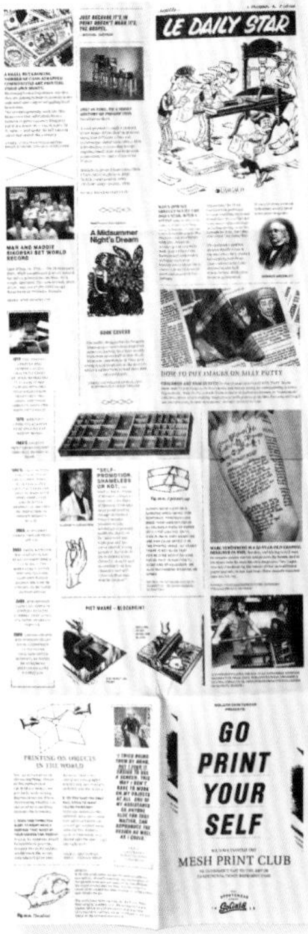

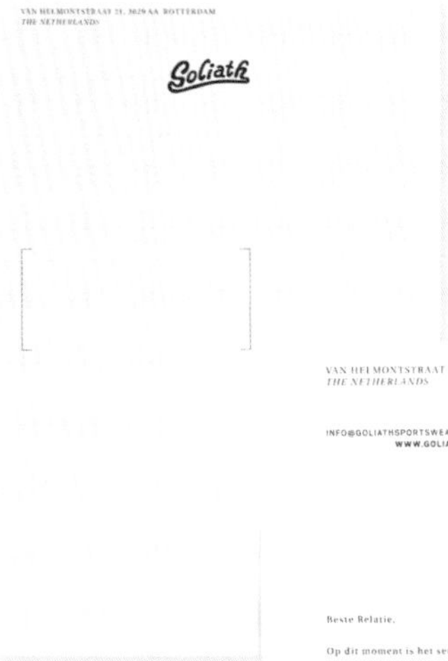

VAN HELMONTSTRAAT 21, 3029 AA ROTTERDAM
THE NETHERLANDS
t +31 (0)10 299 0506
f +31 (0)10 299 9494
INFO@GOLIATHSPORTSWEAR.COM
WWW.GOLIATHSPORTSWEAR.COM
Goliath

Beste Relatie,

Op dit moment is het seizoen weer van start gegaan met de aftrap op de Bread & Butter (Urban Superior Men Area: Booth 33.1) in Berlijn. Ook zullen wij op 17 en 18 juli op de Modefabriek (Industry Hall: Booth 914) in Amsterdam aanwezig zijn. Wij zouden het leuk vinden jullie te ontmoeten op onze stands, waar we vol trots onze nieuwe zomerse collectie presenteren.

Om alvast in de juiste stemming te komen, ontvang je hierbij onze nieuwe Productguide, die een mooie impressie van Goliath en de nieuwe collectie weergeeft.
Ik plan graag op korte termijn onze inkoopafspraak in, hiervoor zal ik binnenkort contact

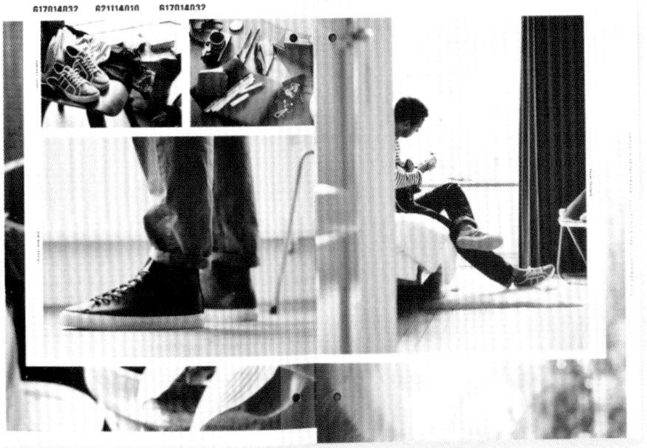

Goliath Sportswear

Eighty-five years ago a shoemaker's son had a most wonderful idea: creating a footwear brand that focuses on people that are passionate about details. Today, almost one hundred years later, we were asked to help the brand redesign their identity. [illegible] without throwing away the old values and traditions, we've created a visual world that exudes the spirit of attention to detail.

Life Uncommon Photography

They say a picture is worth a thousand words, so it made sense to give the photos by David Tsai a voice. Design Ranch accentuated David's candid, journalistic style of photography by pairing shots with creative dialogue from a captured moment. The business collateral and marketing piece for Life Uncommon Photography give a glimpse into the sappy, silly and sweet details of life and love.

LIFE UNCOMMON PHOTOGRAPHY
FOR EVERY SHOT A STORY.
HERE'S TO YOU AND YOURS.
LIFE UNCOMMON PHOTOGRAPHY
FOR EVERY SHOT A STORY.
STORY.

LAZONA

Identity design for the cinema production company Lazona. The black line shows the limitations of the zone and is used on all applications, even in the windows of the office.

ESTE SOBRE HA SALIDO DE
LAZONA
LAZONA
LAZONA
LAZONA
ESTE DOCUMENTO
HA SALIDO DE
LAZONA
LAZONA
LAZONA

ESTE DOCUMENTO
LAZONA

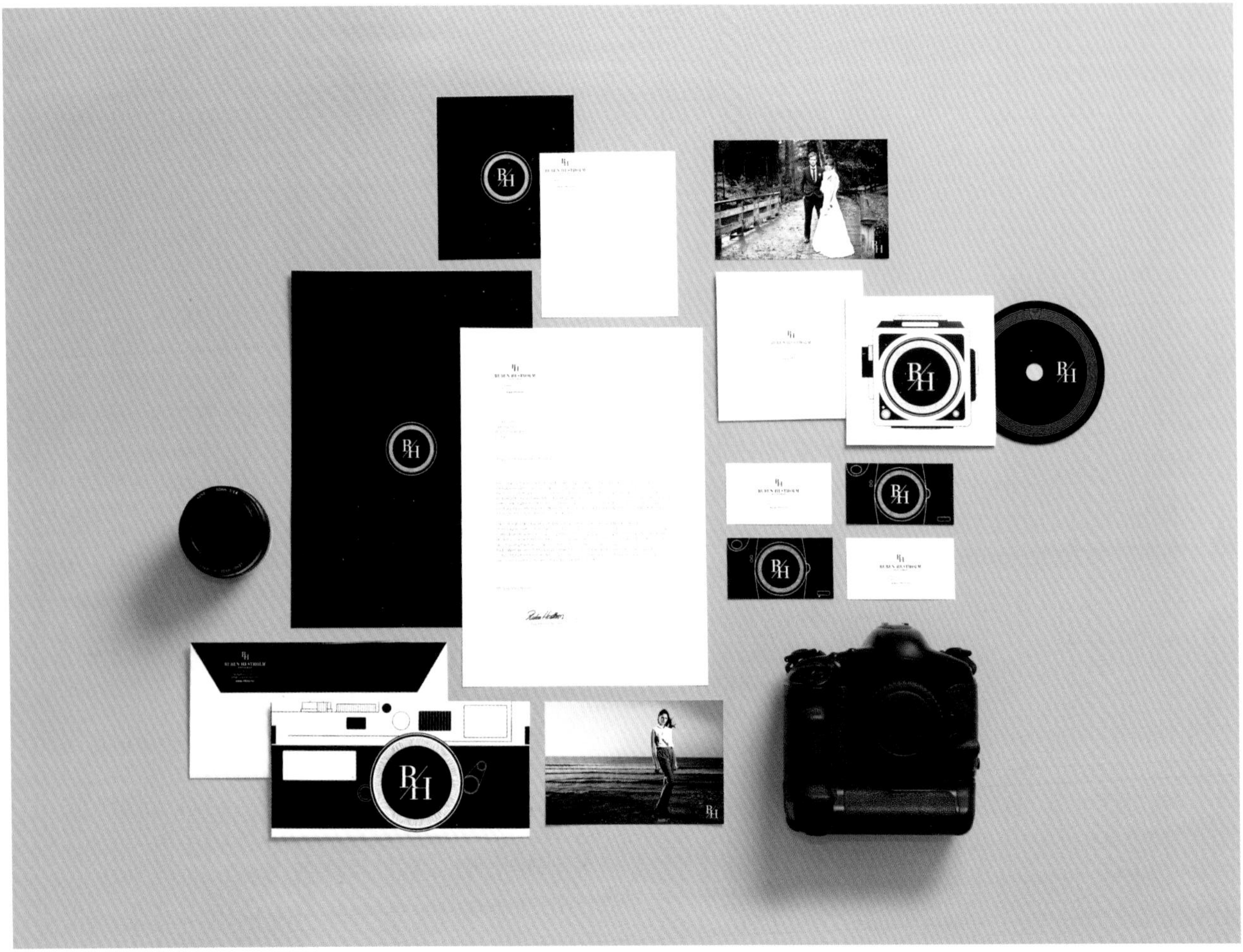

Ruben Hestholm Identity

Ruben Hestholm is a Norwegian photographer in the Sandnes, Stavanger area. He mainly focuses on family, youth, pregnancy, and childhood portraits. When he approached Daniel, he explained he wanted to enter the commercial market, but the first step was to get an overhaul on his visual identity and style. A cleaner, stylish modern profile was created to appeal to a new audience, but the design also took care not to alienate current customers by being too radical. The identity is created around images of different cameras.

RUBEN HESTHOLM
www.rhfoto.no
Josse Lund
Løkkegata 2
4003 Stavanger
Norge
UTVIDELSE AV FOTO STUDIO

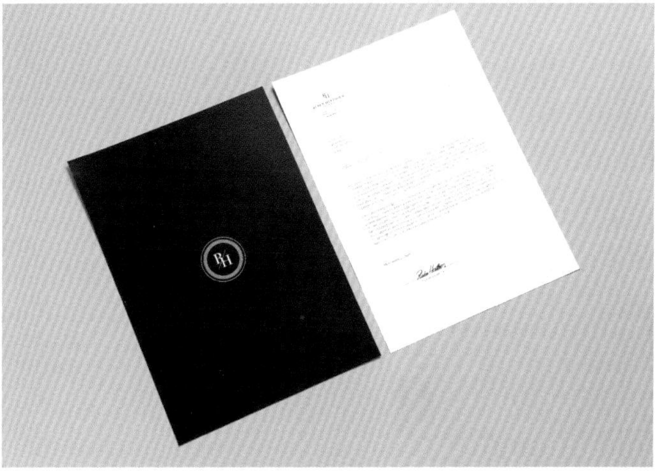

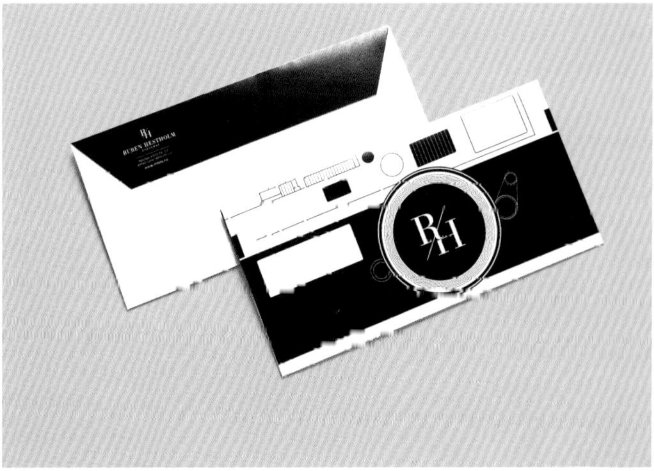
RUBEN HESTHOLM

Erste Private Banking

This project is about corporate collateral for Erste Bank's Private Banking Sector. Dark blue "skin" folders use a custom designed laser-cut pattern in order to show what is housed within the folder. The design enhances the tactile nature of the service Erste Bank offers to its Private Banking customers.

ERSTE
Private Banking

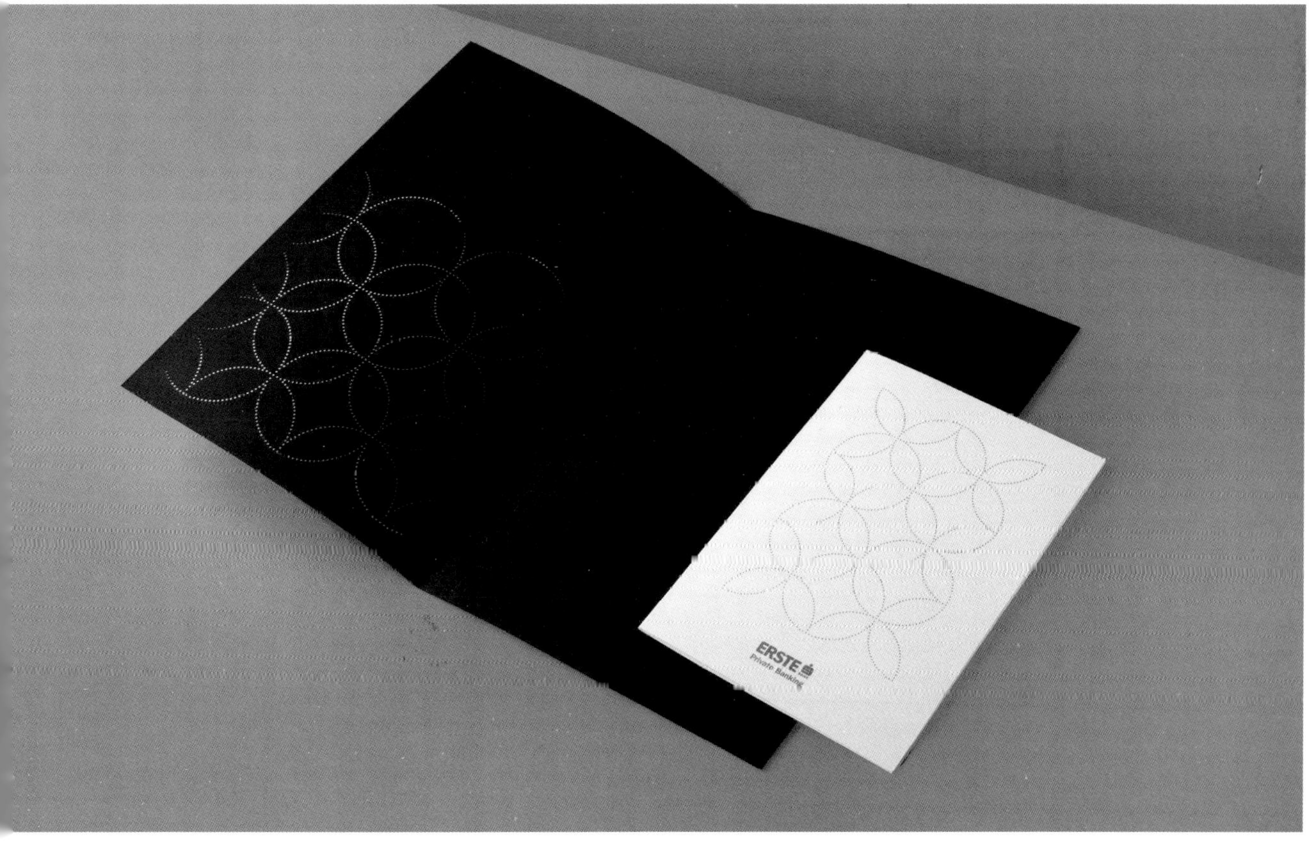
ERSTE
Private Banking

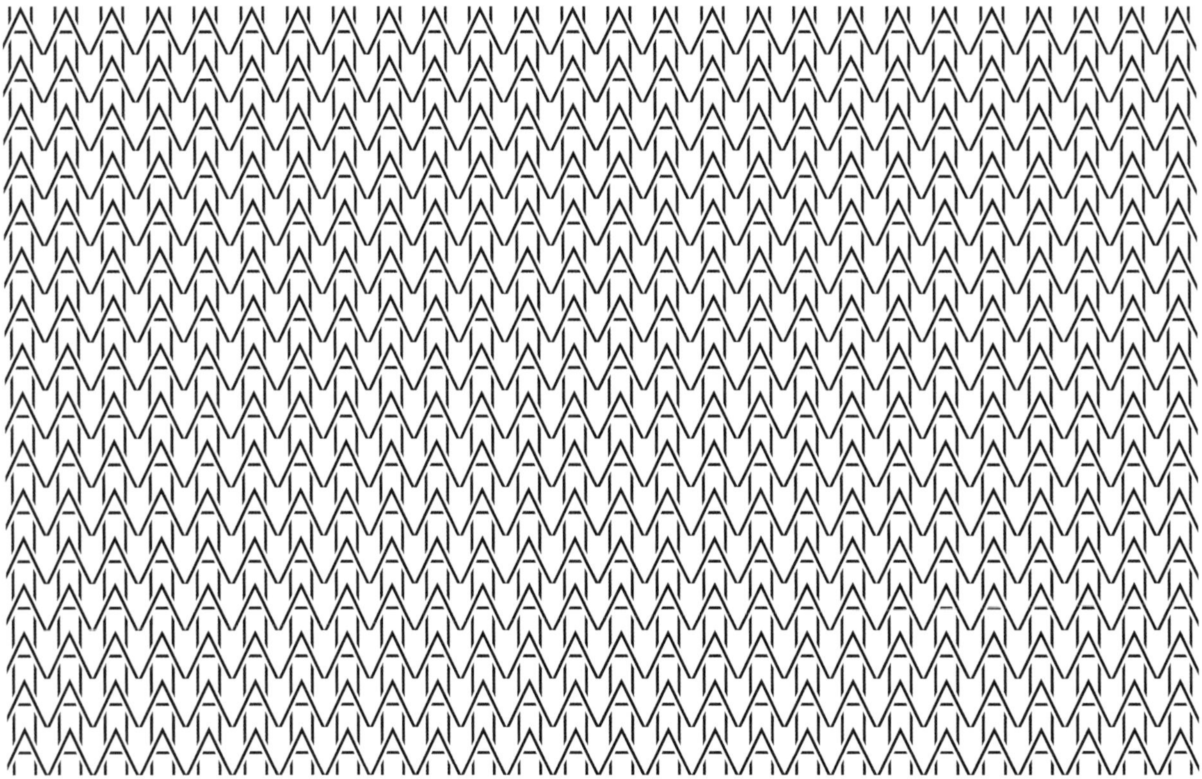

Archabits

Archabits comes from Architecture and other Habits. This small and powerful studio is doing not only architecture but also product design and interior design. That's why Dimo decided to make a modular monogram logo that describes their work using simple icons for each category.

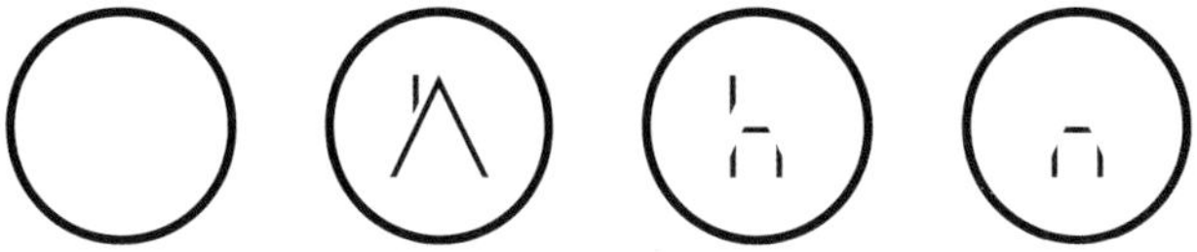

Focus / Unity / Completion

Architecture

Home / Interior

Product design

Archabits
Atanas Mirchev
Architecture & Other Habits
+359889346372
+359886346372
mail@archabits.com
www.archabits.com
54 Petrova Nina str.
Plovdiv, Bulgaria
Archabits
Architecture & Other habits
Archabits
Architecture & Other habits
Archabits
Architecture & Other habits
Archabits
Architecture & Other habits

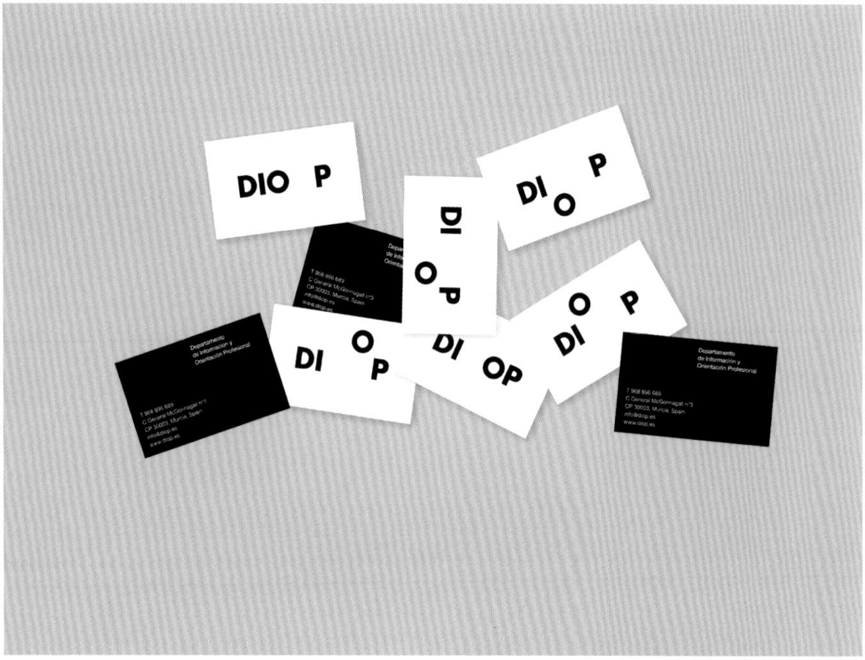
DIO P
DI O P
DI O P
DI O P
DI OP
DI O P
Departamento
de Información y
Orientación Profesional
T 968 896 689
C General McGonnagall nº3
CP 30003, Murcia, Spain
info@diop.es
www.diop.es

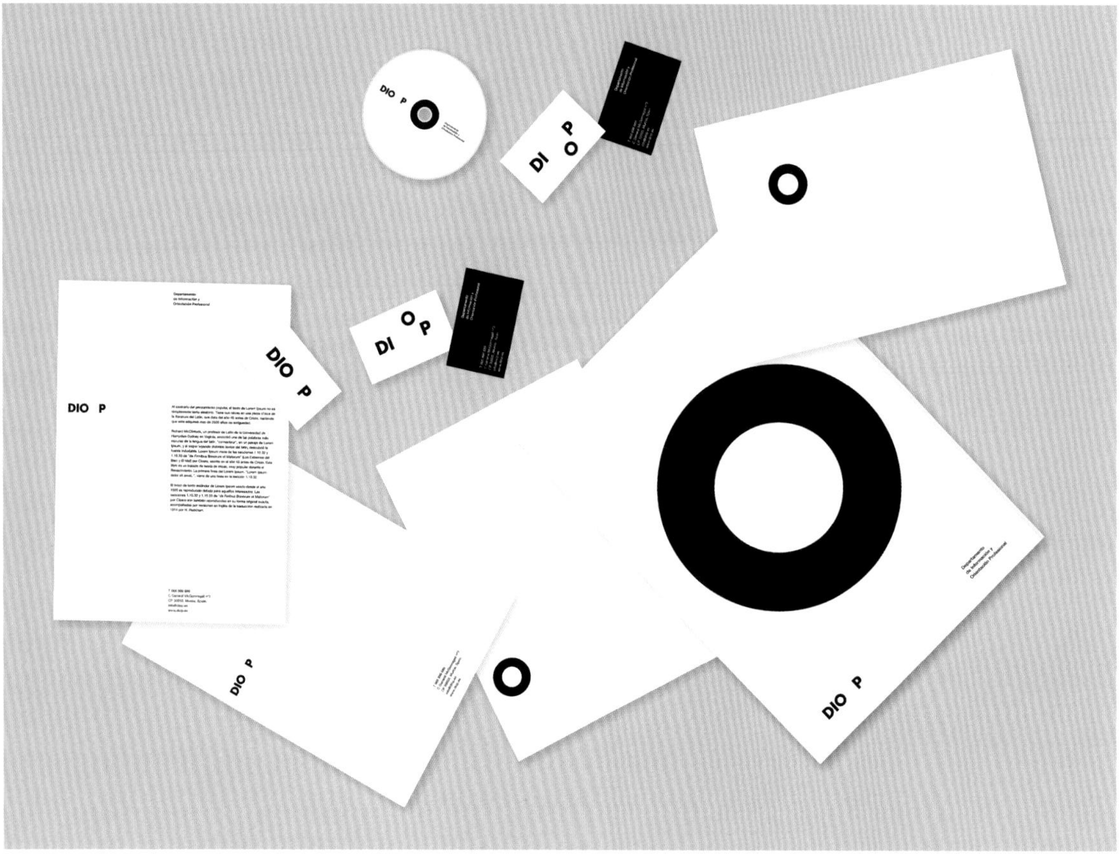
DIO P
DI O P
DIO P

DIOP

The DIOP, Departamento de Información y Orientación Profesional (Department of Information and Vocational Guidance), develops a series of actions consisting of courses, conferences and publications, and from the department office, it connects the education community with the real demands of society. Career Guidance and Continuous Training are the main functions. To develop the identity, I started from the concept of "Possibilities", the infinite possibilities of the future that a person can have. Why make a unique and static identity when there are so many options? I played with the possibilities of the position of the letter "O" in the logo. The letter "O" is us, is our endless options, is our unwritten future. The contrast between black and white is because DIOP is a light in the darkness, is a solution and support system when we don't know what to do with ourselves and our future.

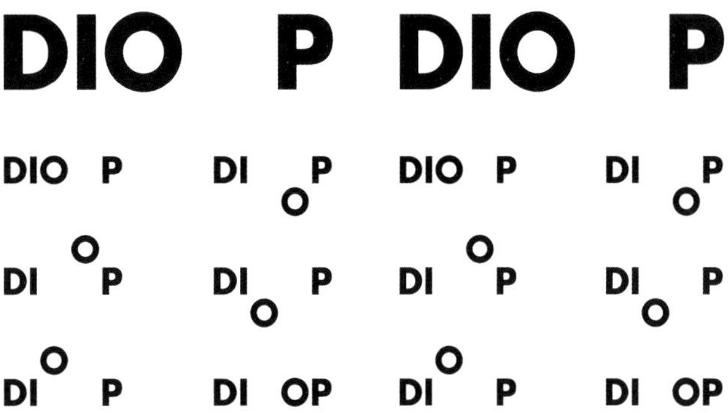

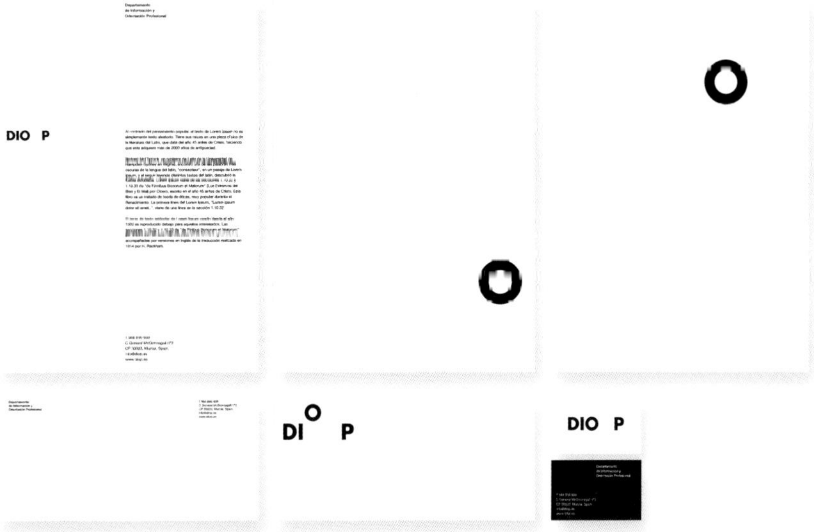

MVA Identity

"MVA" stands for "Manuel Ventura Architects", which is an architecture atelier based in Oporto, Portugal. In order to redesign the atelier identity, we created an identity that would differentiate it from the competition, while still identifying it inside its market. Thus, we proposed the design of a new brand, which could be young, fresh and irreverent, without losing the essence of the structure, the beauty of the shape, and the minimalism which we automatically identify with the field of Architecture. We started to play around with the initials of the atelier, shaping them into basic elements in the form of a "v". The final logotype is the combination of this symbol with the name of the brand, but there will be specific situations where the symbol can be used alone, when desired.

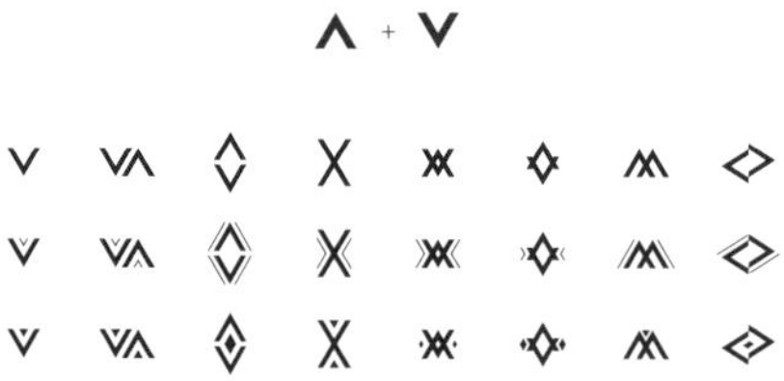

> CONVITE <
Lançamento de Empreendimento
Porto, Setembro 2010
Numa organização conjunta da Manuel Ventura, Arquitecto Lda, e PP-Empreendimentos Imobiliários, Lda, irá ter lugar no próximo dia 17 de Dezembro pelas 19h no Porto, o evento que reúne o lançamento comercial do empreendimento "TUPI CLUB RESIDENCIAL" e a inauguração das novas instalações do gabinete de arquitectura.

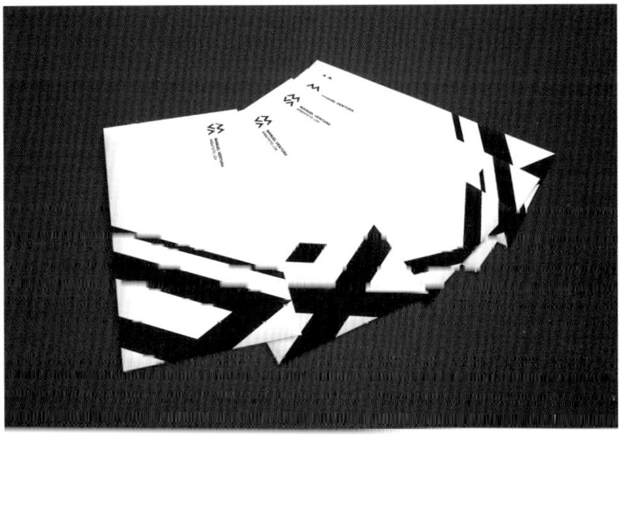

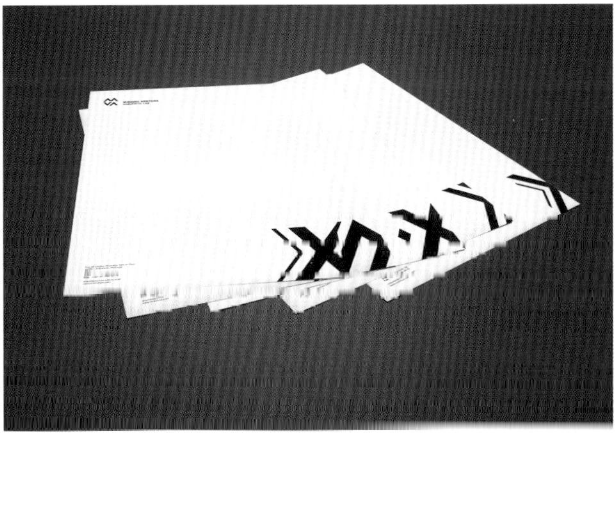

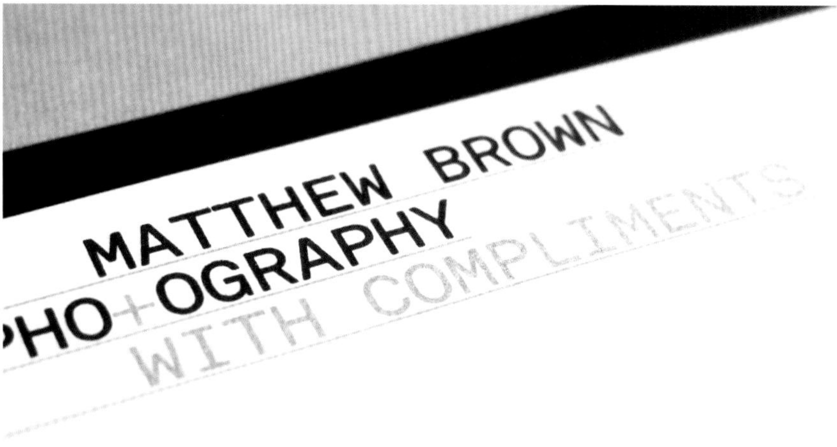

Matthew Brown Identity

The "+" symbol is traditionally used in photography to mark the centre of a camera's viewfinder to assist with composition. We've chosen to include this familiar, balanced icon as a part of the identity to reinforce an association with the industry. The "+" also brings a feeling of positivity and confidence to the brand, whilst promoting a professional message to the consumer.

The Matthew Brown identity uses black and metallic silver to create a strong visual impact and contrast. The focus is on a simple type based mark; it is uncluttered, easy to absorb and recognizable at a glance. The classic and sophisticated identity system is given room to breathe and is complemented by the "+" symbol where appropriate. Designed to stand alone and against photographic imagery this simple yet effective mark is the basis of the brand's personality.

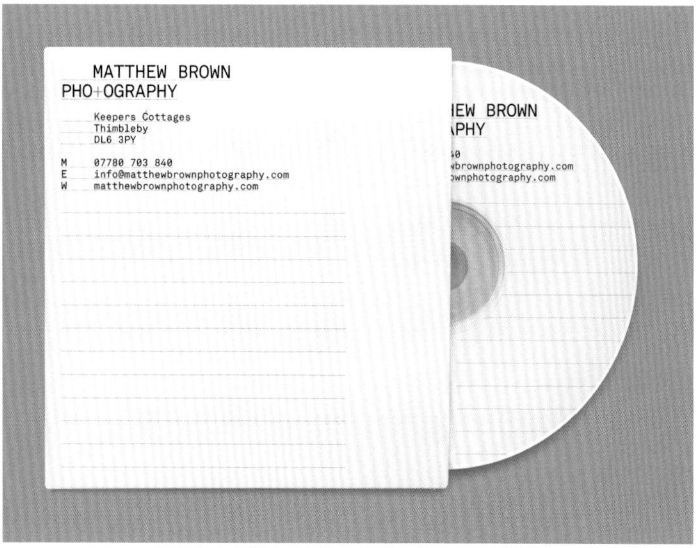

MATTHEW BROWN
PHO+OGRAPHY
MATTHEW BROWN
PHO+OGRAPHY
M 07780 703 840
E info@matthewbrownphotography.com
W matthewbrownphotography.com
MATTHEW BROWN
PHO+OGRAPHY

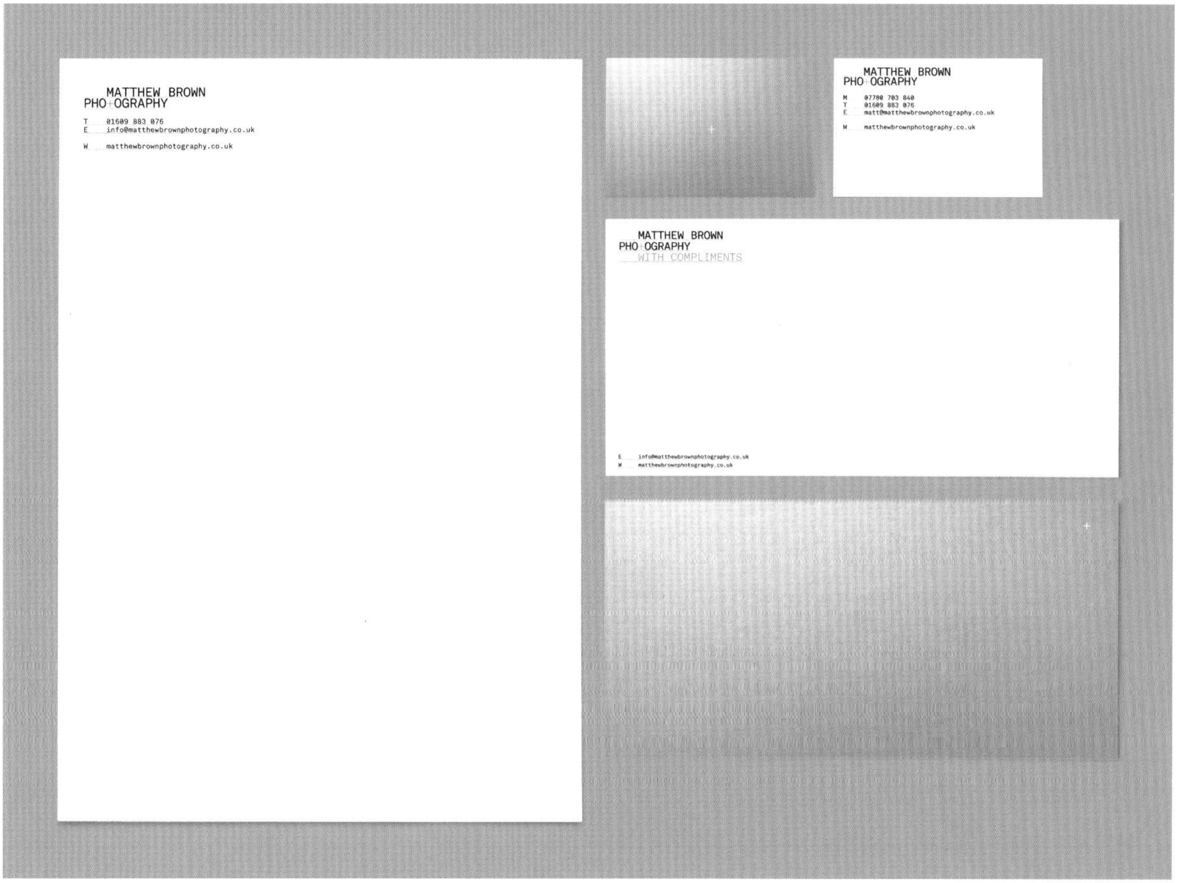
MATTHEW BROWN
PHO+OGRAPHY
T 01609 883 076
E info@matthewbrownphotography.co.uk
W matthewbrownphotography.co.uk
MATTHEW BROWN
PHO+OGRAPHY
M 07780 703 840
T 01609 883 076
E matt@matthewbrownphotography.co.uk
W matthewbrownphotography.co.uk
MATTHEW BROWN
PHO+OGRAPHY
WITH COMPLIMENTS
E info@matthewbrownphotography.co.uk
W matthewbrownphotography.co.uk

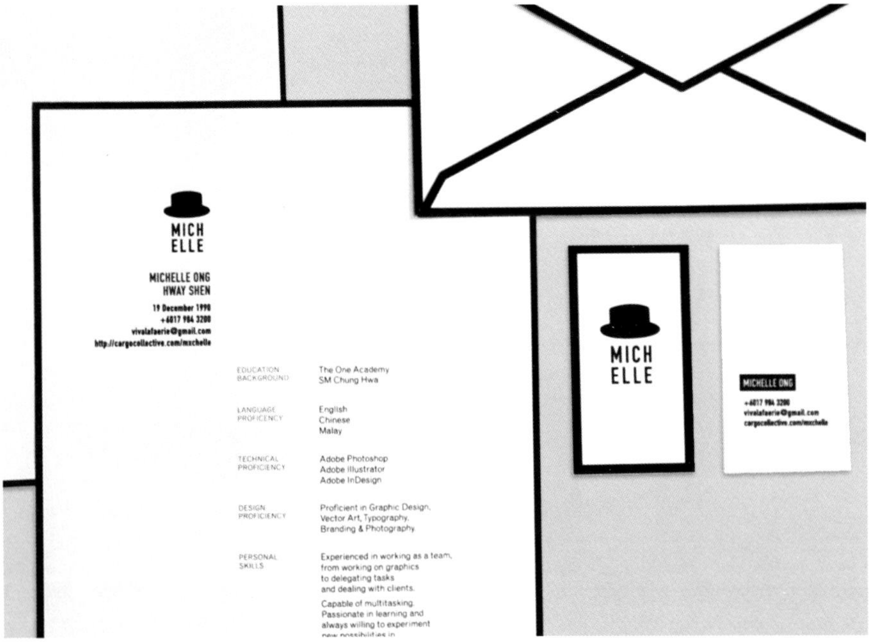

Michelle Ong Identity

As part of the self-promotional package, this identity design was developed to communicate what makes Michelle unique as a designer. It consists of a set of stationery with business card, letterhead, and envelope, along with a mailer and a portfolio that share the same visual identity. The concept behind the identity was to create a visual metaphor of a thinking cap, to convey that Michelle is a designer that thinks during her design process. Coincidentally, the hat is also a signature look of her everyday style. She decided to make a simple yet memorable design with a minimalistic approach. A contemporary sans-serif typeface was used, and only black and white was used for the whole identity program as she didn't want the design to lose its own aesthetics.

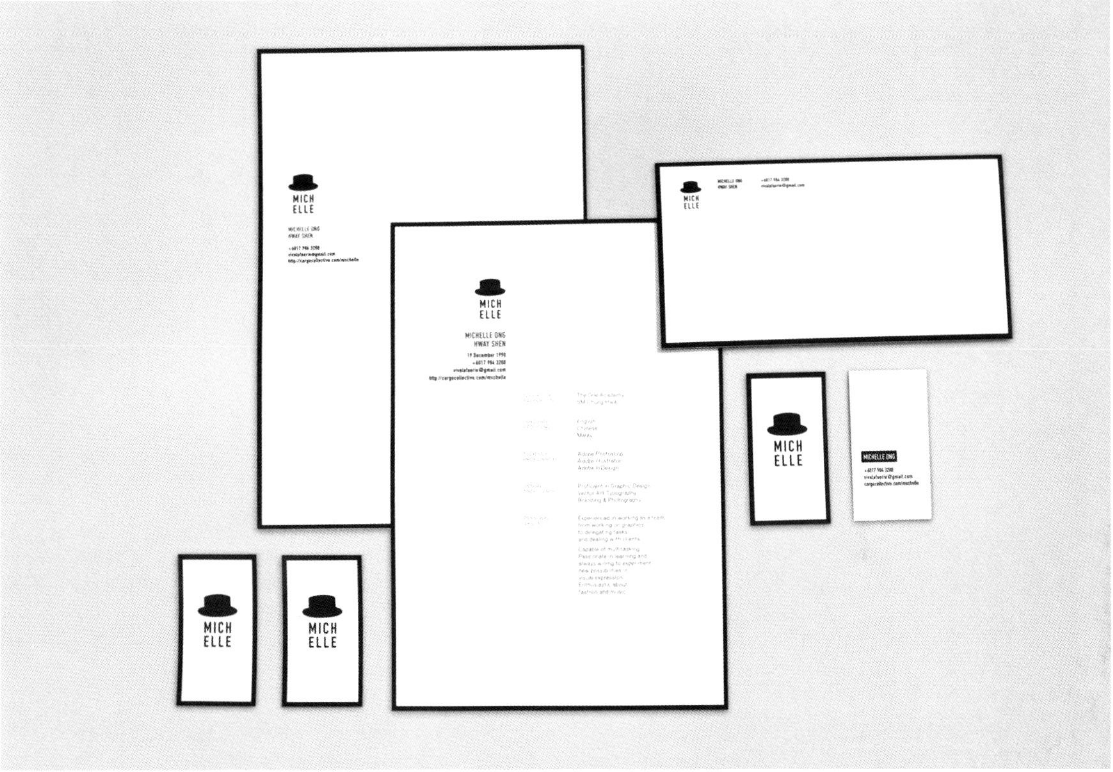
MICH
ELLE
MICHELLE ONG
HWAY SHEN

RANDOM STUFF
ABOUT ME:
And here's my résumé:
MICH
ELLE
MICHELLE ONG

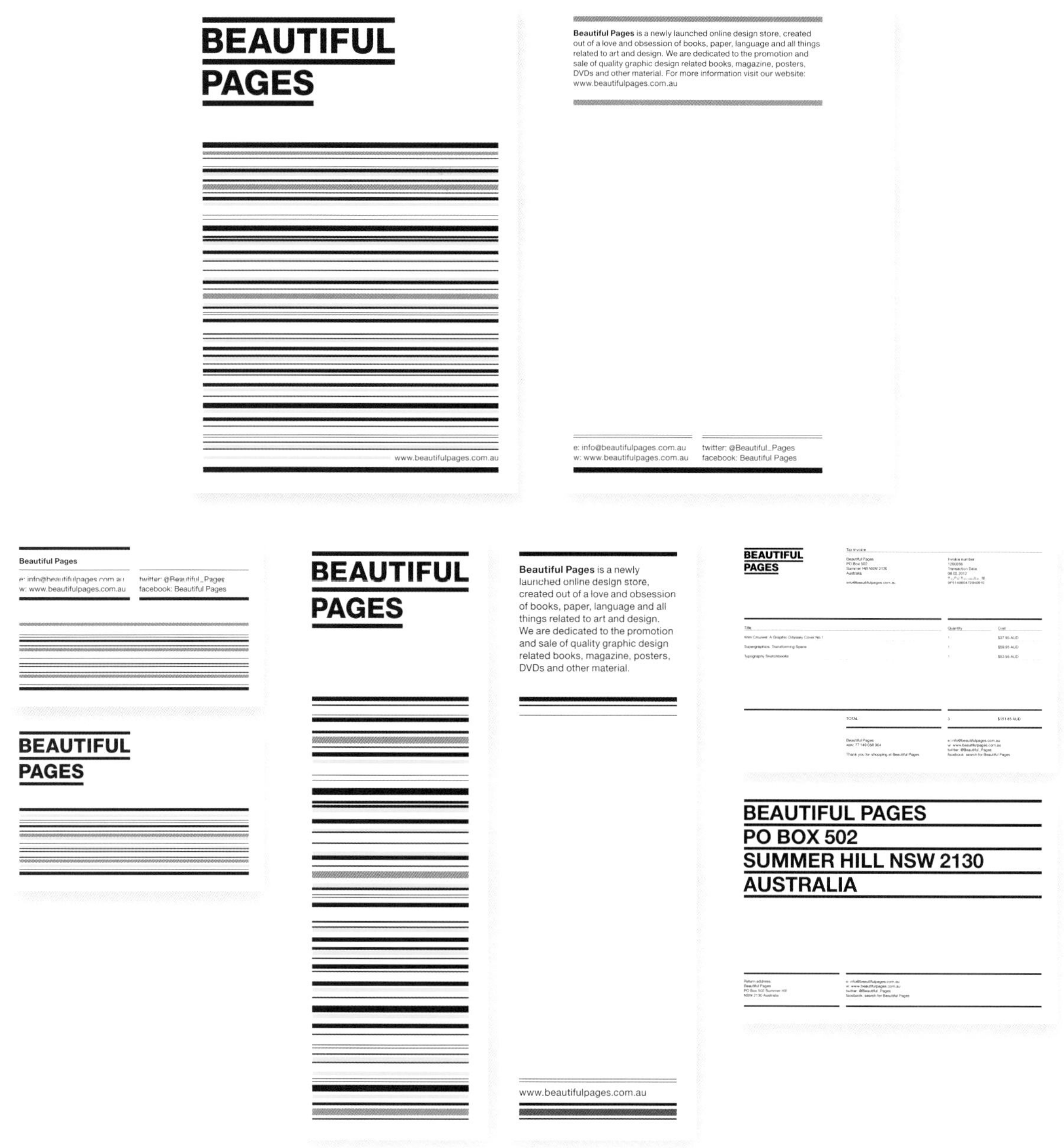

Beautiful Pages Stationery

Beautiful Pages is a newly launched online design store born out of a love for and obsession with books, paper, language and all things related to art and design. The store is dedicated to the promotion and sale of quality graphic design related books and materials. This project involved naming, developing the brand, stationery, packaging, email newsletter and website for the online store. The final brand identity is visually appealing, simple, friendly and flexible. It is unique in style, instantly creating a strong and memorable brand, whilst communicating the importance that the company places on design. The responses have been very positive from the first day. Sales have been increasing steadily since the launch of the store in 2011.

Paraules i bits

The corporate identity revolves around the peculiarity of the double concept: the written letter (in black and white) and the digital letter (the white on the black). Day and night, white and black, Núria and Juanjo. Núria is a translator, corrector and linguist and Juanjo is an IT engineer. The "bits" are words. The graphic image incorporates a random code programmed in the language Python to generate a series of prints.

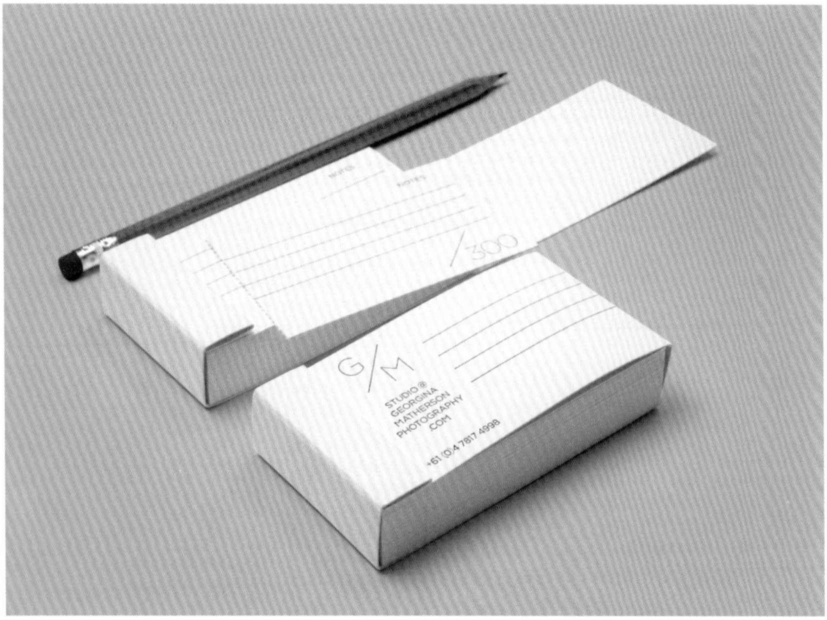

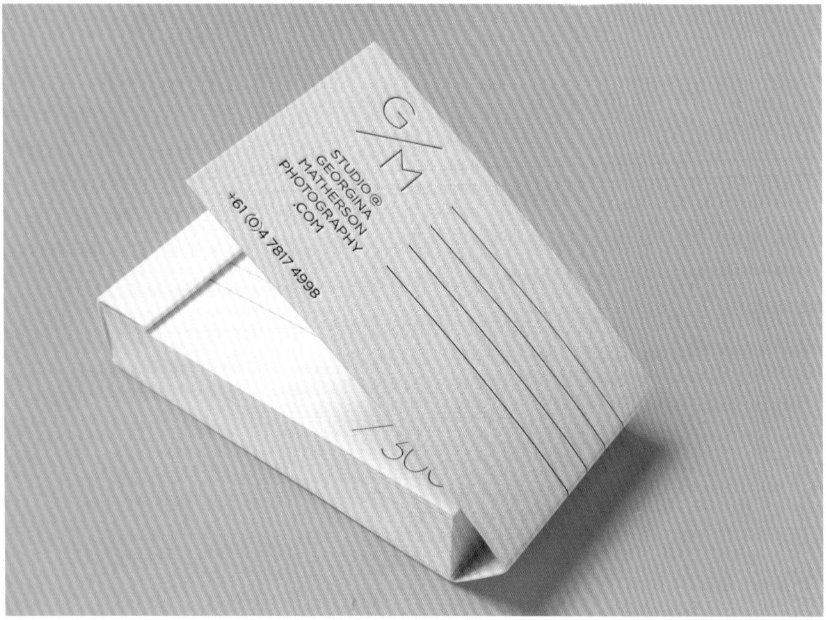

Georgina Matherson Identity

Georgina Matherson approached us as she wanted to make the transition from Artist/Photographer to commercial photography. Georgina also wanted a way to make each piece of her collateral personal and therefore memorable to whoever she was communicating with. The idea of artist's editions and numbered prints became the cue for her identity combined with a series of lines on which to write her message. The same block was used to letterpress all collateral items and allowed us to produce the business card books with perforated cards.

NOTES
STUDIO @
GEORGINA
MATHERSON
PHOTOGRAPHY
.COM
+61 (0)4 7817 4998
/300

G/M

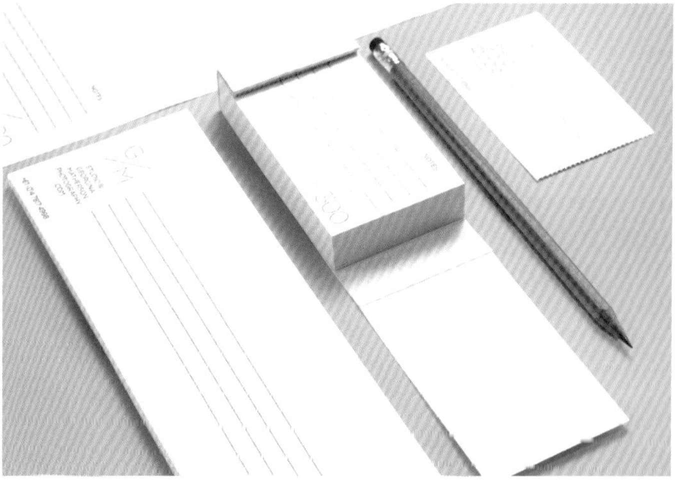

Modern Library Rebranding

This project was a proposed rebranding for the literary imprint Modern Library. Modern Library is a publishing company that has a collection of some of the greatest works of the 20th century. Rachel decided to give the company a more "contemporary" look while not forgetting its roots. Focusing on clean, modern elements Rachel built a new brand. The logo design reflects the structure of a bookshelf and exists on a grid that lends itself to different arrangements and lots of flexibility based upon its application. Combining this fresh and colorful logo with classical etchings of famous authors and thinkers, Rachel expanded the brand to highlight the history of the books as well. The branding serves as a bright, iconic, and easy to navigate system that people will hopefully begin to recognize and embrace on their bookshelves at home.

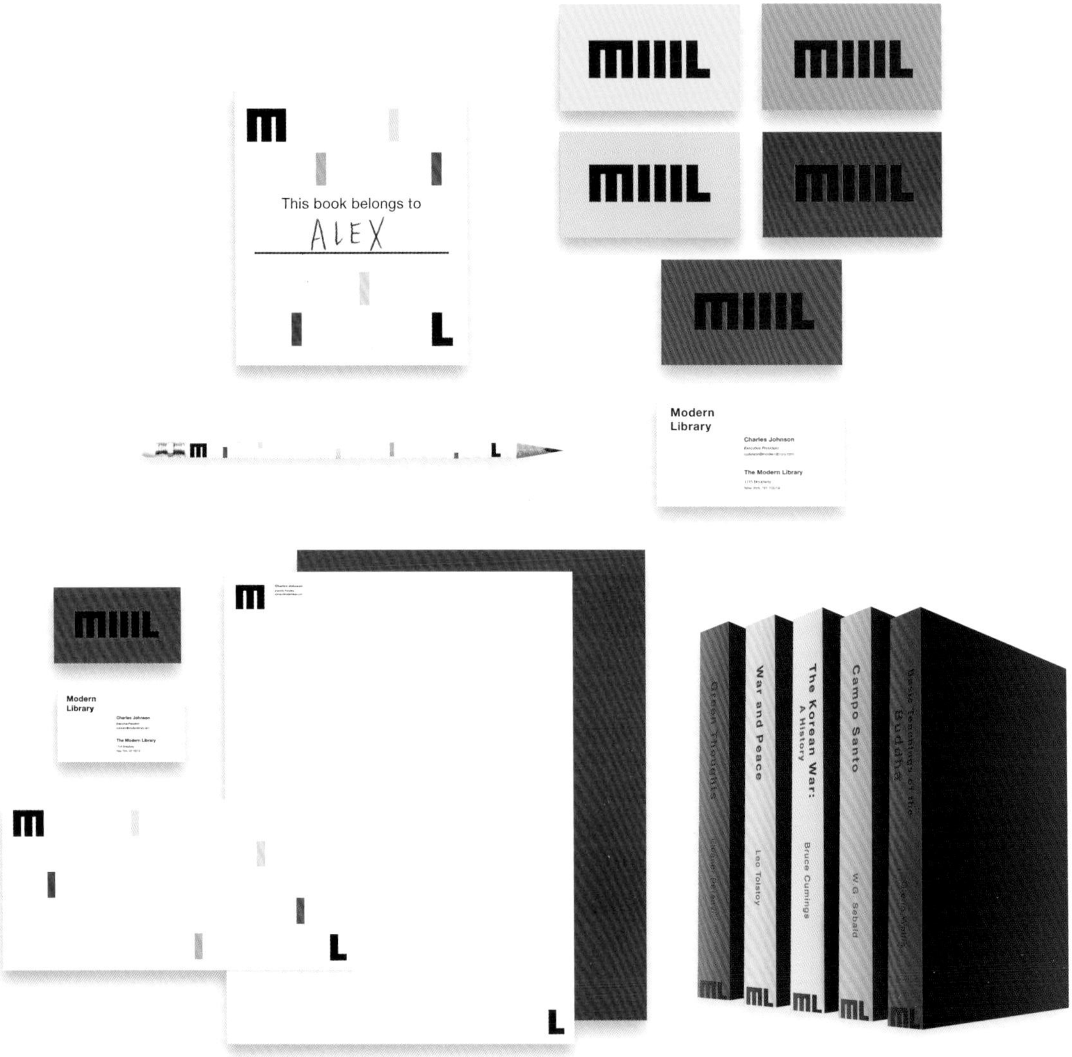

Modern
Library
100 Novels
Shakespeare
Reading Guides

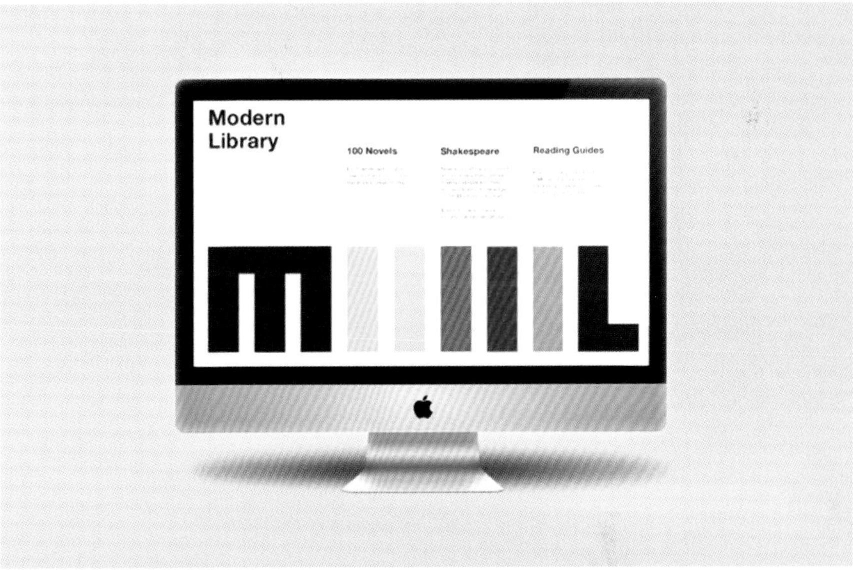
Modern
Library
100 Novels
Shakespeare
Reading Guides

Modern
Library
Shakespeare
Complete Works
Modern
Library
Jane Austen
Complete Works
Modern
Library
Charles Darwin

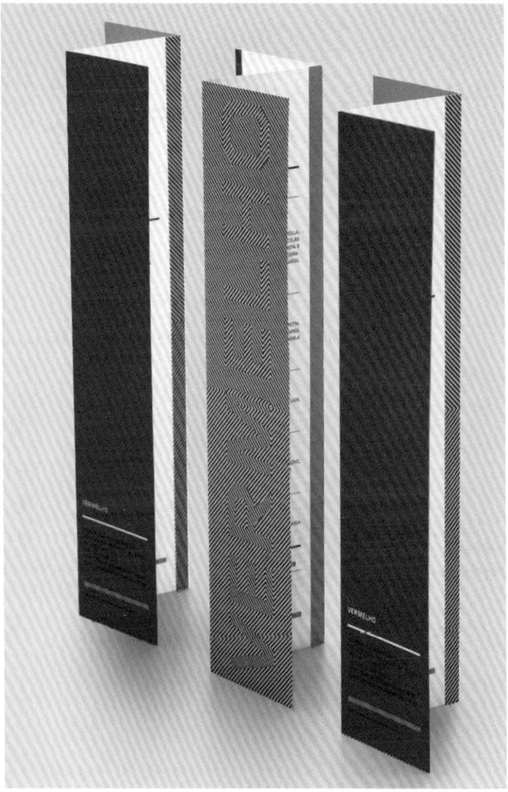

Visual Identity for Vermelho art gallery

The identity was built with the colors: Pantone 812, Black and White. The graphic project is very simple and each piece carries the following technical information printed below the address of the gallery: paper type, weight, shape, typography, colors.
Two formats of envelope were designed for the stationery: one for A4 sheets and the other in a multiple format, which serves three different functions, as it is folded and closed with its system of tabs and holes: it serves to carry CDs and DVDs, a complement card (A5 format) and, without folding, like a traditional letter envelope. We also designed letterhead, certificates of authenticity for works of art, printed publication, directory and business cards. The business cards were printed in silk screen on paper vellum 240 gs/m2.
Photography by Edouard Fraipont.

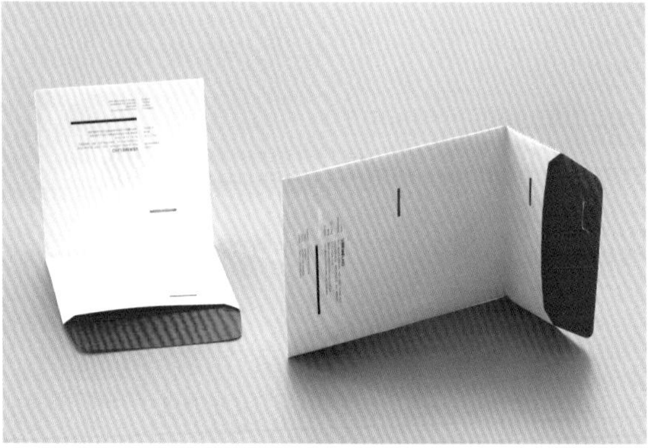

VERMELHO
MARINA BUENDIA
marina@galeriavermelho.com.br
TEL: 55 11 3138 1522
Rua Minas Gerais, 350
São Paulo / SP / Brasil
CEP: 01244-010
www.galeriavermelho.com.br

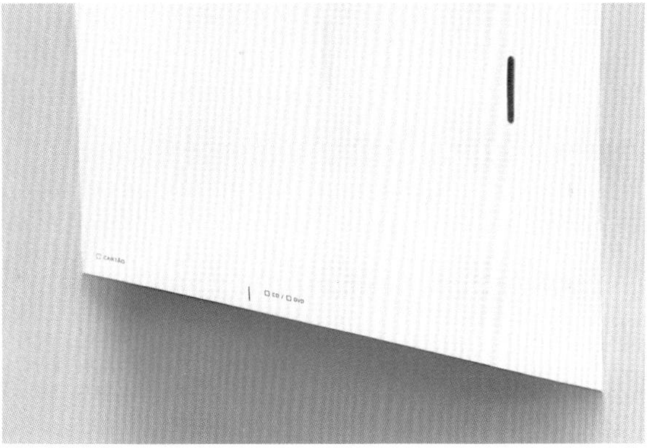

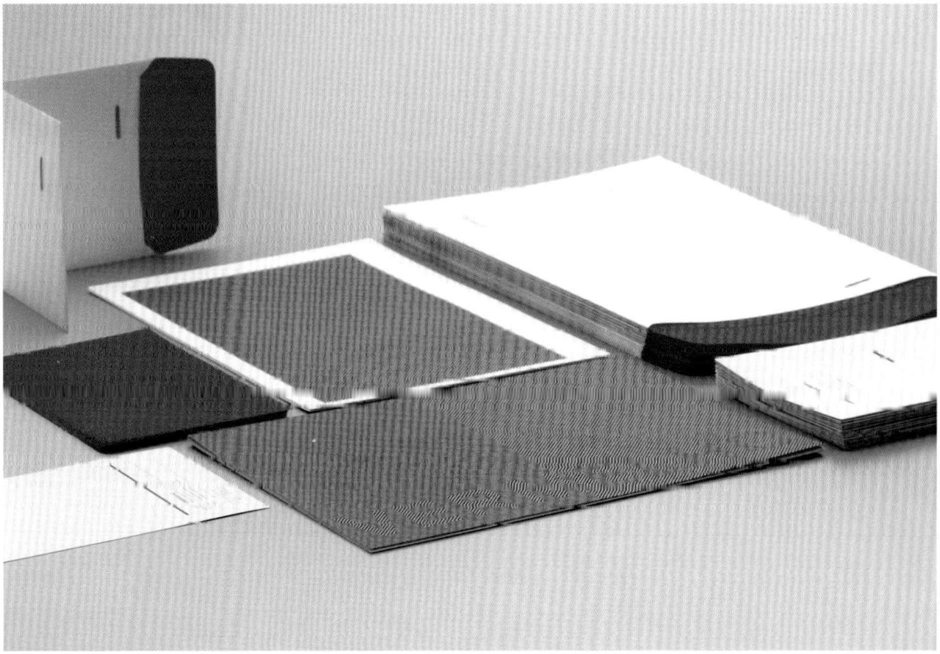

Ihr Mehrwert

Ihr Mehrwert ("Your Added Value") is a successful Austrian sales and management consulting company. The graphic design with the focus on colors emphasizes its business concept: "Your added value due to self-value". Increased appreciation of each employee helps increase business success. The color sequence between red and magenta suggests openness, courage and eagerness to make decisions. At the same time, it provides space for intermediate steps. You might want to discover how much more there is behind "Ihr Mehrwert" as shown in the 3D tip effect of the business cards. Product photography by Marion Luttenberger.

Ihr
Mehrwert
dank
Selbstwert

Ihr
Mehrwert
dank
Selbstwert

Ihr
Mehrwert

Ihr
Mehrwert
dank
Selbstwert

Sales Desk Polen

Sales Desk Polen offers a range of practical solutions to foreign companies wishing to operate in Poland. The company emerged from several years of professional experience of its founder, Patrycja Kosta, in assisting German companies in entering the Polish market.
A long term cooperation with German Lower Saxony and the exchange of ideas and solutions between the region representatives from around the world was also significant.
Sales Desk Polen asked us to design their complex corporate identity. We decided to develop the logo based on the characteristic Lower Saxony symbol: a red horse. However, we wanted to design it from scratch, in a modern, minimalistic way, concentrating on the upper part of the horse.
After elaborating the logo and its technical details we began designing corporate materials. The idea was to keep it as clean and simple as possible, so that the logo was the main point of identity. Additionally we made the wax stamp (in red) to seal envelopes, with an embossed horse symbol. The next step was a photo session with employees in business casual style. The photos complemented by selected quotes were used in the key visual and in the last phase of our work – in a website design.

SALES
DESK
POLEN

La Fonda del Sol

Mirko Ilić Corp. created the identity design and menus for La Fonda del Sol, a Spanish restaurant in New York. La Fonda del Sol means "the small restaurant of the sun" in Spanish, thus they created the logo representing the sun out of a gold circle that is used throughout the restaurant. Photography by Eric Laignel.

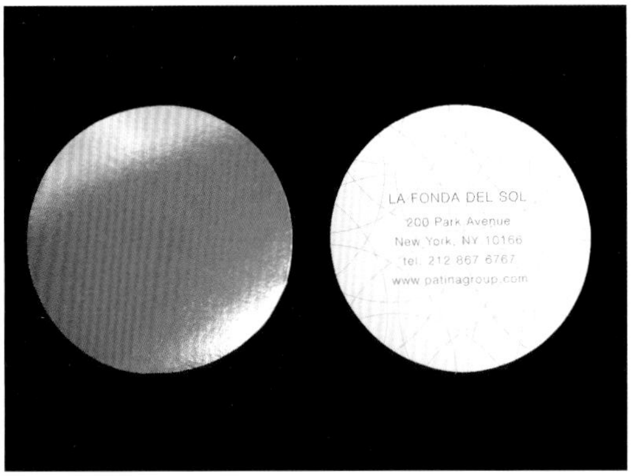
LA FONDA DEL SOL
200 Park Avenue
New York, NY 10166
tel. 212 867 6767
www.patinagroup.com

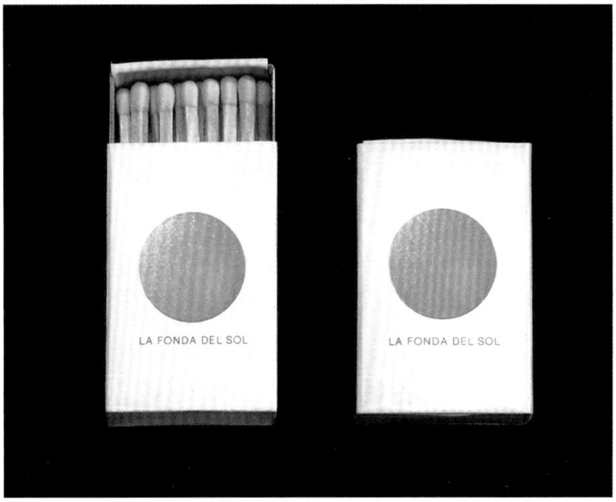
LA FONDA DEL SOL
LA FONDA DEL SOL

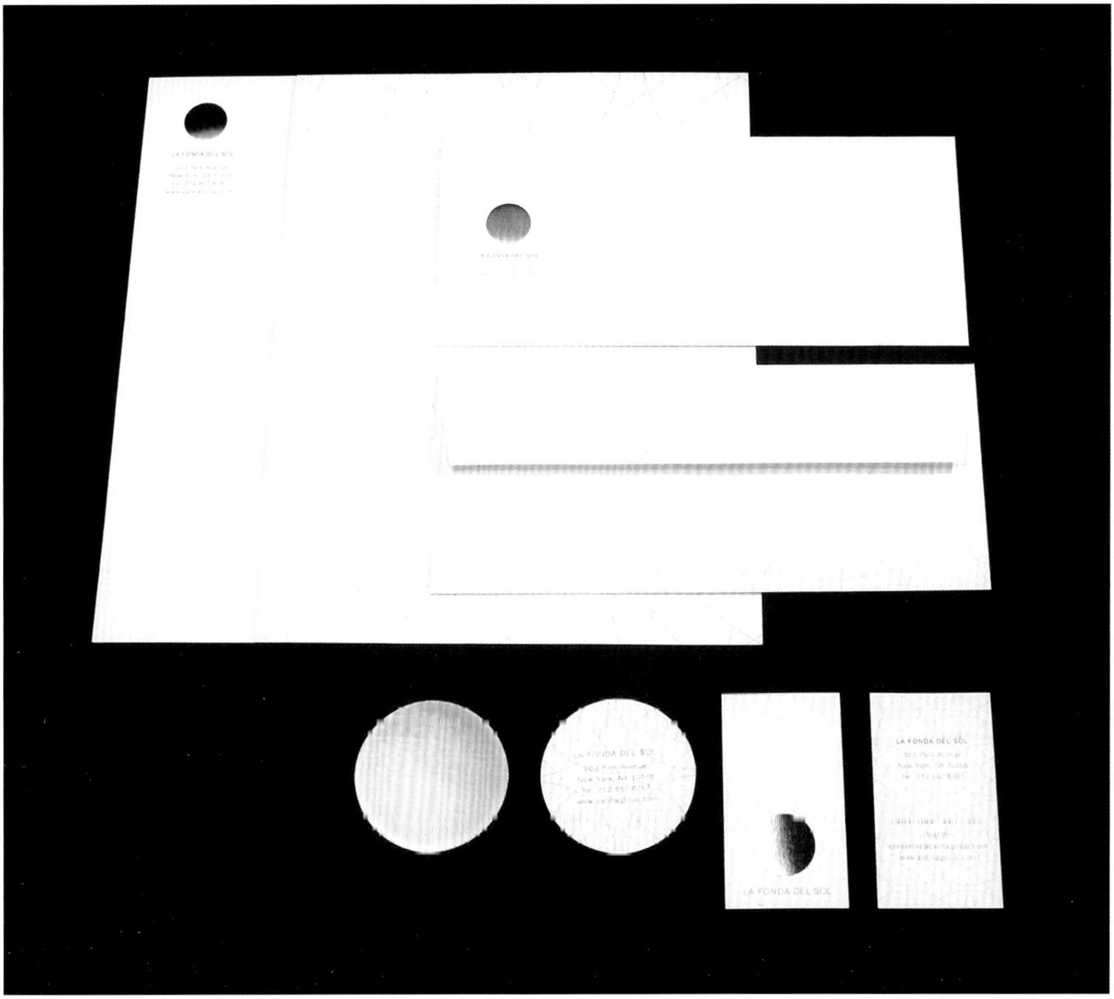
LA FONDA DEL SOL

FUGA

FUGA is an architecture center in Budapest and its identity is the result of an open design competition won by Hungarian graphic designer István Szugyiczky.
István intended to design an abstract logotype that carries the possibility of easily constructing a pattern, which can be integrated in the interior design of the building as either two or three dimensional elements. The logotype consisting of the word FUGA, which translates to plaster in English, or grout - is present in a kind of static form with a vibrating solution, as the lower part of the F forms the top of the G at the same time. This graphic structure is intended to communicate the idea of one of the main possibilities of architecture: the dynamism inherent in basically static constructions.

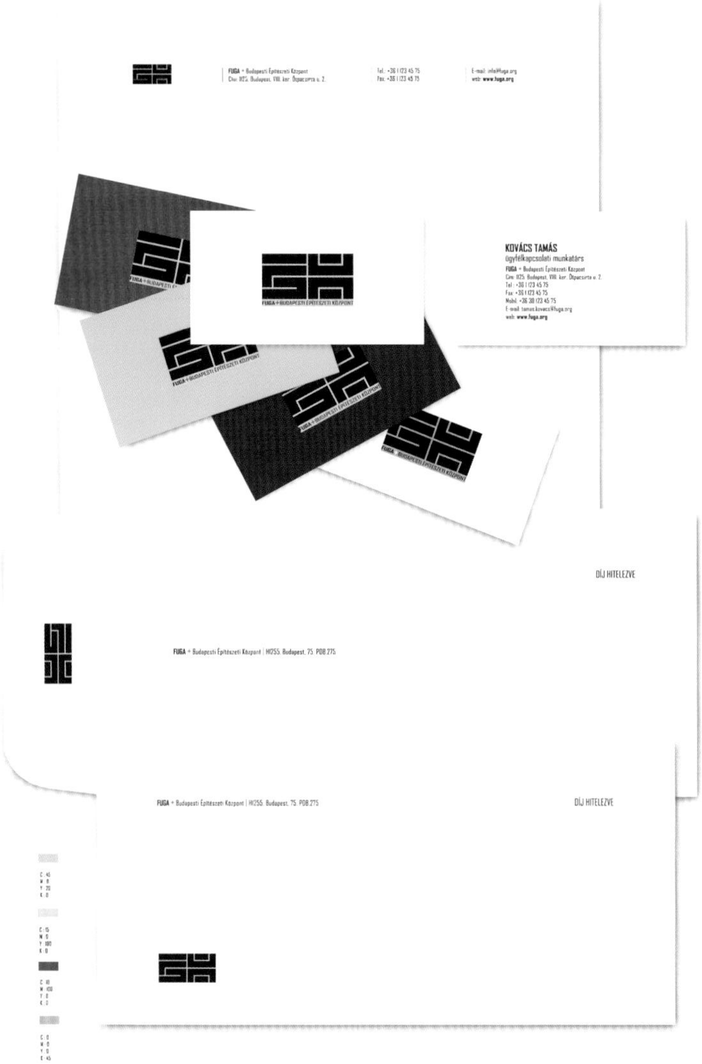

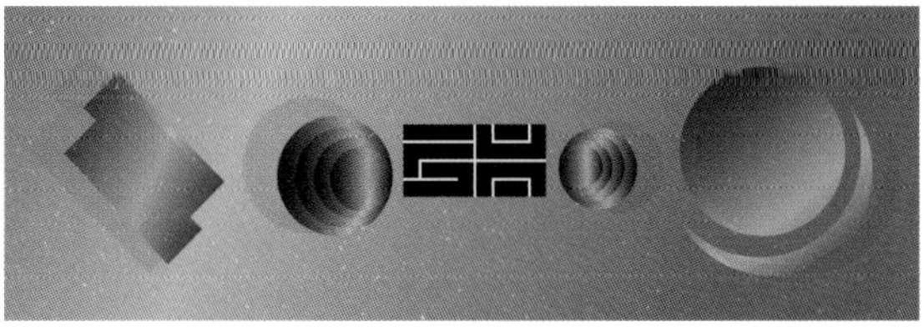

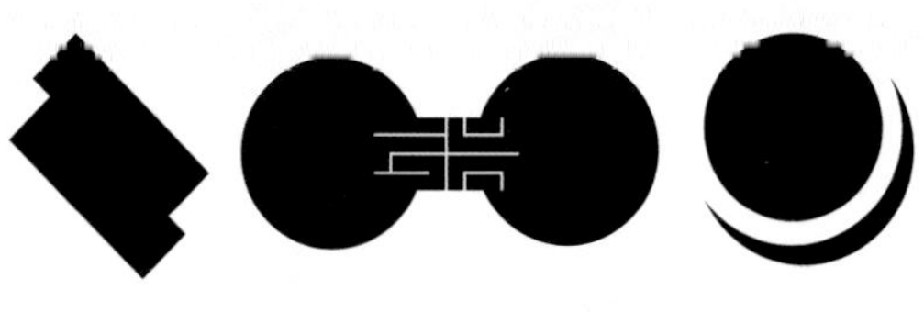

341 Gallery

341 is a gallery and art advisor which is inspired by Alfred Stieglitz's 291. We wanted to make sure the identity had a contemporary feel and based the system on mathematics.

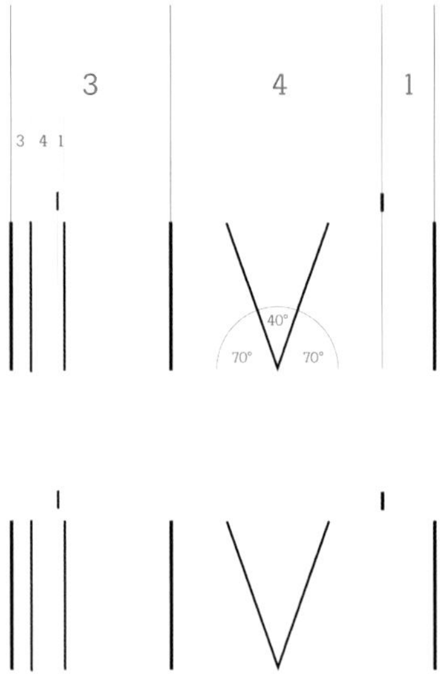

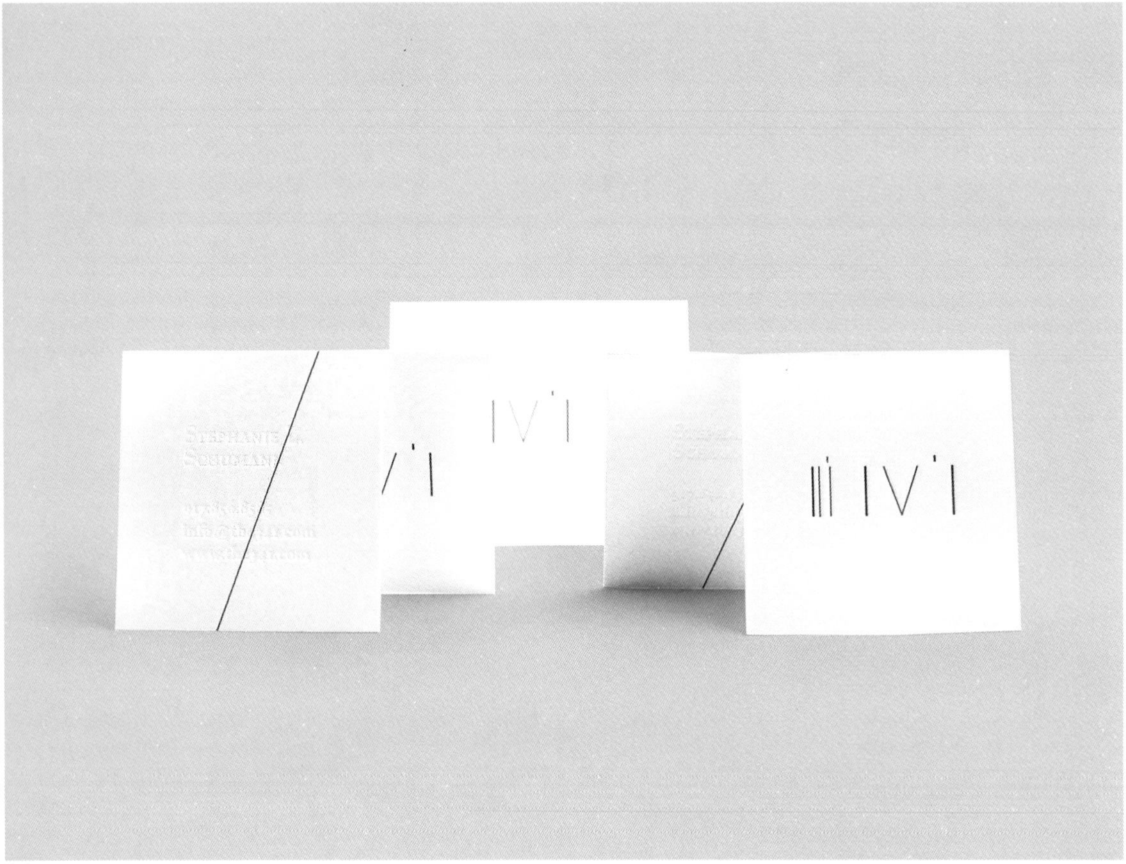

EURA NOVA Brand Identity

EURA NOVA is a Belgian IT company founded in 2008. I approached them creatively as a space where IT consultancy (specific to their clients' needs) meets a research centre (surfing on the highest and most advanced knowledge waves). EURA NOVA is a young and very dynamic team, who try to be different in the very strict and closed world of IT. Their philosophy is based on involvement: we were bound to meet. The acquaintance met all my expectations, as they offered me the best "carte blanche" ever. I chose Olin rough high white 300 gr Magnific and constant white paper for the business cards.

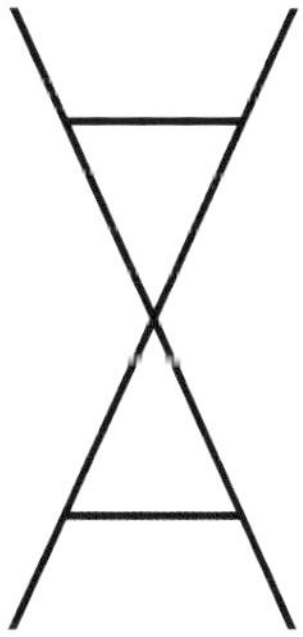

Parad Rebranding

Proekt Communication Agency performed the rebranding of Parad boutiques. The essential aim was to focus the corporate ID elements on the female audience, as Parad had to abandon the male product line. The visual aesthetics of the new Parad is based on the intrigue and the process of in some way paradoxical communication. The logo is designed like the women's lips — the source of passion and wisdom.

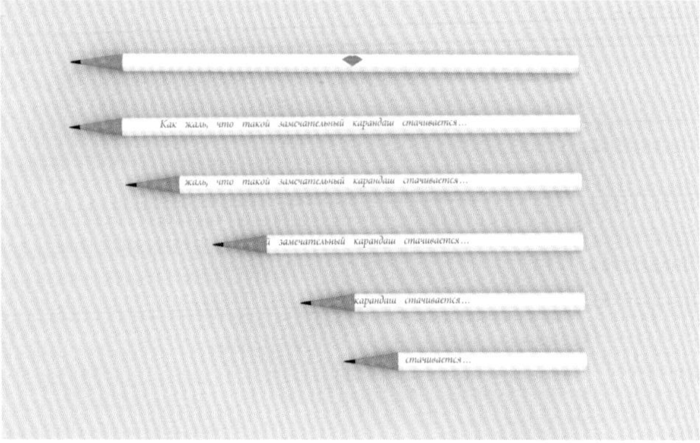

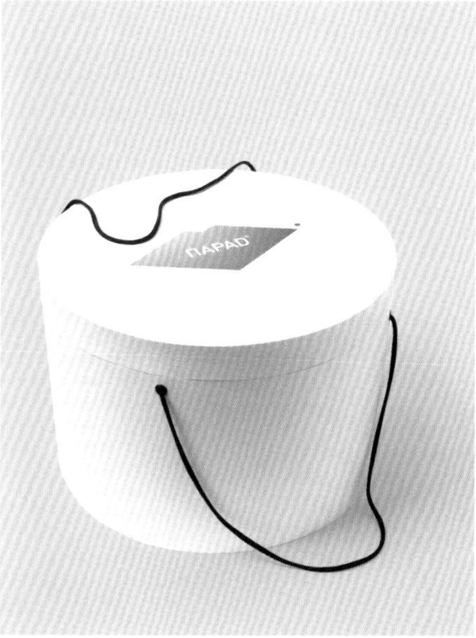
ПАРАD®

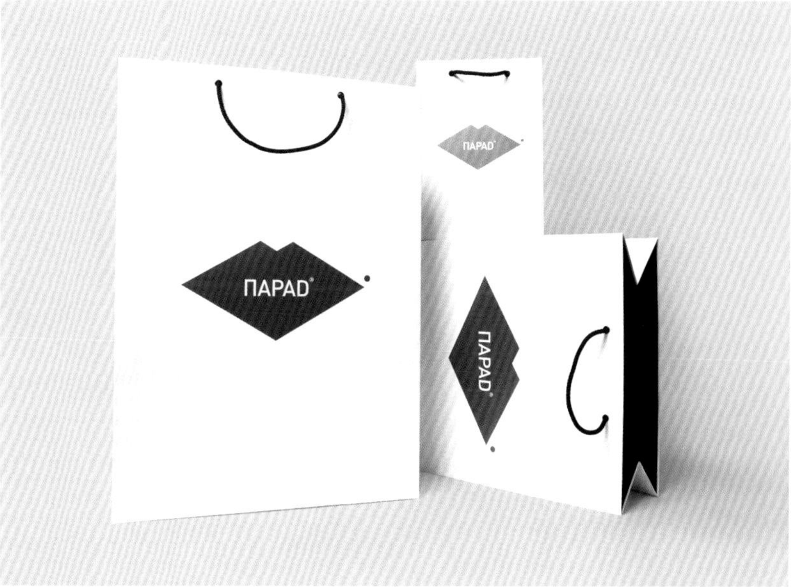
ПАРАD®
ПАРАD®
ПАРАD®

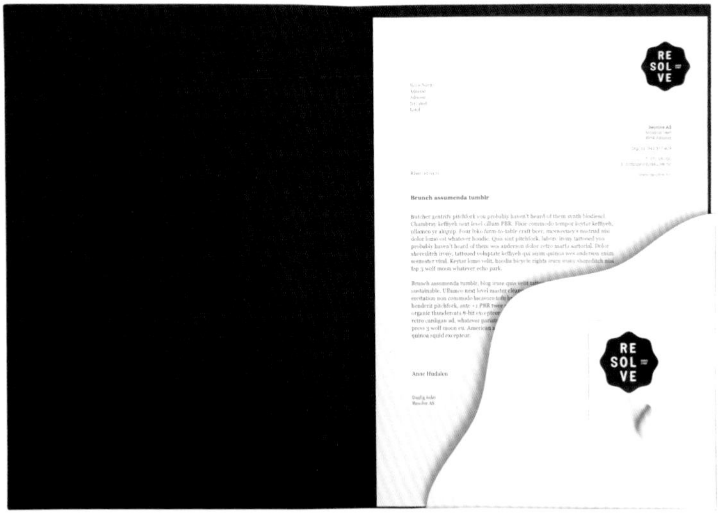

Resolve Identity

Resolve is a supplier of cleaning and damage restoration services, which has a strong commitment to its employees and craft. Through this identity, we aimed to emphasize Resolve's distinct personal and proud approach in an industry that often portrays itself as sterile, with no particular emotion. The result is soft, warm and professional. Photography by Kimm Saatvedt.

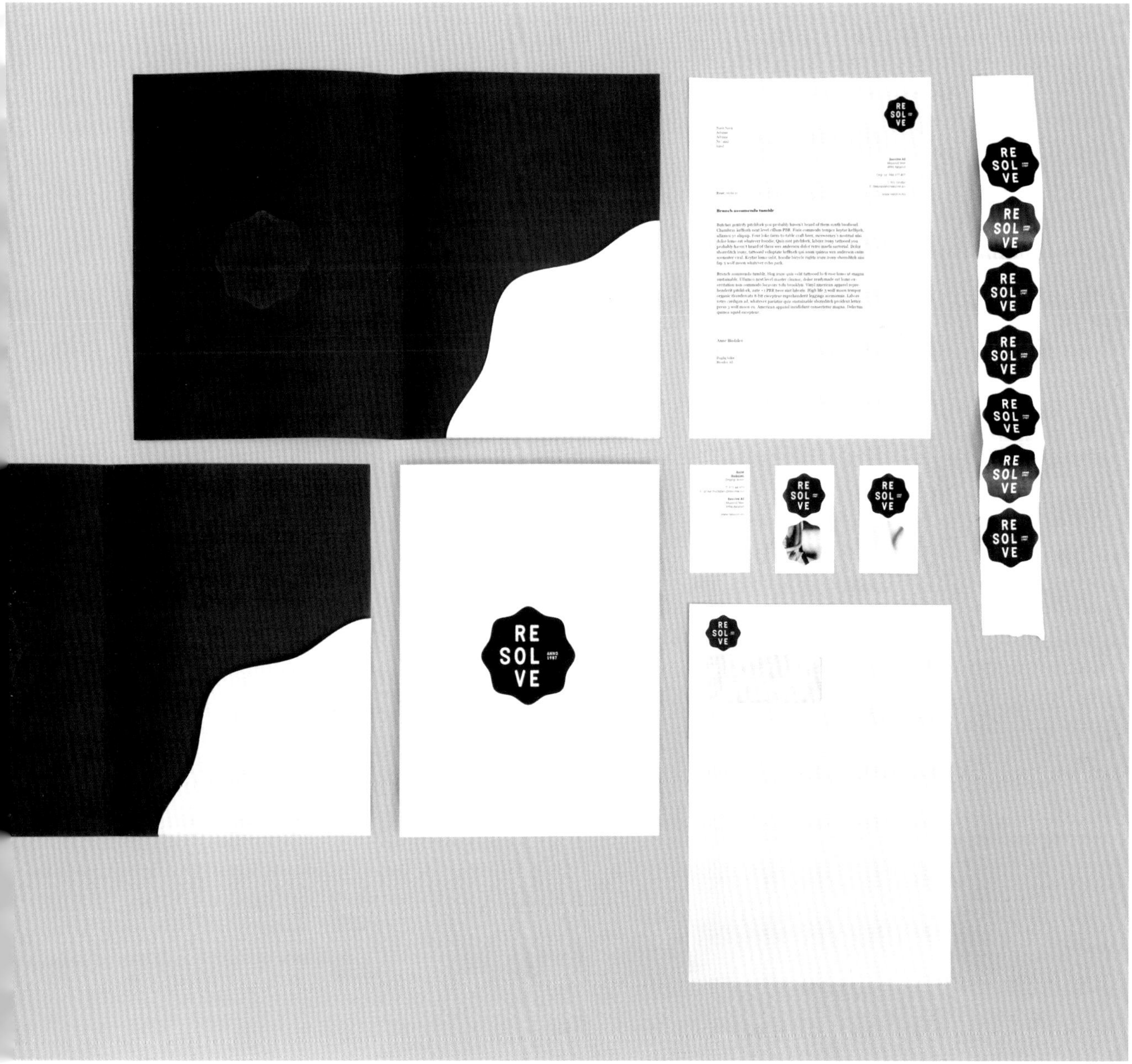
RE
SOL
VE
ANNO
1987

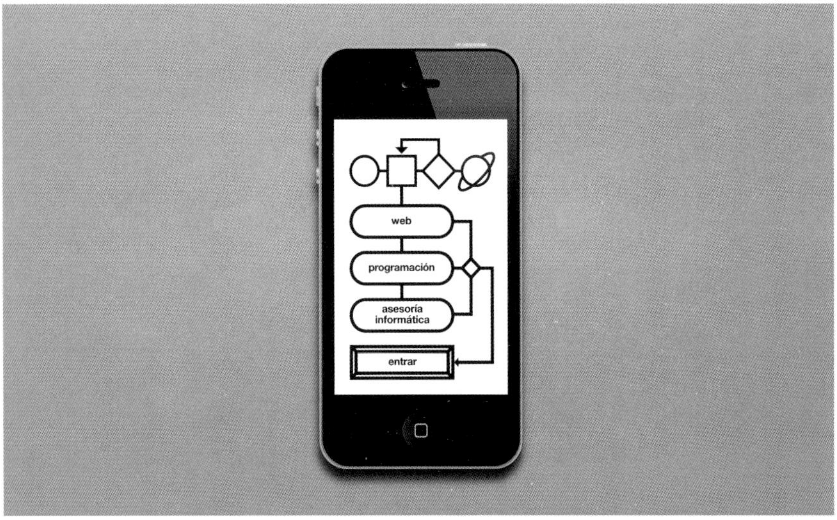

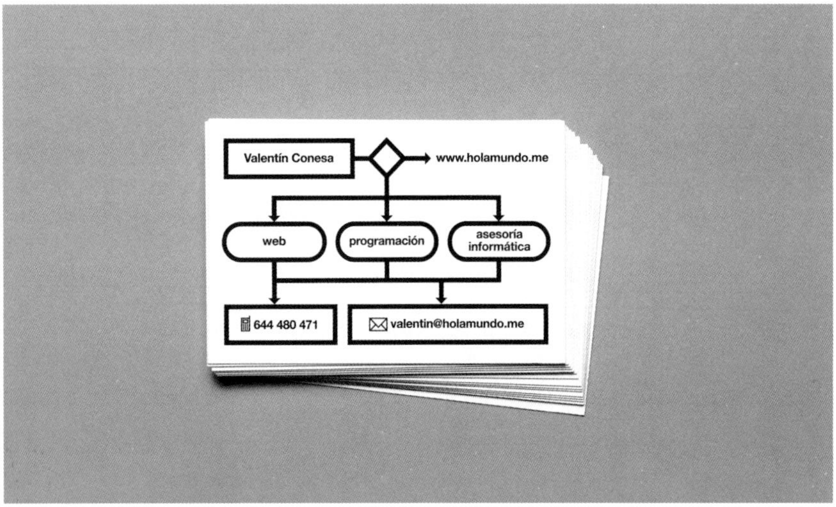

Hola Mundo

Frequently, "Hello World" (Hola Mundo) is the first application we experiment with while we are learning a new programming language. It is a friendly and funny way to make yourself known for an enterprise that is specialized in programming and computing services.
The client demanded a corporate identity that conveyed how his enterprises worked.
Thanks to computing consultancy, programming, and web design, the way other enterprises work becomes easier and more effective.
It is clear, then, that through a combination of all three aspects, we save the client time and money. Then again, this is why the graphics are based on flowcharts. These diagrams are used to schematize information and facilitate the resolution of problems. By simplifying the different graphic elements that make up the diagrams, we arrive at what is to be the brand symbol. This flowchart is, indeed, quite simple, as we can see here. There are four stages:
1. The beginning (Circle)
2. The process (Square)
3. The decision (Rhombus)
4. The end (World)
The graphic style is based on pure geometric figures. To prioritize the information and to facilitate the reading order we use boxes and arrows. A sequence of pictograms allows variations in the logo for its different applications (an envelope in the mail, CD packaging, etc.).

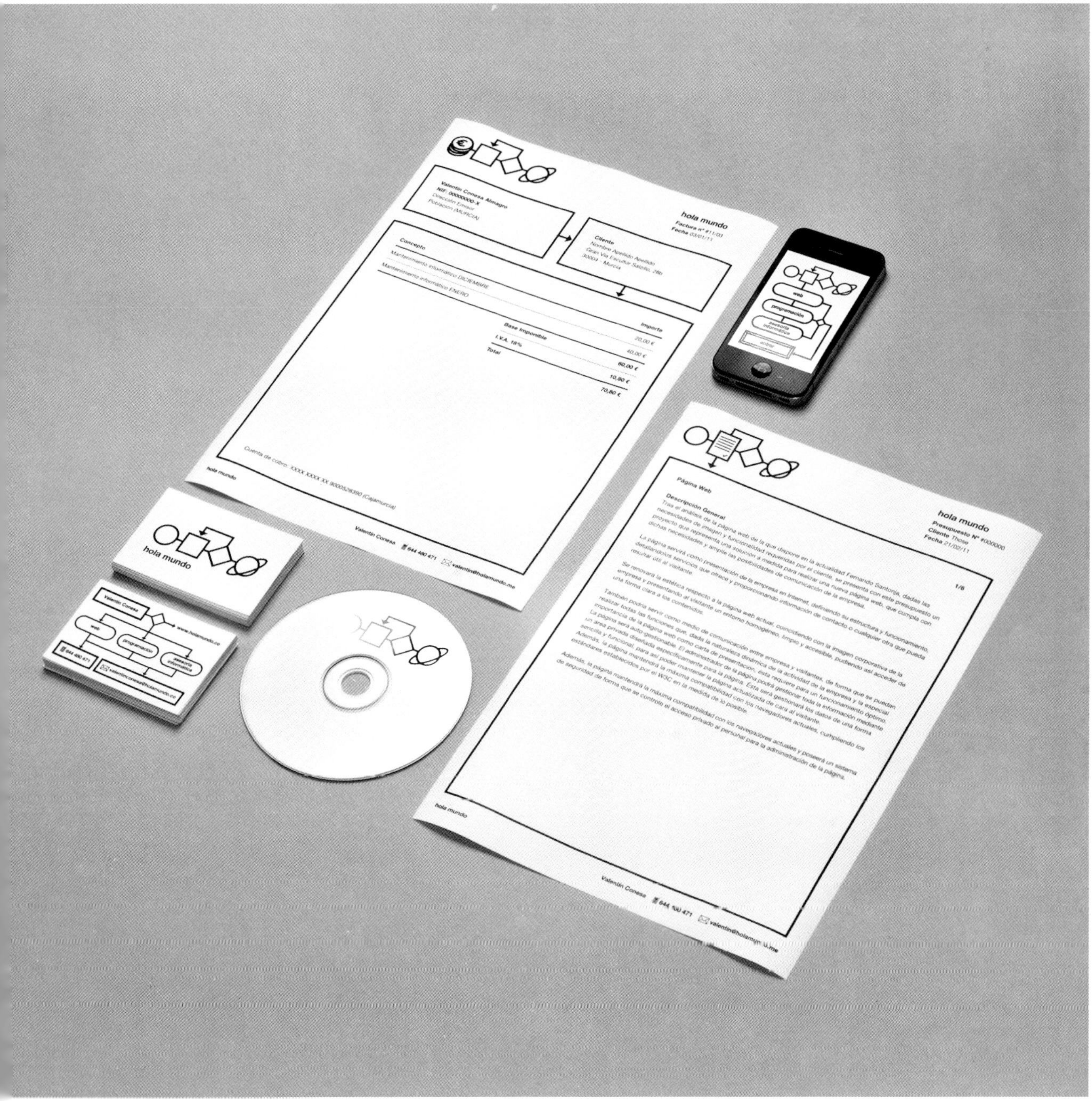
hola mundo
Factura nº #11/03
Fecha 03/01/11
Valentín Conesa Almagro
NIF: 00000000-X
Dirección Emisor
Población (MURCIA)
Cliente
Nombre Apellido Apellido
Gran Vía Escultor Salzillo, 28b
30004 - Murcia
Concepto
Mantenimiento informático DICIEMBRE
Mantenimiento informático ENERO
Importe
Base imponible
I.V.A. 18%
Total
20,00 €
40,00 €
60,00 €
10,80 €
70,80 €
hola mundo
Valentín Conesa
644 480 471
valentin@holamundo.me
web
programación
asesoría informática
hola mundo
Valentín Conesa
www.holamundo.co
644 480 471
valentinconesa@holamundo.co
hola mundo
Presupuesto Nº #000000
Cliente Those
Fecha 21/02/11
Página Web
Descripción General
1/6
hola mundo
Valentín Conesa
644 480 471
valentin@holamundo.me

SDA Identity Design

SDA = SYNTHESIS Design and Architecture, London, UK. SYNTHESIS is an emerging contemporary design practice with over a decade of professional experience in the fields of architecture, infrastructure, interiors, installations, exhibitions, furniture, and product design. SYNTHESIS's Founding Director is Alvin Huang. He is an award-winning architect, designer, and educator specializing in the integrated application of material performance, emergent design technologies and digital fabrication in contemporary architectural practice. I designed a logotype with a new font, which adapts Alvin's architectural ideas. Thank you to Imprvd design agency (Remo Kommnick and David Ottlik), which gave scope to my abilities.

SDA
SYNTHESIS
DESIGN + ARCHITECTURE
SWOOSH
PAVILON
tel: +44 (0)207 193 7263
fax: +44 (0)207 681 1107
www.synthesis-dna.com
Unit 2.6, Rockwell House,
10-14 Hewett Street,
London EC2A 3NN
£ 3 000 000
£ 100 000
£ 400 000
£ 3 500 000
SINCE
2011
Dear Kiss Miklos
Best Regards,
Budapest, 2010. 06. 22
CHELSEA
WORKSPACE
ITECTURE

Felani Yap Identity

This project is about self discovery and self understanding. While most people have an idea of what they want to show to people about themselves, I am also finding my own identity. Being a mature designer, I have to explore various design styles to suit the work and understand the personality behind each. I've gained knowledge in the design filed and have found things to express my viewpoint. I always love to be original and be known by people in different ways. I am not into anything cliché and am always honest in everything I do. As a person, I have a strong personality and love to be organized in every way. Somehow this is where the idea of Periodic Table of Chemistry is applied. When I was in high school, I was fascinated by chemistry as a subject in terms of the ability of the molecules to combine themselves with each other. It is not only about the chemical reactions, but also their composition, structure and properties which relate to design. The initial "FE" not only come from my name but also from one of the elements in the Periodic Table that belongs to Iron. This might sound unusual but the originality of the idea has caught my attention.

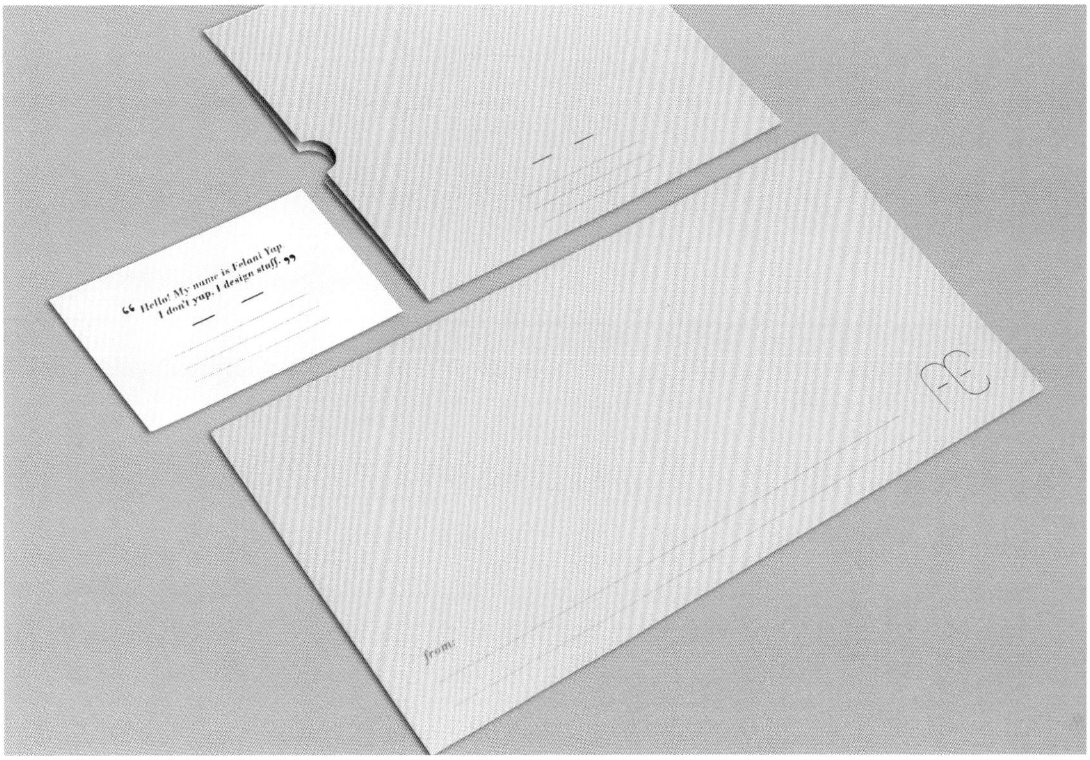
“Hello! My name is Felani Yap. I don't yap, I design stuff.”
from:

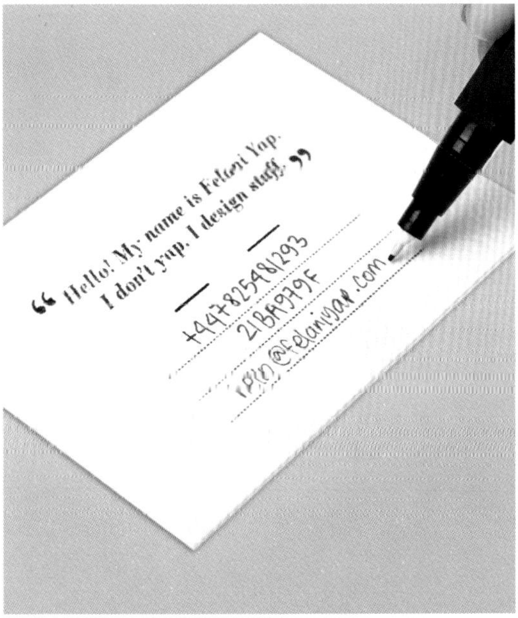
“Hello! My name is Felani Yap. I don't yap, I design stuff.”
+447825481293
21BA979F

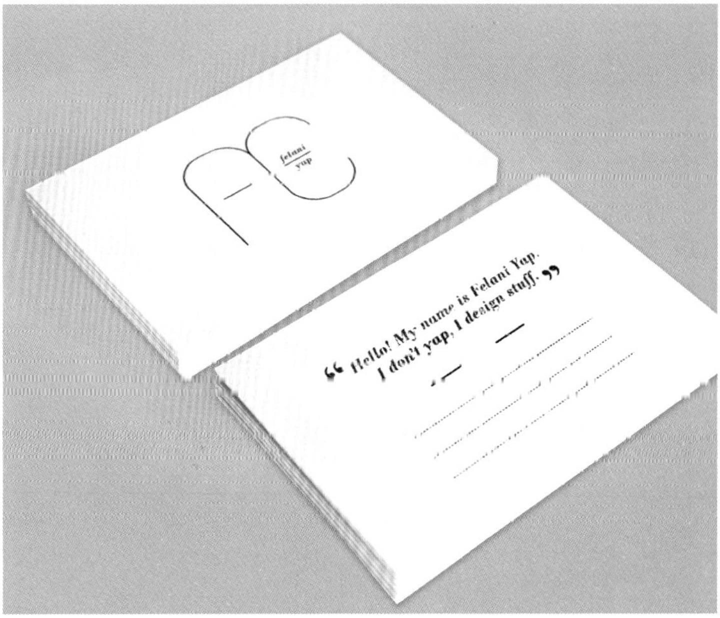
felani
yap
“Hello! My name is Felani Yap. I don't yap, I design stuff.”

Megan Sheerin

For corporate communications consultant Megan, a new brand identity increased the visibility of her business, along with its value. Aligning Megan's primary planning, training and writing services with a single descriptor — communication strategist — clarified her capabilities. Using language and typography, an innovative logo was designed to reflect Megan's personality. The result was some of the "The Year's Best Work", according to industry publication *Australian Creative.*

OneSource Visual Identity

This identity project was designed bearing in mind the physical nature of the client's business. OneSource provides computer network consulting, implementation and management services. The cables frequently used to physically build the networks were the starting point for the project. This key element, in the form of a line, became part of a flexible graphic language. Different developments of the original logo and visual language were designed with lines having different thicknesses, adapting well to the size of the object where the identity is then used. On larger objects versions of the logo with more and thinner lines can be used. Photography by Daniel Santos.

New Frontier Group

New Frontier Group is a network of globally thinking and locally acting IT companies across state borders and is very flexible! It specializes in the IT solutions field for central and eastern Europe as well as Russia. In addition to the logotype, the generative pattern in the corporate identity – created by moodley – depicts the dynamic, multinational networking as well as the internal processes of the group; New Frontier Group combines wide and deep competence with the ability to adjust solutions to very specific markets. Product photography by Marion Luttenberger.

new
frontier
group

new
frontier
group
Mit den besten Grüßen

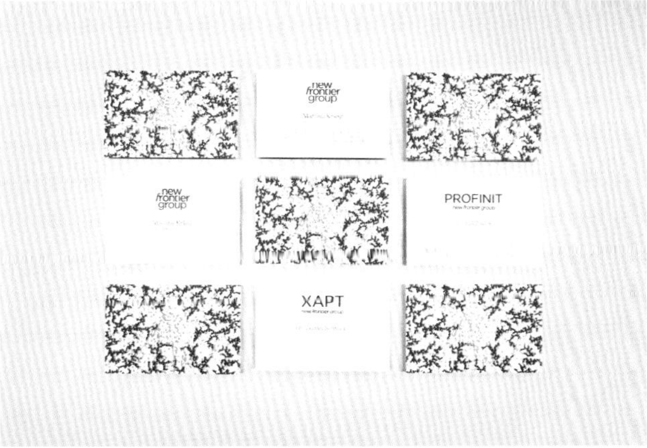
new
frontier
group
PROFINIT
XAPT

Dear
Executive of
Deutsche
Telekom AG
Dear
Executive
of Telenor
Group

A GREEN NEW DEAL
ENRIC RUIZ-GELI
CAT
_RTS S_NT_ MÒNIC_
MARÇ-JUNY 2010
ANTÀRTIDA. TEMPS DE CANVI
MIREYA MASÓ
2.587 PERSONATGES
I 311 DEFINICIONS DE DÉU
VALÈRE NOVARINA.
EL TEATRE DEL DIBUIX
LA RAMBLA.IN/OUT.
BARCELONA.
JORDI BERNADÓ/
CAT
_RTS S_NT_ MÒNIC_
DESEMBRE 2010-MARÇ 2011
PENSAR ART – ACTUAR CIÈNCIA
SWISS ARTISTS-IN-LABS

Arts Santa Mònica Stationery

Creating the identity for a contemporary art centre is always a complex job and an exciting challenge. It's even more of a challenge when the centre is not only restricted to fine arts, but incorporates three other disciplines: science, thought and communication. We created a logo which works as a visual poem, as the four A's are missing from the name, corresponding with the four arts which coexist at the centre. These letters are recomposed, forming a very simple, eye-catching, abstract and highly recognizable symbol.

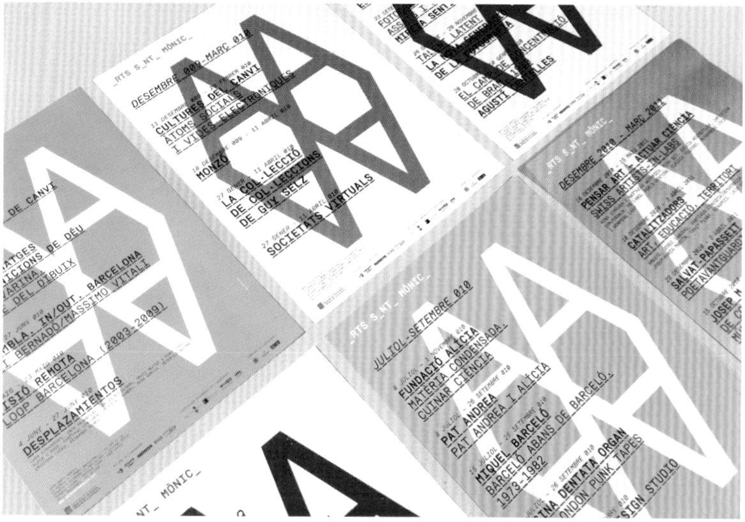

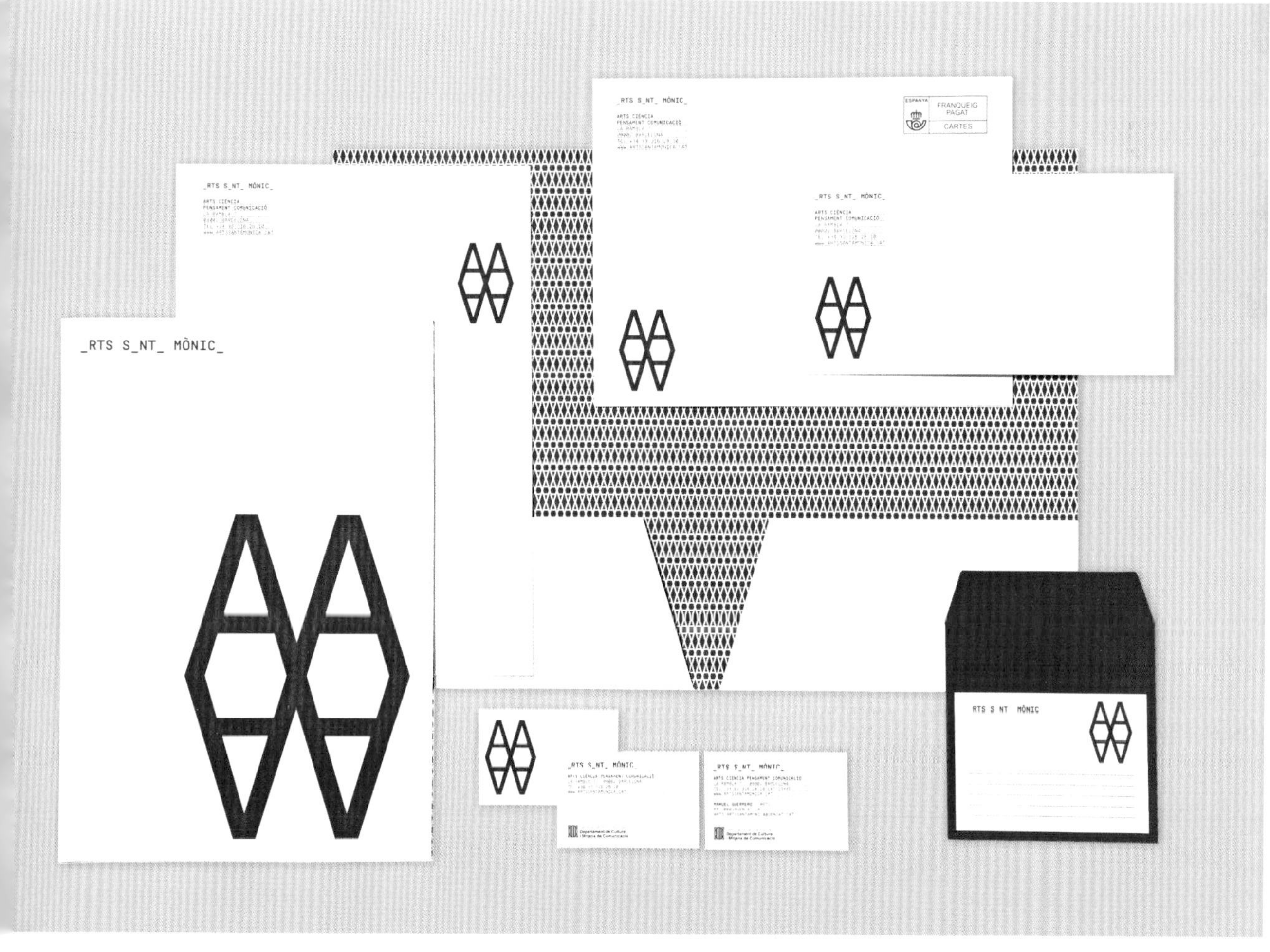

Carpet Sign

Carpet Sign is one of the leading producers of high-end design rugs. Studio Laucke Siebein was asked to develop a new brand strategy, visual identity and a redesign for all its communication tools and product presentations as well. Within an accurately defined creative concept based on a fresh and sober no-nonsense approach, all items become a dignified representative of the beautiful and precious products of Carpet Sign.
The project was in cooperation with Studio Müller en van Tol industrial and interior design.

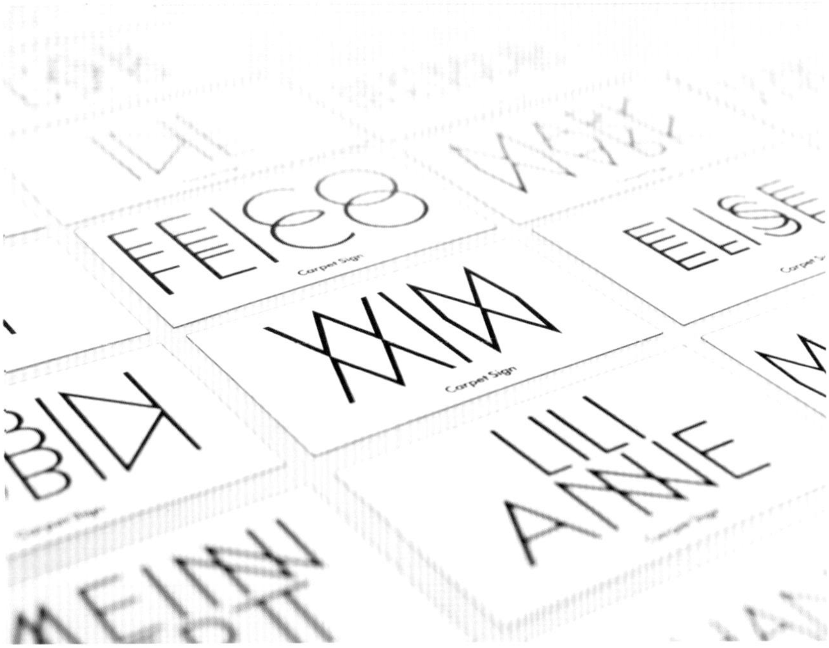

Carpet Sign
Lilain
www.carpetsign.nl

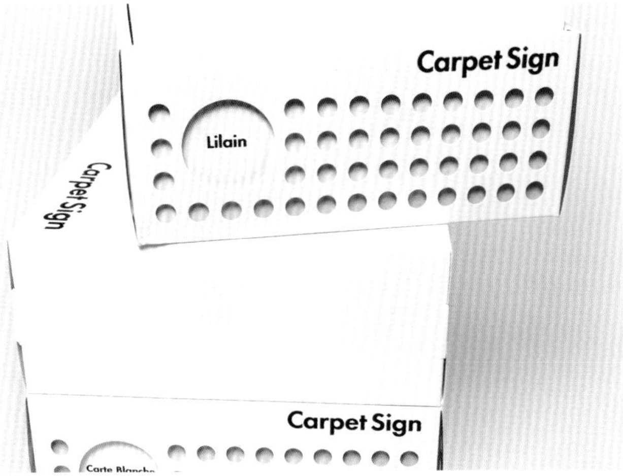
Carpet Sign
Lilain
Carpet Sign
Carpet Sign

Carpet Sign
METRO
POLIS
Design by:
Carpet Sign Studio
Colours by:
Christiane Müller
Carpet Sign
C-Sign Creation
CUSTOM
MADE
In addition to the strong standard collection, custom made rugs are offered: the Carpet Sign Studio is
Carpet Sign
T. +31 (0)493-69 67 23
F. +31 (0)493-69 72 16
info@carpetsign.nl
www.carpetsign.nl
METROPOLIS
Carpet Sign
MADE
Metropolis 270050

arkray
arkray
arkray
arkray
arkray,inc

arkray
arkray,inc

arkray

Deeming "precision" to be the ideal image for a medical testing equipment manufacturer, I strove to express this in the identity for arkray. The logo, grounded in grey, is to laid out as grandly as possible, with ample negative space. The color grey acts to stifle any air of arrogance, while nurturing composure and rational thinking. Our thorough design management extends to every package and testing tools, no matter how small. We feel stifled by excessive cleanliness, but for those products in which we entrust our lives, a sense of cleanliness is necessary. If both customers and employees value cleanliness and an atmosphere in which that is cherished and nurtured, trust will only accelerate.

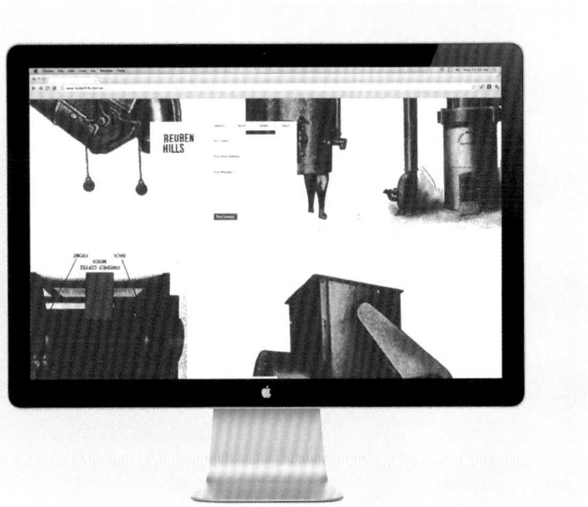

Reuben Hills

Identity design and roll out for Sydney based cafe Reuben Hills. Thanks to Douglas Lance Gibson for the location photos. Architecture design by Herbert & Mason. Additional coffee machine shots by Florian Groehn.

REUBEN
HILLS

Russell Beard
61 Albion Steer
Surry Hills 2010 NSW
02 92115556
+61 402 404 908
russell@reubenhills.com.au
REUBEN
HILLS

REUBEN
HILLS

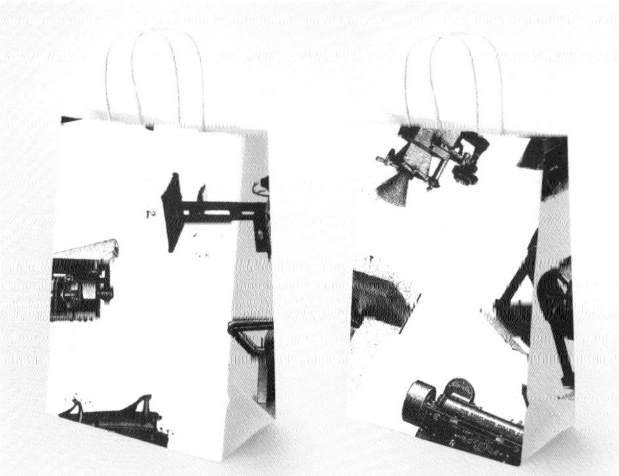

Onde Sonore

Onde Sonore Identity was created for a music festival featuring several bands that took place on a beach during sunset.
Silvia Giulianini was asked to create a visual identity that appealed to a young target audience. As the name of the festival was a play on the word "waves", referring to both the sound waves and the sea waves, Silvia decided to use simple geometric graphic shapes related to the sun and the wave shape, with a colour palette drawn from the colours of the sunset.

Franco Rossi
Rotonda Cadorna, 7
48015 Ravenna
Mobile +39 348 7455540
www.ondesonore.com
ONDE SONORE
ONDE SONORE
Elena Bianchi
Rotonda Cadorna, 7
48015 Ravenna
Mobile +39 348 7455540
www.ondesonore.com
ONDE SONORE
Spett.le Franco Rossi
Rotonda Cadorna, 7 | 48015 Ravenna
Tel. 0544 993045 | Mobile +39 348 7455540
franco@ondesonore.com | www.ondesonore.com
ONDE SONORE

ONDE SONORE
ONDE SONORE

The Apollo Restaurant

We worked in collaboration with a team of visionaries to bring the creative vision of the restaurant to life, including Jonathan Barthelmess - Manly Pavilion, in partnership with Longrain's Sam Christie and architect George Livissianis. Our creative challenge was to align classic beauty and rustic charm with an urban edge. Our solution used modernist typography with a 1930s echo - playing off the architecture of the building. We tested the use of bold fluorescent ink as a branding colour, printing silk screen on simple box board. The menu needed to be both durable and updateable; our solution was to brand a robust, heavy backing board combined with in-house printed sheets – updated daily and fastened with an industrial stationery clip. The Apollo has achieved high ratings in the Sydney Morning Herald and Sydney Magazine.

THE APOLLO
THE APOLLO
THE APOLLO

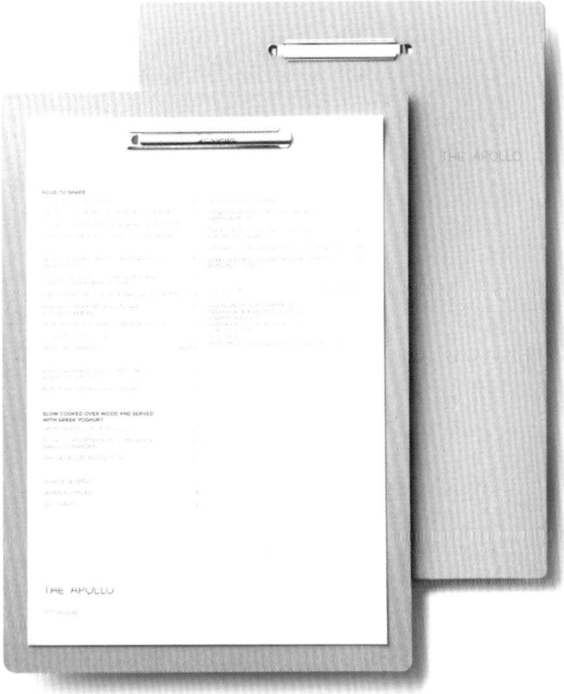
FOOD TO SHARE
SLOW COOKED OVER WOOD AND SERVED
WITH GREEK YOGHURT
THE APOLLO
THE APOLLO

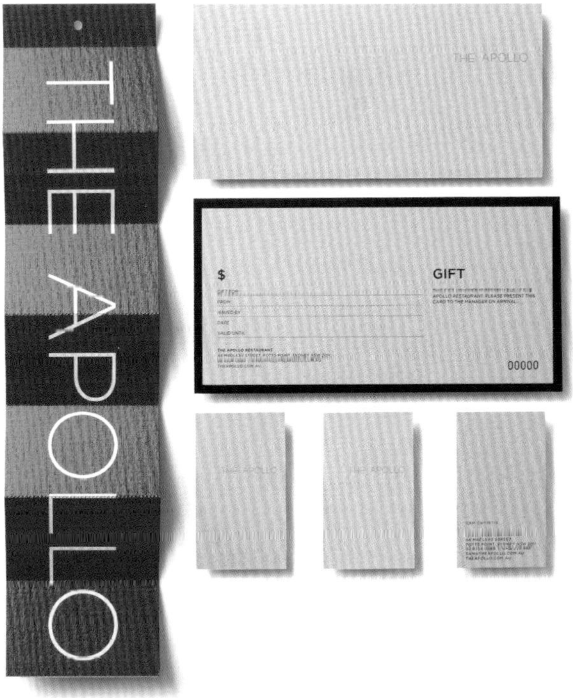
THE APOLLO
THE APOLLO
$
GIFT
THE APOLLO RESTAURANT
00000

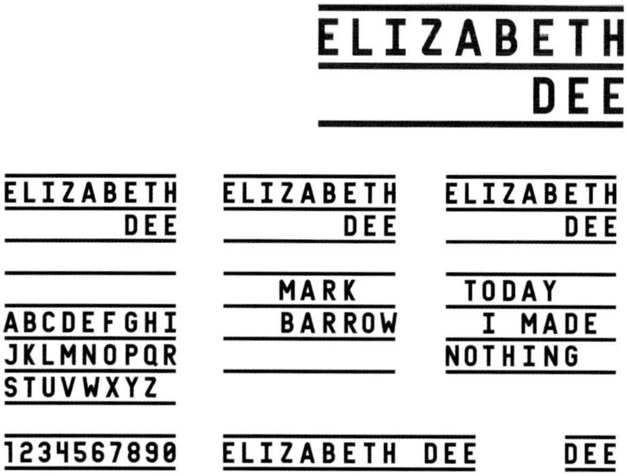

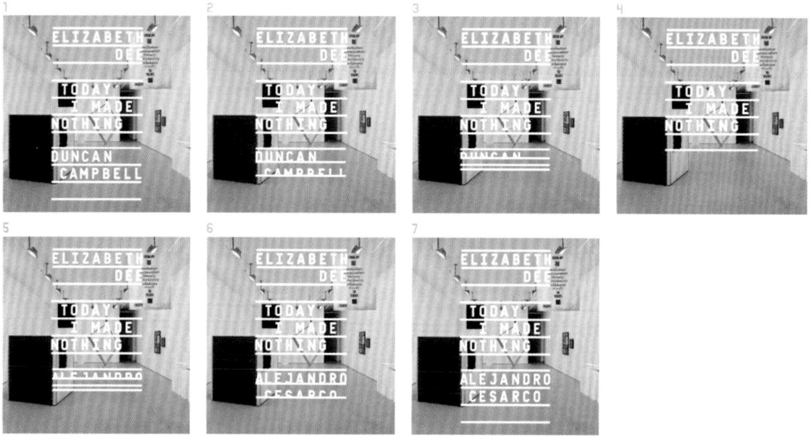

Elizabeth Dee Visual Identity

Jeff designed the visual identity, custom typeface and extensions for an amazing gallery located in Chelsea, NYC.

ELIZABETH
DEE

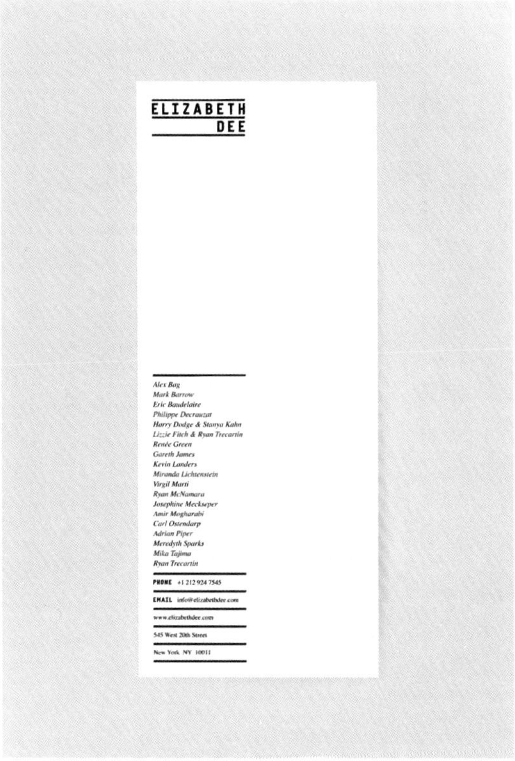
ELIZABETH
DEE
Alex Bag
Mark Barrow
Eric Baudelaire
Philippe Decrauzat
Harry Dodge & Stanya Kahn
Lizzie Fitch & Ryan Trecartin
Renée Green
Gareth James
Kevin Landers
Miranda Lichtenstein
Virgil Marti
Ryan McNamara
Josephine Meckseper
Amir Mogharabi
Carl Ostendarp
Adrian Piper
Meredyth Sparks
Mika Tajima
Ryan Trecartin
PHONE +1 212 924 7545
EMAIL info@elizabethdee.com
www.elizabethdee.com
545 West 20th Street
New York NY 10011

ELIZABETH
DEE
Tim Saltarelli Director
PHONE +1 212 924 7545
MOBILE +1 347 668 7278
SKYPE timsaltarelli
EMAIL tim@elizabethdee.com
545 West 20th Street
York NY 10011

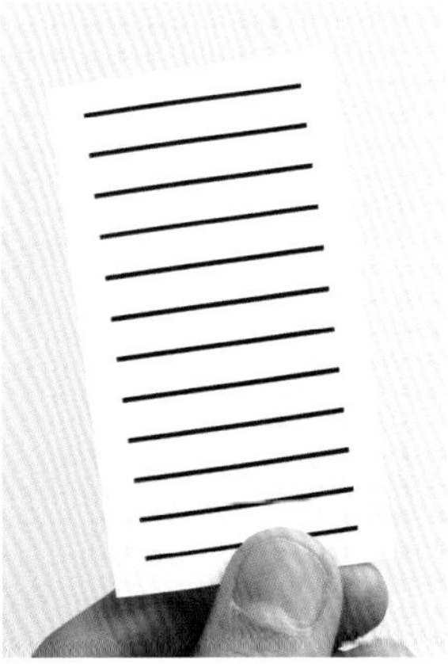

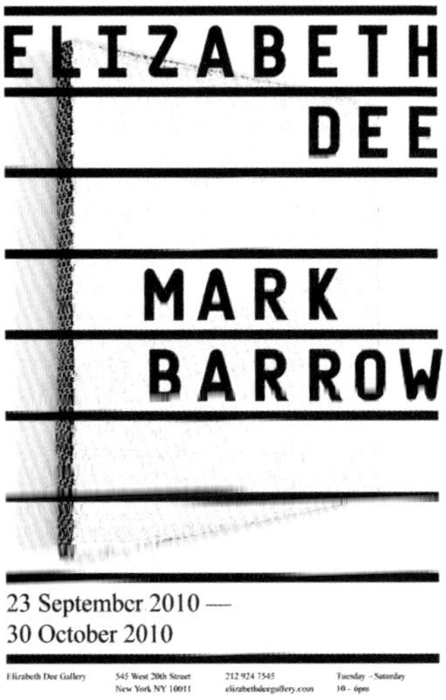
ELIZABETH
DEE
MARK
BARROW
23 September 2010 —
30 October 2010
Elizabeth Dee Gallery
545 West 20th Street
New York NY 10011
212 924 7545
elizabethdeegallery.com
Tuesday – Saturday
10 – 6pm

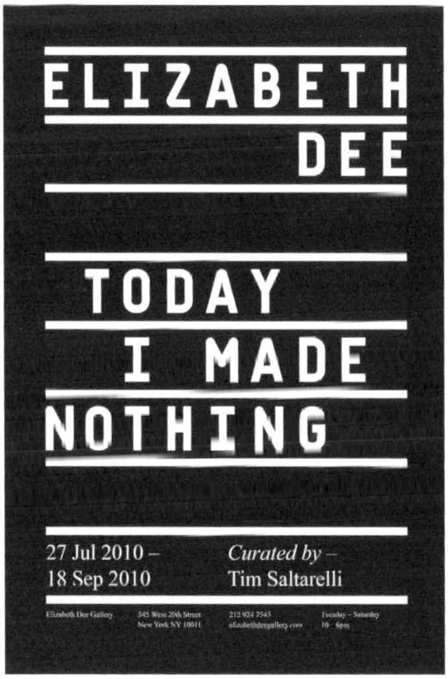
ELIZABETH
DEE
TODAY
I MADE
NOTHING
27 Jul 2010 –
18 Sep 2010
Curated by –
Tim Saltarelli
Elizabeth Dee Gallery
545 West 20th Street
New York NY 10011
212 924 7545
elizabethdeegallery.com
Tuesday – Saturday
10 – 6pm

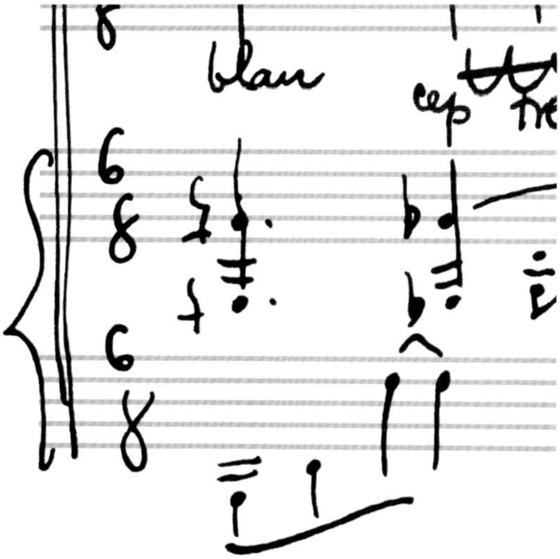

"CANTICEL"
CANÇÓ PER A VEU I PIANO, 1923
LLETRA: JOSEP CARNER
MÚSICA: EDUARD TOLDRÀ
PARTITURA ORIGINAL: BIBLIOTECA

Eduard Toldrà Auditorium

The City Council of Vilanova launched a new music amphitheater for the city in spring of 2011. The corporate identity is based around the identity of the musical score-the starting point for a musician. The five lines of the staff represent the creation of the musician. The building is named after Toldrà Eduard (1895-1962), a famous composer and musician of Vilanova. The logo is accompanied by a horizontal straight line graph and the score, undulating like the sea, pointed like the mountains of Garraf and vertical as the vertical architecture of the new building. Pieces have been published as a handbill, a bookmark, banners and informative signage in the auditorium. One of the most well known musical creations of Eduard is the original score for "Canticel," which is sculpturally represented in the center hall of the building.

AUDITORI
EDUARD
TOLDRÀ
VILANOVA I LA GELTRÚ

AUDITORI
EDUARD
TOLDRÀ
VILANOVA I LA GELTRÚ

AUDITORI
EDUARD
TOLDRÀ
VILANOVA I LA GELTRÚ

L'AUDITORI EDUARD TOLDRÀ
ET CONVIDA AL CONCERT BENÈFIC,
DEL PROPER DIA 20 DE GENER DE 2012,
"LES NITS"

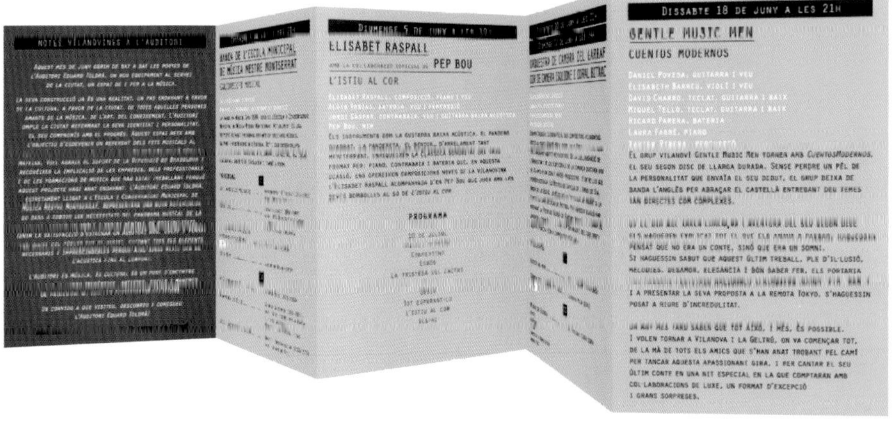
DISSABTE 18 DE JUNY A LES 21H
GENTLE MUSIC MEN
CUENTOS MODERNOS
ELISABET RASPALL
PEP BOU
L'ISTIU AL COR
PROGRAMA

CoPlanner

The new corporate design of CoPlanner, a specialist in the field of "Business-Software for Controlling and Corporate Management", reflects the excellence of the company in two respects. On one hand moodley brand identity tried to accentuate the serious software solutions by using pictures showing architectural and landscape structures. On the other hand those images communicate at the same time openness and breadth, which stand for the flexibility of CoPlanner and their ability to react quickly and effectively to individual customer requirements. The colour gradient used for the stationery reflects the same mix of competent seriousness and animated open modernity as do the textured paper and the mix of typographies used in the editorial design of the magazine. Photography by Gerald Liebminger and Marion Luttenberger.

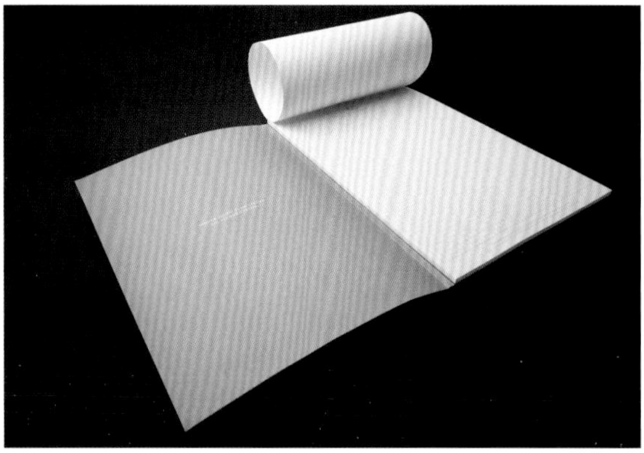

FREIRÄUME

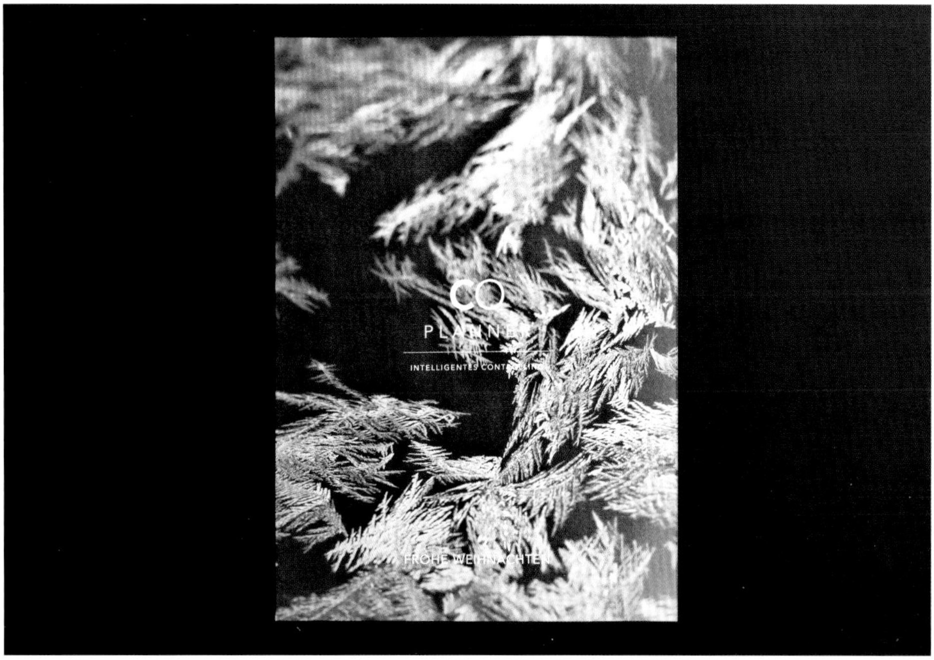
CO

CO
PLANNER
INTELLIGENTES CONTROLLING

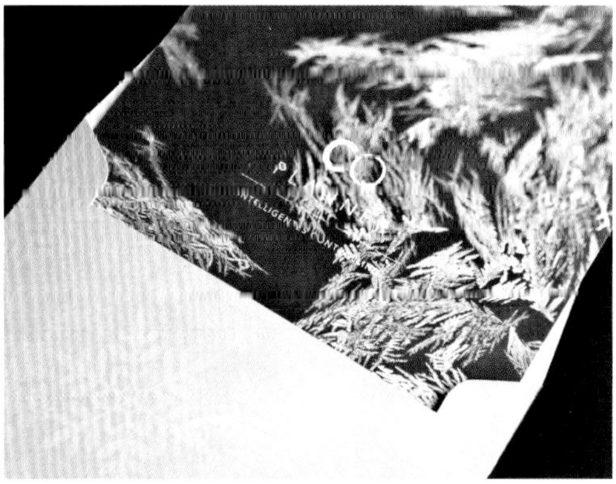

Muñoz Joyeros 1943

Corporate identity for a well-known jewelry brand based in Murcia, which wanted to renew its image. The concept focused on adornment.I wanted to represent this idea on our future identity through adornment with the basic elements and resources of graphic design, typography, colour, basic shapes and glitter. In this way an abstract, flexible, and unusual identity was created.

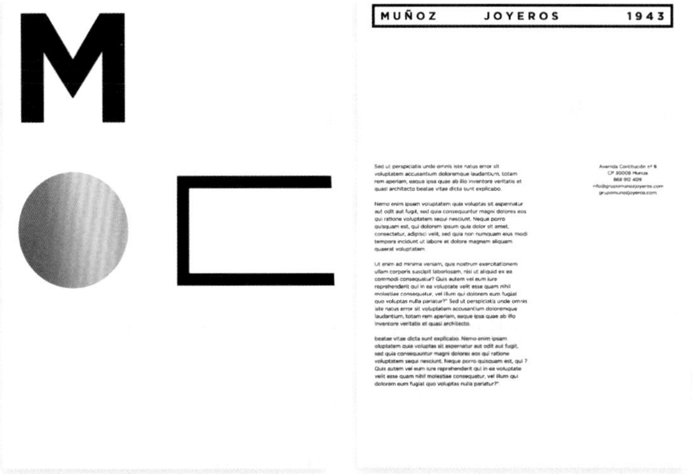

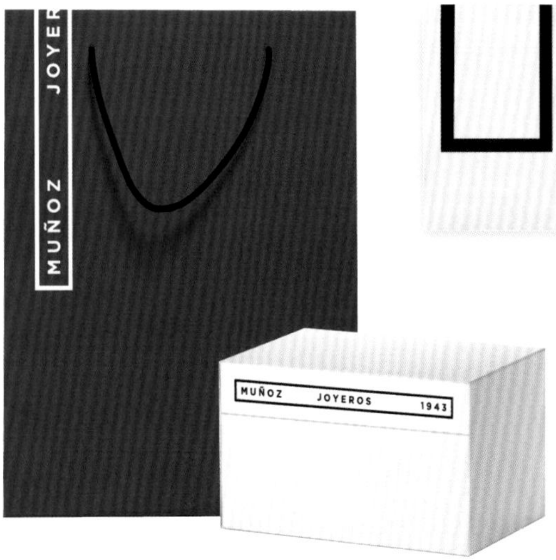

AND Museum

Conceptual rebrand for the Architecture and Design Museum in Los Angeles, a research and education organization dedicated to promoting students and designers through exhibitions.
The Architecture and Design Museum is a leading destination for new designs and concepts in architecture *and* design. The proposed identity embraces the unique personality of the museum, and allows the identity to expand easily into various applications. The transmedia identity includes the website, collateral, environmental design, poster and exhibition catalog.

Bertholo Consulting Identity

Identity and branding for a consulting company. Black foil stamp on gray Sirio Color paper. QR Code detail with a website link on the business card.

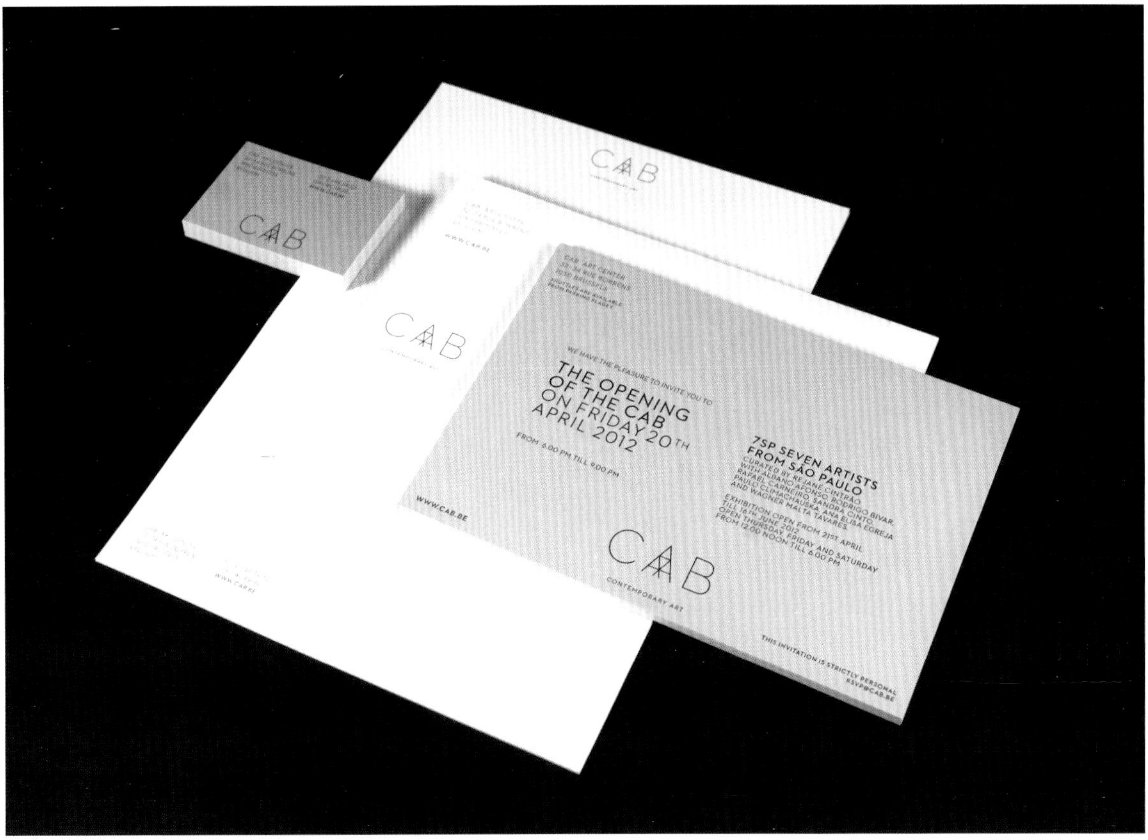

CAB ART CENTER

Visual identity for a new art center in Brussels: logo, website, stationery, invitation…

CAB is a private contemporary art center that opened in April 2012. The center is dedicated to the promotion of contemporary art through the promotion and organization of exhibitions and residencies in its gallery space in Brussels. The goal of the CAB is to actively participate in the diffusion and exchange of Belgian and international contemporary art.

Nederlands Fotomuseum (The Dutch Photomuseum)

The Nederlands Fotomuseum strives to realize outstanding exhibitions in the field of photography. They also manage several national and international collections, as well as the largest archive of Dutch phtography. Studio Beige was asked to restyle and restructure NFM's corporate identity. The new website will be realized at the end of 2012.

EUGÈNE ATGET
VIEUX PARIS

24.SEPT.2011_08.JAN.2012

"I CAN TRUTHFULLY SAY THAT I POSSESS ALL OF VIEUX PARIS"

Met deze grootse tentoonstelling brengt het Fotomuseum voor het eerst ruim 200 foto's van de beroemde Franse fotograaf Eugène Atget (1857–1927) naar Nederland. Atget fotografeerde rond 1900 in Parijs op plaatsen waar de stad nog niet door afbraak en modernisering was aangetast.

Het beeld van het oude Parijs dat uit de foto's van Atget oprijst is uniek, zowel in detaillering als in sfeer, die romantisch en surreëel tegelijk is. Atget behoort tot de internationale top en wordt gezien als de grondlegger van de documentaire fotografie. Hij komt in ieder geschiedenisboek over fotografie voor. Zijn werk inspireerde talloze andere grote fotografen en beeldend kunstenaars, zoals Walker Evans en Man Ray.

Dit is de eerste keer dat werk van Atget in Nederland uitgebreid te zien is. Foto's van Atget zijn uiterst fragiel en mogen zelden reizen. Een unieke kans om dit bijzondere werk van deze meesterfotograaf te zien.

With this ambitious exhibition, the Fotomuseum brings over 200 photographs by the French photographer Eugène Atget to The Netherlands for the first time. Atget photographed in Paris around the turn of the last century, where the city had not yet been affected by demolition and modernisation. The image of the old Paris that emerges from his photos is unique, both for the details and in its atmosphere, which is romantic and surreal at the same time. Atget belongs to the top of international photography and his work inspired countless other great artists, including Walker Evans and Man Ray. Prints by Atget are extremely fragile and are seldom permitted to travel. This is a unique chance to see this exceptional work by a master photographer.

DE DONKERE KAMER
BIJZONDERE VERHALEN

VASTE PRESENTATIE

Ruim 185 jaar Nederlandse fotografie in 22 verhalen, verteld aan de hand van de rijke collectie van het museum. Ontdek hoe de eerste foto's werden gemaakt, volg het liefdesverhaal van Ed van der Elsken en ga mee op jacht met de camera. Beleef het allemaal in *De Donkere Kamer*, de enige tentoonstelling in Nederland over de Nederlandse fotografiegeschiedenis.

Ontwerp Kossmann.dejong
Doe-boekje voor kinderen
5x Springen | € 5
Met dank aan VSBfonds | SNS | REAAL Fonds | Erasmus-stichting | Stichting Bevordering van Volkskracht

STEENBERGEN STIPENDIUM 2011

03.SEP_30.OKT.2011

Gevarieerde tentoonstelling van de genomineerden voor het Steenbergen Stipendium 2011, de 'high potentials' onder Nederlandse fotgrafie studenten. Bezoekers kunnen meestemmen voor de publieksprijs.
Uitreiking 25.okt.2011

ERIK WESSELO
MAASVLAKTE 2

26.NOV.2011_14.JAN.2012

Foto- en filmproject over Maasvlakte 2 in opdracht van het Fotomuseum, Havenbedrijf Rotterdam en SKOR. Wesselo combineert zijn werk van *Maasvlakte 2* met beelden die hij maakte van grote landaanwinningprojecten in het zuiden van India, Zuid-Korea en Dubai.

FOTO NATIONAAL

20.NOV.2011

De jaarlijkse nationale fotosalon voor amateurs van de Fotobond.

National Photo Salon for the Dutch amateur photographers.

VERWACHT | EXPECTED

HET NEDERLANDSE FOTOBOEK 1945 TOT NU

21.JAN_29.APR.2012

nederlands fotomuseum

UITNODIGING | INVITATION

EUGÈNE ATGET
VIEUX PARIS

DE DONKERE KAMER

OPENING 25.SEP.2011_12 UUR

nederlands fotomuseum

EUGÈNE ATGET VIEUX PARIS
24.SEP.2011_08.JAN.2012

STEENBERGEN STIPENDIUM 2011
03.SEP_30.OKT.2011

FOTO NATIONAAL
20.NOV.2011

ERIK WESSELO MAASVLAKTE 2
26.NOV.2011_14.JAN.2012

TENTOONSTELLINGEN NAJAAR_WINTER 2011

Public Gallery Identity

Bark was asked to design the brand identity for this groundbreaking Will Alsop designed arts space in West Bromwich, UK. The brief was to design an identity that would represent the space on an international as well as a national stage. The iconic architecture inspired identity reflects the clean lines of the building allied with bold colours — giving a sense of a "fresh" and modern space within a post industrial area. Bark designed the identity, website, signage and opening collateral.

PUBLIC
GALLERY
PUBLIC
GALLERY
THE PUBLIC GALLERY LTD
1 OVEREND STREET
WEST BROMWICH
WEST MIDLANDS
B70 6EY
UK
SWITCHBOARD: +44 (0) 121 524 2109
WEB: www.publicgallery.org
EMAIL: info@publicgallery.org

PUBLIC
GALLERY
B70 6EY
UK

PUBLIC

Senteurs d'Ailleurs

Senteurs d'Ailleurs is a niche Parfum & Cosmetic Store located in Brussels. The idea behind the logo was to convey different sources of inspiration related to the imagery or myth we all have of a journey into the world of perfumes and scents… The key words for the project were: myth, mystery, alchemy and geometric forms, visual codes and rebuses, diamonds, pirate treasures, literature, and engravings. The visuals within the logo, in the shape of diamond, can be swapped so the logo can be reinvented constantly.

HAUTE PARFUMERIE
SENTEURS D'AILLEURS
HAUTE COSMÉTIQUE
OFFICE
SHOP
DIMITRI MOUTON

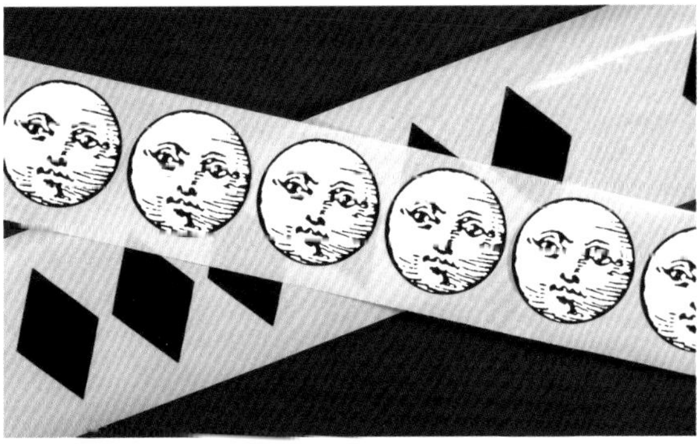

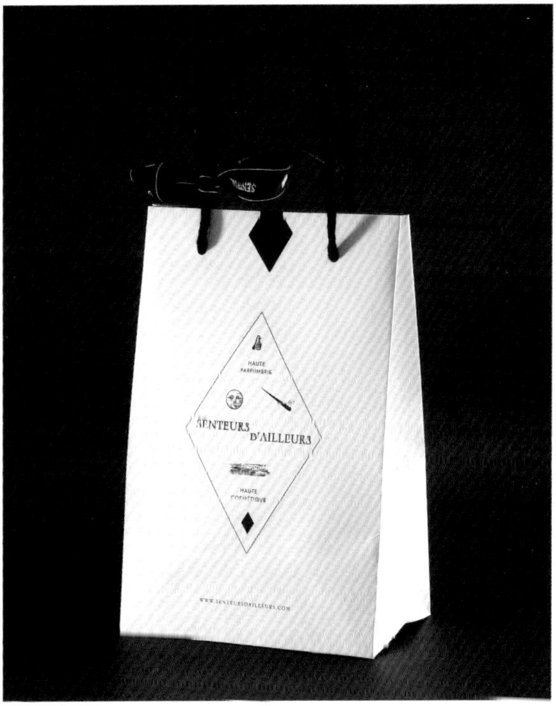
HAUTE PARFUMERIE
SENTEURS D'AILLEURS
HAUTE COSMÉTIQUE
WWW.SENTEURSDAILLEURS.COM

Orange Hive

Emanuele created this branding design for a new creative agency based in Frankfurt. It includes a logo design, print stationery, website layout and the art direction of photography. The company decided to keep the logo but the concept for printed material and the website was changed later on. Photography by Daniel Sax.

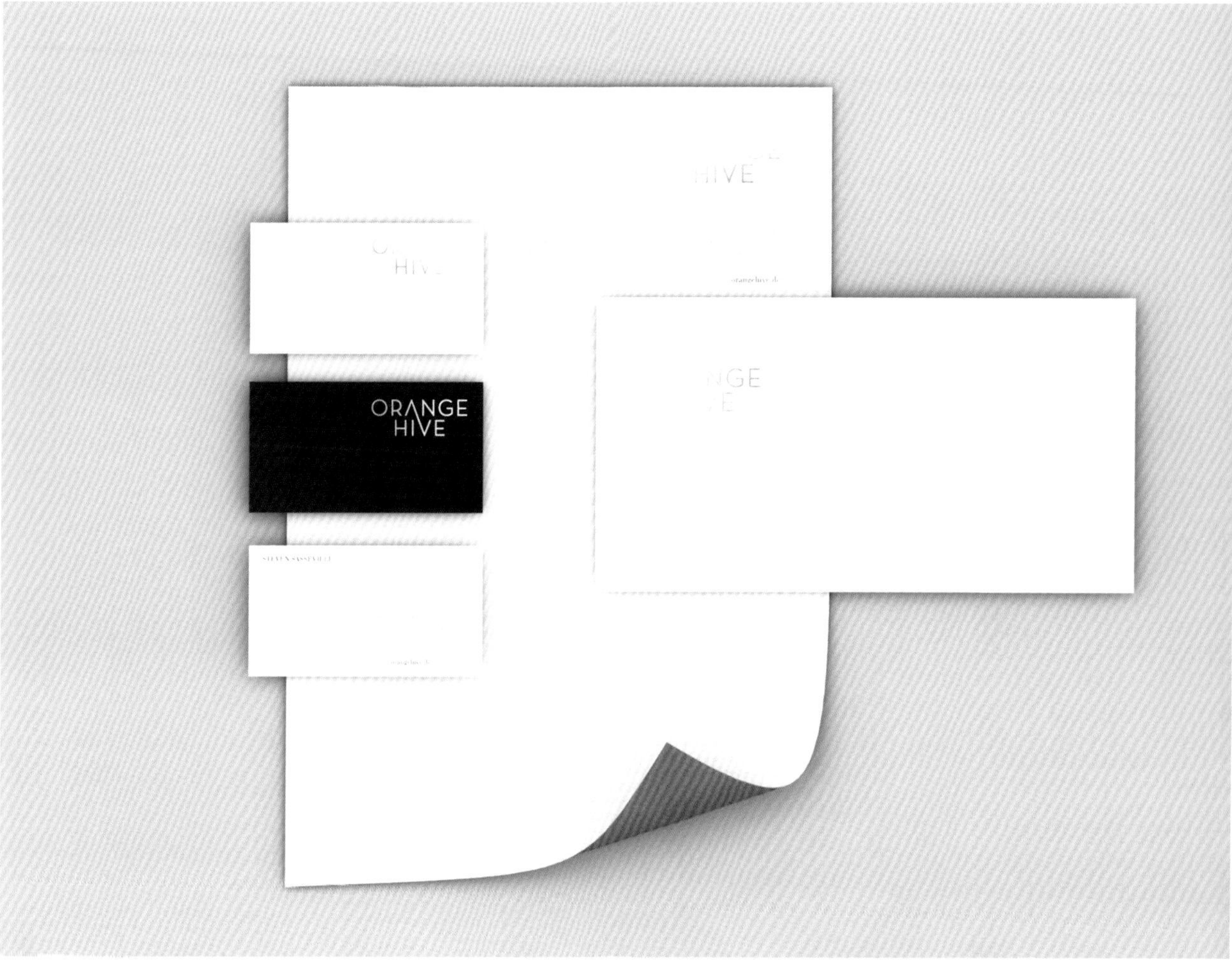
ORANGE
HIVE

ORANGE
HIVE

ORANGE
HIVE

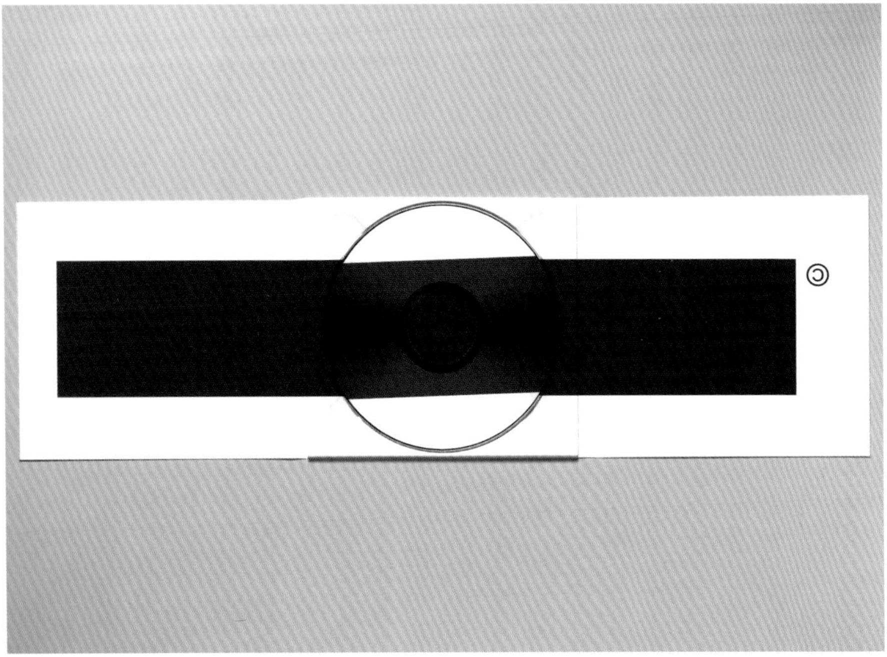

Anonymous

As an exercise in the visual language I asked myself "What if Anonymous went corporate!?" The group would need to button up and streamline its appearance to appear more professional whilst unifying the brand experience. The logotype is anti-authoritative and obviously completely illegible to stick with the roots of the anarchistic group. Colors are used minimally for optimal effect and focus is on the content and logo. This project is neither for nor against the actions by Anonymous, but simply is exploring and playing with the power of visual identity.

[redacted]

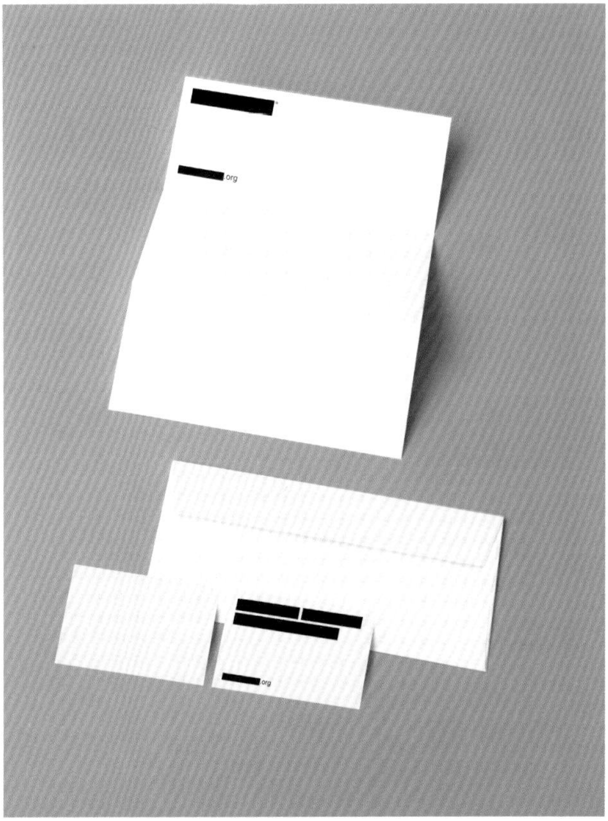
[redacted]
[redacted].org
[redacted]
[redacted].org

[redacted]

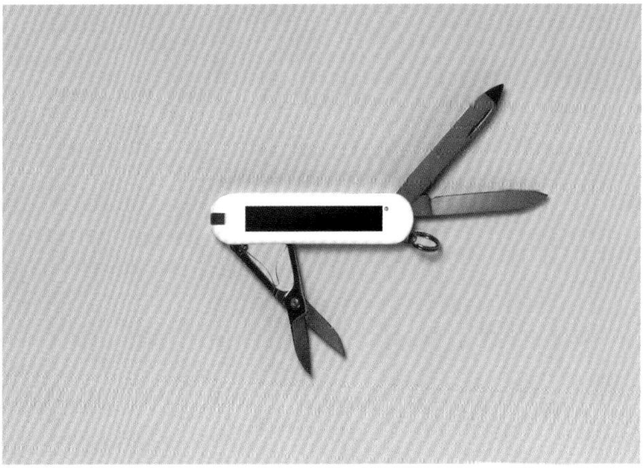
[redacted]

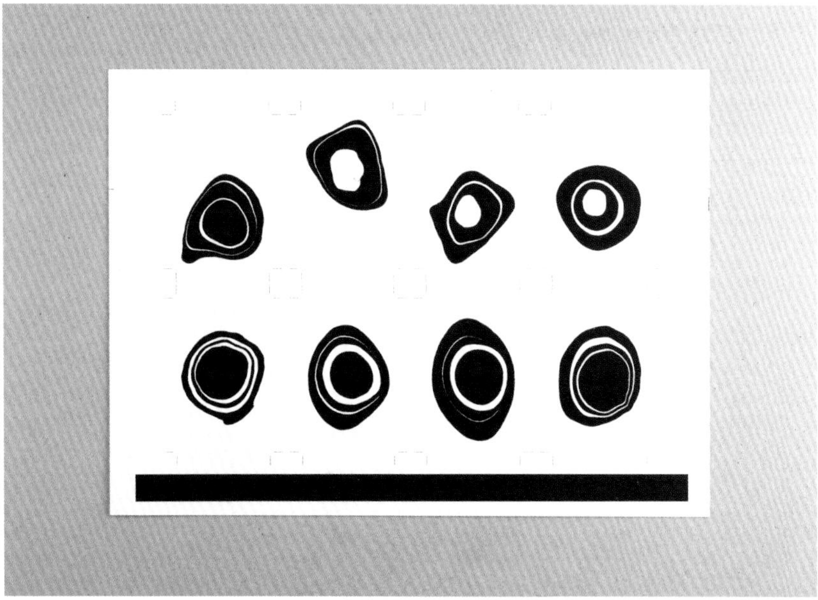

Almighty

Almighty is a company specializing in interior design and home staging that needed a flexible and contemporary approach to its identity while maintaining its classic traditions. We focused on the idea of decoration, and after some research we found an analogy between book covers and wallpaper. We set about creating a pattern of organic shapes using the Japanese technique of Suminagashi marbling. Helped by a connoisseur of this old technique, we experimented with oil, ink and water and ended up with a beautiful random series of signs, similar overall but each one very unique. In post production, we then contrasted the original print material to allow it to be reproduced by an offset machine. The choice of the typeface "Gravur" (designed by Cornel Windlin), gives a technical and industrial feel, contrasting with the free form of the Suminagashi technique. Photography by Yvain Genevay.

•Almighty

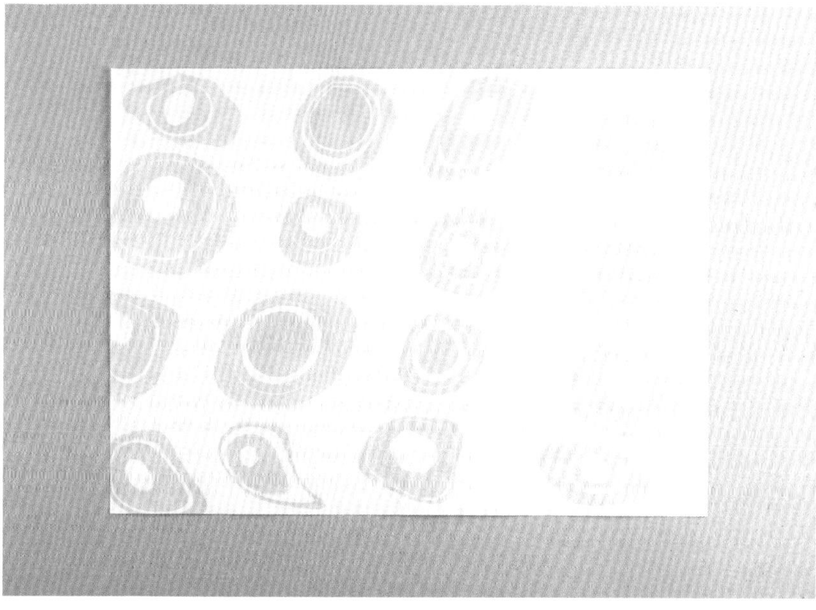

ZOO Praha / ZOO Prague

The competition proposal of corporate design ZOO Prague works on the basis of animal pictograms. The logotype is variable and can operate independently or together with pictograms. Animals in the logo can change as needed; color can be changed as well. These animal pictograms are very important and a characteristic feature of the concept.

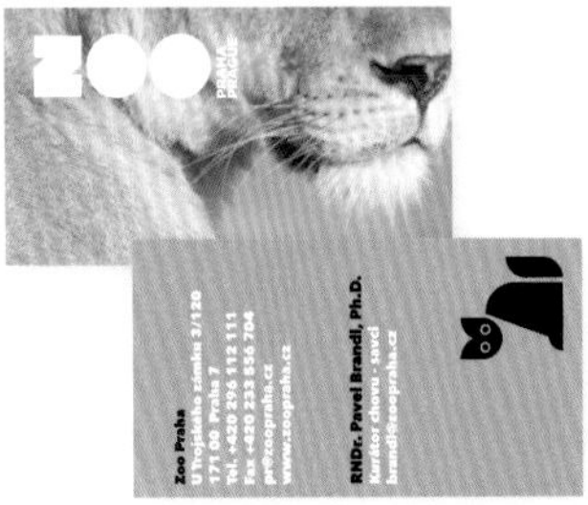

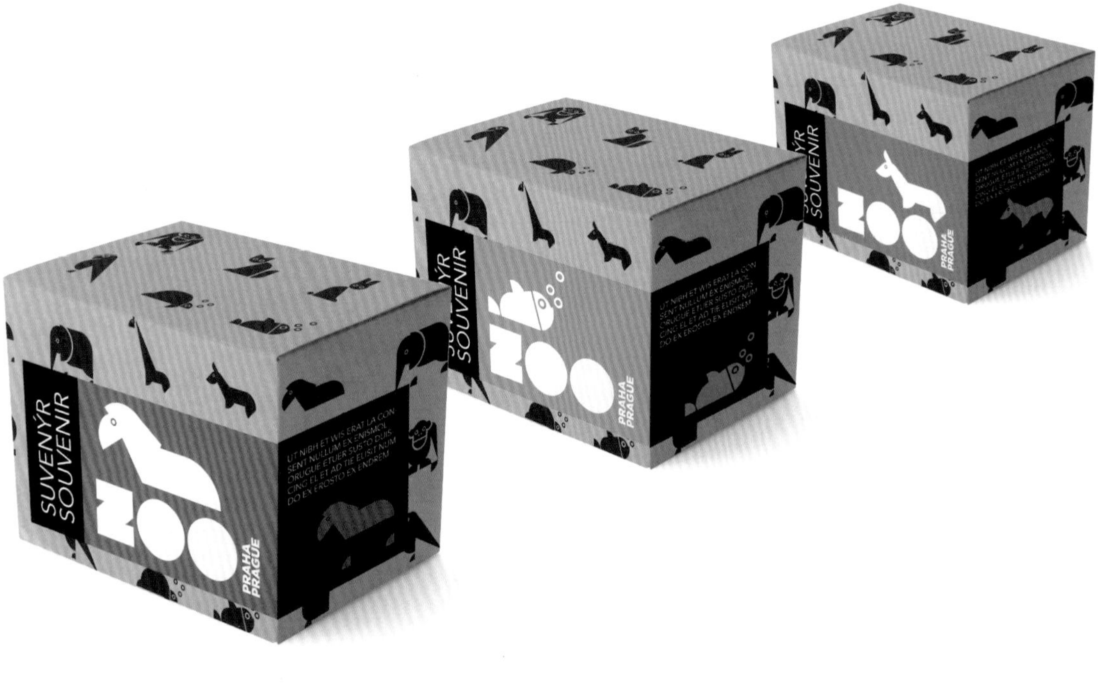

ZOO PRAHA PRAGUE
PTÁCI ZOO PRAHA
EIDUISI BLA CONSE
VULPUTE DEL INIBH.

ZOO PRAHA PRAGUE
PTÁCI ZOO PRAHA
EIDUISI BLA CONSE
VULPUTE DEL INIBH.

ZOO
PRAHA
PRAGUE

JSEM VELMI VZACNY
KUŇ PŘEVALSKÉHO
CHLOUBA ZOO PRAHA!
ZOO PRAHA PRAGUE
ZOO PRAHA PRAGUE

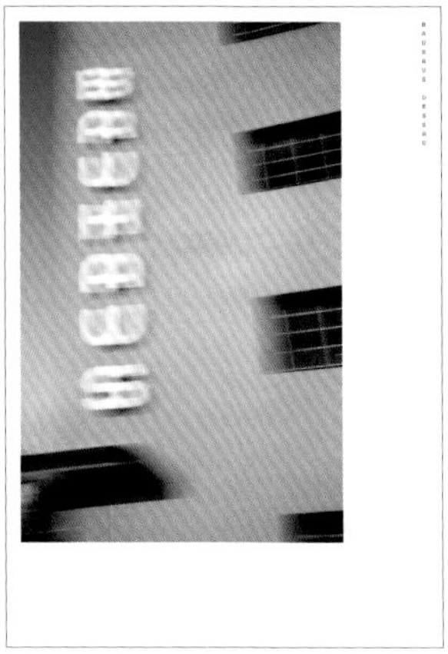

Stiftung Bauhaus Dessau Corporate Identity

The Bauhaus Dessau Foundation commissioned us to develop and design their new corporate identity.
We decided to search for a solution that would relate more to the original ideas of Germany's most influential Modernist school instead of relying on the visual clichés connected to Bauhaus - it seems almost impossible to use circles, squares and triangles nowadays without it coming across as ironic or historicist. Apart from stationery, brochures, posters, tickets, website etc. the new identity also included the redesign of the signage of Gropius' famous Bauhaus building. This factor made it even more important that a clear distinction could be made by visitors between what was a part of the original structure and what new additions we had made.
We thought a generic design would work best in order to make this distinction. The new identity was created by using strict typography, a minimalist layout, standardised formats and no colour. Being the most generic and incidental typeface, Courier was selected as the new corporate font. To guarantee a unique identity we changed the capital "A" of Courier according to Herbert Bayer's well-known logo on the front of the Bauhaus Dessau building. Additionally, the new Bauhaus Dessau logotype is always set vertically. The entire typographic system consists exclusively of common system fonts, an approach connected to the original Bauhaus ideology that demanded functionality and designs based on the potential of mass-production.
Selected Photography by Ola Kolehmainen.

Stiftung Bauhaus Dessau

Stiftung Bauhaus Dessau
Gropiusallee 38
06846 Dessau-Roßlau
Telefon: +49-340-6508-250
www.bauhaus-dessau.de

B A U H A U S D E S S A U

Freikarte
Preis: 0,00 €

30.07.2010 11:02 Frau Gäbler
036943

B A U H A U S D E S S A U

Titel:

Projektleiter:

Datum: Format:

Copyright:

Sommerwerkstatt
„Jugend braucht Zukunft"
10.1.-16.1.2011, Fotodokumentation
© Hans Sommer 2011, Stiftung Bauhaus Dessau

Stiftung Bauhaus Dessau
www.bauhaus-dessau.de

Stiftung Bauhaus Dessau
Gropiusallee 38
06846 Dessau-Roßlau
Germany

www.bauhaus-dessau.de

B A U H A U S D E S S A U

Sommerwerkstatt
„Jugend braucht Zukunft"

10.7.-16.7.2011, Fotodokumentation
Projektleiterin: Elisabeth Kremer
Datum: 27.10.2011
Datenformat: JPG- und PDF-Dateien
© Hans Sommer 2011, Stiftung Bauhaus Dessau

B A U H A U S D E S S A U

Prof. Philipp Oswalt
Direktor

Telefon +49-(0)340-1234-567
Fax +49-(0)340-1234-567
E-Mail abcdefg@bauhaus-dessau.de

Stiftung Bauhaus Dessau
Gropiusallee 38
06846 Dessau-Roßlau
Germany
Telefon +49-(0)340-6508-250
Fax +49-(0)340-6508-226
www.bauhaus-dessau.de

An: HORT
Eike König
Hagelberger Straße 52
10965 Berlin

Betreff: Neukonzeption des visuellen Erscheinungsbildes

Dessau-Roßlau, den 5. Juli 2010

Lieber Eike König,

Die aktuelle Brisanz des Bauhauses liegt nicht in konkreten Objekten oder Formen, sondern in seiner Programmatik, in den Bauhausideen und -methoden. Genau genommen müssen wir hierbei vom Plural sprechen, von den Bauhäusern, und nicht dem Bauhaus. Soweit sich das Bauhaus aus der Bewegung der klassischen Moderne heraushebt und vielleicht tatsächlich einzigartig ist, so deshalb, weil es dem historischen Bauhaus gelungen ist, eine Vielfältigkeit und Widersprüchlichkeit von modernen Gestaltungspraktiken im Rahmen eines Projektes zu bündeln, wie es sonst nie erreicht wurde. Das ungemein fruchtbare lag nicht zuletzt darin begründet, dass an einem Ort Maler, Grafiker, Architekten, Typografen, Theatermacher, Medienkünstler, Stadtplaner, [illegible] und auch Wissenschaftler, Techniker und Ingenieure zusammenwirkten, sich austauschten, stritten und immer wieder [illegible]

Wir haben geordnete Vorstellungen von der Moderne, der Architektur der modernen Sachlichkeit, der abstrakten Kunst, des funktionalen Designs usw. Doch das Eigenwillige des Bauhauses war, dass es eben genau diese Kategorien überwand und die heterogene Gleichzeitigkeit der modernen Avantgarden nicht nur akzeptierte, sondern auch operativ nutzte. Um es mit den letztendlich untauglichen Stilrichtungen und Moden zu umreißen: Es gab am Bauhaus Expressionismus, Konstruktivismus, Funktionalismus, DeStijl, Neue Sachlichkeit, ja auch Dadaismus und vieles mehr. Obgleich es in den einzelnen Phasen der Bauhausgeschichte dominante Haltungen gab, so ist der [illegible], dass diese Widersprüchlichkeiten an einem Ort gleichzeitig präsent waren.

mit freundlichen Grüßen

Prof. Philipp Oswalt

[illegible]
1/1

Stiftung Bauhaus Dessau
Postfach 1405
06846 Dessau-Roßlau
Germany

An: HORT
Eike König
Hagelberger Straße 52
10965 Berlin

B A U H A U S D E S S A U

Prof. Philipp Oswalt Direktor

Stiftung Bauhaus Dessau
Gropiusallee 38
06846 Dessau-Roßlau
Germany
Telefon [illegible]
Fax [illegible]
E-Mail abcdefg@bauhaus-dessau.de
www.bauhaus-dessau.de

Diana Schmidt Servicebereich

Stiftung Bauhaus Dessau
Gropiusallee 38
06846 Dessau-Roßlau
Germany
Telefon +49-(0)340-1234-567
Fax +49-(0)340-1234-567
[illegible]
www.bauhaus-dessau.de

&Larry
www.andlarry.com

&Larry begins every project by putting the name of our client or creative partner before our own. This spirit of collaboration and mutual respect is reflected in the thinking that goes into each piece of work. We believe that art and design shouldn't exist in separate vacuums. Be it commercial or experimental, &Larry always seeks to create works that are honest, functional and expressive beyond aesthetics. The studio has adopted the Eames motto of "Take your pleasure seriously" and examples of this philosophy can be seen in a diverse body of work from posters and print campaigns to our series of Singapore-inspired art objects.
P058-059

2 ONS
www.studio2ons.nl

We are driven by our passion for visual communications. The combination of thinking in systems and grids on the one hand and designing intuitively on the other, results in effective solutions for complex design tasks.
P042-043

A.Stein
astein.fr

A.Stein lives and works in France as a freelance graphic designer. Several years of practice, while he worked for architecture studios, photographers, and art galleries enabled him to develop an orderly methodology and develop his passion for beautiful printed objects. He thinks in terms of functionalism and timelessness, and strongly believes that a well considered use of materials and print processes makes an important difference to the end project. The attention to detail, the use of a simple aesthetic and search for clever and effective solutions are the basis of his approach to design.
P208-209

A3 Collectif
www.a3collectif.ch

Founded in 2010, A3 is a small design studio based in Lausanne (Switzerland), composed of two graphic designers and a communication designer. Basically, three enthusiasts who share common goals: cooperation and creation. A3 is specialized in visual identity, editorial design, illustration and poster. The group also meets the demand for creative publishing, record covers, and labels. Animated by the same impulses, A3 group regularly participates in events of illustration, street art and gallery exhibitions. Attracted by design, contemporary art, photography and more generally urban trends, the artistic desires of A3 have no limits.
P226-227

Akihiro Kumagaya
alekole.jp

Born in 1984, Akihiro Kumagaya is a designer and director of ALEKOLE. During his design career, he has won several design awards, which demonstrate that his woks can leave people deeply impressed. In 2011, he was an award winner of the Sign Design Award 2011 in Japan.
P050

Alex Dalmau
alexdalmau.com

Alex Dalmau is an art director based in Barcelona. He is specialized in graphic design, branding and corporate identity. After graduating from Image and Design School (IDEP), he worked at various advertising agencies and design studios like Animal-BCN, Larsson-Duprez, Creatica and began working as a freelancer in 2011. He has worked for clients like Progess, Mandarin Oriental Barcelona, Carolina Herrera, Adidas, Ricola, Font Vella, Reig Capital and others.
P012-013

Alonglongtime
www.alonglongtime.me

Alonglongtime is a Hong Kong based multi-disciplinary design house. We are dedicated to brand identity, printed matter, and packaging for clients from corporate, leisure, retail and art & cultural areas. We do believe not everything can stay forever there are some things worth fighting for.
P156-157

Andfold Studio
www.andfold.co.uk

Andfold is an independent design studio established by Brett Wilkinson in 2010. The studio specializes in creative services for print, branding, digital media and advertising. We're passionate about our work, approaching every project with an open mindset and a strong focus on practical, engaging and carefully considered visual communication. We work in partnership with our clients, encouraging involvement right from the start of each project whilst our collaborative approach allows us to work with a growing network of photographers, artists, illustrators and designers to further our creative output.
P108-109

Andrés Guerrero
www.behance.net/aannddeerr

I am a graphic designer born in Murcia (Spain) in 1983. I completed my Superior Studies in Design in Murcia in the year 2008. I combined design studies with my professional activities. I started my career with three of the companies which were the best known in my city. During my years of experience I have specialized in corporate identity, packaging and editorial design. In my projects, I think the concept is more important than the graphic aspect. I synthesize untill I get a convincing image, I take great care with typography and I try to avoid trends so that each project survives the passing of time.
P278-279

Angel Souto Creative Studio
www.angelsouto.es

We are a multidisciplinary creative studio with over 12 years experience. We specialize in the creation and development of complete brand identity, design and web development and graphic design. Our work has been recognized internationally at conferences, magazines, art publications and renowned websites of the world specializing in design.
P128-129

Aoki
www.aoki.se

Aoki, founded in 2009, is a small design agency located in Gothenburg, Sweden. Today there are 5 people in the studio. We work a lot with fashion and different culture projects. Our biggest client is Polarn o Pyret, a Swedish retailer concern established in Europe.
P181

ARE WE DESIGNER
www.arewedesigner.com

We are ARE WE DESIGNER, a Cologne based design studio founded by Janina Braun, Daniela Kempkes and Sascha van den Bloock and completed with the outstanding Graphic Designer Ruth Biniwersi. We don't have a circle of advisors, client managers, hordes of interns, or even a human resources department. We're much smaller; we're more efficient, which allows our clients to benefit from our professionalism, our courage, our honesty and authenticity. We love what we do and we take each project to heart. Our clients should be bold, because we are, too.
P220-221

artentiko
www.artentiko.com

We were born for brands, to create new ones and revitalize those that already exist.

We design for brands; we carry the visual aspect of their identity.

We think for brands; we use our knowledge to support their growth.

We realize ourselves for brands, because we love being surrounded by good things.
P080-081, 266-267

Ascender
www.ascender.com.au

How many design consultancies really explain what they do? At Ascender, we clarify and communicate what your business stands for, helping it stand out. We make messages visible and meaningful, by giving them shape and life – and the power to inform and persuade people. It takes clear, inspired communication and consistency across all visible expressions of a business, supported by trusted relationships and 30 years of combined experience. What it does is move minds and behavior in ways that meet business goals.
P284, 298-299

atipo
atipo.es

atipo is a small multidisciplinary studio founded in early 2010 by Raúl García del Pomar and Ismael González and based in Gijón, Spain. After several years working for others in branding consultancy, web design and graphic design we thought it was time to launch a personal project that allowed us to develop the work from a personal point of view. Our background in Fine Arts allows us to combine different disciplines, such as typography, photography, painting, illustration and video and produce each work using experimentation.
P198-199

Atipus
www.atipus.com

Atipus is a graphic communication studio, created in Barcelona in 1998. We are a team of expert professionals, trained in various disciplines; corporate identity, art direction, packaging design, and web services. Our aim is to communicate through good graphic work that is both simple and conceptual.

P224-225

Barfutura
www.barfutura.com

Barfutura is a Madrid based creative studio founded in 2003. We are a multidisciplinary team that prioritizes the concept, execution and attention to detail in order to find the most effective solution for every project. The broad range of skills we have in all aspects of design from corporate identity to animation, interactive design, exhibitions and events means we are able to produce work for every platform of communication. As a result, we are able to explore what is possible for a project and ensure that every client has a well rounded outcome and can reach their audience in the best possible way.

P240-241

Bark
www.barkdesign.net

Bark is a design agency founded on the belief that good design can drive revenue for clients and inspire growth. Bark is a small team providing bespoke branding solutions for a broad range of clients. We design what you want when you need it.

P312-313

be-pôles
www.be-poles.com

be-pôles is a creative studio dedicated to the graphic representation of brands. With its "Graphik Design™, Identity & Culture" global approach, be-poles creates lasting visual identities that respect the universes of its clients. be-pôles's prior clients include Agnes b., Colette, Louis Vuitton, Merci, Sotheby's, Théâtre des Champs Elysées, and Wool and the Gang.

P034-035

Berger & Föhr
bergerfohr.com

Berger & Föhr is a Boulder, Colorado based multidisciplinary design studio. We practice cohesive visual communication characterized by modernism, minimalism and the search for objectivity. We employ a comprehensive methodology emphasizing clear and concise communication – to create lasting, considered work. Our studio exists to support businesses, organizations, and brands dedicated to the development of socially and environmentally responsible products, ideas, information and assets. We are committed to the triple bottom line — people, planet and profit and run our studio accordingly.

P018-019

Beyond the Pixels
btpdesign.com

Beyond the Pixels is a full service design consultancy. Our local and international clientele includes listed companies and start-ups, as well as various cultural and government organizations.

We work on a broad range of projects, from building brands and concept development to solving complex design problems for screen, print, products and environments. At Beyond the Pixels we establish lasting relationships with clients who respect our professional advice, values and creative expertise. Our permanent team is comprised of professional designers Che Douglas, Kareen Clark and Tass Gyenes. Collectively we possess a breadth of expertise and a wealth of experience in all things design.

P144-145, 162-163

Bielke+Yang
www.bielkeyang.com

Bielke+Yang is an ambitious and creatively driven graphic design studio specializing in identity, branding, art direction and web interaction. We believe in captivating long-term design solutions, strategic problem solving and precise communication. Attention to detail and a strong conceptual base is key as we endeavor to produce design with intelligence, integrity and effectiveness.

P154-155, 234-235

Biquini
www.estudiobiquini.com

Biquini represents a small design studio founded by two graphic designers Álex Sánchez and Sergio Palao. Being passionate about graphic design, we offer a wealth of experience through every stage of our projects; from concepts in the creative process to the physical production of pieces. We believe that design is a creative, sensitive and powerful tool capable of offering us different points of view on the world we live in. Design makes the world a better place that's more stimulating, understandable and attractive.

P070-071

Blank
www.blank.com.pt

Blank is Alexandra Mendes' independent design consultancy, offering services of. creative direction, branding, packaging, print, editorial, writing, and design thinking. Blank focuses on making tailored projects to find engaging design solutions to implement meaningful communication strategies. From concept to completion, by filling the blanks with fresh, provocative ideas, Blank intends to bring content to the table. The aim is to communicate!

P021, 074-075

Blok Design
www.blokdesign.com

Blok is a design studio specializing in brand identities and experiences, packaging, exhibit design, installations and editorial design. We steep ourselves in the world around us, seek out the normal, the abnormal, the mundane, the exciting, the current, the obsolete, the inspiring, and the disheartening and then use what we see to create surprising, compelling ways to move people. And we do it by collaborating with highly talented thinkers from around the world, taking on initiatives that blend cultural awareness and a love of art and humanity to advance society and business alike.

P026-027

Bomo Grafistas
www.bomo.es

Patricia Bolinches and Beatriz Montañana have been partners of Bomo Grafistas for 10 years. Their customers are mostly small firms, however they have also worked for significant public entities.

In short, their work focuses on corporate identity and editorials, but they do not strictly adhere to the professional area, and always look for new opportunities and challenges. Hence, they continue to submit their personal projects to competitions in order to explore and develop their interests and ideas. Among their recent awards are two silver LAUS, for naming and corporate identity.

Their purpose is to never stop doing what they do best: keep learning.

P179

Bond
www.bond.fi

We are a creative agency focused on branding and design. We work for clients who value creative and practical ideas. We demonstrate our expertise through our work rather than talking, because design is, first and foremost, a craft for us. We design, visualize and define brands in a way that helps companies differentiate themselves from the competition. This can mean creating brand identities, branded environments, packaging, experiential web services or advertising.

P014-015

Branch
thelondonbranch.com

Branch is an independent design consultancy based in the heart of London. We are an experienced team working across many disciplines and believe that the key to good design and communication is simplicity. Our services include identities, branding and strategy, design for print, web, art direction and advertising.

P068-069, 180

BRUNSWICKER
www.brunswicker.dk

BRUNSWICKER is an interdisciplinary design studio established in [illegible]. Based in the heart of Copenhagen, BRUNSWICKER works primarily on art direction, identity design and graphic communication for brands within the fashion, lifestyle, design and media industries. Furthermore, the studio cooperates closely with major players in communication and product development to ensure a streamlined process and a cohesive result.

P090-091, 134-135

Bunch
www.bunchdesign.com

Bunch is a leading creative design studio offering a diverse range of work, including identity, literature, editorial, digital and motion. Established in 2002 with an international reach, from London to Zagreb, Bunch has an in-house team of specialists to deliver intelligent and innovative cross-platform solutions of communication design. Over the years they have been commissioned by many blue chip companies as well as younger brands and artistic industries. They've built an impressive client base that covers many styles and disciplines, such as BBC, Nike, Diesel, Sony, Sky and Red Bull and others...

P244-245

BÜRO UFHO
www.ufho.com

BÜRO UFHO is a creatively-led design studio focusing on developing creative solutions for clients across the fields of art, fashion, music and the advertising industry. A boutique studio specializing in providing creative and art direction, brand development, graphic design, and illustration services, BÜRO UFHO helps clients define and position their brand in an ever increasingly saturated market. BÜRO UFHO also collaborates with advertising agencies to help some of the world's most famous brands in their advertising and branding efforts by providing unique art direction and cutting-edge imagery.

P048-049, 082

busybuilding
www.busybuilding.com

busybuilding is a multi-disciplinary design agency based in Athens, founded in 2007 by Dimitris Gkazis. busybuilding's diverse team of specialized experts consists of creative people working to build brands. Their main objective is the creation and implementation of contemporary visual communication concepts, through print, spatial and digital design services and solutions. busybuilding is a member of EDEE, the Greek association of advertising and communication agencies and also belongs to Design lobby.

P130-131, 132-133, 210

BVD
www.bvd.se

BVD was founded in 1997 by Catrin Vagnemark and Carin Blidholm. It is a design and branding agency specialized in every physical touchpoint of a brand, in and around a retail environment. Our approach is based on a combination of consumer insight, business focus, ideas and design. We view design as a strategic marketing tool. As such, its primary role is to communicate the brand in a relevant way, and to deliver concrete and measurable results.

P216-217

clase bcn
www.clasebcn.com

clase bcn is a graphic design and visual communication studio in Barcelona made up of a team of ten young, international, multidisciplinary professionals whose work has won a number of awards. We work on all areas of design, but pay particular attention to typeface and the element of surprise. When we take a project on, we see to all phases of the strategic and creative process and come up with specific, innovative and distinctive languages following a coherent, exacting approach in accordance with the needs of each project.

P288-289

Cocolia
www.cocolia.cat

Cocolia creative studio is located in a small street of Palm Baix, in Barcelona. Specializing in corporate identity, art direction, editorial design, illustration, advertising and website design, Cocolia differentiates itself by a restless spirit, a will for self-improvement in each project, personal attention to the client and a Mediterranean sensibility. Cocolia likes to solve every job with creative solutions and new graphic forms, taking into account the needs of every client, always with the same high level of motivation. At Cocolia, we aspire to do things well and enjoy the creative process and end result.

P257, 302-303

Codefrisko
www.codefrisko.be

Codefrisko is a graphic design and art direction studio specialized in culture, fashion, architecture, design and the food industry. Our expertise ranges from acting as a think tank to doing graphic design and photo shoots to providing online solutions, and much more.

P309, 314-315

Daniel Brokstad
www.danielbrokstad.com

Daniel Brokstad is a 24 year old graphic designer and photographer from Stavanger, Norway. He is currently employed full time at Procontra, but still does freelance in his spare time. Graphic design and photography is not only his work, but a lifestyle he has chosen to follow. He likes to do things a little different, put his own style to print which gives him a good sense of achievement and usually makes the client happy with getting something out of the ordinary as well.

P242-243

Demian Conrad Design
www.demianconrad.com

Created in 2007, the Demian Conrad Design studio is based in Lausanne, Switzerland. Working mainly in the cultural field and the leisure industry, the studio lends its expertise to everything related to events communication and visual identity. Multidisciplinary, the studio favors a "lateral thinking" approach with the aim of finding creative, destabilizing solutions and forms of avant-garde, cutting-edge, hard-hitting communication. Projects successfully carried out by the studio include the identity of the Gabbani brand, the campaign for the Lausanne Underground Film Festival.

P138-139, 320-321

Design Ranch
www.design-ranch.com

Design Ranch is a nationally recognized design agency, specializing in lifestyle branding and corporate collateral. We don't pitch hay, we pitch ideas. We love what we do. Logos, print, packaging, art direction, and interactive design... the whole shebang. As a small but saucy design firm, we're allowed to do things a little differently. That means, while the other guys are doodling on their cocktail napkins, we are cranking out Grade-A, high quality work.

P238-239

Designbydave
www.designbydave.co.uk

Designbydave is a small independent design consultancy based in Manchester, UK. I work with a number of clients from small businesses through to larger companies. My work is often mainly focused on identity work — specializing in creating ideas based on print and web work for lovely people!

P182-183

DEUTSCHE & JAPANER
www.deutscheundjapaner.com

DEUTSCHE & JAPANER studio was initiated in 2009 and offers expertise in various disciplines, such as graphic design, product design, interior design, illustration and scenography as well as conceptual creation and strategic brand escort. The studio focuses on communication, regardless of its physical condition, environmental, haptical or visual, but always with regard for sustainable experiences.

P114-115, 116-117

Dimo Trifonov
www.di-t.com

Born in Bulgaria, Dimo Trifonov is currently living in London, UK. He has been doing all kinds of visual arts since 2006. For the last couple of years he has gained some experience in advertising, art direction and photography. He is simply exhilarated by everything visual.

P246-247

Elaine Michell
www.elainemichell.com

After graduating from the acclaimed University College Falmouth's BA (hons) in Graphic Design, Elaine became a designer at Allies Design, the leading design agency for independent food retailers and producers. Elaine is now a freelance designer working with international agencies, brands and private clients alike. Her expertise and experience allows her to work with projects ranging from brand strategies & concepts, to identities, packaging and web design. Although stationery will always remain a firm favorite!

P185

Emanuel Cohen
www.26lettres.com

Emanuel Cohen is a Montreal-based multidisciplinary graphic designer who graduated in 2011 from the Université du Québec à Montréal (UQAM), with a B.A in graphic design and a B.F.A in design & computation arts from Concordia University in Montreal. He currently works for the Montreal based graphic design firm Paprika.
P060-061

Emanuele Cecini
www.emanuelececini.com

Emanuele Cecini is an Italian Art Director who has been living and working in Milan, London, Copenhagen and Frankfurt. He has an eye for details and simplicity, with belief that clean, simple and well finished design can communicate strongly, more so than elaborate design.
P150-151, 316-317

Eskimo
www.eskimodesign.ru

Design studio "Eskimo" (Murmansk) works in the field of creation of logos, identities, websites and illustrations. We give much prominence to each client, helping to solve the goals of promotional development for business.
P092-093

Estúdio Campo
www.estudiocampo.com.br

Estúdio Campo was founded in 2009 by São Paulo designers Carolina Aboarrage and Paula Tinoco. Estúdio Campo's work is characterized by a focus on research: each project is approached individually, involving an intense period of searching for and testing the right references and solutions to help clients achieve their ambitions. Aboarrage and Tinoco's vast experience and repertoire play a key role in the research process, producing innovative and functional designs.
P262-263

F33
www.fundacion33.com

F33 is a group of agencies in that is present in Madrid, Santiago de Compostela and Murcia. It was founded in 2006 and since that year it has been collaborating with clients from the artistic sector. F33 works closely with architects (Barbarela Studio, Ecoproyecta) on different projects such as Taller de Arquitectura de la Universidad de Alicante. F33 has won national and international [illegible] which earn the agency great trust from clients.
P178

Face
www.designbyface.com

Founded in 2006, Face is an intelligence-driven super modernist design studio, based in Monterrey, Mexico, with work including design solutions, advertising, editorial projects and custom publishing, corporate identity, web design and brand development. As sensible creators, who understand brands and their undeniable emotional connection to humans, we form a close connection between our client and its target market. Through this personalized process, and based on our expertise and know-how, our clients achieve an outstanding and desirable end result.
P084-085, 232, 233

FBA. – Ferrand, Bicker & Associados
www.fba.pt

FBA. is a Coimbra, Portugal based design studio with print, identity, exhibition, signage and interactive work developed with clients of different sizes and status from both the private and public sectors. FBA's permanent team's competencies and experience are further expanded by professionals hired for specific projects as well as by our direct linkage to a number of partner companies working in complementary sectors.
P285

FBDI STUDIO
www.estudiofbdi.com

FBDI is a creative studio with its offices located in Buenos Aires, Argentina. Our goal is to provide every project and client with original ideas that express and represent the brand´s potential. We believe in the high impact of ideas and design and apply this concept to branding and brand communication. Federico Batemarco, the studio's director, founded FBDI over ten years ago with the intention of creating and enhancing national and international brands through graphic and industrial design and art direction. With incalculable experience in luxury and fashion brands, the studio works in different industries and segments.
P164-165, 218-219

FEB Design
www.feb-design.com

FEB Design is a design collective based in Oporto, Portugal, that has been developing multidisciplinary projects since 2009, specializing in corporate identity, branding, signage systems, websites, packaging, exhibition and book design.
P051, 062-063

Felani Yap
www.felaniyap.com

Felani Yap is a graphic designer from Indonesia, currently residing in Birmingham, United Kingdom. She has been interested in fashion photography and typography ever since high school, which is why she chose design when she [illegible] in college. However, after learning more about the design field, she realized that she loves to portray personality in design more than capturing great photos. Thus she is now into branding and editorial design, though she loves to explore other fields as well - as long as they include creativity and good visuals.
P282-283

FIBA Design
www.fibadesign.com

FIBA is a design studio specialized in products, identities, publications, posters, books, exhibitions, websites, and signage systems.
P051, 062-063

FÖDA Studio
www.fodastudio.com

FÖDA Studio is a brand consultancy and graphic design studio in Austin, Texas.
Unique amongst their competitors, FÖDA is led by multi-disciplinary designer, lecturer, entrepreneur and creative director Jett Butler, who has nearly two decades of experience producing award-winning work in architecture, brand development, graphic design, and other related mediums.
FÖDA prides itself on thoughtful work and careful research that produces a marked return on investment for their clients and garners peer recognition both domestically and internationally. Since 2003, their unique brand of "decadent minimalism" has earned FÖDA dozens of Design Awards, collegiate or professional invitations to lecture or critique, and international publication in over 30 books and magazines.
P206-207

Foreign Policy Design Group
www.foreignpolicydesign.com

Foreign Policy Design Group is a team of idea makers and story tellers who help clients and brands realize and evolve their brands with creative and strategic deployment of traditional terrestrial channel and digital media channels. Helmed by Creative Directors Yah-Leng Yu and Arthur Chin, the group works on a good smorgasbord of projects ranging from creative art direction and design, branding, brand strategy, digital strategy, strategic research and marketing campaign services for luxury fashion and lifestyle brands, fast-moving consumer goods brands, arts and cultural institutions, and think tank consultancies.
P148-149, 228-229, 230-231

Fórmula P
www.formulap.com.br

Fórmula P is an integrated communication company, focused on creating and developing unique solutions for each customer, in order to generate significant results and new market opportunities. It is medium size with over 60 direct employees and over 30 indirect, working in the areas of Administrative and Financial, Account Manager, Media, Budget, Internet, Public Management, Electronic Production and Graphic Production. Fórmula P is one of the largest agencies of the state Minas Gerais and serves customers all over Brazil. Beyond that, it is one of the most awarded with more than 120 regional awards, both national and international .
P166-167

Fuse Design
www.fuse-design.co.uk

We excel in original, intelligent and effective visual solutions in graphic design, brand development and website design. Making ideas happen and delivering them to the highest standard is an essential part of our design service. Our expertise and thinking are never restricted to one specific style; we focus on delivering innovative design ideas that obtain results.
P067

Gold & Wirtschaftswunder
www.gww-design.de

Gold & Wirtschaftswunder: the name of this Stuttgart Communication and Design Agency, which has existed since 2005, recalls Germany's "economic miracle". Their design projects include the internationally successful Stuttgart club Rocker33 and the Self Service Gallery as well as many other projects for clients in the fields of architecture, culture and art. Free projects within these fields have also been created with photographers, curators and artists working together in varying interdisciplinary combinations. This ensures that individual notions of design are continually challenged while new approaches and concepts are developed. G&W bases its role on dialogue, working with the client to evolve new permutations and offering flexible, open and complex design solutions.
P024-025

Greenspace
www.thegreenspace.com

We are Greenspace, a brand consultancy based in Bethnal Green, London. We help companies reach their business objectives, and how we deliver this is unique to each client and each challenge. We are a small team of senior staff, who have worked for some of the biggest advertising, experiential and branding agencies in the world. We've worked across many sectors with clients including Amnesty International, Aston Martin, Bentley, Heineken, Friends of the Earth and Nokia.
P186-187

Heng Aik-soon

Heng Aik-soon Wilson is a Chinese Designer born in Malaysia who graduated from Melbourne's RMIT University, Australia in 1988. Having amassed over a decade of experience in renowned international advertising agencies and brand solution companies in Singapore (DIA, London base - Europe top 10) and Hong Kong (Head of Kan and Lau Design Consultant, Shenzhen), Wilson established his own firm - 5W.1H Brand Solution Ltd in Hong Kong in 2005.
The company's scope of business ranges from corporate identity, environmental graphics, literature, packaging design and last but not least, design education. His clientele spans Greater China (The Mainland, Hong Kong & Taiwan), Malaysia and Singapore.
P152-153

Hey Studio
heystudio.es

Hey is a multidisciplinary design studio based in Barcelona, Spain, specializing in brand management, editorial design, packaging and interactive design. We share the profound conviction that good design means combining content, functionality, graphical expression and strategy. As a result, we offer our clients a personal service based on mutual understanding and trust, working to innovate from rationality and directing advice to meet actual needs.
P083

Heydays
heydays.no

Heydays is an Oslo-based design studio that creates strong visual concepts that trigger curiosity, create excitement and show ambition. We listen, research and challenge. We remove noise to add value. A dynamic and effective design studio founded in 2008, we are large enough to take on a leading design role, but small enough to follow projects from start to finish.
P016-017

Hort
www.hort.org.uk

HORT began its inhabitance back in 1994, under the previous stage name of EIKES GRAFISCHER HORT. Who the hell is Eike? Eike is the creator of HORT. HORT - a direct translation of the studio's mission. A creative playground. A place where 'work and play' can be said in the same sentence. An unconventional working environment. Once a household name in the music industry. Now, a multi-disciplinary creative hub. Not just a studio space, but an institution devoted to making ideas come to life. A place to learn, a place to grow, and a place that is still growing. Not a client execution tool. HORT has been known to draw inspiration from things other than design.
P324-325

Hype Type Studio
www.hypetype.co.uk

Formed in 1999 by Paul Hutchison, Hype Type is a multi-disciplinary graphic design and communications studio with over 10 years experience working closely with local, national and international clients. With offices in both the UK and the US, Hype Type Studio has built a reputation for producing relevant, memorable and effective creative solutions. Our experience extends across many areas including arts, leisure, consumer goods and services, government, healthcare, media and entertainment, youth culture, technology, retail, music and fashion industries.
P170-171, 252-253

Isthar Marcon
www.istharmarcon.com

Isthar Marcon is an Italian independent graphic designer and art director, settled in Spain, working for private clients and collaborating with advertising and communication agencies. In 2004 she graduated from Visual Communication Design with honors (1999-2004. Politecnico di Milano University). After a few years working in different communication agencies in Italy and Spain, she started working independently, complementing a multidisciplinary network of professionals.
P188

István Szugyiczky
www.szugyiczky.com

István Szugyiczky is a Hungarian graphic designer who graduated from Academy of Fine Arts with an MA in graphic design. He has since then worked for several design agencies as art director for many clients. István also makes posters for charity organizations and his work has been featured in many social and environmental poster exhibitions worldwide. His work has been published in Computer Arts, CA Projects, IdN, Beautiful Decay and Semi-Permanent. Working as an independent graphic designer, nowadays, he is interested in illustrated typography, lettering and illustration and has worked for clients including Financial Times.
P270-271

IYA Studio
iyastudio.co.uk

IYA is an independent creative studio in London working across a broad spectrum of projects covering commercial interiors, digital and graphics. Having an ever expanding network of expert partners enables us to push our creativity without constraint. Our experience and knowledge of working on projects large and small means we're very much open for new challenges whatever the size or budget. We truly believe that creative partnership is the key to a successful outcome.
P202-203

Jeff Jarvis
www.jefftjarvis.com

Jeff Jarvis is a designer living and working in Brooklyn, NY. He's a graduate of the University at Buffalo and the Portfolio Center.
P300-301

John Barton
www.johnbarton.co.uk

John Barton is a recent graduate who now freelances at a number of well-established UK-based design studios.
P078-079

Jorge León
www.leonjorge.com

Jorge León is a 25 year old graphic designer from the Canary Islands, Spain. He has been working for two of the most influential studios in Spain for the last two years: Folch Studio and Clase BCN, both in Barcelona. Since March 2012, he has been running his own studio from the Canaries to the world, carrying out several projects for different international clients like Lacoste. Specializing in art direction, identity, communication, fashion, typography, editorial and web design, he has combined commercial projects with personal projects and collaborations with other designers, photographers, illustrators, artists and even bookstores and art galleries.
P088-089

MEMOMA
www.memoma.tv

MEMOMA is a motion graphics house where the Sunday matinee fills the sky. No vacation. No rest. Just faith and intelligence. We explore visual culture from different art disciplines, using live action, design, and animation techniques to create breathtaking imagery for TV, entertainment, brands, advertising and the music industry.
P052-053

MgA. Iva Návojská Pechmanová
www.pinxit.cz

Iva Návojská Pechmanová works as a freelance graphic designer. She lives in the Czech Republic where she studied Faculty of Fine Arts VUT in Brno. Previously she studied at Art high school in Brno. Her main activity is the creation of logos and integrated visual styles (corporate design). Shea also creates T-shirts and the custom jewelry brand PIN.X.
P196-197, 322-323

Micaela Barrero
www.micaelabarrero.com

Micaela Barrero is a graphic designer who currently lives and works in Texas, USA. Micaela is originally from La Paz, Bolivia where she grew up and attended the Universidad Catolica Bolivia to get a degree in Mass Communication and Advertising. She enrolled in the Art Institute of Houston to get a degree in Graphic Design in 2006 and graduated in 2010. She won the best portfolio award of her graduating class. Micaela has participated in many graphic design contests, winning a gold award at Graphis among other awards. She has been published in several magazines, such as CMYK and Vanidades Bolivia, as well as newspapers.
P110-111

Michelle Han
michellehan.net

Michelle Han is a communication designer based in Los Angeles. Michelle graduated from Art Center College of Design in 2011 and holds a Bachelor of Fine Arts in Graphic Design. Michelle's identity and packaging design has been selected as an ADAA Semifinalist and her work is featured in: The Dieline, Creative-inspiration, UK, Packaging of The World, Sandu, and Design Inspiration.
P307

Michelle Liv
www.michelleliv.com

Michelle Liv is a graphic designer based in New York with a background in Comparative Literature and French. She finally decided to pursue her interest in graphic design after a fortuitous encounter with a small bookshop in Lyon that introduced her to the world of book design. She appreciates thoughtful design and finds creative outlet in Elsewhere Magazine, an art collaboration with Debra Ohayon.
P098-099

Michelle Ong
cargocollective.com/mxchelle

Born in Malaysia, Michelle graduated with a Second Upper Class BA (Hons) Graphic Design & Illustration in 2012. She strongly believes that every design is beyond just visuals, and every design should have an intention. She's a passionate learner and has a strong interest in experimenting and exploring visual expressions. She's particularly excited about publications and hopes to do cross-disciplinary work in the fields of music and fashion. She also wishes to get involved in social change campaigns to someday help make a difference.
P254-255

Mike Collinge
www.mikecollinge.com

Mike Collinge is an award-winning designer and art director with over twelve years experience. He is well versed in a wide range of disciplines, including brand identity, brand design, corporate communication, art direction, packaging, and publication design. Mike's work is reductive in approach, led by the belief that the idea should always determine the form and that the purity of the idea is maintained through rigorous graphic application. He has a deliberate, considered and crafted aesthetic that is often typographically driven. Now working for himself, Mike is an independent designer and brand consultant.
P036-037

Miklós Kiss
www.kissmiklos.com

Miklós Kiss is a designer and visual artist. Currently architecture, design and graphic design are his work fields. There is an outstanding aesthetic quality and strong artistic approach characterizing his implementation of work. His fine artworks define his work just as much as the individual perceptional corporate identity designs and graphics listed under his name.
P096-097, 280-281

Mind Design
www.minddesign.co.uk

Mind Design is an independent London based graphic design studio founded in 1999 and run by Holger Jacobs and Romilly Winter. Mind Design focuses on integrated design which combines corporate identity, print, web and interior design. Our philosophy and approach is based on a passion for craftsmanship and typography. We offer practical and friendly design solutions and believe that content and form are inseparable. It is important for us to work in close collaboration with clients, ideally right from the start. Every project is seen as a new challenge and we never follow an already established graphic house style.
P140-141

Mirko Ilić Corp.
www.mirkoilic.com

Mirko Ilić Corp. was established in 1995 as a multi-disciplinary studio specializing in graphic design, 3D animation, motion picture titles, and illustration. The studio is especially known for its strong visual concepts. Mirko Ilić Corp. has received awards from various organizations including the Society of Illustrators, the Society of Publication Designers, the Art Directors Club, I.D. Magazine, Print Magazine, HOW magazine, the Society of Newspaper Design, and more.
P038, 268-269

moodley brand identity
www.moodley.at

moodley brand identity is an owner-led, award-winning strategic design agency with offices in Vienna, Graz and Shanghai. Since 1999 we have worked together with our customers to develop corporate and product brands which live, breathe and grow. We believe our key contribution is to analyze complex requirements and develop simple, smart solutions with emotional appeal – whether corporate start-up, product launch or brand positioning. Our team currently consists of 32 employees from 7 different countries.
P103, 264-265, 286-287, 304-305

MusaWorkLab
www.musaworklab.com

MusaWorkLab is a multi-disciplinary design and communication consultancy studio founded in 2003 by Raquel Viana, Paulo Lima and Ricardo Alexandre, located in Lisboa, Portugal. Our focus is to be unconventional, to innovate, and to go beyond traditional studio work by integrating an international creative professional's network with diverse backgrounds and talent. Every project is treated uniquely based on the special needs of our client – one solution does not fit all. We strive to give our clients successful brand communication strategies and state of the art graphic concepts providing relevant and creative solutions.
P308

My name is
www.mynameis.fr

My name is is an independent graphic design and art direction studio based in Paris, Montmartre. Since 2007, we have worked on a wide range of media such as visual identities, editorial design, art direction, music covers, websites, photos and videos. Focusing on the context and specificity of each project, every solution we create is the result of a unique collaboration between us, designers, and our client.
P030-031

MyORB
myorangebox.com

We create identities, websites, typefaces, books and brochures, design exhibitions, produce short films, and make other things. The aim of our work is to be curious, intriguing and playful. The goal of our practice is to create mutually-beneficial relationships with people and organizations whose work we admire. Some of our clients: Audi, American Institute of Graphic Arts, Anthony Logistics for Men.
P136-137, 272

Nahuel Marín Luriaud
www.behance.com/nahuelmarin

Nahuel Marín Luriaud was born in Buenos Aires, Argentina, in 1989. He immigrated to Spain in 2001, and in 2012 finally he completed his Higher Education in Design (ESD) in Murcia, Spain. Nahuel worked in two agencies while he was studying and currently he is working as a freelance graphic designer at one of the most important advertising agencies of Spain. In these intense years he specialized in are corporate identity, editorial and print design.
P248-249, 306

Neue Design Studio
www.neue.no

Since its establishment in 2008, Neue Design Studio has created visual communication with the belief that insight and creativity are equally necessary in the process toward creating engaging, long-lived concepts. Working from their 6th-floor studio with its overview of Oslo, they develop strategies and make editorial design, brand identities, packaging and illustration for both print and screen.
P276-277

Noeeko
www.noeeko.com

We are a multi-disciplinary design studio founded by Art and Creative Director Michal Sycz. We are passionate about producing creative projects of the highest quality across digital, print, branding and interactive media. The aim is to create a coherent, original and distinctive design solution that communicates clients' key messages. We love to experiment with new materials and techniques to keep our work fresh. Our design process goes through four phases: research, creative base, visual base and unique solution. We are pretty lucky to come to our studio and do something that we really enjoy every day.
P102

Pacifica
www.thisispacifica.com

Pacifica is a forward thinking studio. Our approach is essentially creative. We believe in ideas, solving problems, and taking opportunities. We focus on the good ideas without barriers, formulas or specific tools. Our method is based on visual thinking. We do branding, graphic design, interactive design, web design, packaging, signage, environments, editorial, motion graphics, mobile design, advertising, events and relationship marketing. Pacifica is an independent graphic design studio based in Porto, Portugal, established in 2007 by Pedro Serrão, Pedro Mesquita and Filipe Mesquita.
P214-215

Pauerr
www.pauerr.com

"Professional whistler and loser of valuable objects, student of all, almost guitarist for a day, writer without orthographic manual, compulsive winner and eternal aspirant to intellectual. I always wake up before the alarm rings to be able to switch it off. My mother says I am special and my shampoo says I am soft and manageable." Pau Garcia Sanchez lives and works in Barcelona and is a graphic designer and copywriter.
P056-057

Pedro Serapicos Studio
www.serapicos.org

Psst stands for Pedro Serapicos Studio. Founded in 2011, Psst is a small graphic design studio based in the north of Portugal. Pedro has been working since 1999 as a designer on his own and as part of collaborative projects. He now is a PHD student at Fine Art School. His work is devoted to several interests and is mainly the result of unexpected but inspiring personalities. From corporate identity to editorial, poster design and illustration, a variety of his works have been published. Teaching is also an important activity. Currently, Pedro is lecturing at ESAD Matosinhos and ESEIG / IPP Vila do Conde. The present moment is marked by an important shift in this graphic journey where he seeks to explore further.
P192-193

Pentagram
www.pentagram.com

Pentagram is the world's largest independent design consultancy. The firm was founded in 1972 and is run by 19 partners, a group of friends who are all leaders in their individual creative fields. Working from offices in London, New York, San Francisco, Berlin and Austin, the firm specializes in different areas of graphic design, industrial design and architecture, producing printed materials, environments, products and interactive media for a wide range of international clients.
P039, 112-113

Priscila Mendoza
www.priscilamendoza.mx

Priscila Mendoza is an Information Designer from Mexico. She graduated from UDLA in 2005 and interned for a year at UCM in Madrid. After graduation she was invited by German Montalvo to the Design Department of UDLA where she worked for 2 years. There she got involved mostly in Editorial and Poster Design. In 2008 she moved to Monterrey and ventured into advertising and branding where she worked for 5 years. She was recently granted a Fulbright scholarship and is moving to Savannah Georgia (SCAD) for the MFA in Design Management.
P190-191

Proekt Communication Agency
proekt.co.uk

Proekt is a Moscow based communication agency. We focus on working with large Russian development companies and international brands such as Toyota, Honda, Nokia, BrunoMagli, Design museum in London and so on. We are interested in advertising the innovative projects of our clients. Whatever we do, whether working with advertising companies, fashion or interior design, we combine all the available media. We are innovators, constructors of the environment around us. We act for the benefit of humanity - without forgetting to successfully increase the profits of our clients at the same time.
P274-275

qián creation
www.qian.be

Olivier Rensonnet, widely recognized for his love of corporate design and never-ending creative enthusiasm, founded the qián agency. He is an identity specialist working with the best professionals in communication for over 15 years. In this period of time, he has managed to develop identities for all sizes of companies and institutions, from the smallest to the largest. qián's motivation is to develop rich visual communication that makes sense, with integrity and completely oriented towards the essence of the clients. qián's expertise ranges from pure identity creation to development of offline and online communication tools, to the creation of conceptual promotion locations to office refurbishing.
P273

Rachel Willey
www.rachelwilley.com

Rachel Willey is a designer from Orange County, California. She is currently living and working in Brooklyn, NY. She recently graduated from the School of Visual Arts in New York City and is now working in publication design.
P260-261

Raewyn Brandon Design
www.raewynbrandon.com

Raewyn Brandon is a passionate web and graphic designer from New Zealand. The saying "less is more" has highly influenced Raewyn's design style, as her work represents simplicity and minimalism with high attention to detail.
P094-095

Ritator
www.ritator.com

This Swedish design and advertising agency was founded in 2007. Ritator deploy unique concepts to create attention and interest for our clients in business, government and the public sector.
P184

Silvia Giulianini
www.cargocollective.com/silvia_giulianini

Silvia Giulianini is an Italian graphic designer, currently based in London, who recently graduated with an MA in Graphic Branding and Identity at the London College of Communication. She has worked as a graphic designer and as a freelancer in New York City, in London and for several years in Italy, thus she has much international work experience. Though she has been involved in different kind of projects, her inclination is mainly towards branding development, corporate identities, print design, and information graphics.
P296-297

SMEL
www.smel.net

Smel, founded in 2001 by Edgar Smaling and Carlo Elias, consists of a dynamic team of dedicated, multidisciplinary creative people. Smel designs strategic corporate identities, magazines, books, corporate identities, websites and illustrious design concepts which subtly

unite quality and imagination. Smel works for a variety of clients, public service, fashion, design, art and architecture.
P064-065

Stockholm Design Lab
www.stockholmdesignlab.se

Stockholm Design Lab is one of European most highly respected design companies. Founded in 1998, the concept and goal of Stockholm Design Lab is to be an important platform for the creation of quality design that matters and makes a difference. Our design philosophy is rooted in Scandinavian tradition and based on the fundamental ideas of simplicity, clarity, openness and innovation. Our belief is that this approach to design will clearly be an asset to corporations by enabling them to further develop and express their position and values. SDL's work is simple, innovative and powerful.
P222-223

Studio Beige
www.studiobeige.nl

Studio Beige is a Rotterdam-based design studio founded in 2003, specialising in concept, strategy and design. We focus on printed matter as well as webdesign and count among our clients commercial and non-profit organisations both large and small. We create visual identities, book designs, magazines, campaigns and websites. At Studio Beige we cherish a love for typography, which tends to show in just about anything we do. Moreover we like to use unusual materials and apply special techniques. As a result we deliver striking, tactile and highly communicative designs.
P020, 066, 072-073, 107, 236-237, 310-311

Studio Constantine
manualelectric.com

Manual: It's craft; attention to detail and a commitment to translating abstract ideas into concrete expressions, through flawless execution. Electric: It's the concept; inspired lateral thinking that excites and delights. We are a boutique design studio based in Melbourne, with representation in Europe. Our work is articulate, original and of highest quality. We foster creative and collaborative relationships that deliver impactful results. We advocate the benefits of being strategic about the process of communication for our clients, in every project, regardless of scale or budget.
P044-045

Studio Laucke Siebein
www.studio-laucke-siebein.com

Studio Laucke Siebein is a design studio based in Amsterdam and Berlin. Its focus is on creative strategy, dynamic identities, graphic, book design and web design within the scope of cultural and commercial projects. Dirk Laucke and Johanna Siebein have been awarded, amongst others, the Art Directors Club NY, The European Design Award, The Best Dutch Books, The Dutch Design Award and the Dutch Corporate Identity Award. Its work has been presented in a large number of magazines and books.
P290-291

Studio Worldwide
studioworldwide.net

Studio Worldwide is a multi-disciplinary design practice specializing in crafted and considered graphic design and art direction. Established by Dutch designer Thijs van Beijsterveldt and British designer Joel Priestland, Studio Worldwide's foundations are based on a combination of international backgrounds with extensive design experience to produce unique, effective and engaging creative work. Their clients range from arts and culture, fashion and luxury to property development and education. They are driven by the relationships with their clients in tailoring intelligent, creative solutions to specific needs.
P258-259

Sublima Comunicación
www.sublimacomunica.com

Sublima was founded in 2002 in the city of Murcia, Spain as a creative communication agency, but it would rather call itself "a company of ideas". All developments in the world - everything around us - comes from an idea, a thought. That is the basis of Sublima: the search for concepts applied to a design which transmits many things just using a few. A search that applies to editorial design, corporate identity, packaging, advertising, direct marketing, street marketing ... and everything that requires implementing a creative idea to solve a problem, generally, of communication.
P174-175

Surya Prasetya
www.suryaprasetya.com

Surya Prasetya is a Melbourne based graphic designer. The main area of design includes but is not limited to printed matter, identity and branding, exhibitions, fashion, websites etc. The approach to our communication is defined by research, simplicity, analytical thinking and clarity, resulting in well crafted design solutions.
P100-101, 120-121

Temple
www.madebytemple.com

Founded by Roberto Crippa and David Nguyen, London-based studio Temple crafts elegant yet stark designs through their signature monochrome palettes, spacious compositions and sharp geometric forms. Combining Classical and Modernist design values, their work includes brand identity, art direction, interactive design and installation projects for clients in the cultural and private sectors. In addition to client work, they also create their own products including fonts and other distinctive design objects.
P158, 212-213

Thorleifur Gunnar Gíslason
thorleifur.is

Having recently graduated from the Icelandic Academy of the Arts, Thorleifur now works as a graphic designer for Jónsson & Le'macks advertising agency in Reykjavík as well as being a member of the multidisciplinary design crew Wolfgang.
P194-195

Tiana Vasiljev
www.tianavasiljev.com

Tiana Vasiljev founded her own design practice, working with a variety of clients and businesses, and occasionally collaborates and freelances for design studios in Sydney. With a special emphasis on typography, attention to detail, a strong conceptual attitude, and a willingness to experiment, she is open to all challenges. Tiana's goal is to create and encourage innovative and meaningful design that promotes thought, interaction and a smile.
P256

Timur Salikhov
www.timursalikhov.com

Timur Salikhov is a 31-year old art director and graphic designer based in Saint Petersburg, Russia. He has been involved in design, advertising and branding for the past 11 years. Graphic design, brand identity, and ads are his major interests. He is confident in his abilities to deliver superior results in these fields. Also he has a notably high success rate at conceptualizing and presenting for pitch. Traveling is his main hobby. It provides him with new ideas for his work. Currently he is working at Brandson branding agency as an art director.
P124-125

Tom Tor Studio
www.tomtor.com

Tom Tor is founder and Creative Director of Tom Tor Studio™. Internationally educated from Switzerland to Southern California, Tom brings ten years of visual arts experience. Having worked with prestigious agencies such as Chiat\Day and Ogilvy& Mather, Tom cut his art direction teeth on many prominent name brands. Tom believes that creative communications bring together typography, colour and form to fulfill the strategic goals of a company, and deliver creative solutions, which generate challenging, intelligent and trend-setting designs that change the marketing landscape. His work exemplifies his commitment to clear communication, without need of translation.
P176-177

Turnstyle
www.turnstylestudio.com

Turnstyle is a graphic design and branding firm founded on the belief that in a crowded marketplace, people gravitate emotionally toward companies and products that project a distinctive style. Design's power is in its ability to craft that stylistic distinction and to communicate on an emotional, visceral level. We emphasize design execution because that's where the analytical rubber meets the emotional road. In a nutshell, we breathe life into products and businesses by infusing clever thinking into impeccably executed branded materials.
P046-047, 147

Un-staged
www.un-staged.com

Un-staged is a design studio based in Oporto, Portugal, led by two graphic designers: Ana Pais and Tiago Resende. They specialize in subjects such as corporate identity, branding and web design. Their approach to communication design has earned them a nice reputation for creating "visually striking work" that is also conceptually well-founded and structured. The term "unstaged" stands for the way they think and consequently how we work, meaning that they cultivate an "anti-design" attitude which allows them to balance between something ruled and something experimental. Un-staged is all about minimalism and a good sense of balance and beauty.

P250-251

Urform Studio
www.urformstudio.com

Urform is a small Amsterdam-based design studio. We produce identities to match the ideas and philosophy of brands or individuals. Our curiosity makes us look beneath or far above the surface to find and refine the essence of a brand's existence. We create a complete language instead of a single word, taking care of every aspect of a brand's creative context by offering a blend of creative thinking, practical solutions and attention to detail. We believe design can be an effective tool to guide people to and through a brand.

P169, 200-201

Vasava
www.vasava.es

In Vasava we understand that the journey is the destination. We, as a studio, take pride in continual learning, creative experimentation, and risk-taking. Every project has to be special, and the process is equally important as the final outcome. Vasava started up in Barcelona in 1997; today we are a communication studio with 18 young designers who specialize in cross-media projects: print, web, motion, 3D animation, and video. We believe in technology in support of creativity. Whether we are programming for the web, editing video, or designing for print, we continually find ways to push the boundaries of our craft, with a passion that shines through in everything we do.

P126-127

Visualism
www.visualism.de

We are Visualism – a multidisciplinary design studio based in Hamburg, Germany with a focus on visual communication, brand identity, art direction and illustration. Coming from various subcultures (graffiti, dj-ing, skateboarding and streetwear) we keep a playful and experimental approach to our work while maintaining an equally professional attitude. Our passion is to create and design, for large or independent clients alike. The foundation for all of our projects is rooted in solid strategic thinking and a strong yet organic conceptual process.

P211

Wayne Tang Design
waynetang.net

Wayne is currently a designer at Addis Creson in Berkeley, California. Growing up in Hong Kong, he maintained a collection of his favorite Japanese snack packages and model kit boxes. As a designer, he finds inspiration across all types of media: the hand lettering on chalkboards at cafes, the curves of an Eames chair, the architecture in Barcelona, or a nicely paced movie title sequence.

Prior to his graphic design career, Wayne worked as an engineer designing aircraft engine components. While it was quite a leap, Wayne has brought the structural sensibility and systematic approach that he learned in engineering to his design work.

P032-033, 189

YAWN
www.weareyawn.com

YAWN means Yeah Awesome Wow Nice. YAWN is Annika and Sandra. We both studied graphic design and have been working together as freelance illustrators and graphic designers since 2009.

We're children of the '80s: we like watercolors, rainbow colors, handmade type, geometric forms and sneakers. We are influenced by music, pop, youth culture, fashion, '80s surf and skate design, high school movies (Brat Pack) and Hedi Slimane's photography.

P054-055

We would like to express our gratitude to all the designers and companies for their generous contribution of images, ideas, and concepts. We are also very grateful to many other people whose names do not appear in the credits but who made specific contributions and provided support. Without you all, the successful completion of this book would not have been possible. Thank you for sharing your innovation and creativity with all our readers around the world.